MONARCHY AND MATRIMONY

Frontispiece The Sieve Portrait by George Gowers. Reproduced by courtesy of Lane Fine Art Ltd, London.

MONARCHY AND MATRIMONY

The courtships of Elizabeth I

Susan Doran

London and New York

First published 1996
by Routledge
11 New Fetter Lane, London EC4P 4EE

Simultaneously published in the USA and Canada
by Routledge
29 West 35th Street, New York, NY 10001

Typeset in Times by
Florencetype Ltd, Stoodleigh, Devon

Printed and bound in Great Britain by
T.J. Press (Padstow) Ltd, Padstow, Cornwall

British Library Cataloguing in Publication Data
A catalogue record for this book is available from the British Library

Library of Congress Cataloguing in Publication Data
A catalogue record for this book has been requested

ISBN 0-415-11969-3

For Alan

'Everyone seems to get married except me.'

Queen Elizabeth in *Blackadder*

The marriage of Queen Elizabeth 'seems to me like the weaving of Penelope, undoing every night what was done the day before and then reweaving it anew the next, advancing in these negotiations neither more nor less than has been done and undone countless times without reaching a conclusion one way or the other'.

The duke of Parma, 3 October 1580, quoted in Charles Wilson, *Queen Elizabeth and the Revolt of the Netherlands* (1970), p.75.

CONTENTS

LIST OF PLATES

ACKNOWLEDGEMENTS

My interest in Elizabeth I's courtships arose in the 1970s while writing a political study of the third earl of Sussex for my doctoral thesis. Conrad Russell, one of my external examiners, encouraged me to concentrate my research interests on the queen's matrimonial negotiations and it is to him I owe this book. In the early stages of its writing, his penetrating questioning of my material proved invaluable; in addition his practical assistance in recommending the project to a publisher and in supporting my applications for research funding provided me with the confidence and means to keep working when borne down by other responsibilities. My gratitude to him is beyond measure.

The completed typescript has been read by three historians to whom I offer my warmest thanks: Christopher Durston whose meticulous editing is a testament of the clarity of his prose and his qualities of friendship; Nicola Sutherland who has put me right on many points of French history and saved me from producing unhelpful end-notes; and Jonathan Woolfson whose witty comments cheered me up during the tedious task of copy-editing. Their contributions have greatly improved the book. I alone am responsible for remaining errors.

I am grateful to St Mary's University College for granting me a year's study leave and some research funding, and especially to my head of department, Jane Longmore, for her consistent support. I am also indebted to the Scouloudi Foundation and the British Academy for providing me with grants to consult manuscripts in the Bibliothèque Nationale at Paris, Simancas in Spain and the National Library of Wales. Thanks are due to the librarians there and at the Bodleian Library, British Library and Public Record Office.

Others who have been particularly helpful to me include Ralph Houlbrooke, David Goodman, Maria Denislow, Ros Durston, and the members of the early-modern English History seminar at the Institute of Historical Research. In the Routledge editorial team I am especially grateful to Claire L'Enfant and Heather McCallum.

ACKNOWLEDGEMENTS

My family have been amazingly supportive – well beyond the call of duty. My daughter Bathsheba had perceptive comments to make about the introduction and literary sources; my son Jacob helped me cope with modern technology and rescued me from panic whenever my printer jammed or 'disc error' inexplicably appeared on the computer screen; and my husband Alan discussed at length early drafts of the text and listened to me trying to unravel some of the more complicated issues. As appropriate for a book about matrimony, this work is dedicated to him.

I appreciate permisson to include extracts from my articles already published in the *English Historical Review* and *The Historical Journal*.

Susan Doran,
March 1995

LIST OF ABBREVIATIONS

AGSE	Archivo General de Simancas Estado
BL	British Library London
BN	Bibliothèque Nationale Paris
Bodl.	Bodleian Library
Codoin	*Colección de Documentos Inéditos para la Historia de España*. Edited by M. F. Navarete *et al.* (Madrid, 1842–95)
Fénélon	Bertrand de Salignac, seigneur de La Mothe-Fénélon, *Correspondance Diplomatique*. Edited by A. Teulot (Paris, 1838-40)
HMC	Historical Manuscripts Commission
NLW	National Library of Wales
PRO	Public Record Office
SP	State Papers

NOTES ON SOURCES

The year has been taken to begin on 1 January and not 25 March, as in the Old Style Calendar.

Spellings of original documents have been retained but I have modernised punctuation and eliminated contractions.

I have used the recognised English version of place-names and people where it exists (for example Henry of Anjou). Otherwise I have used the style and title used in the place or by the person concerned (for example, the duchesse de Nevers de Montpensier).

Wherever possible I have looked at the printed or manuscript Spanish version of the documents in the *Calendar of State Papers Spanish*. Where the wording is especially important I have put the Spanish quotation in the notes. To indicate in the notes that the calendar translation is not entirely accurate I have used the formula 'with a translation in . . .' and if required provided my own translation in the text.

1

INTRODUCTION

This book re-opens the question of Elizabeth I's attitude to marriage and the place of her various courtships in the political and religious history of the reign. Too often in the past, biographers and historians dismissed the queen's courtships as 'empty charades', 'political dalliance' or 'diplomatic games', which had no chance of success because of her intransigent opposition to marriage.[1] Instead of anachronistically dooming each matrimonial scheme to failure, this work will treat seriously all those marriage negotiations that were taken seriously by Elizabeth and her contemporaries, and place them within the context of court politics, religious developments and international diplomacy in order to assess their historical significance.

Until 1581 Elizabeth's marriage was a dominant and often divisive political issue in England, and was treated with such importance by contemporaries that it provoked both polemical debate and political unrest. Elizabethan observers realised, even if later commentators have since forgotten, that the final outcome of the courtships was uncertain and could affect the political stability of the realm, determine its religious future, and influence the direction of England's relations with her neighbours abroad. By focusing on the matrimonial issue, therefore, a new window is opened onto the outlook and concerns of early Elizabethan England. Furthermore, only a detailed examination of the individual courtships can provide a full explanation of why Elizabeth did not marry. Certainly there is very little evidence to support the view, which appears in so many biographies, that from the very beginning of her reign the queen had made a conscious decision to remain unwed either because of her implacable hostility to matrimony or her determination to rule alone.

It is now generally recognised that the story of Elizabeth swearing an oath to follow a life of virginity soon after her accession is little more than a myth. It was based on the version of Elizabeth's 1559 speech to parliament which first emerged in William Camden's early seventeenth-century history of the reign. According to Camden, when a small parliamentary delegation presented her with a petition to marry in 1559, the queen responded with the announcement:

But now that the publick Care of governing the Kingdom is laid upon me, to draw upon me also the Cares of Marriage may seem a point of inconsiderate Folly. Yea, to satisfie you, I have already joyned my self in Marriage to an Husband, namely, the Kingdom of England. And behold (said she, which I marvell ye have forgotten) the Pledge of this my Wedlock and Marriage with my Kingdom. (And therewith she drew the Ring from her Finger and shewed it, wherewith at her Coronation she had in a set form of words solemnly given her self in Marriage to her Kingdom).[2]

John King, however, has demonstrated that this version of Elizabeth's speech and behaviour is highly suspect; in Cecil's papers (Camden's source) there is no copy of the speech in question nor any record of the vow he described.[3] In addition, Elizabeth's words as presented in Camden's history differ in both style and substance from the official answer which she read out in the House of Commons on 10 February 1559. In this statement, which appears in several manuscript copies, Elizabeth was more ambivalent about marriage, promising the MPs that if 'it may please God to enclyne my heart to an other kynd of life, ye may well assure your selves my meaning is not to do or determyne anie thinge wherwith the realme may or shall have iuste cause to be discontented'.[4] Furthermore, as Carole Levin has pointed out, even married monarchs used the metaphor of marriage as a rhetorical device to describe their relationship with their kingdoms; thus in 1559 Elizabeth was claiming that her body politic was the spouse of her country but not that her body natural would never marry.[5]

In her many other statements and speeches during the first half of the reign, Elizabeth at no time ruled out the prospect of marriage. Responding to a second marriage petition from parliament in 1563, she told the Speaker: 'yf anie thinke I never meant to trade that [single] lief, they be deceaved; but yf I may hereafter bende my minde thereunto the rather for fullfillinge your request I shal be therwith very well content'.[6] When later in 1563 she discussed with the Scottish envoy Mary Stuart's claim to the throne and right to the succession, Elizabeth allowed for the possibility that she might marry and have a child: 'As for the title of my crown, for my time I think she will not attain it, nor make impediment to my issue if any shall come of my body'.[7] In 1564 she wrote to the duke of Württemberg:

Although shee never yet was wearie of her maiden and single life, yet in regarde shee was the laste issue her father lefte, and only of her house, the care of her kingdome, and love of posteritie did ever councell her to alter this course of life.[8]

Thus, although Elizabeth frequently expressed a preference for a life of celibacy, throughout the first half of her reign she always appreciated and admitted that she might have to marry in the future to satisfy her subjects' need of an heir. As she well knew, marriage and childbirth provided the only hope of producing a clear and unchallenged Protestant line of succession to the English throne and of averting the dangers of a civil war on her death. Although there were Protestant claimants in the first decade of the reign in the persons of Catherine and Mary Grey, the grand-daughters of Henry VIII's younger sister Mary, the Roman Catholic Mary Stuart, who had descended from Henry VIII's elder sister Margaret, had the best title by right of heredity.[9] Mary's claim, moreover, was strengthened during the 1560s by the disgrace of the Grey sisters, caused by the illicit union of Catherine to the earl of Hertford in 1561, the bastardisation of their two sons, and the misalliance in 1566 of the dwarfish Mary to a lowly servant of the court, who was reputed to be over six feet tall. As Elizabeth consistently refused to name her heir, and was especially unwilling to exclude Mary Stuart from the throne, which would satisfy her Protestant subjects, she was in no position to rule out marriage as a way of resolving the problem of the succession.

It was precisely because of the succession that Elizabeth was exhorted to marry time and time again in the early part of the reign. As part of their advice for dealing with the dangers posed by Mary Stuart, the Privy Council as a body called on Elizabeth to take a husband in late December 1559.[10] In 1559, 1563, 1566 and 1576 her parliaments sent her petitions urging marriage in order to provide an heir from her own body. Sometime around 1560, Matthew Parker, the archbishop of Canterbury, Edmund Grindal, the bishop of London, and Richard Cox of Ely 'thought it our parts for our pastoral office, to be solicitous in that cause which all your loving subjects so daily sigh for and morningly in their prayers desire to appear to their eyes', for they could not 'but fear that this continued sterility in your Highness' person to be a token of God's displeasure towards us'.[11] During her summer progress of 1565, the Recorder of Coventry greeted her with an oration which included the wish that 'like as you are a mother to your kingdom . . . so you may, by God's goodness and justice, be a natural mother, and, having blest issue of your princely body, may live to see your children's children unto the third and fourth generation.' More oblique petitions were also directed towards the queen: court masques were performed before her in the mid-1560s which harped on the theme of the superiority of marriage over celibacy; and as a New Year's gift for 1560, the diplomat Sir Thomas Challoner presented and dedicated to the queen a book in praise of Henry VIII, which ended with a sentimental call, that barely masked a hard political reality, begging her 'to bestow the bonds of your modesty on a husband. . . . For then a little Henry will play in the palace for us.'[12]

Elizabeth was also exhorted to take a husband who could protect the realm against its enemies. In the 1560s the candidature of the archduke

Charles of Austria was supported as a way of easing the tensions between England and Spain, and binding the Habsburgs to Elizabeth rather than Mary Stuart. As time went on and childbirth became less likely, Elizabeth's councillors came to urge marriage predominantly in order to seal a league with the French king and provide protection against Mary Stuart's allies, the Guises and Philip II. Thus, when the earl of Sussex listed seven advantages to the Francis of Anjou match in August 1578, only one related to the possibility of producing an heir, and this was the last one he mentioned; the remainder concerned the beneficial effects that would arise from a dynastic alliance with the house of France.[13]

Elizabeth's failure to marry despite her subjects' entreaties and the urgent need for an heir apparent has been viewed as extraordinary. Her ostensible neglect of duty seems to be totally out of character for a monarch usually noted for her dedication in defending the interests and unity of the realm.[14] For this reason no doubt some biographers and historians have tended to put forward a variety of extraordinary explanations to account for her unmarried state, all of them built on the premiss that Elizabeth *chose* to remain single.

In the past, it was sometimes suggested that Elizabeth refused to marry because she knew that she suffered from some physical impediment to intercourse or some mysterious disease, possibly syphilis, that made her infertile. The evidence for this view, however, is now recognised as weak and unconvincing.[15] Instead, in recent years, psychological explanations have become more fashionable with biographers. Some of their diagnoses are quite straight-forward, such as when they detect in Elizabeth an antipathy to marriage stemming from an emotional block to any kind of change or an almost pathological inability to take a decision; others, however, seek to explore the depths of Elizabeth's psyche to discover a cause of her 'choice' to remain single.[16]

It is easy to find in Elizabeth's childhood experiences a ready explanation for an irrational and pathological aversion to marriage. After all, her mother, Anne Boleyn, was executed by her father on a charge of adultery when Elizabeth was not yet three years old; Anne's supplanter, Jane Seymour, died from puerperal fever soon after giving birth to Prince Edward in 1538; and in 1542, a third step-mother, Catherine Howard, was also executed for adultery. No wonder that some historians have argued that these early traumas naturally led the young Elizabeth to associate sexual relations with death and develop a hysterical reaction against marriage. In the words of Alison Plowden: 'It would be hardly surprising if by the time she was eight years old, a conviction that for the women in her family there existed the inescapable correlation between sexual intercourse and violent death had taken root in her subconscious.'[17]

If such a conviction did indeed exist, the experiences of her troubled adolescence could only have reinforced it, since when she was in her early

4

teens Elizabeth fell victim to the lustful advances and political ambitions of Lord Thomas Seymour, a maternal uncle of the new king, Edward VI. While the details of the affair are somewhat unclear, it would appear that Seymour began indulging in open sexual banter and romps with Elizabeth while she was living with him and his wife, her final step-mother, Catherine Parr. He frequently came into her bedchamber in his night-gown, and 'One mornyng he strave to have kissed hir in hir bed'. What evidence there is suggests that Catherine colluded in the sexual harassment for a time, even to the extent of holding onto Elizabeth while 'in the Garden, he [Seymour] wrated with hir, and cut hir Gown in an hundred Pieces'. Later, however, she sent her young charge away perhaps out of jealousy.[18] In September 1548 Catherine died of puerperal fever and immediately afterwards Seymour began courting Elizabeth. In early 1549 he was arrested on the grounds of seeking to marry an heiress to the throne and in March he was executed for attempted treason. Elizabeth herself was closely interrogated for her part in encouraging Seymour's matrimonial schemes, while her closest servants spent some time in the Tower of London. It could logically be argued that this unsavoury episode confirmed Elizabeth's earlier negative feelings about sex, marriage and childbirth. Moreover, if Elizabeth were indeed the victim of a degree of sexual abuse and especially if she had found Seymour's advances exciting or even enjoyable, she might well have internalised intense guilt at the subsequent fates of both Catherine and Seymour.

Psychoanalytical theories have been used to bolster this view of Elizabeth as a damaged human being. Using a Freudian psychoanalytical model, Larissa J. Taylor-Smither has postulated that Elizabeth suffered all her life from an 'irresolution of the Oedipal complex', and argued that just when she must have been entering 'the phallic stage of development' and experiencing hostile feelings towards her mother and desire for her father, her mother was permanently removed through her father's action. In this historian's view, the extreme guilt that must have been provoked by this Oedipal wish-fulfilment would have stunted Elizabeth's emotional development and prevented the formation of a mature sexual relationship in the future. To make matters worse, the Seymour episode was 'a stimulating and terrifying replay of the Oedipal romance', as Thomas, who was about thirty-eight years of age in 1547, was a man old enough to represent her father. What is more, according to Taylor-Smither, these childhood experiences had another important effect in that they taught Elizabeth that 'maleness mattered' and left her with a 'masculine identification'. Had she been born a boy, her mother would not have been destroyed while she herself would have retained her father's affections. As a result, explained Taylor-Smither, Elizabeth came to value and adopt the masculine qualities of dominance, aggression and fearlessness, which made it impossible for her to assume the subservient role expected of a wife.[19]

These kinds of arguments have proved extremely popular, because they seem to explain not only why Elizabeth did not marry, but also why she appeared to have such an implacable hatred of matrimony in general. Her attempts to curb clerical marriage, her opposition to the marriages of her courtiers and ladies-in-waiting, and her fury when she found out that their clandestine marriages had taken place despite her wishes, seem to be more readily understandable in the light of some psychological disorder. The uncontrollable rages Elizabeth frequently displayed on such occasions (as when she broke the finger of Mary Shelton on discovering her secret marriage to James Scudamore) only seem to make sense if we accept that her behaviour was clinically hysterical and the result of unconscious anxieties stemming from childhood disturbance.

None the less, these arguments are simply psychological speculations, which, though fascinating, are suspect, based as they are on unproved models of human behaviour and inadequate evidence. There is no factual information at all to indicate how the deaths of her mother and step-mothers affected the young princess, and it could equally well be argued that their emotional impact was slight. Queen Anne was a very remote figure in Elizabeth's early childhood; the young princess had, moreover, stable surrogate mothers in the persons of first Lady Bryan and then Katherine Champernowne, later to be Mrs Ashley. Attitudes to parent-hood and death in the sixteenth century were in any event quite different from those of today, and it is ahistorical to transpose late twentieth-century sensibilities to the past. Furthermore, in adult life Elizabeth showed herself capable of forming relationships with male courtiers and advisers on a range of levels of intimacy, which suggests that she was not the emotion-ally stunted woman depicted by Taylor-Smither and others. Finally, Elizabeth's hostility to the marriages of her subjects had its own specific explanations. Antipathy to clerical marriage stemmed from the queen's religious conservatism, while her anger at the secret weddings of her ladies and courtiers often had a political cause. In general terms, she wanted her privy chamber to be apolitical and consequently required her ladies to be free from loyalties to a husband and his kin.[20] By marrying, her ladies were risking their political neutrality; furthermore, when they married secretly (often of necessity), they were demonstrating to their mistress their untrustworthiness and divided loyalties.

For these reasons, other historians have discarded psychological expla-nations and tended instead to see Elizabeth's decision to remain unwed as the deliberate, rational response of an intelligent woman to the practical problems of being a female ruler. Joel Hurstfield, for example, described Elizabeth as a career woman who chose to sacrifice the chances for marriage and motherhood in favour of ruling the country: 'Marriage and motherhood would deprive her temporarily – perhaps permanently – of the authority and power to rule. To share power she would hate. To renounce it she would find intolerable.'[21] As a mere woman in a patriarchal society, it has been argued, Elizabeth would be expected to hand over power to her husband or at the very least to follow his wishes over policy.

In recent years, mainly thanks to the influence of American scholars writing from a feminist perspective, the problem of marriage for a female ruler has been placed within a wider context of sexual politics.[22] In several articles which examine sixteenth-century attitudes towards gynaecocracy – female rule – historians have shown that politicians were bound to fear that a female ruler's marriage might jeopardise her authority, since they believed that a wife should always defer to her husband when making decisions, given that women were naturally inferior to men and that God had ordained female subordination to men in all private relationships. Anxieties about a queen regnant's marriage had consequently been present when Mary I planned to wed Prince Philip of Spain and Burgundy in 1553, and her councillors had therefore taken care to negotiate a marriage-treaty which would fix clear limits on Philip's political power in England; thus, while he was to enjoy all Mary's titles, policy-making and the exercise of patronage were reserved for the queen. It is often argued, however, that Mary failed to abide by the treaty, as she wanted her husband to share in her rule. In particular she has been criticised for allowing him to take control of foreign policy which resulted in the untimely French war and loss of Calais. According to Constance Jordan, had Mary adhered to the terms of the marriage-treaty, Elizabeth might have been able to marry without questions being raised about her own power, but:

> The failure of the legislation intended to limit Philip's power seems to have been largely due to the queen herself, who must have repeatedly declined to exercise the independence of mind that the law had authorized. Her fate doubtless weighed upon Elizabeth, who would have had to reflect on the extent to which such instruments of policy, when they relate to sexual politics, are only as binding as the strongest party to them determines they should be. By refusing to marry, Elizabeth avoided risking the loss of control that Mary had experienced.[23]

For some feminists, this decision of the queen to remain unmarried was admirable. Susan Bassnett, for example, viewed Elizabeth as a role-model, 'a symbol of active female assertiveness for future generations', and praised her for choosing virginity as 'her statement of what we might term feminist attitude'.[24] For more radical feminists like Allison Heisch, on the other hand, Elizabeth represented the typical token woman who accepted 'male notions of how the world was or should be organised' and who reinforced rather than eroded 'those systems which oppress and exclude women'. Instead of questioning or challenging patriarchy, claimed Heisch,

Elizabeth chose to become 'an honorary male' in a patriarchal society in order to hold onto political power, and she therefore could not possibly marry and sink back into the feminine role.[25]

All historical writings inevitably reflect historians' contemporary concerns, but there has perhaps been too great a tendency in recent years to impose on the past a feminist perspective which assumes that Elizabeth had a twentieth-century appreciation of sexual politics and which judges her by today's standards of political correctness. More particularly, it is a mistake to assume that Elizabeth could only deal with the issue of her gender by remaining celibate, and that she had to remain unmarried because she did not wish to share power with a husband. In his treatise, *An Harborowe for Faithful and Trew Subiectes* (which was written in 1559 as an answer to John Knox's *First Blast of the Trumpet Against the Monstruous Regiment of Women*, the most famous work denying the legitimacy of gynaecocracy) John Aylmer, later to be bishop of London, argued against those who said that a married queen regnant should always display uxorial subordination in line with God's law and defer to her husband on all matters of state:

> Yea say you, God hath appoynted her to be subject to her husband
> ... therefore she maye not be the heade. I graunte that, so farre as
> perteining to the bandes of mariage, and the offices of a wife, she
> must be a subjecte; but as a Magistrate she maye be her husbande's
> head. ... Whie may not the woman be the husbande's inferiour in
> matters of wedlock, and his head in the guiding of the common-
> welth.[26]

Aylmer saw a queen regnant as two persons, one private and one public. As a wife she would be subordinate to her husband in private affairs, but as a magistrate she would be dominant and could command and even punish her husband if he broke the law. Since her obligations as a wife would not take precedence over her regal responsibility, Elizabeth could thus retain her powers when married.

There were few practical obstacles to this political theory. It was in the obvious interests of all Elizabeth's advisers and servants to exclude her husband from power, and the means were at hand in the marriage-treaty of Mary and Philip. Consequently, they all agreed that any marriage-contract negotiated for Elizabeth should be based on the treaty of 1553; as Sir Nicholas Bacon explained, this would ensure that her husband 'shall not intermeddell with any parte of the governement of the realme to move any suspicion'.[27] The experience of the previous reign was also a reassuring precedent, for Mary had not been the weak, dependent woman characterised by Constance Jordan. On the contrary, recent research is revealing that the queen had not allowed power and authority to slip from her hands into those of her husband. For one thing, she placed difficulties in the way of Philip playing an effective role in government by denying him a personal patrimony in England, which would allow him to build up an independent patronage base.[28] For another, she made little attempt to push his coronation through parliament, an investiture which would have enhanced his status as king. Furthermore, all the court rituals and ceremonies of the reign asserted Mary's role as sovereign and emphasised that Philip was merely her consort: her throne was larger than his and placed at a higher level; she was served off gold while he was served off silver.[29] The treaty itself was upheld in every detail. Philip had to pay the total costs of his huge household and, even when it came to the war against France, the Council did not automatically approve England's participation on the side of Spain but only agreed entry after the French raid on Scarborough Castle. The Marian precedent, therefore, did not suggest that it was necessary for Elizabeth to remain unmarried in order to rule rather than reign.

But some historians argue, in addition, that the decision to remain a virgin gave Elizabeth opportunities to play a role and develop an image, which could help her overcome the obstacle of her gender in asserting her rule.[30] Unlike her sister, Elizabeth was aware of the value of symbols, fictions and drama in the exercise of political power, and it is often said that she fashioned for herself a public persona as a virginal goddess, which would give her a special mystique as a female ruler and allow her to command the respect and awe reserved for kings. In courtly pageantry she acted out the roles of the *beldame* of mediaeval chivalry or the Petrarchan mistress of Renaissance poetry, who was beloved and served by male courtiers without any loss to their honour. In this way, the queen could keep in line male courtiers chafing at the obligation to obey a female monarch. Similarly, through the image of the Virgin Queen she was able to present herself as no ordinary woman, but as an exceptional woman whose purity made her worthy of devotion, even adoration. Her virginity allowed her to be cast in portraits and literature as the moon goddesses, Diana, Phoebe and Cynthia, as well as Astraea, the virgin who in Virgil's poetry had once presided over the Golden Age and would return again to restore it. Her virginity also enabled her to exploit the coincidence of her birth date, 7 September, with the feast of the Nativity of the Virgin Mary and claim a symbolic kinship with the mother of Christ. These public personae were obviously incompatible with marriage. Quite simply, as Christopher Haigh has explained so succinctly, 'how could she admit that she was just the same as the rest, and submit herself to a husband? ... Elizabeth had refused to be a mere woman, and was not going to be a mere wife.'[31]

Elizabeth, however, did not have to remain unmarried and chaste to appear exceptional to her subjects, nor did she need to develop the secular cult of the Virgin to create for herself a special mystique. Instead, she could and did derive a special status as a female monarch by emphasising her position as the instrument of God's purpose and identifying herself with providential figures in the Bible. Most Protestant publicists described Elizabeth in this fashion. In his treatise of 1559, Aylmer asserted that God had ordained Elizabeth to rule, as a special woman, when he provided for no male heir through the succession: 'it is a plain argument that for some secret purpose he [God] myndeth the female should reign and governe'.[32] John Calvin also believed that Elizabeth's accession was 'ordained by the peculiar providence of God'; although accepting the contemporary assumption that female rule was a 'deviation from the original and proper order of nature', he acknowledged that 'there were occasionally women', like Elizabeth, who 'were raised up by divine authority' to be queen in order to become 'the nursing mothers of the church'.[33] In John Jewel's *Apology of the Church of England* of 1562 and John Foxe's *Acts and Monuments* of the following year, the authors argued that all the signs of scripture and history confirmed the providential nature of the queen's rule. Both elitist poetry and popular verses expressed the same argument. From Edmund Spenser's *Faerie Queene* came the lines:

> But vertuous women wisely understand
> That they were borne to base humilitie
> Unlesse the heavens they lift to lawfull soveraintie.[34]

Meanwhile, the verse of the Protestant balladeer John Awdelay proclaimed:

> Up, said this God with voice not strange,
> Elizabeth, thys realme nowe guyde,
> My wyll in thee doo not hyde.[35]

Elizabeth also liked to project herself in this providential mould; in her parliamentary rhetoric, for example, she frequently described herself as a woman raised by Providence to be a monarch, one who was thus exceptional in nature, quite unlike other women.[36]

It was to mark the rule of a providential queen that the anniversary of Elizabeth's accession, 17 November, was celebrated 'in forme of a Holy Day' throughout the realm from the late 1560s onwards. The joyous festivities were accompanied by prayers and sermons that drew attention to the providential divide in England's history between the captivity of popery and the promise of God's true Church, and gave thanksgiving to 'her, to whom under God, we owe all our service upon earth'. While at court the emphasis was on chivalric display, most parishes commemorated Accession Day as 'a day wherein our nation received a new light after a fearful and bloody eclipse'.[37]

The image of the Virgin Queen, in fact, appeared relatively late in Elizabeth's reign; one of its earliest manifestations seems to have been the entertainments performed before the queen at Norwich in the summer of 1578. Until then, Elizabeth had found a model for active female rule in the scriptural figures of Deborah, the Israelite Judge of the Old Testament, and to a lesser extent Judith, the killer of Holofernes in the Apocrypha, both of whom were married women. Deborah, a providential ruler and the rescuer of the Israelite chosen people from Canaanite idolatry, could readily be identified with Elizabeth in her attempts to uproot popery and build up the Protestant Church in England; Judith in her victory over Holofernes was another divinely inspired champion of the true faith against its foes.[38] This imagery appears as early as January 1559, when in one of the coronation pageants presented before the queen, the figure of Deborah appeared and Elizabeth was told: 'A worthy precedent, O worthy Queen! thou hast!', while the published description of the procession reminded its readers that 'God, ofttimes, sent women nobly to rule among men, as Deborah which governed Israel in Peace, the space of forty years'.[39] Both Deborah and Judith continued to be portrayed as representations of Elizabeth in woodcuts and pageantry until late in the 1570s, and it was only then that the imagery of the Virgin Queen emerged and grew in popularity. As will be seen in later chapters (6 and 7) Elizabeth herself did not initiate this 'cult'. Rather, it was an image first used extensively between 1578 and 1581 by some of her subjects who were opposed to her plans to marry the duke of Anjou. Only later did she adopt and exploit it for her own political benefit.

In the following chapters, I follow through the argument that Elizabeth did not reject marriage from either psychological motives or political reasons associated with her gender. Indeed, I question whether Elizabeth *chose* at all to remain single. It is clear to me that she did want to marry on two occasions: once on the death of Lord Robert Dudley's wife in September 1560 when most contemporary observers believed that she was seriously contemplating marriage to her favourite, and again in 1579 when she demonstrated a strong desire to wed Francis duke of Anjou. Furthermore, in response to intense pressure from her councillors and parliaments, she showed a readiness to marry two other suitors, though admittedly without the enthusiasm displayed during the Dudley and Anjou courtships. In the mid-1560s she agreed to open negotiations with the archduke Charles of Austria and from late 1570 through to the autumn of 1571 she encouraged matrimonial negotiations with Henry duke of Anjou. On both these occasions there was no dallying with her suitors for political advantage; on the contrary Elizabeth exhibited a serious intent to get down to the business of drawing up an acceptable matrimonial contract and at times was ready to offer concessions on areas of disagreement. To appreciate why these negotiations failed, we have to turn our eyes away from the character and gender of the queen and focus instead on the debates surrounding the courtships, the sticking-points in the attempts to reach a matrimonial settlement, and the political tactics employed by the opponents of the various matches to ensure their ultimate failure.

2

EARLY SUITORS

The usual fate for a king's daughter in the sixteenth century was an early dynastic marriage. Elizabeth's two aunts, the daughters of Henry VII, for example, had both been espoused to foreign kings, Margaret to the king of Scotland at thirteen and Mary to the king of France at eighteen. Elizabeth, on the other hand, succeeded to the throne of England unbetrothed and unwed, although she had already turned twenty-five. During her childhood and adolescence there had been several suitors for her hand, but matrimonial schemes had come to nothing, largely as the result of her uncertain legal status.

Henry VIII had shown an early readiness to treat Elizabeth as a tool to further his diplomacy. When she was sixteen months old in January 1535, he opened discussions for her marriage with the duke of Angoulême, the third son of Francis I, in order to foster a closer alliance with France. Although Elizabeth's legitimacy was denied by the Habsburg relations of Catherine of Aragon because she had been born during the ex-queen's life-time, Francis was content with the match as he recognised Henry's second marriage as legal and believed that the king would 'treat Elizabeth as his only heiress'. By July, however, the negotiations had broken down over three main areas of contention. Most importantly, Francis was unwilling to meet Henry's demand that he should make a public statement defending the Boleyn marriage, but he also disagreed with the English insistence that Angoulême be educated in England until the espousals took place. On his side Henry was aggrieved that Francis wanted as part of the dowry to cease giving him the pension which the French were accustomed to pay the English monarch.[1]

Although Anne Boleyn's downfall in the spring of 1536 had little immediate effect on Elizabeth's day-to-day circumstances, it introduced a change in her rank and status which inevitably blighted her future marriage prospects. Soon after Henry's marriage to Anne was annulled, a new Succession Act passed through parliament which bastardised their daughter and debarred her from 'any inheritance as lawful heir'.[2] At a stroke, Elizabeth lost her position as a royal princess at home and her

13

value as a partner in a dynastic alliance, and it soon became clear that unless and until she 'be made of some estimation', no man of importance would take her hand in marriage.[3] For Charles V, Catherine of Aragon's nephew, the 1536 statute only served to confirm his earlier judgement that the Boleyn child was a bastard and he therefore dismissed Henry's suggestion in 1538 of betrothing Elizabeth to one of his nephews by merely noting 'the life and death of her mother'. Francis I, however, seemed to be initially unaware of Elizabeth's changed legal position and continued to view her as a potential bride for one of his sons, until he learned otherwise. In the summer of 1541 he suggested a marriage between her and his son, the duke of Orleans, but he hastily withdrew his informal proposal on hearing from the duke of Norfolk that Elizabeth had been declared illegitimate by parliament and that, while plans were afoot to restore her half-sister to the succession, Elizabeth would remain debarred, since only in Mary's case 'did we not know the father and the mother, and consider the marriage good?' For Francis, the question of his prospective daughter-in-law's legitimacy was of paramount importance, and he claimed that 'he believed it, that it was more honourable for the son of France to marry the poorest gentlewoman, being legityme, than a dame of the noblest parentage, being illegytyme'.[4]

None the less, Henry did not give up trying to exploit his second daughter's marital eligibility for diplomatic advantage. In April 1543, he endeavoured to arrange her marriage to the eldest son of James Hamilton, second earl of Arran, who in the previous January had been proclaimed the governor of Scotland during the minority of Queen Mary Stuart. Henry's aim was to use Elizabeth as bait to keep Arran loyal so that he would agree to the removal of Mary to England and her marriage to Prince Edward. Thus, Arran was to be told that the matrimonial alliance had been 'devised for the advancement of his blood that he may have cause to rejoice in his conformity to the King's proceedings'.[5] Initially, the earl agreed, probably in good faith, to both his son's marriage and that of Mary to Edward, but by September 1543 he had found it impossible to keep his promises to Henry and therefore deserted the English cause, calling off the marriage of his son to Elizabeth.[6]

Arran had originally been content to accept Elizabeth as his heir's bride, because he believed that the king would soon restore her legitimate status and rights of inheritance. In this view he was soon to be proved partially correct, as in 1544 she was recognised as third in line to the throne by an act of parliament, although the taint of bastardy was not removed. Yet despite this improvement in her legal position, there was little opportunity for a dynastic marriage during the rest of Henry's reign. At war with France and Scotland, Henry could only offer Elizabeth to a Habsburg prince, but Charles V had little interest in a matrimonial alliance with England and in any event, as the protector of his cousin Mary, he still refused to consider Henry's second daughter as anything other than a bastard.[7]

On Henry VIII's death Elizabeth's matrimonial prospects remained poor. The international situation continued to work against a foreign marriage concluded for diplomatic gain, as the Lord Protector Somerset escalated the war in Scotland and consequently remained on hostile terms with France under its new king Henry II. At the same time a betrothal to an Englishman was so politically sensitive that it was out of the question. Henry VIII had probably been aware that ambitious Englishmen might set their sights on his daughters, and so he laid down in his will that Mary and Elizabeth would lose their place in the succession if they married without the consent of the Privy Council. Dominated by the duke of Somerset, the early Edwardian Council would never sanction any marriage which might elevate a potential political rival to the Lord Protector.

For this reason, there was no chance that councillors would approve a marriage between Elizabeth and Somerset's brother, Baron Thomas Seymour of Sudeley, who saw marriage to the king's sister as a means of gaining greater influence in the government. The secret courtship he carried out in 1548 was therefore highly dangerous to both parties. Although only fourteen years old, Elizabeth seemed to have had the wit to realise the true situation, and she remained aloof from Seymour's advances, unlike her household servants Katherine Ashley and Thomas Parry, who foolishly encouraged him in his schemes to marry their charge. Predictably, the affair ended with Seymour's execution, and for a time Elizabeth feared for her own life; in fact she only suffered a temporary disgrace, as thanks to her coolheadedness nothing treasonable could be proved against her.

Elizabeth soon returned to favour with the king and Privy Council. During months of retreat in her country homes, she was able to throw off the scandal of the past by working to present herself as a modest, pious, serious-minded scholar who was committed to the Protestantism of the Edwardian government. By the end of 1550, the Council was ready to bring her back to court and find her a foreign husband. In December, Sir John Borthwick, an English agent in the Baltic, was instructed by the Council to open unofficial talks for a marriage between Elizabeth and the son of the king of Denmark and to stress the learning, 'godly profession' and appearance of the young princess. Nothing came of these negotiations, perhaps because the Council told Borthwick to speak of the marriage 'that it maye seeme of your owne heade' and not to admit to the Danes that the initiative behind his overture came from the government.[8]

Between 1551 and the summer of 1553, conditions for arranging a dynastic marriage for Elizabeth improved. She was treated by the Privy Council as an honoured princess and recognised as second in line for the throne. Peace was negotiated with France in 1550, and soon afterwards overtures were being made for Elizabeth's hand in marriage by minor foreign princes, who were often the allies of France: thus the duke of Guise mooted a marriage on behalf of the son of the duke of Ferrara in 1551, and in early 1553 the second son of John Frederick of Saxony expressed an interest in courting the princess.[9] Rumours were also heard about marital projects with M. d'Aumâle (a son of the duke of Guise) and the eleven-year-old son of the duke of Florence.[10] The sources do not indicate why these suits proceeded no further, whether the princes themselves lost interest or whether the Council rejected them. It seems likely, however, that John Dudley, the duke of Northumberland, Lord President of the Council and effective ruler of England, was unwilling to allow Elizabeth to marry and live abroad, while Edward was unwed and the succession to the throne uncertain.

Northumberland decided to bypass Elizabeth when he made plans to keep power on the death of Edward by marrying his son Guildford to a royal princess and diverting the succession to their son. Lady Jane Grey, the great-niece of Henry VIII, was chosen as Guildford's bride and Northumberland's pawn, while Elizabeth along with her sister was excluded from the throne by Edward's letters patent. Possibly, Northumberland had reason to know that Elizabeth was less amenable than Jane: that she could not be easily bullied into an unwelcome marriage, let alone treason, and that, once queen, she would not be content to give up effective power to her husband, son or father-in-law. Had Northumberland used Elizabeth rather than Jane, it would have strengthened his legal and political case. Declaring both of Henry's daughters illegitimate seemed both illogical and illegal, while excluding the Protestant Elizabeth from the succession made his actions look like a crude bid for power rather than the idealistic defence of Protestantism which his propaganda proclaimed. The duke may well have realised this himself, as he thought to keep Elizabeth in reserve, in case the Council would not rally around Jane. In May 1553, just before the wedding of Guildford to Jane, rumours were spreading about the court that the duke might annul the existing marriage of his eldest son, marry him to Elizabeth, and claim the throne by that route.[11]

Elizabeth's loyalty during the crisis of Mary I's accession made little impression on the new queen who had always resented and came increasingly to distrust her half-sister.[12] From the very first, Mary was keen to right the wrong inflicted on her mother, and her earliest parliament passed an act invalidating Henry's divorce from Catherine of Aragon, which in effect reinforced Elizabeth's illegitimate status.[13] Mary also showed an eagerness to remove Elizabeth from the succession, 'because of her heretical opinions, illegitimacy, and characteristics in which she resembled her mother'.[14] In these circumstances she was loath to see Elizabeth married to either an Englishman or a foreigner who might assert and fight for his wife's claim to the English throne if the queen died without issue. But not all of Mary's councillors felt the same way. Some, like Lord William Paget, not only believed that Elizabeth's right of inheritance was enshrined in statute law but also feared the consequences if she were excluded from the succession. There was first the danger that the king of France would claim the throne on behalf of Mary Stuart queen of Scotland, and second the concern that the English Queen Mary's intended husband, Philip of Burgundy and prince of Spain, would seize the throne for himself on the death of his wife. To avoid foreign domination, therefore, Paget recommended that Elizabeth be married to an Englishman and then formally designated Mary's heiress presumptive.[15] For Elizabeth's husband, Paget put forward the name of Edward Courtenay, the great-grandson of the Yorkist king, Edward IV, who had pretensions of greatness and had hoped to marry Mary rather than her sister.[16]

In late November 1553 Paget tried to persuade Simon Renard, the Imperial ambassador, to support a Courtenay match with Elizabeth. Using arguments which he thought would appeal to the queen and Habsburgs, he explained that the marriage and settlement of the succession would assist Mary's security, as it would turn Elizabeth and Courtenay away from political intrigues and make her own marriage to Philip more acceptable to those Englishmen who feared that her husband might otherwise take the throne on her death. He argued that there was no need to worry that Elizabeth would turn the country once again to Protestantism, as Courtenay seemed to be a sincere Catholic and would keep Elizabeth 'in the religion she now professed' (for under pressure from her sister she was reluctantly attending Mass). Although Renard accepted the logic of Paget's case, he was not entirely convinced by it, while Mary made it perfectly clear that she did not want Elizabeth to succeed her. Her only concession was that she agreed to think it over further and to ask the advice of her mentor and future father-in-law, Charles V.[17]

Within a month, on 24 December 1553, Charles came out very firmly against the matrimonial project, arguing that it would strengthen Mary's opponents and even encourage assassination attempts against the queen.[18] In the knowledge of this, Paget immediately began to distance himself from the scheme, and Courtenay was advised to to leave it well alone by Lord Chancellor Gardiner.[19] While the official project was thus killed off by the emperor's opposition, a number of disaffected noblemen and gentlemen at court continued to see merit in the proposed match, but for a different purpose. Instead of seeking to settle the succession, this group of conspirators aimed to depose Mary, marry Elizabeth to Courtenay, and place them both on the throne. Their plan involved four simultaneous risings in Kent, Leicestershire, Devon and Herefordshire, but it was prematurely uncovered, and only one rising in fact took place: Wyatt's rebellion in Kent. Elizabeth probably knew something about the plot but sensibly avoided giving the conspirators any indication of her knowledge or support, in order that she could deny any involvement in the event of its failure. Again her caution served her well, but it did not prevent her imprisonment in the Tower of London and later house-arrest at Woodstock on suspicion of treason. She had her enemies at court, including Mary herself, and consequently her life hung by a thread, but she could rely on her powerful Howard relations to protect her as well as those councillors who feared that her death would destabilise the succession. Gardiner's affection for his protégé, Courtenay, also worked to her advantage, as he could hardly shield the earl from retribution and at the same time urge the execution of Elizabeth.[20]

Although no evidence implicated Elizabeth in the rebellion, it was obvious to all that she was a potential source of danger to the queen. In later years, when justifying her refusal to name a successor, Elizabeth stated her belief that she had inadvertently been a focus for plots in her sister's reign because she was next in line to the throne. This was only partially true, however, as it was the uncertainty about the succession that had helped to provoke conspiracies to place Elizabeth on the throne. Many of those who participated in Wyatt's rebellion and the later Dudley plot feared that Mary would disinherit Elizabeth and leave England with a disputed succession and opportunities for a Spanish or French seizure of power. Had they been assured that the Protestant Elizabeth would succeed to the throne, the plotters might well have waited for their middle-aged queen to die naturally, instead of seeking to oust her from power.

While Elizabeth was a prisoner in the Tower in the spring of 1554, some of Mary's councillors who wanted to protect her from execution thought in terms of finding her a husband to keep her out of harm's way. Once married, they reckoned, she could safely be set free to live under super-vision or surveillance in her husband's house, preferably far away from London. Obviously Courtenay was no longer thought to be a suitable candidate, but the earl of Arundel put forward his son, Lord Maltravers, while Lord Paget favoured a foreign match with Emmanuel Philibert, prince of Piedmont and duke of Savoy, who was a cousin of Philip and governor of the Imperial troops in Flanders.[21] Unconvinced by Elizabeth's protestations of innocence in any plots, Mary preferred the option of imprisonment, and was no doubt relieved to find that Charles V also opposed Paget's proposal for a Savoy match.[22]

Towards the end of 1554, Paget again proposed a foreign match for Elizabeth. Taking advantage of the supposed pregnancy of Mary, he was able to argue that Elizabeth was no longer 'of any great account', and so 'she might be married off to some poor German prince; for that would be the safest way to dispose of her'. His real concern, however, was to safeguard Elizabeth's succession in case the queen died in child-birth, for the princess would have to be recognised as Mary's heiress before a matrimonial alliance could be concluded. This time Charles V agreed with Paget; he was also by no means convinced that Mary would produce a healthy heir and he preferred Elizabeth as the future queen to the French claimant, Mary Queen of Scots, Henry II's prospective daughter-in-law. Charles, therefore, recognised that it would be in the Habsburg interest to wed Elizabeth to a Catholic prince who would have neither the will nor means to 'try to start intrigues in England' during Mary's life-time, and would keep England tied to a Habsburg alliance on her death. He would have chosen the Spanish duke of Segorbe's son for the purpose but feared that Elizabeth's heresy might lead her into trouble with the Inquisition, and so he fell back on a German. First he contemplated the marquis of Baden, 'as he is of their Majesties' kindred, and his states are far from the sea and near here', but in early 1555 he began to consider seriously his nephew, Archduke Ferdinand of Austria, as the better candidate for keeping England within his family if Mary and Philip remained childless.[23] Philip, however, soon made clear his opposition to Ferdinand's suit, which he feared would work against Spanish interests. At this time there were tensions between the Austrian and Spanish branches of the Habsburg family over the inheritance of Charles V, and Philip believed that an English match for his cousin would strengthen Austrian claims to the Netherlands because of England's close commercial links with Antwerp.[24] Philip's choice fell, instead, upon Paget's original candidate, the duke of Savoy, who had impeccable testimonials as an ally of Spain, since his father had lost almost all his lands in supporting the Habsburg cause in Italy. Emmanuel Philibert seemed an excellent choice on other counts too; he was the right age, of royal blood, a staunch Catholic, good at languages and not too powerful to appear a threat to the English.[25] There were only two obstacles to the match, but these were overwhelming; neither Mary nor Elizabeth would sanction it.

Philip worked for the Savoy suit in earnest during his stay in England from March to July 1557 against the opposition of Elizabeth and Mary.[26] Whatever her feelings about marriage in general, Elizabeth did not want to be identified with the Habsburg or Catholic cause which acquiescence in the Savoy match would entail. Mary for her part was still resisting the inevitable and refusing to acknowledge Elizabeth's legitimacy and status as heiress presumptive, a necessary concomitant of the Savoy match. Philip attempted to break down the opposition of his wife by using his confessor to persuade her that it was her duty to her realm and religion to allow the marriage. At the same time, he tried to trample over Elizabeth's objections by frog-marching her off to Flanders, where Savoy was governor, accompanied by the duchesses of Parma and Lorraine. Both tactics failed. Mary faltered briefly, under pressure from her husband and the confessor, but then held firm against the match, possibly through the influence of Cardinal Pole, while Elizabeth was able to take refuge behind her sister's implacable opposition and unexpected protection.[27]

The Savoy matrimonial project was raised several times again during the reign, sometimes with Mary and sometimes Elizabeth but, distracted by the war against France, Philip could not apply consistent pressure to either of them. Briefly in early 1558 he urged his wife to follow his will in the matter, but she would only agree to put the scheme before parliament, an unsatisfactory concession as Philip had already been told that most Englishmen opposed any foreign match for the heiress to the throne.[28] In June 1558 when Philip's temporary representative in England, the count of Feria, held an interview with Elizabeth, he may have offered her the recognition of her rights of succession in return for her marriage to Savoy. He certainly touched on the Savoy match in a second interview with the princess, which took place shortly before her accession, but he did not dwell on it at length, explaining 'I do not believe the time is ripe to raise the matter with her.'[29]

While Philip was pressing the suit of his kinsman, another matrimonial proposal reached Elizabeth, one which was as unexpected as it was unwelcome to Mary and the Habsburgs. In November 1557 King Gustavus Vasa of Sweden sent an envoy to England to settle some differences over commerce and to seek Elizabeth's hand in marriage for his son Prince Eric. On his arrival, before presenting himself to the queen, he went directly to Elizabeth to deliver a letter from the young prince. Mary was furious and calmed down only when she learned that Elizabeth had turned him away unsatisfied and had 'never heard of his Majestie beffore this tyme'.[30] Clearly, the queen's rage was less a reaction to the Swede's unwitting breach of etiquette than the result of her fear that Elizabeth might be tempted to encourage Eric's suit and so come under the protection of a Lutheran king. Elizabeth, however, was too canny to fall into that trap. Believing that if she played a careful waiting game the crown would eventually be hers, she wrote and told the queen that she had no intention of marrying the Swedish prince nor indeed any other.[31] The Swedish ambassador, however, did not return home and he consequently aroused some concern in Philip. Suspecting that Gustavus Vasa might make another bid for Elizabeth after the death of Mary, Philip made inquiries about the Swedish king and his realm.[32]

During Mary's reign, Elizabeth several times declared her preference for the single life. While these statements may have been expressions of her true feelings, it is more likely that they were made for a political purpose, since it was wiser to rule out marriage in general terms than to reject and risk offending individual suitors. She had no wish to tie herself to any of the men who were offered to her, as they could give her neither security nor political advantage; had she encouraged either Edward Courtenay or Prince Eric she would have been vulnerable to charges of

20

treason; had she agreed to the suits of Archduke Ferdinand or the duke of Savoy she would have lost all freedom of action once queen. Elizabeth's statements therefore did not mean that she intended to remain single for ever, and both foreigners and Englishmen fully expected her to marry. Only Paget sounded a note of caution when he warned Feria in November 1558 'that there was no one she could marry outside the kingdom nor within it'; but as the unsuccessful broker of both kinds of marriage for the princess, Paget was jaundiced in his views.[33]

Once she became queen in November 1558, Elizabeth was considered to be 'the best marriage in her parish'.[34] During the first years of her reign she attracted matrimonial suits from the kings Philip II of Spain and Eric XIV of Sweden, the archdukes Ferdinand and Charles of Austria, the dukes of Savoy, Nemours, Ferrara, Holstein and Saxony, and the earls of Arran and Arundel.[35] It should be remembered, however, that most of these men had already sued for her hand under Mary, that many of them were of relatively minor rank for a queen regnant, and that at least two of them put forward their proposals of marriage very reluctantly. None the less, the arrival at Elizabeth's court of so many princes' envoys to seek a marriage was a great propaganda victory for the new queen, since it showed that their masters were implicitly accepting her legitimacy and right to rule at a time when other monarchs were questioning or challenging it. While Elizabeth based her right of accession on parliamentary title, Henry II of France claimed the throne for Mary Queen of Scots, now married to the *dauphin*, in accordance with the fundamental law of inheritance.[36] Henry encouraged Mary to quarter the arms of England with those of Scotland and many believed that he was pressing the pope to declare Elizabeth illegitimate. In these circumstances, the presence of so many suitors at her court was of great value to the queen. It is consequently not surprising that during 1558 and 1559 she took the opportunity, whenever she could, of making a public display of these courtships – not necessarily out of vanity, as is so often alleged, but for political advantage.

During the early months of the reign many in Elizabeth's court wanted her to marry an English subject rather than a foreign prince. Among those thought suitable were the leading peers of the realm, Westmorland, Norfolk and Arundel. Sir William Pickering's name was also mentioned although he was just a courtier and minor diplomat. Of these only Henry Fitz-Alan twelfth earl of Arundel thought himself a serious candidate. In December 1558, it was rumoured that he was borrowing money on the strength of his matrimonial prospects and using some of it to bribe the queen's ladies-in-waiting to speak well of him; at the beginning of the following January, he was said to be selling 'all he has' to spend on Christmas banquets and a jewel as a New Year's gift for Elizabeth.[37] Eight months later when Elizabeth spent a few days of her summer progress at his house at Nonsuch, his lavish entertainment aroused comment and was widely believed to be another move in his bid for the queen's hand.[38] Elizabeth, however, never took him seriously as a candidate, perhaps because of his Catholicism, his age (he was some twenty years older than her) or his character (Feria viewed him as 'a flighty man of small ability' and the Imperial diplomat, Baron Breuner, was equally uncomplimentary).[39]

Several of Elizabeth's other early suitors – the duke of Savoy, King Philip and the Austrian archdukes – were candidates supported by the Spanish Habsburgs in their quest to keep England both Catholic and pro-Spanish. Philip's attitude towards Elizabeth's marriage after her accession was a continuation of his policy under Mary but conducted with more urgency. Feria shared his view:

> The more I think about this business, the more certain I am that everything depends upon the husband this woman may take. If he be a suitable one, religious matters will go on well, and the kingdom will remain friendly to your Majesty, but if not it will all be spoilt.[40]

Philip II's preferred choice was still the duke of Savoy, provided that he was not needed for a dynastic marriage in France.[41] The Spanish king was prepared to distribute bribes or pensions to win support for the match, but by the end of the year he had to admit defeat and accept the withdrawal of the duke's candidacy. Feria had assured him that the English councillors were reluctant to allow another foreign match for their queen, and especially one with the duke as 'they fear he will want to recover his estates with English forces and will keep them constantly at war'.[42] At the same time, the French were insisting on the duke's marriage to a French princess before they would agree to the restoration of his lands as part of the peace settlement at Câteau-Cambrésis.[43]

The Spaniards, therefore, had to find a new Habsburg candidate quickly. Although Archduke Ferdinand was being mooted unofficially, neither Philip II nor Feria was keen on an Austrian match. As a result, they both came to the conclusion that it was preferable for Philip to marry the queen himself.[44] Philip, however, had grave reservations about this project too. He knew that he would have to reside in his other dominions, and that the English would object to his long absences abroad. He was also worried that the French would see the marriage as an act of provocation and consequently continue the wars against Spain. Most important of all, he feared that the queen held heretical opinions and he refused to take her as his wife unless she were a Catholic.[45] Eventually, however, he set aside his doubts and decided that it would be his Christian duty 'to render this service to God' and marry the queen, provided that certain conditions were met. First and foremost, Elizabeth would have to regularise her position with the pope, by requesting and receiving his absolution:

so that when I marry her she will be a Catholic, which she has not hitherto been. In this way it will be evident and manifest that I am serving the Lord in marrying her and that she has been converted by my act.

Second, Philip wanted agreement that once wed he would not have to live in England. Finally he wanted to improve the terms of the marriage-treaty signed with Mary and ensure that the Netherlands would not be inherited by any child born of the English marriage, but instead pass to his existing son, Don Carlos.[46] Yet, even with these safeguards, Philip felt uneasy about the prospect of marriage to Elizabeth; in a secret letter written on 10 January 1559, the same day on which he announced his decision to Feria, Philip described himself as 'a condemned man, awaiting his fate', and a little later he declared: 'If it was not to serve God, believe me, I should not have got into this. . . . Nothing would make me do this except the clear knowledge that it would gain the kingdom [of England] for his service and faith.'[47] A little later he explained to Feria that he was going through with the proposal not for any political advantage but 'what has forced me into it is the conservation of our religion'.[48]

Despite the unpopularity of the Spaniards after the loss of Calais in the French War, there was some support among Englishmen for a second Anglo-Spanish match. In particular many English merchants based in Antwerp favoured a matrimonial alliance with the ruler of the Netherlands 'for hyr hone wellthe and for ye wellthe of ye relme'.[49] Elizabeth and her Privy Council, however, were bent on a religious policy that ruled out marriage with Philip II; far from changing her religion or submitting to papal authority as Philip required, they were preparing a legislative programme for a Protestant Church Settlement, which was introduced in the House of Commons during the second week of February 1559.[50]

All too aware of the intended changes in religion and Elizabeth's extreme reluctance to marry, Feria was slow to put forward his master's suit. He delayed speaking to the queen about it until after a parliamentary delegation had petitioned her to marry, and even then he conducted the negotiations with little sense of urgency.[51] None the less, he continued to write in favour of the projected marriage to the king and played down the importance of the proposed religious changes, as when he claimed that 'if the marriage is carried out the rest will soon be arranged, and all will proceed in accordance with the glory of God and the wishes of your Majesty'.[52] The news from England, however, was making Philip increasingly despondent. Unwilling to marry the queen if the Protestant legislation passed through parliament and unconvinced that Elizabeth wanted to marry him at all, he began to consider making a French marriage to seal the treaty being negotiated at Câteau-Cambrésis. He therefore told Feria to settle the negotiations with Elizabeth quickly so that he could press ahead in that alternative direction if he had to, and even before he had heard from his ambassador of Elizabeth's final rejection of his proposal, he had arranged a marriage with Elisabeth de Valois.[53]

While few believed that Elizabeth would want to marry Philip II, some suspected that she would encourage his suit if only to keep intact the Anglo-Spanish entente and isolate France at the peace conference at Câteau-Cambrésis. The French were particularly concerned that she would 'toutefois donner espérance, et l'entretenir par ce moyen, afin qu'il ait occasion de tenir plus fort et plus roide au fait de Calais'.[54] Yet in this they were mistaken. From the earliest mention of the Spanish marriage, Feria was given the same negative response; Elizabeth repeatedly told him that 'she had no desire to marry' as indeed 'she had intimated from the first day'.[55] In each of her interviews with him, she rehearsed all her old prejudices against marriage in general, reiterated the by then familiar case against marriage to a foreign prince, and went on to produce a new and compelling argument against marriage to Philip in particular. The Spanish king, she pointed out, was her brother-in-law and her marriage to him would be invalid, as forbidden in the scriptures; nor would she accept a papal dispensation to remove this prohibition, since she initially questioned and then 'denied point-blank' the pope's right to overturn scriptural injunctions.[56] This objection was unanswerable in political terms; for were she to accept the legitimacy of a papal dispensation in this case, Elizabeth would be *de facto* recognising the validity of her father's marriage to Catherine of Aragon and hence her own bastardy. This point had already been realised by the French as early as 7 January 1559, when their ambassador to Rome had reassured Henry II that the Anglo-Spanish marriage was most unlikely to take place since 'la dicte royne entendra bien difficilement au mariage d'elle et du roy Philippe, ne pouvait contracter avec luy, à mon jugement, qu'elle ne confesse par cet acte là que la royaume d'Angleterre ne luy appartient de succession'.[57]

As Feria did not seem to appreciate that Philip's offer of marriage had been gently rebuffed in his early interviews with the queen, she spelled out her refusal unambiguously on 14 March 1559, when she told him that she could not marry Philip as she was a Protestant, and in order to avoid any misunderstanding she repeated the words several times.[58] The date of this conversation was significant, as it took place at the time when the government's bill introducing the royal supremacy and liturgical changes was struggling for survival in the House of Lords. The bill ran into difficulties at its second reading and was committed on 13 March. Thus on the day that Elizabeth spoke to Feria there seemed a strong possibility that the bill would either be lost or amended beyond recognition; certainly a few day afterwards it was pruned of its liturgical clauses and redrafted to express the royal supremacy in terms which failed to give parliamentary sanction to her title.[59] This Bill of Supremacy which then passed through the Lords was an emasculated version of Elizabeth's original measure and its contents were unacceptable to the queen and her Protestant councillors. By turning down Philip's suit at this time on religious grounds, Elizabeth was signalling her intention to stick to her ground despite the opposition of her bishops and some lay peers in the Upper House.

It is clear then that Elizabeth had rejected Philip II's suit well before she overcame the Catholic resistance to her Church Settlement and also before she had signed the Treaty of Câteau-Cambrésis on 2 April 1559. This makes a nonsense of the view of some historians that the queen found it expedient to dally with the king of Spain both in order to stop him giving a lead to the Catholic opposition in England and to gain his help in the negotiations with the French.[60] As shown here, Elizabeth chose rather to bring the Spanish courtship to a swift conclusion in the knowledge that the legal impediments and her chosen religion made marriage with the king impossible, even though she had need of Philip's friendship in early 1559. She was prepared to take the risk of offending him, because in the short term she knew that Calais was lost, marriage or no marriage, since the French would not surrender it willingly and the Spaniards would not fight for its recovery; in the longer term, she was reasonably confident that Philip would not withdraw his protection from her and leave her undefended against his French rivals, despite the introduction of Protestant worship in England.[61]

In early April 1559, however, when the news of Philip II's impending marriage to the daughter of the French king was relayed to her, it seemed that Elizabeth and her advisers had misjudged the king badly. Alarmed by this development, Elizabeth angrily complained to Feria that the king had jilted her since she had given no formal reply to his proposal.[62] But, despite the Franco-Spanish marriage, Elizabeth's original assessment of Philip was not mistaken. No matter how deeply he hated the religious changes in England he could not afford to give succour to her enemies. He would not agree to help English Catholics for risk of stirring up political instability which could be exploited by the French. Direct military intervention was also out of the question, as he needed to concentrate his limited resources on countering the military threat from the Turks in the Mediterranean.[63] He opposed a papal crusade in support of Mary Queen of Scots for fear of a French seizure of the English crown, and he urged Pope Paul IV in April 1559 to hold back from proclaiming Elizabeth a bastard and excommunicating her until he had seen the results of 'measures that I shall be putting in hand'.[64] Although not specified, these 'measures' were undoubtedly the negotiations for a marriage between Elizabeth and one of the Austrian archdukes, which Philip was now prepared to back in a final resort to return Elizabeth to the Catholic fold.

The Austrians had shown some interest in a marriage project between Archduke Ferdinand and Elizabeth during Mary's reign, possibly because they believed that it would strengthen their claim to the Netherlands, and soon after Elizabeth's accession the emperor made delicate enquiries to see if the queen was prepared to enter into matrimonial negotiations with one of his two sons, Ferdinand or Charles. In February 1559 he sent his ambassador in Brussels, Count George von Helfenstein, to England, officially to offer bland assurances of friendship but primarily to discover 'whether this Queen and the Lords of her realm have a preference for one of our sons'.[65] During his stay at court, Helfenstein gained the distinct impression that Elizabeth was personally interested in the suit of Archduke Ferdinand and that the English would far prefer their queen to marry one of the archdukes than the king of Spain. At the same time he gave reassuring reports about the queen's religion. 'Throughout England', he wrote, 'the form of the Catholic religion is preserved'; and in any case, 'the Queen was such a sensible woman that if she obtained such a husband, she would certainly not prescribe to him in religious questions but follow him along all paths.'[66]

Encouraged by these observations and by the news that Philip II was to marry elsewhere, Emperor Ferdinand decided in April 1559 to send over to England another envoy to open formal marriage negotiations with the queen. At the same time he asked Philip to use his influence to forward the match. The Spanish king's response was positive, since by then it was obvious that this marriage would provide the last peaceful means of securing England for the Catholic Church and Habsburg interest. In addition, it would allow him to show Pope Paul IV that he was taking some action on behalf of the Catholic cause in England and thereby forestall papal intervention against Elizabeth.[67] Feria, however, had his doubts about the matrimonial scheme. First, he was suspicious about the way that the Austrians were carrying out independent negotiations, and irritated that the emperor and archdukes 'apparently will not understand that your Majesty's influence in this matter is so great that it may be said to be in your gift'. Feria's concern was not simply a matter of etiquette but rather an anxiety about the future; he worried that after the wedding the Austrians would continue to act independently and not in accordance with Spanish interests. Second, Feria was not convinced that Elizabeth could be won back to the Catholic faith, as she had already told him that she was a Protestant and wanted the Lutheran Augsburg Confession or something very like it to be maintained in the realm. Finally, he was doubtful about the likelihood of Elizabeth accepting the archduke's proposal, since he had noticed as early as April 1559 that the queen 'is in love with Lord Robert and is never separated from him'. Feria suspected that she was waiting for Dudley's wife to die so that she could then marry her Master of the Horse.[68]

Notwithstanding Feria's reservations, the Austrian suit carried on. By early May 1559 the emperor had settled on the younger Archduke Charles as the queen's suitor, since Ferdinand could not be persuaded to put aside his morganatic wife, and at the end of the month his envoy, Caspar Breuner baron von Rabenstein, arrived in England to open talks with the queen about the marriage before official ambassadors were sent to negotiate a treaty.[69] By this time Feria had been recalled to Spain, and it was his replacement, Don Alvaro de Quadra, bishop of Aquila, who gave Breuner assistance at the English court in accordance with Philip's instructions.[70]

Elizabeth's early responses to the Habsburg proposal were negative, but not final. In her interviews with the Imperial and Spanish ambassadors, it was reported that her answer was:

> she has not yet made up her mind to marry anyone in this world. She had, it is true, not forsworn marriage, as her mind might for various reasons change, but she could not at the moment come to any resolution and was also unwilling to bind herself for the future.[71]

On 5 June 1559 Elizabeth wrote to the emperor in a similar vein, telling him that although she could not speak for the future, at the present 'we have no wish to give up solitude and our lonely life, but prefer with God's help to abide therein of our free determination'. Meanwhile, Cecil instructed his agent in Germany, Christopher Mundt, to discover all he could about the archduke, including information about his appearance, temperament, religion and attitude towards Protestants.[72] By this time, however, the emperor was having doubts himself about the projected marriage. Alarmed by reports of the change of religion in England and of Elizabeth's affection for Dudley, he was no longer sure that he wanted 'to give her my son even if she asked for him'.[73] But instead of with-drawing Charles's candidacy, he decided to keep a representative in England officially to continue the negotiations but with a brief to keep a close eye on political developments there and to obstruct the suit of any other candidate who might be harmful to Habsburg interests, in particular a Protestant or an ally of the French. If Elizabeth did change her mind about marriage to Charles, then his ambassador could insist upon strict religious conditions before the match was taken any further.[74] Philip II agreed with this plan.[75]

During the summer months the courtship made no headway, and by early September 1559 de Quadra was expressing his belief that the marriage would never take place. A few days later, however, his mood switched to one of optimism, as suddenly and unexpectedly he began to detect a more positive attitude towards the archduke match at court. An unnamed nobleman together with Elizabeth's favoured lady-in-waiting, Lady Mary Sidney, the sister of Lord Robert Dudley, came to tell him and Breuner that the queen had resolved to marry in the winter and that it was therefore an opportune time to renew Charles's suit with more vigour and send him over to seek her approval. Their story was confirmed by Sir Thomas Parry, and at the same time Dudley offered his services to Philip in encouraging the match. The queen's change of attitude, they all claimed, had been sparked off by a new sense of insecurity created by a recently discovered plot to poison her and Dudley, political disturbances in Scotland, and deteriorating relations with France after the death of Henry II in July 1559. Although de Quadra was by this time inclined to distrust the queen, he did think that Lady Sidney was sincere in her message, and was prepared to believe that there was an opportunity for the archduke if action were taken quickly.[76]

Soon afterwards, the queen herself spoke to both the Spanish and Imperial ambassadors in an attempt to revive the courtship. While she would not commit herself either to marriage in general or to the archduke in particular, she told them that she could not possibly marry a man whom she had not seen, and intimated that she would be pleased to welcome Charles if he came over to England. By mid-October 1559, de Quadra had come to the conclusion that 'she is really as much set on this marriage as your Majesty is', and had also told the duchess of Parma that 'her intentions were good in this business'. Apart from the messages he had received from her closest household servants, de Quadra was encouraged by signs that Elizabeth was standing out against her Protestant clergy in her determination during the autumn to keep a cross and candlesticks on her 'altar' in the royal chapel. As a result of this optimism, both ambassadors urged the emperor to send Charles immediately to England, if necessary in disguise, so that negotiations for a marriage-treaty could proceed.[77]

De Quadra was far keener on the match than his predecessor, Feria, had been, and he was certainly guilty of 'wishful thinking' when making his assessment of the queen's attitude in the autumn of 1559. It is hard to believe that Elizabeth intended to marry the archduke at this time; if court gossip is to be believed, she was deeply attracted to Robert Dudley, and may even have been hoping to marry him at some time in the future when his wife, who was rumoured to be ill, died.[78] Her political aim in breathing life into the archduke's suit in September 1559 was to neutralise the Spanish Habsburgs in the anticipated conflict with France in Scotland, not to bind them permanently to her with a matrimonial alliance. She may also have hoped that re-opening negotiations with the Habsburgs would placate influential religious conservatives at home, like the earl of Arundel and duke of Norfolk, who were becoming increasingly disgruntled with the new Protestant regime and anxious about the direction of future policy decisions. Perhaps, too, she wished to divert attention from the growing scandal of her relationship with Dudley.

Elizabeth's ploy had some success. By raising hopes of a Habsburg marriage, she strengthened Spanish resolve to protect her against France:

thus in early October 1559, de Quadra told the Spanish ambassador at Rome that 'he must take care the French do not get at the new Pope [Pius IV] and cause him to proceed against the Queen [Elizabeth] on the Scotch queen's claims. It would do much damage both here and elsewhere before the marriage.' The French, moreover, well aware of the discussions with the Habsburgs about a marriage alliance, had to be cautious about plans to take military action against Elizabeth on behalf of Mary Stuart, their new queen on the accession of Francis II.[79] Although Elizabeth could not feign interest in the archduke's suit indefinitely, she was able to keep discussions going until the spring of 1560 without committing herself to anything or indeed giving very much encouragement to the Habsburgs.

In November 1559 news came from Emperor Ferdinand that he would not allow his son to make a state visit to England to be inspected for approval or even to travel there in disguise:

> For if you and the Bishop of Aquila think that we could have sent our son *incognito* with Count Von Helfenstein, you are greatly mistaken in thinking that it could have been done in secret. We will not say how unworthy, puerile and unseemly a journey so made would have been for us, for our son and for the whole glorious House of Austria.[80]

Apart from the dishonour and the uncertainty involved, Ferdinand still had doubts about the marriage and particularly wanted clarification about the religious issue. As he told Philip II, he was determined not to do anything that was not in the interests of God and the Habsburgs. Despite these reservations, he sent Helfenstein back to England with instructions to work out the terms of a matrimonial alliance, but he had little hope of success.[81]

By the time of Helfenstein's arrival at court Elizabeth had once again cooled towards the match and throughout the winter she refused to negotiate any terms before seeing the archduke or to agree in principle to marry him. For their part the Austrians refused to let Charles come to England before the religious difficulties were resolved and an assurance had been given that the marriage would take place if he pleased her. Not surprisingly, de Quadra grew increasingly frustrated with both the queen and the Austrians, whose diplomacy he considered inept, and he began to urge a more forceful approach to break through the deadlock. Time seemed short, as he feared for the fate of Elizabeth's Catholic bishops who had refused to take the Oath of Supremacy, and believed that Elizabeth was set on a collision course with France in Scotland.[82] He therefore advised Philip II to put more direct pressure on the queen or call her bluff by sending over the archduke to England straightaway, but the king disagreed.[83] Ferdinand too refused to give way on this point and recalled Helfenstein in May 1560. By this time all were agreed that the archduke's suit was over.

Archduke Charles's main rival for Elizabeth's hand was Eric of Sweden, the eldest son of King Gustavus Vasa, who was keen to renew the courtship begun in Mary's reign. Although Elizabeth gave him no encouragement at all prior to 1561 and little thereafter, he was the most persistent of her early suitors from abroad and only ceased his attentions in 1562. The first advance was made soon after Elizabeth's accession by Dionysius Beurreus, who had been acting as the resident Swedish ambassador at the English court since March 1558. Showing an ignorance of diplomatic protocol, Beurreus requested an answer to the proposal from Eric which had previously been presented in Mary's reign, instead of obtaining from his king a new letter addressed to Elizabeth as queen. As a result of this gaffe, he was left without any reply or indication of the queen's attitude for several months.[84]

At last on 6 May 1559 the Council informed the Swedish ambassador formally that the queen could not agree to matrimony with the prince. Nevertheless, in the summer of 1559 Gustavus sent an embassy to England led by two Swedes, Gustavus Johansson and Charles Holgersson, and a Frenchman, Charles de Mornay. The embassy attracted considerable comment at court, as they made a fine show with their 'livery, displaying some hearts pierced by a javelin on the lapels of their red velvet coats, symbolizing the passion of their sovereign', but their alien manners led them to be treated with derision by both courtiers and the queen herself.[85] Although Elizabeth again rejected the offer of marriage, the Swedes had already dispatched another embassy, this time headed by Gustavus's second son, Duke John of Finland, to plead Eric's suit.

John arrived at Harwich at the end of September 1559 with a retinue of fifty men on horseback and was escorted to court in early October by the earl of Oxford and Lord Robert Dudley.[86] The duke's tactics were to win over the queen and courtiers by his courtesy, charm and largesse, so as to demonstrate that Sweden was not a poor and backward country but that on the contrary its future king was worthy of a royal bride. Duke John proved an excellent ambassador for his brother. Many at court and in London were impressed by his command of Latin, his 'very civill and modest behaviour', and his ease in adopting English ways and customs. At the same time his wealth and generosity were noted by all. He kept an open house at his lodgings in the bishop of Winchester's residence in Southwark, 'was very liberal to the poor', and distributed sumptuous presents as bribes to courtiers. Among the many gifts he offered was a ring presented to Elizabeth which was thought to be worth some five or six thousand crowns.[87] The Swede's only mistake was to allow his rivalry with the Imperial ambassador, Baron Breuner, to get out of hand, which incurred the displeasure of the queen.[88] Despite all his efforts, Elizabeth again rejected the suit firmly and even refused to accept the proffered ring. Yet still Duke John continued to stay on at court, and on 14

December 1559, he formally presented the details of the Swedish proposal for a matrimonial alliance with England.[89]

In many ways the match was an attractive proposition. Eric was a Protestant (though admittedly Lutheran, whereas Elizabeth's new bishops tended to follow Swiss Reformed doctrines and forms of worship) so there appeared to be no major incompatibility over religion. The alliance would both assist Elizabeth in forging closer relations with the Lutheran princes of Germany and benefit English merchants who were seeking to open up commerce with Muscovy. The terms offered by the Swedes, moreover, were very advantageous to the queen and answered the main English objections to a foreign match. The Swedes were prepared to pay the expenses of Eric's houschold, to limit its size as specified by the queen, to allow Eric to reside permanently in England even when crowned king of Sweden, and to accept that he would not interfere in English matters of state. To safeguard the independence of both realms, they agreed that the two countries should continue to operate as entirely separate states. Nor did there seem to be any danger that the union of the two crowns would be permanent. Since the Swedish throne was elective, it was quite likely that a son born of the marriage and reared in England would not become a future king of Sweden; and it was perhaps for this reason that nothing was said about the inheritance of any issue from the marriage in the terms forwarded to Elizabeth. Finally, the Swedes proposed an offensive and defensive alliance, whereby each of the realms should send to the other up to eight thousand men, if and when required.

Even these terms could not tempt Elizabeth into marriage with Eric. If she had to agree to a foreign match she seemed to prefer one with the Archduke Charles, although he was Catholic and unlikely to offer such favourable conditions. At a political level, a Habsburg match could provide protection against France and the friendship of Spain, while a Swedish marriage would upset the Catholic powers, isolate the queen in Western Europe and embroil England in Baltic politics, including a war with Sweden's historic enemy, Denmark. Although there were some economic benefits from a Swedish alliance, Baltic trade was far less important to English merchants than commerce with the Netherlands, and the powerful lobby of merchants trading with Antwerp 'much misliked' the Swedish match, preferring Elizabeth to marry the archduke.[90] At the personal level, Elizabeth continued to think the Swedes alien in their habits; and in addition she considered that marriage to their king would be a form of disparagement, since Gustavus had usurped the crown from the king of Denmark and his monarchy was elective rather than hereditary.[91]

The queen's refusal to marry Eric, however, fell on deaf ears. On 3 April 1560 the resident Swedish ambassador regaled the Council with arguments in favour of the match and at Easter Duke John returned home full of enthusiasm for it.[92] Soon after his departure, Elizabeth heard that

Eric was thinking of visiting her personally. Presumably, the Swedes erroneously believed that Elizabeth's reply to the Habsburgs also applied to them: that she was not inclined to marry at that particular time but might change her mind in the future, that she would only marry a man whom she had met, and that she would welcome a personal visit from her suitor. Although Elizabeth told Eric that there was no point in his coming and that he should look elsewhere for a bride, news reached England in June 1560 that he was intending to set sail for England with about ten thousand men and a massive quantity of gold. By the summer, London, Edinburgh and Paris were buzzing with rumours of an impending marriage between Elizabeth and the Swedish prince.[93]

In Sweden, however, King Gustavus was reluctant to spend further large sums on Eric's matrimonial project, but the combined pressure of his two sons persuaded him grudgingly to consent to another embassy to England. John had his own motives for backing the match with such energy following his return to Sweden in the spring of 1560. Not only would it benefit him as ruler of Finland if his brother were to be an absentee king of Sweden, but he had also made an agreement with Eric to help him win Elizabeth in return for receiving sibling support for his own ambitions in Livonia.[94] Both brothers clearly believed that the match was possible and that if they acted quickly they could seize the initiative from the Imperialists, whose suit had initially looked more hopeful but was by then foundering owing to the emperor's veto on his son's visit to England.

In September 1560, however, Gustavus died, and on his accession to the throne Eric XIV started to rethink his matrimonial plans. Although he continued to favour an English marriage as part of a wider project of building up a political and commercial power-base in the Baltic, he was less inclined to offer such great political concessions in order to obtain it. Furthermore he could not afford to leave Sweden to woo Elizabeth personally, as earlier intended, since he needed to consolidate his position at home.[95] At first he may have thought of returning Duke John to the English court but in the event he sent over his Chancellor, Nils Guildenstern, in early 1561 with new, less favourable, terms for a marriage-treaty.[96]

Meanwhile in England, there had also been some reconsideration of the Swedish matrimonial proposal and a few men who had been previously indifferent or hostile to the match began in 1561 to see its merits. Their change of attitude was the result of two new circumstances. The first was the sudden and mysterious death of Robert Dudley's wife in September 1560 and the widower's devious and dubious manoeuvres to obtain Spanish support for his own marriage to the queen. For Protestants like Sir William Cecil and Sir Nicholas Throckmorton who dreaded a Dudley marriage, the embassy of Guildenstern seemed propitious as a means of promoting a Protestant match as an alternative to the one with her favourite.[97] The second circumstance was the death of Francis II in December 1560 and the uncertainty of the marital future of his widow, Mary Queen of Scots. Rumours reached England in the spring and early summer of 1561 that Eric was also making advances to the Scottish queen, and Elizabeth as well as her advisers grew alarmed at the prospect of a Swedish–Scottish alliance.[98] The Swedes were quick to exploit the more favourable climate for their suit and encouraged propaganda which presented Eric as an acceptable suitor to those who disliked accommodation with the Catholics at home and abroad.[99] For these reasons, Guildenstern was warmly welcomed at court at the outset, and Elizabeth even granted a safe-conduct for Eric to visit her personally.[100]

During the summer of 1561 rumours were rife in England and abroad that Eric was on his way to London with another mass of bullion, and that a marriage would soon follow his arrival. Merchants were anticipating with pleasure the distribution of Swedish treasure, while London stationers were selling images of Eric and Elizabeth side by side as if they were a married couple, much to the dismay of the queen.[101] Excitement about the match also encouraged the publication of tracts describing Sweden's history and culture of which George de Corth's *The Description of Swedland, Gotland, and Finland* was but one.[102]

Eric's plan to visit the queen was scuppered by the weather. After leaving Sweden escorted by some thirty or so vessels, his fleet was twice beaten back by storms to the Scandinavian coast and the king was forced to retire from the venture. Only three of his ships arrived safely in England, one of them containing twenty-four horses of which six had died from lack of drinking water. The vessels were brought to London, the surviving horses were stabled at the Cross Keys in Gracechurch Street for public display and admiration, while the bullion on the ships was unloaded at the Tower.[103]

As a result of this misfortune, Eric began to have second thoughts about his romantic mission and told the queen that he would need to see more positive signs of her interest in the match before setting off again; but instead of receiving any indication that she wanted the courtship to continue, Eric was treated to rumours of her scandalous relationship with Dudley. Consequently, the king began to lose interest in his suit and started to look elsewhere for a powerful bride.[104] When the Swedish ambassador put forward his proposal for a last time in December 1561, the conditions demanded were so uncompromising that many at the English court believed that the king wanted to break off the negotiations so that he could seek the hand of Mary Stuart. Against the wishes of the queen and possibly at the instigation of Dudley, who wanted to see an end to Eric's courtship, the English responded by trying to humiliate the Swedes publicly. According to an anonymous chronicler, who was usually very well informed about court life, Robert Dudley, his brother Ambrose, Lord

Admiral Clinton, the earl of Pembroke, Lord Chamberlain Howard of Effingham and the earl of Bedford, all boycotted a great feast held by the Swedish ambassador in January 1562.[105] The mayor and aldermen of London, who had initially accepted his invitation, also stayed away, sending word that they had a prior engagement, although 'some thought they durste not or that they were otherwyse comanded'.[106] The ambassador clearly could not operate in these conditions and soon afterwards planned to return home, but the queen tried to detain him for fear that he would go straight to Mary Stuart in Scotland. It was therefore not until early April 1562 that he left England.[107]

The failure of the Swedish courtship in early 1562 disappointed all those who were anxious to see Elizabeth wed to almost anyone other than Dudley. Also displeased were some merchants engaged in the Baltic trade who had been active in promoting the match. One of these was John Dymock, a London merchant, who during a business visit to Stockholm in 1561 began acting as a semi-official intermediary between the two courts and encouraged Eric to believe that Elizabeth only needed careful wooing to be won over to the marriage. Although these efforts brought Dymock into trouble with the queen and Council, he began dabbling in the Swedish match again on his return to England. Exploiting an acquaintance with Katherine Ashley, chief gentlewoman of the Bedchamber, he made contact with her in order to dig out information about Elizabeth's intentions towards both Eric and Robert Dudley. From talks with Katherine and more particularly her husband, Dymock concluded that the queen was 'well-minded' towards the Swedish king. Consequently, when he went back to Sweden in early 1562 to sell the king some jewels and was asked for news of Elizabeth, he spoke encouragingly of the marriage and urged Eric to send the queen still more valuable presents as tokens of his love, including some of the jewels which Dymock was trying to sell.[108]

Dymock's account of Elizabeth's feelings was backed up in July 1562 by several letters written from England which were addressed to Guildenstern and some Englishmen in service at the Swedish court. At least two of these were penned by English adventurers seeking profit from contact with the wealthy and reputedly generous Swedish king, but a third was written by Katherine Ashley and another lady of the Privy Chamber, Dorothy Broadbelt, whose motives were to encourage a great match for their mistress and save her from a scandalous marriage with Dudley.[109] These letters, however, fell into the hands of the Privy Council, who on the queen's instructions immediately told Guildenstern that his informants were 'idle cheats' whose tales should not be believed. Ashley and Broadbelt were confined to their chambers, while the men were interrogated and sent to the Tower for fear that a plot was afoot. It was rumoured that the affair was part of a wider anti-Dudley campaign, possibly involving the earl of Arundel, the marquis of Northampton and other enemies of the favourite, though in truth if any councillor were involved it was probably Cecil.[110] Dudley himself may well have taken this view, as it appears that he took the initiative in exposing Dymock's scheme. The Spanish ambassador reported that a Dudley spy had recovered the letters, and Dymock told Cecil that the guards who had come to arrest him had been overheard saying that they would watch out for him all night, since 'they do losse my Lord Robert's favour for ever' if he were not taken.[111] The interrogations, however, uncovered no political conspiracy and by September 1562 the two women were restored to their places in the Privy Chamber. Dymock in the meantime had eluded the guards sent to arrest him, and escaped abroad.[112]

By this time Eric XIV was looking elsewhere for a matrimonial alliance, first towards Mary Queen of Scots, without success, and then towards the daughter of the Landgrave of Hesse, to whom he became betrothed in the autumn of 1562.[113] This did not stop him, however, from continuing his suit of Elizabeth by correspondence. At the end of October 1562 he sent her a letter declaring that his love for her remained unabated; and again in the October of the following year he wrote marvelling at her constancy in remaining single so long on his account and asking for a safe-conduct so that he could come to her court and woo her in person.[114] On the first occasion he was angling to obtain some trade concessions and on the second he was looking for an ally in his war against Denmark, which had broken out the previous May.[115]

Eric's long pursuit of Elizabeth was looked on with suspicion by the Austrians and Spaniards, who feared that the negotiations might end in a marriage which would confirm the queen in her heresy and result in a Lutheran alliance. At the same time, however, it was disliked by the Lutheran king of Denmark, who himself claimed the throne of Sweden, as well as by the French and Scots who feared that an Anglo-Swedish union would make Scotland vulnerable to attack. Their diplomatic activity against the match included presenting their own candidates for the hand of Elizabeth.

The main Danish contender was the uncle of King Frederick II, Adolphus duke of Holstein, who, despite his meagre lands and status, had several notable points in his favour. He was generally thought to be exceptionally good-looking, and Thomas Randolph commented on 'the nobilitie of hys howse, the goodliness of hys personage, his power, hys frendes, and also that he professethe the same religion'.[116] His friends included the Habsburgs for whom he had long been acting as a mercenary, although in fact they did not believe that he would suit their purpose as husband of the queen. At the end of March 1560 the duke visited England to enter royal service, and formally put forward his marriage proposal. Although Elizabeth turned him down, Cecil was anxious not to offend the duke whose troops he wanted to use in the war then taking place in Scotland,

and so Adolphus was greeted with great courtesy, honoured with the Order of the Garter and told that no final answer could be given until the Scottish campaign was concluded.[117] Once the peace of Edinburgh ending the war was signed in July 1560, Holstein intimated that he would send over envoys to pursue his suit, but was put off by Cecil who wrote telling him that the queen had no interest in marriage.[118] At the end of the year, possibly perturbed by the rumours of Elizabeth's emotional entanglement with Dudley which were spreading across the courts of Europe, Holstein wrote to the queen directly to request a firm answer to his proposal. In her reply she dealt the final blow to his hopes.[119]

While it is true that the French were most hostile to the matrimonial schemes of their Habsburg rivals, they also disliked the suit of Eric of Sweden.[120] Although Cecil and the Spanish ambassador believed that they would favour an Anglo-Swedish matrimonial alliance to thwart the Austrians, the French had in fact good reason to be suspicious of the Swedes, who 'ne fust de longue mains amy ou allié', and to see the marriage as 'un danger trop grand et chose grandement préjudiciable' to the king of France.[121] It was not easy for Henry II, however, to find a suitable alternative candidate who could tie England to the French interest: his three unmarried sons were far too young for Elizabeth, and he was reluctant to put forward another French suitor in case it would signify the recognition of her title, thereby prejudicing the claims of his daughter-in-law to the English throne. Consequently, he was ready to give clandestine encouragement to the suit of his ally, John Frederick duke of Saxony, but not to support that of the Frenchman, the duke of Nemours, on the grounds that it would imply that he recognised Elizabeth as the legitimate queen of England.[122] After his death, the French court supported a range of candidates to spoil the Swedish match: the son of the duke of Nevers, the duke of Ferrara and even the earl of Arran.[123]

It was the Scots who expressed most concern about the prospect of a Swedish marriage, which they feared could result in their own encirclement and 'd'avoyr un voysin si grand qu'il seroyt s'il peult conjoindre la force d'Angleterre avec la sienne'.[124] For this reason as much as any other, the Protestant Scottish Lords of the Congregation pressed Elizabeth to accept James Hamilton, third earl of Arran, as her consort in the summer of 1560, and urged the king of France to advance Arran's cause.[125]

As early as June 1559, there had been some interest in Arran as a possible suitor amongst both English and Scottish Protestants, since he and Elizabeth were 'mariable both and the chief upholders of God's religion'.[126] In March 1560, while English troops were struggling to oust French garrisons from Scotland as allies of the Lords of the Congregation, Cecil told the English ambassador in Scotland to raise the marriage with the Scots as a means of cementing a league between the two realms. In response to this overture and also because of anxieties about the Swedish courtship, Arran's suit was discussed in the Scottish parliament in August 1560, and the following November an embassy of Scottish lords arrived in England to present a formal proposal to the queen.[127] In the knowledge that Arran's main rival was Eric, the lords tried to persuade the English that a Scottish match would bring far greater political rewards than a marriage with the Swede. In the words of one of them: 'theyr ostentation may be greatar and they themself ar able to make a greatar shewe off richesse then we, but fynde I not wherin theyr frendship shall stand England in soche stede as ouris may do'.[128] As the Scots saw it, the political benefits for Elizabeth included not only amity and co-operation between neighbours 'once so much in discord', but also a possible future union of the two realms, since Arran was the son of the heir presumptive to the Scottish throne.[129]

By this time, however, Cecil's interest in the match had cooled. Neither he nor Elizabeth could see any immediate political advantage in the offer. The Scots were already her allies and there now seemed no likelihood that the French would retain a presence in Scotland, as Cecil had feared when he had originally suggested the match. The marriage would bring no other alliances, since the Habsburgs opposed it and the German Lutherans would be dismayed were Elizabeth to prefer a Calvinist husband over a Lutheran. In the longer term there was in fact no guarantee that a marriage would unite the two realms. Arran was only second in line to the Scottish throne and would succeed only if Mary Stuart had no child and he outlived both his father and the queen; but since Mary was his junior by ten years and quite likely to remarry and conceive, the earl's accession was uncertain at best. As the Spanish ambassador to the French court observed, marriage to Arran would bring Elizabeth only his person, for she would gain neither foreign allies nor any great prospect of securing the succession to Scotland.[130] There existed the danger, moreover, that once the earl was married to Elizabeth, the Scottish lords would seek to depose their rightful queen to put him on the throne, a move which would involve Elizabeth in an illegitimate and unwelcome attack on Mary's rights and lead to a renewed struggle against France. For all these reasons Elizabeth immediately turned down the suit and soon afterwards Arran looked towards Mary Stuart for the satisfaction of his marital ambitions, thereby following the same path as so many other of Elizabeth's rejected suitors.

Until the Dudley romance disturbed the political scene, the early courtships of Elizabeth aroused few strong feelings at court. Although the rival suitors and their ambassadors squabbled among themselves, most of the English courtiers and councillors showed little inclination to take sides. While they had their preferences, many were probably content to consolidate their own political positions before a royal consort was chosen.

Others simply could not make up their minds between the different candidates; one of the latter was the earl of Sussex, who wrote to Cecil in 1560:

> I have heard the opinions of the most and greatest discursers of England touching the Quene's Mariage. And I confesse that some tyme the great amytie, some tyme the gret ryches that myght be gotten by forein marriages, some tyme the exampell of King Philip, some tyme the knitting with Scotland, and some tyme the dowte of the desire of domesticall persons to exalte or overthrowe olde friends or foos according their affections have drawn me diiversely in opinion so as I have been much dowtefull where to settle whilest these persuasions wrought in my head.[131]

The Archduke match could only command the support of Norfolk and possibly Paget. Although Parry and Dudley had seemed to back it in the autumn of 1559, it is probable that they were merely carrying out the queen's instructions; Parry was thought to favour an English marriage with Sir William Pickering, another favourite of the queen, whereas Dudley was playing his own game. The most vocal support for a Habsburg marriage came from the English merchants who traded with the Netherlands and the diplomats based in Antwerp who represented their interests: Sir Thomas Gresham and Sir Thomas Challoner.[132] Support for the Arran match was similarly limited. Cecil appears to have favoured it for a time, as did various ambassadors abroad, including Throckmorton in France and Thomas Randolph in Scotland. Its attraction lay in hopes that it might result in a union of the two realms, for history had demonstrated that 'estats hath by no one thing growed so greate, and lastyd in their greatnes, as by mariages, which have united countryes that do confyne together'.[133] Its weakness lay in that dynastic union could not be assured. The Swedish match enjoyed more support particularly in late 1560 and 1561 when Eric seemed to Cecil and some of his friends a far better choice of husband than Dudley. Had the Swedish ambassador, Nils Guildenstern, conducted the negotiations with more skill and offered better terms, there might well have emerged a strong and united pressure group in favour of the match, which Elizabeth would have found difficult to resist. As it was, Elizabeth could take refuge behind her surfeit of suitors to evade marriage with any of them. Those desperate for a Protestant heir did not lose heart when she rejected each courtship in turn, even though they may have lost patience, as there always seemed to be another possibility of a matrimonial alliance amid the steady stream of suitors.

Even in her own lifetime Elizabeth was accused of dalliance with her suitors. In response to this criticism, she was to protest in early 1571:

> whilest we continued, as it were settled by natural disposition in a determination not to marry, we did so also plainly answer all persons,

and required that the motions might be stayed; wherewith if the parties or their Ministers would not be satisfied, but would continue rather still their motions; what default was this in us? Yea, it is very true, that some parties being answered by our own mouth, and that deliberately and frequently, yet would they not accept the same for a final answer; wherein as we could not but esteem their affection very great towards us, so truly did we give them no new cause to hope of any change of our mind of marriage.[134]

Her self-justification was neither disingenuous nor cynical, but the simple truth. As seen from this account, Elizabeth did not play diplomatic games with her suitors, with the possible exception of the Austrian archduke briefly in the autumn of 1559, and during this courtship the emperor was almost as guilty of dalliance as the queen. In all her other courtships she did not prolong the negotiations unnecessarily, but on the contrary told each suitor without delay of her intention to stay single for the present and urged them to look elsewhere for a bride. Some, like the dukes of Saxony and Ferrara, listened and disappeared quickly from the marital scene; but others, most notably Eric of Sweden, could not believe that a queen regnant would risk the succession by remaining unwed and therefore decided to bide their time and woo her either by persuasive arguments or romantic gestures. Elizabeth's consistent refusal to be moved stemmed in part from political considerations, for each of the candidates had his own disadvantages; it suited her, moreover, to remain single while establishing her rule and religious settlement; but the overall impression, from reading the correspondence of contemporaries, is that Elizabeth turned down the opportunity of marriage to a foreign prince so readily in the early years of her reign, because she was deeply in love with her own subject, Robert Dudley.

3

THE DUDLEY COURTSHIP

Robert Dudley was born in 1533, a few months before Elizabeth. Although his grandfather was attainted for treason at the accession of Henry VIII, his father, John Dudley, gained influence and rewards in the king's service, including the title of Viscount Lisle. At the beginning of Edward VI's reign, participating in the political scramble for new honours, the viscount was promoted to be the earl of Warwick, but it was after the fall of Lord Protector Somerset that he became the dominant figure on the Council and in 1552 was awarded the prestigious dukedom of Northumberland. At the beginning of Mary I's reign, however, for engineering the abortive coup of Lady Jane Grey, it was his turn to be attainted for treason, while his five sons were incarcerated in the Tower for their active role in his conspiracy. Guildford, the husband of Lady Jane, went to the scaffold immediately after Wyatt's rebellion, another son died in prison, but Robert and his two remaining brothers were released and pardoned in January 1555. With this personal history, Robert Dudley found it well nigh impossible to lose the stigma of being the heir to a line of traitors, even after his subsequent loyal service to both Mary and Elizabeth.[1]

Almost nothing is known of Robert Dudley's relationship with Elizabeth before she became queen. In 1566, he told the French ambassador that they had been friendly even before she was eight years old: 'ayant commencé a la cognoistre familierement devant qu'elle eust huit ans'.[2] Building on this evidence, some writers have seen them as childhood playfellows, but, while it is certainly possible that they knew each other when he was part of the household of Prince Edward, it is most unlikely that they were ever close companions as children. It is equally unlikely that they had any contact with each other when they were both prisoners in the Tower, another popular but unsubstantiated belief. Nor is there strong evidence that towards the end of Mary's reign Robert sold some of his land in order to help Elizabeth who was then in some financial difficulties at Hatfield.[3] None the less, just before Mary's death, Dudley was picked out by Feria as one of the men in favour with Elizabeth and likely to benefit from the new regime.[4]

On Elizabeth's accession, Robert and his sole surviving brother, Ambrose, were given office at court. On the first day of the reign Ambrose was made Master of the Ordnance, an office previously enjoyed by his eldest brother, and in January 1559 Robert was appointed Master of the Horse, a position which had been held by his father. Their promotion reflected Elizabeth's general determination to reverse the policies of her sister and restore the fortunes of those who had suffered in the previous reign; it was not their personal reward for past friendship or favours, as is sometimes said. Neither man in fact made gains as great as several other political figures whose families had been prominent in the government of Edward VI and lost out under Mary. Robert received no substantial grants of land until March 1561 and Ambrose was not granted his father's and elder brother's titles, Viscount Lisle and earl of Warwick, until December of the same year.[5] It has been suggested that Elizabeth was unwilling to provide them with a power-base until she could be sure that they would not seek to avenge their father's death, but it is also probable that she did not identify them immediately as her long-term supporters or as opponents of the previous regime. After all, they had intended to exclude her, as well as her sister, from the throne in 1553. She may also have felt that they were too closely associated with the Marian regime, since after their royal pardon they had given loyal service to Mary and Philip and volunteered to fight in the war against the French in 1557, an adventure in which their brother Henry had died at the battle of St Quentin.[6]

As Master of the Horse Robert had frequent access to the new queen. With responsibility for her stables he was Elizabeth's regular companion at her favourite pastimes of hunting and riding and, with lodgings at court, he attended royal suppers and entertainments. Very soon it became noticeable that he had come into great favour and was enjoying a special place in Elizabeth's affections. Early in April 1559 gossip began to spread about their relationship, some of it scurrilous, and by the autumn a scandal was fermenting. In the spring of 1559 it was being said that Elizabeth was visiting him in his chamber day and night and showing him so many signs of affection that it was clear she would marry him, were his wife to die; by November it was being whispered that Dudley intended to help his wife on her way by means of poison.[7] Rumours of Dudley's intimacy with the queen not only spread through the English court but were carried by foreign ambassadors to those abroad, inevitably tarnishing her reputation. To some extent Dudley was blamed for the incipient scandal as his conduct was thought to be 'uncomly' for a married man but Elizabeth was also held to be at fault: 'a yong princesse canne not be to ware what contenance or familiar demonstration she maketh more to oon than to another', wrote Sir Thomas Challoner to Cecil.[8] Katherine Ashley, too, believed that Elizabeth could do more to scotch the malicious tales in circulation, and begged the queen to marry one of her suitors and so 'put an end to all these disreputable rumours' about Dudley, 'for she showed herself so affectionate to him that Her Majesty's honour and dignity would be sullied'.[9]

As well as touching the queen's honour, Dudley's pre-eminence with Elizabeth was creating unhealthy rivalries at court. He was particularly resented as a *parvenu* whose family contained three generations of traitors, but he was also feared as a potential faction-leader whose ambition knew no bounds and whose vengeance against his late father's enemies would be great.[10] His sudden rise made him so unpopular that rumour succeeded rumour of plots to assassinate the favourite: an attempt to poison him at the earl of Arundel's house; threats to kill him uttered by a courtier called Drew Drury; and a murder conspiracy led by the duke of Norfolk.[11] Tensions ran particularly high in late 1559, not only due to jealousy but also because Dudley's relationship with the queen was believed to be affecting policy. Norfolk in particular blamed Dudley for the failure of the Archduke matrimonial project, a decision which he believed would have serious repercussions for England's security and lead to a disastrous war against France in Scotland.[12]

Court gossip about Dudley and the queen subsided for a time during the first half of 1560 while Elizabeth and her ministers were preoccupied with the military expedition sent to Scotland to help the Protestant Lords and flush out the French. There is hardly any reference to the relationship of queen and favourite in the correspondence of the late spring and early summer months of 1560. None the less, once the crisis in Scotland was over Elizabeth again began spending most of her leisure-time with Dudley, hunting with him 'dayly from morning tyll nyght' and showing evident delight in his company.[13] By August 1560, their intimacy was once more causing concern and stimulating calumny. At court there was a renewed rumour, possibly initiated by Cecil, that Dudley intended to poison his wife, while in east Essex a woman from Brentford was spreading stories of Elizabeth's supposed pregnancy by the Lord Robert.[14] By early September it looked as if political change might be brewing as a result of the rise of Dudley as royal favourite. Cecil was feeling increasingly marginal at court and began to hint to his friends and to the Spanish ambassador that he intended to resign his office.[15] It was in this climate of suspicion and uncertainty that the news of the death of Amy Dudley hit the court and country.

Unquestionably the death of Dudley's wife on 8 September 1560 had a number of unusual, not to say suspicious, features but it is unlikely that it would have aroused such a stir had it not been for its timing.[16] Amy Dudley had broken her neck after a fall down 'a paier' of stairs (a staircase with two landings) 'which by reporte was but eight steppes', not a likely occurrence, especially if her head-dress was undisturbed by the accident as was later claimed.[17] At the time of the tragic incident, moreover, she appeared to have been alone in the house, Cumnor Place, where she was living as the guest of her husband's steward or treasurer, since she had sent away her gentlewomen, maid-servants, and companion Mrs Odingsells to a fair at Abingdon for the day. It was all too easy to believe that one of the gentlemen living in the house, either Anthony Forster or Sir Richard Verney, both friends of Robert Dudley, had orchestrated or personally carried out her murder.

In these circumstances no-one was surprised that Amy Dudley's death gave rise to 'grevous and dangerous suspition, and muttering' throughout the country, nor was anyone in any doubt about how important it was for Elizabeth and Dudley to clear their names from any suspicion of conspiracy to murder.[18] Dudley especially was aware 'what the malicious world will bruit' and consequently decided to stay away from Cumnor while the investigations into the death were taking place, so that none could say he had tampered with the evidence there or used his influence to obtain a favourable verdict from a coroner's inquest. Instead he urged his servant and kinsman, Thomas Blount, to charge the coroner to call a jury of 'no light or slight persons, but the discreetest and [most] substantial men', who would be seen to scrutinise every piece of evidence thoroughly and impartially in order that 'shall it well appear to the world my innocency'.[19] For her part, Elizabeth immediately distanced herself from her favourite and sent him to his house at Kew, until the inquest had reached its verdict and declared Amy Dudley's death an accident.

Even though Blount believed that the jury had taken 'great pains to learn the troth' about the cause and circumstances of Amy's death, rumour persisted that the outcome was a cover-up. A contemporary chronicler, who was admittedly no friend to Dudley, implied that the foreman of the jury, a Mr Smith, was neither independent nor trustworthy, by pointing out that he had once been 'the Quene's man, being lady Eliz., and was putt owte of the howse for his lewd behaviour'.[20] It was the chronicler's impression also that 'the people saye she was killed by reason he [Dudley] forsocke her company withowte cause', despite the findings of the jury that it was death by misadventure. He himself seemed to believe that Verney had ordered his man to do the deed, though whether or not at the direct instigation of Dudley he left unclear.[21] At the French court, too, the rumours persisted that Amy Dudley had not 'by mischaunce' broken her own neck but that 'her neck was broken', and 'dishonorable and naughty reaportes' circulated there for much of the autumn:

one laugheth at us, an other threateneth, an other revileth her Majestie, and some let not to say what religion is this that a subiect shall kill his wief, and the prince not onely beare withall but mary with him, not sticking to reherse the father and the grandfather.[22]

For the rest of his life, Dudley was never able to shake off completely the imputation that he was responsible for either a cover-up operation or the actual murder of his wife. After a quarrel with the favourite in September 1561, the earl of Arundel made arrangements to delve into the testimonies given at the inquest in the hope of turning up some incriminating evidence.[23] In 1567 Amy Dudley's half-brother, John Appleyard, who had been present at Cumnor while the inquest was proceeding, 'said that for Dudley's sake he had covered the murder of his sister', although later, when his accusation was investigated further and the case brought before Star Chamber, he retracted his statement and admitted that it had been made 'only of malice'.[24] In 1584, the virulently anti-Leicester tract known as *Leicester's Commonwealth* accused Verney of killing Amy Dudley on orders from her husband.[25] On the whole, however, historians have judged Dudley innocent of both charges, or at least found the case against him both unproved and unlikely. Since few think that Amy could have met her death by falling down a mere eight stairs, whether accidentally or as an act of suicide, a medical theory has been put forward that she was suffering from a form of breast cancer which caused her bones to fracture or crumble spontaneously, and almost by default this has gained general acceptance.

More than four hundred years after the event, there is no possibility of determining the precise cause of Amy Dudley's death. The evidence placed before the inquest is no longer extant; the staircase at Cumnor cannot be seen at first hand as the whole building was destroyed by fire; even the bodily remains have disappeared and cannot be exhumed and examined to determine the nature of a fatal injury or the existence of a degenerative disease. The mystery remains, especially as there are strong objections to every theory that has been posited to explain the death, whether it be suicide, murder, accident or death by natural causes. If pressed, I would judge suicide to be the most likely explanation. There was a motive for Amy Dudley taking her own life, the opportunity of the empty house and some evidence of an unsound mind. Thomas Blount had noted the early testimony of her maid, 'who doth dearly love her', that her mistress had prayed to God to deliver her from desperation, and he had heard other tales of the victim which led him to believe that she was 'a strange woman of mind'. Even if the method of suicide seems a little amateur and unusual, it did have the merit of making the death look accidental which would be necessary to ensure a decent and Christian burial.[26] Dudley would be anxious to stifle suggestions that he had driven his wife to such a desperate act, an anxiety which would sufficiently explain any attempt to make contact with the foreman of the jury or influence its proceedings, if indeed such interference ever took place. Though less likely, murder cannot be completely ruled out with Dudley playing the role of Henry II at the time of the murder of Archbishop Thomas Beckett.

For a short time Dudley played the part of the grieving widower, spending some £2,000 on his wife's funeral and wearing black for about six months after her death, but on his return to court in early October 1560 it was widely believed that he was 'in greate hoope to marry the Quene'. He continued to receive many marks of her favour and expected to be raised to the peerage. In many parts of London 'the Reporte whas that hyr Hygness shoolde marry him', and at court everyone was in a state of nervous uncertainty about Dudley's future.[27] The opposition to his matrimonial plans was overwhelming, however, and, apart from Dudley's own following, support came only from Lord Paget, who was ill and without office, and the earl of Sussex, who could do little to promote the match as he was engaged in royal service in Ireland.[28] Rumours were soon heard that the nobility would rise if the marriage took place; according to one account, Arundel, Northampton and Pembroke would lead the opposition to the marriage.[29] De Quadra thought there might be plans afoot to make the earl of Huntingdon successor and to reopen the Habsburg matrimonial project.[30] In the event, the crisis passed without any major incident, but feelings were obviously running high and at the end of November a great affray at court broke out between the retinues of Dudley and the earl of Pembroke.[31]

Throughout this period of tension, Dudley's position with the queen remained unassailable. Although she was undecided about their future and showed signs of emotional stress during the autumn months, Elizabeth did not waver in her affection and support for her favourite.[32] He remained her trusted confidant and anyone who dared to slander or slight him was in danger of disgrace or detention. A servant of the earl of Arundel was punished for uttering 'Lewde and unfytting Wordes', including a reference to Dudley's attainted blood; two servants of Cecil were reported to the queen for not lifting their caps when Lord Robert passed by; and Throckmorton was warned off criticising the Dudley match by his friends, as his advice was being 'taken but practice of your own hand rather of ill will than well meaning to the state'.[33] In this political climate, all politicians needed to display caution and Cecil proved the most successful at revealing little of his true feelings. In the knowledge that his letters were being intercepted, he avoided putting in writing his views on the projected marriage to ambassadors abroad, while at court he continued to act on friendly terms with Dudley, so much so that a messenger used by Throckmorton described him as 'the only minister for my Lord Robert and so hath ben a good tyme'.[34] In reality, Cecil was as opposed to the marriage as anyone; not only did he fear it would damage the queen's reputation and stir up factional unrest, but he was also concerned about his own position as her leading adviser.

Some time during the autumn and winter of 1560 Elizabeth seems to have made up her mind that a marriage to Dudley could not be risked, as it would endanger her throne and discredit her abroad. In November 1560 she had drawn back from ennobling Dudley, thereby depriving him of a status deemed necessary for a prospective royal consort, and her behaviour in taking a knife to slash the patent at the very last moment suggests that this was a decision which caused her considerable distress.[35] The following January, she again deliberately decided against enhancing Dudley's power and importance, when she awarded to Cecil rather than her favourite the lucrative and influential office of Mastership of the Court of Wards, which had fallen vacant on the death of Sir Thomas Parry.

In these circumstances Dudley recognised that he could no longer rely on his personal magnetism with the queen to realise his ambitions but instead had to find some powerful allies elsewhere to act on his behalf and so persuade Elizabeth that a marriage with him would not lose her the throne. With little possibility of obtaining the support of the Council or nobility, he turned to Philip II of Spain in the hope that Habsburg advocacy of the match might well win over to his side religious conservatives within the English peerage like Norfolk, Arundel and Lord Howard of Effingham, who were long-standing friends of the Spanish king. According to his political calculations, he had a fair chance of procuring Spanish support for the match, since he had worked hard to ingratiate himself with Philip during Mary's reign and on many occasions after Elizabeth's accession had tried to present himself to de Quadra as 'the best servant that His Majesty has here'.[36] At first the ambassador was inclined to trust him. Early in 1559 he courted Dudley as the royal favourite, and during that autumn believed that Dudley was working for Habsburg interests, when he seemed to be promoting the Archduke Charles match. After its collapse, however, he came to view Dudley with contempt and repeated to Philip all the scandalous gossip attached to his name.[37] None the less, de Quadra was prepared to listen carefully to the proposal made by Dudley in January 1561. Dudley's brother-in-law, Sir Henry Sidney, made the initial contact. According to de Quadra's report of 22 January 1561, Sidney approached him and expressed his amazement that Philip did not seize the opportunity to put Dudley in his power by supporting the marriage, so that the English lord would serve and obey him as his own vassal.[38] As the conversation progressed, Sidney went on to say that religion in England was in a very bad state and in need of remedy, and that Dudley and the queen were determined to restore it by way of a Council. Sidney explained that he had not spoken on his own initiative but had been sent by Dudley with, he believed, the consent of the queen.[39]

On 13 February, Dudley himself had an interview with de Quadra in the presence of Sidney, and implored the ambassador to speak to the queen in favour of the marriage. When de Quadra did so two days later, Elizabeth confessed that she had some affection for Dudley but that she had at no time in the past decided to marry him or anyone else, although she could see every day how necessary it was that she married and knew that her subjects preferred her to marry an Englishman. She then asked what Philip's reaction would be if she married one of her servants, as had the duchesses of Suffolk (either Mary Tudor who had married Charles Brandon or the present duchess married to Richard Bertie) and Somerset (the widow of the Lord Protector who had married a certain Francis Newdigate). The following day Dudley, who had been given an account of the conversation by the queen, begged de Quadra to speak to her again on his behalf, offering in return for Spanish aid to send a representative to the third session of the Council that was being convened by the pope at Trent, adding that if they could not find anyone else to send he would go there himself.[40]

Historians have disagreed markedly about the significance of these conversations. Marie Axton could not accept de Quadra's account at face value as it conflicted with her view of Dudley as a Protestant activist and patron.[41] Kenneth Bartlett, on the other hand, has claimed that during the early 1560s Dudley was engaged in a cynical plan to restore the Catholic religion as the price for papal and Spanish help in realising his ambitions, and 'was willing to sacrifice his political and religious connections with the reformers in order to secure Elizabeth as his wife and the crown matrimonial'.[42] Wallace MacCaffrey, meanwhile, has suggested that Dudley, in agreement with the queen, was prepared to promise the restoration of Catholicism in return for Philip II's support for the marriage, without having the slightest intention of keeping to it once the wedding had taken place.[43]

There is no reason to discount de Quadra's reports. It is out of the question that so experienced a statesman could be mistaken in his understanding of a number of different and important conversations. Nor is there any strong argument for considering Dudley's behaviour to be in any way out of character. In the early 1560s he gave his patronage to both sides of the religious divide and it was not until several years later that he was exclusively identified with the Protestant cause.[44] At the same time it seems unlikely that Dudley and the queen thought that they could get away with such a sleight of hand in their dealings with Philip II by making promises that they could have no intention or means of honouring. A closer examination of what was being offered is needed in order to find a more convincing explanation for their conduct.

First of all Sidney and Dudley did not offer the Spaniards a 'restoration of Catholicism' but 'to restore religion by way of a general Council'. In the context of political events in 1561 this meant something else altogether. In November 1560 Pope Pius IV had called for a General Council of the Church to meet at Trent the following January, and sent nuncios to the German Lutheran princes with an invitation to attend. Shortly afterwards, in January 1561, he appointed Abbot Martinengo as his nuncio to take a formal invitation to the English court.[45] The Protestants on the Privy Council were naturally suspicious of this papal initiative and reluctant to admit the nuncio, but they also recognised the dangers involved in rejecting the Council out of hand, especially as they were not sure what policy the Lutheran princes or the French government intended to follow. Cecil, therefore, wanted to co-ordinate a response with the Germans and French along the lines that they would all refuse to attend a Council presided over by the pope but would agree to send representatives to a free and general Council of the Church. To this end he sent his agent, Christopher Mundt, to an assembly of the German Lutherans gathered at Naumburg in early January 1561 to discuss their joint response to the papal invitation. Mundt was instructed to tell the princes that they should not assent to the council unless it were held in Germany, and to recommend that the German princes and English government should keep each other informed about their resolutions, 'so as consydering both their cause in that point is but one, their aunswer and dealing may be also one'. In addition he was told to communicate Elizabeth's desire for an accord in doctrine and 'perfect amity and frendship' in the form of a league with the Lutherans.[46] At the same time, the earl of Bedford was sent to Paris with instructions to persuade the French to work 'either to procure suche a lawfull generall Counsell as may be proffitable to Christendome, or ells to stay this papal [Council] for a time' and to take into account the responses of the German Lutherans and English queen before they made a final decision.[47]

By making his proposal to de Quadra in the midst of these negotiations, Dudley was offering to use his influence in favour of an alternative strategy: attendance at the Council of Trent as convened by the pope and the admission of the papal nuncio. He was aiming to move the queen away from Cecil's policy of organising opposition to a papal Council and building up closer links with the Lutheran princes. As no-one could be sure what the Lutheran or Huguenot response to the papal invitation would be, Dudley might well have been hoping in January 1561 that they too would agree to send representatives to a Council, which could then work to reform the Church and end the schism in Europe. Even if they ultimately decided against attendance, he could still recommend that Elizabeth should accept the papal invitation in the belief that, given the fluid nature of the religious situation in Europe and the irenic temperament of Pope Pius IV, English representation at the Council would show a conciliatory attitude to the Catholics without committing the queen to any major religious change. Whether or not in the last resort Dudley would have been prepared to compromise or surrender the 1559 Church Settlement in exchange for marriage to the queen is an unanswerable question, but in early 1561 he was clearly not making that offer.

As a result of the overture to de Quadra, the issue of the Dudley marriage became inextricably enmeshed with the question of the entry of a papal nuncio to England and English representation at Trent. On the Spanish side, Philip II was prepared to continue negotiations along the lines proposed by Sidney, but insisted that Elizabeth demonstrate her sincerity first. He demanded that she free the Marian bishops who had been imprisoned for refusing to take the Oath of Supremacy and send one or more of them to the papal Council, before he would even consider making any statement supporting her marriage to Dudley. As for de Quadra, he planned to treat Martinengo's entry as the test of Elizabeth's honesty in her dealings with him.[48] On the English side, Elizabeth's behaviour indicates that she was ready to allow the entry of Martinengo to England, provided that her reception of him did not imply any recognition of papal authority. She was also prepared to give serious consideration to English participation in a general council which was not dominated by the pope, as a means of ending the religious divide in Europe and safeguarding her own position with the Catholic powers.[49] As for marrying Dudley, she refused to make any firm statement of intent, saying only that she would not marry him against the wishes of her subjects.[50] She allowed his intrigues with the Spaniards to continue and gave him considerable encouragement throughout the early months of 1561 – in marked contrast to her treatment of all her other early suitors. Dudley, therefore, had good reason to hope that she would marry him if he were successful in winning over the nobility.

In the middle of March 1561 Elizabeth brought Cecil into the negotiations. By then Cecil had learnt that the German Lutherans had decided to boycott the Council and were expecting a similar negative response from Elizabeth, whereas Catherine de Medici, the queen-mother and regent in France, had expressed her readiness to send a representative to the Council of Trent without imposing any conditions on the pope. In these circumstances, English acceptance of the papal invitation would align Elizabeth with the Catholic powers in Europe, and Cecil therefore disliked all the elements of the Sidney proposal. Reading between the lines, it seems that instead of openly denouncing the policy, he launched a damage-limitation exercise by taking charge of it and moving it into a different and less dangerous direction. He almost certainly dissuaded the queen from sending a special negotiator to Spain, as Dudley had wanted, and successfully advised her to allow him to discuss the matter with de Quadra. He also worked out with her a procedure which would publicise Philip's support for the match but not make her and Dudley entirely dependent on Spain. At his interview with the ambassador in March 1561, Cecil suggested that Philip write a personal letter in support of the marriage, which could then be presented before a meeting of some twenty representatives of the three estates (bishops, peers and burghers), 'all of them confidants of Robert and informed of the Queen's wish' so that the marriage could then be arranged 'with the accord of these deputies'. Although Cecil did not mention religion during this interview, he took whatever opportunity he could afterwards to discuss with de Quadra the means of reconciliation with Rome and conditions for an English presence at a general council. The terms he laid down held firm to the Protestant position and would have ensured the continuation of the 1559 Settlement in England; as such they were ultimately unacceptable to Philip II and the pope.[51]

None the less, in early April 1561 de Quadra was still hopeful that Martinengo would be allowed entry into England and that agreement would be reached about representation at the Council. Elizabeth had said that the nuncio could come, provided that he obeyed the laws of the kingdom (meaning that he would not publicly hear Mass) and was called 'the ambassador of the Bishop of Rome' (not the papal nuncio).[52] She had moved de Quadra to lodgings at Greenwich where the nuncio could be received without having to face a hostile crowd as he travelled through the streets of London, and Dudley had assured him that there was no difficulty in the way of Martinengo's visit. At the same time, the matrimonial plans were progressing, and a meeting of the Knights of the Garter on St George's Day was being considered as an opportune time for proposing the match to representatives of the realm.[53] By a skilful and unexpected manoeuvre, however, Cecil suddenly sabotaged these plans and gained the initiative. Informed of the damning depositions of a Catholic priest who had been arrested at Gravesend, Cecil saw a way to whip up an anti-papal scare, which would demonstrate to the queen the dangers of Dudley's policy, make the arrival of a papal nuncio politically impossible, and thus deter Philip II from supporting Dudley's marriage to the queen.

The Catholic priest was a chaplain of Sir Edward Waldegrave, named John Coxe, who had been en route to deliver money and letters to English Catholic exiles in Flanders. His testimony implicated several notable Catholics, including two Marian ex-councillors (Waldegrave himself and Sir Thomas Wharton), who were immediately arrested and charged with violating the Act of Uniformity. Several other priests, meanwhile, were accused of working spells to compass the queen's death. During the investigations that followed, a letter was found in Waldegrave's house which contained information about the arrival of the papal nuncio and expressed the hope that it would be soon followed by the release of the Marian bishops and the granting of toleration to English Catholics.[54] This gave Cecil the opportunity to claim that the prisoners were involved in seditious political activity with de Quadra and the Marian bishops, and were hatching a plot which aimed to restore England to the papal fold and overturn Protestantism. Playing on this fear, he was able to frustrate Dudley's plans by persuading Elizabeth and the Council that Martinengo should be denied entry into England. Cecil's crucial role in the affair cannot be doubted, as he admitted it openly to Throckmorton in May 1561:

> This Bishop of Aquila [de Quadra] had entered into such a practise with a pretence to furder the grete matter here, meaning pryncipally the Church matter, and percase accidentally the other [marriage] also. . . . When I sawe this Romish influence towards about one month past I thought necessary to dull the papists' expectation by discoveryng of certen massmongars and punishyng of them. . . . I take God to record I meane no evill to any of them, but only for the rebating of the Papists' humours which by the Quene's levity grow too rank. I fynd it hath done much good.[55]

On 25 April 1561 Cecil informed de Quadra that an extensive conspiracy had been discovered and that consequently the nuncio could not possibly be admitted. A few days later, Elizabeth complained to the ambassador of tales being spread by the papists that she had promised him 'to turn Catholic at the instance of Lord Robert'.[56] In this climate of hostility towards Catholics and fear for the future of the Church Settlement, Cecil and his 'best pillors', Lord Keeper Bacon, the earl of Pembroke, and the marquis of Northampton, persuaded the Privy Council to agree unanimously to refuse admission to the papal nuncio; 'not that any counsellor was outwardly unwilling, but no man was found so earnest and bold as to adventure the advising of such as were of other minds'.[57] The resolution was taken on 1 May 1561 and notice of the decision was sent immediately to France and the Lutheran princes of Germany.[58] A few days afterwards, Elizabeth told de Quadra that no English representatives would attend the Council of Trent since it was not general, universal or free.[59] Clearly, Cecil had won the struggle at court for control over policy and foiled the schemes of Dudley and the ambassador. As he told Throckmorton in a note of triumph, de Quadra 'findeth all his conceptions and practices unjointed and underfoot', and 'as for me I can see no certain disposition in her Majesty to any marriage'.[60]

The final plank in Dudley's stratagem came unstuck at the annual meeting of the Knights of the Garter held around St George's Day in April 1561. The earl of Sussex, on leave from Ireland, proposed there that the Order should petition the queen to marry Dudley, but Norfolk, Arundel and Lord Montague objected strongly and would only allow a petition to go forward in more general terms, urging that she marry but without saying whom.[61]

Elizabeth and Dudley had been cleverly outmanoeuvred in the spring of 1561 by Cecil and his supporters. With the benefit of hindsight, it can be seen that the failure of Dudley's Spanish intrigues marked an important change in his relationship with the queen; although she could retain him as her favourite, she was forced to surrender the idea of making him her consort. Her awareness of this development allowed her mood to lighten and her feelings for Dudley to appear less intense. She could even afford to joke about their relationship, as when she jested with de Quadra that the Spaniard could act as a minister at their wedding if only he knew enough English.[62] None the less, few at court appreciated that Dudley's position with the queen had changed, and his courtship vied with the Swedish match for public attention, until the latter faded away at the end of the year. Courtiers noticed that Elizabeth's 'goodwyll and favour contynwyth styll' towards her favourite, and reported stories which illustrated her fondness for his company.[63] In August 1561 there was a rumour that Elizabeth intended to put the Dudley marriage before her parliament, as she was of the opinion that no-one would dare to speak out against it.[64] It was generally believed that Dudley would soon be raised to the peerage as a preliminary to marriage, and when his brother was made earl of Warwick in December 1561, several comments were made that his elevation was an encouragement for Lord Robert.[65] By the end of 1561, Dudley's men were boasting of his matrimonial prospects with the queen, and after her final rejection of the Swedish ambassador's proposal of marriage in December, it looked as if they had cause for their optimism.[66] Although many of the nobility together with Cecil continued to be unhappy at the prospect of his marriage to the queen, Dudley was making new political friends and eroding some of the opposition to his suit.

The arguments in favour of a Dudley match were expressed in several literary works which appeared at various times between the death of Amy Dudley and the beginning of 1562. Always an effective self-publicist, it is likely that Dudley was the patron of these works, although in only one case – the play and entertainments performed by the lawyers of the Inner Temple in January 1562 – is there evidence of active patronage, and the others may have been written to attract his attention rather than at his behest. One of them, a *Dialogue on the Queen's Marriage*, was written by Sir Thomas Smith, a young diplomat who had recently quarrelled with Cecil and was looking for a new patron to help him advance in royal service. Although not printed at the time, the *Dialogue* appears in many manuscript copies and was probably widely circulated at court.[67]

Following the Renaissance convention of framing arguments in the form of a rhetorical conversation, the *Dialogue* discussed the relative merits of Elizabeth staying single, marrying a foreigner, or wedding an Englishman. Marriage at home was the course favoured and its case was presented by Axenius or Homefriend. Part of Homefriend's argument was intended to appeal to xenophobic instincts and national pride, particularly when he praised the natural superiority of Englishmen in their attitude to marriage.

'I pray you, what nation is there, where matrimony is so indifferently of each, and so godly of both kept, as in England?' he asked, before reciting the marital faults of other nationalities in Europe: the jealousy of the Italians, French and Scots, and the drunken habits of the Dutch, Danes and nations of Germanic origin. At the same time, however, Smith, *via* Homefriend, articulated deep-seated fears about the political repercussions of a foreign match on England. Drawing on the experience of Mary's reign, he could argue that a foreign husband might well use England's resources to finance his own territory's wars, 'then shall he covet to enrich that, and to impoverish ours'. Equally alarming, he might 'bring in the manners and conditions of that country which he liketh best' to England, and so 'to frame her Majesty, as they call it, to his bow which he thinketh best'. The danger with this lay not so much in matters of taste, such as clothes, diet or pastimes, but in laws and institutions, which he shall 'by all means study to bring them hither'. An English consort, on the other hand, would have none of these political disadvantages and he would moreover provide Elizabeth with the better chance of a happy married life. Instead of taking 'a pig in the poke', she would be choosing a man whose qualities she had seen with her own eyes; instead of settling for a man with alien habits, which could cause discord, she would enjoy the companionship of a man from a similar background, and 'likeness of tongue, behaviour, manners, education be those which make love, bring fruit, and cause amity'.

Although Smith did not mention Dudley by name in his discourse, he did discuss and dismiss the two arguments most usually raised against marriage to her favourite: first that it was disparagement for a queen to marry a subject; and second that it would lead to faction, since 'envy naturally kindleth amongst equals'. As to the former, Smith's answer was that there was no dishonour for Elizabeth to marry within the ranks of the English nobility. An English duke, earl or baron, he wrote, was 'as noble as the nobility is of other realms. . . . How then should the Queen's Majesty be more disparaged, marrying here one of that degree than there?' As the kings of England had suffered no disparagement on the many occasions when they had married a female subject, why, he asked, should it be disparagement for Elizabeth to wed an Englishman? Concerning factional strife, he denied the validity of the one historical example which his contemporaries usually cited as proof that marriage within the realm would bring in 'envy, strife, contention, and debate' (that of Edward IV to Elizabeth Woodville), and he claimed that there were better examples of dissension produced by foreign marriages (such as that of Henry VI to Margaret of Anjou).[68]

The issues of disparagement and faction were raised in another literary work written at about the same time, *The Play of Patient Grissell* by John Phillip.[69] Little is known about the play's provenance, but from internal evidence it appears to have been written sometime between late 1560 and 1561, though not licensed for public performance until sometime after July 1565. The plot would be familiar to an educated audience, as it was taken from a story in Chaucer and Boccaccio, but in order to give his play political relevance Phillip changed its emphasis away from the actual trials of Grissell after her marriage to Prince Gautier, which had dominated the earlier versions, and instead devoted the first half to the deliberations which had led the prince to marry a peasant girl.[70] The contemporary references to the queen and Dudley were clear from the text. At the beginning of the play, Gautier expressed his preference for a life of celibacy in lines reminiscent of those used by Elizabeth, while the words spoken by his councillors to persuade him to marry echoed the fears of contemporary Elizabethans about the succession:

> That after you your sead of rule, might have the dignite
> For wher ther is no ishue left the wise man saieth plaine
> That every man in Lordlie state, doth covit for to raigne.
>
> (ll. 179–82)

When Gautier agreed to marry for the good of the realm, he insisted on choosing his own spouse and selected, not a lady of noble birth, but Grissell, a maid of peasant stock; and here the playwright made much of the disparity in rank between the two. While Grissell was of 'poore degree' and 'poore estate', Gautier was of 'hie estate':

> Your Noble state, your dignitie, your honor and your name
> Your worthie birth, your parents race, atchivinge troump of fame.
>
> (ll. 668–9)

As a result, the Vice, Politic Persuasion, who disliked the match, raised objections to it, on grounds of disparagement:

> In her ther is no iot of noble sanguinnitie,
> Therfore unfitly that her seed should rule or have dignitie.
>
> (ll. 926–7)

Grissell and Gautier, however, demonstrated by both their words and actions that the peasant girl was a worthy bride of the noble prince. Grissell showed that she was not an ambitious upstart, an accusation usually levelled at Dudley, by urging the prince to take another woman as wife:

> Therfore goe chuse a better choice, elleckt ameeter mate
> Which may increase and ample make, thy worthy sanguine state.
>
> (ll. 678–9)

Gautier, meanwhile, extolled the virtues of his lover in words which countered the contemporary accusations against Dudley that, once king, he would usurp the government and provoke factional unrest at court.

> She feareth God, she dreads his name, she leads a Godly life,
> And dayly sekes for to subdue contensyon and stryfe
> She will as dutie byndes, hir spoused mate obaye.
>
> (ll. 393–4)

Thus Gautier married Grissell in the knowledge that 'it shall no whit abase my state, nor minishe my renowne'.

The third work written to promote the Dudley match was produced for the stage in late 1561 by the lawyers of the Inner Temple. A year previously, Dudley had successfully used his influence with the queen on their behalf in a jurisdictional dispute with the Middle Temple. In gratitude they erected the Dudley coat of arms in their hall 'for a perpetual monument', vowed that they would never permit one of their members to be 'retained' against him, and chose him to be their Christmas Prince for 1561, a position which allowed him to commission plays and preside over their revels.[71] The masques and play, produced first for their Twelfth Night entertainments and then taken to court on 18 January 1562, were designed to promote Dudley's suit with the queen. In the afternoon the lawyers performed the play, *Gorboduc or Ferrex and Porrex*, written by Thomas Norton and Thomas Sackville, which was intended to show the dire consequences for England if Elizabeth were to reject Dudley's hand; in the evening they participated in the masques of the Prince of Pallaphilos and of Beauty and Desire, which presented Dudley's credentials to be a royal consort.

The plot of *Gorboduc* concerned the fate of Britain after its king, Gorboduc, decided against the advice of his council to divide his kingdom between his two sons, Ferrex and Porrex.[72] A succession dispute followed, the two princes were murdered, civil war raged and the realm became prey to foreign invasion. In focusing on this story, the authors followed the precepts laid down in *A Mirror for Magistrates*: that all monarchs should look into the mirrors held up through poetry and drama to learn how to behave wisely and morally. They thereby sent out a message to Elizabeth that a similar disaster could befall England if she were to imitate the actions of Gorboduc. Just as he had acted against the natural order in dividing his kingdom, so Elizabeth would be acting against nature if she refused to marry, and just as his action had led to a country bereft of an obvious heir and to a consequent civil war, so would Elizabeth's rejection of matrimony. Disorder arose for the Britain of Gorboduc:

> when lo unto the prince
> Whom death or sudden hap of life bereaves,
> No certain heir remains, such certain heir,
> As not all – only is the rightful heir,
> But to the realm is so made known to be.
>
> (Act V, ii, ll. 246–50)

Political disturbance could shake it again if Elizabeth were to die without issue and deprive the state of the most 'certain' and 'rightful' heir – a child from her own body.

No special reference was made in the dialogue of *Gorboduc* to Dudley as a candidate for the queen's hand but the allusion was clear. In the dumbshow before the second act the king was offered an ordinary glass of wine which he refused and then a golden chalice filled with poison, which he took, with predictable results. The moral of this mime was later picked up by the chorus:

> Lo, thus it is poison in gold to take
> And wholesome drink in homely cup forsake.
> (Act II, ii, ll. 107–8)

The golden chalice here represented the king of Sweden whose envoys had ostentatiously distributed gold in their bid to win the queen's hand, whereas the 'homely cup' was Dudley, the home suitor, whose wealth and status were so much more modest. As explained by one member of the audience who recorded his reactions to the play, this dumbshow signified 'howe that men refused the certen and tooke the uncerten, wherby was ment that yt was better for the Quene to marye with the L[ord] R[obert] knowen then with the K[ing] of Sweden'.[73]

One of the speeches made in the final act of the play was similarly a recommendation of Dudley's suit. When the character Eubulus spoke out in favour of the native line of succession, he uttered the words:

> Such one, my lords, let be your chosen king,
> Such one so born within your native land;
> Such one prefer; and in no wise admit
> The heavy yoke of foreign governance.
> (Act V, ii, ll. 169–72)

It is usually assumed that these lines were intended to support the claims to the succession of the English-born Catherine Grey over those of the Scot, Mary Stuart.[74] Catherine was at that time confined to the Tower as a punishment for her secret marriage to Edward Seymour, earl of Hertford, and many Protestants were anxious that the queen would refuse to recognise her and her son as rightful heirs to the throne. The lines, however, can equally well be interpreted as a statement in favour of an English consort for the queen, as they reflect an argument frequently used by Dudley's supporters against a foreign match. Likewise, the speech of Eubulus at the very end of the play, which lamented the failure to call a parliament during Gorboduc's lifetime to resolve the succession and thus save Britain from civil war, should not automatically be taken as another indication that the play was written to promote the Grey claims to the succession on the grounds that the House of Commons was known to favour her as the legitimate heir. The chronicler who sat in the audience certainly understood the reference differently: 'Many thinges were handled of marriage and that the matter was to be debated in parliament, because yt was much banding that hit ought to be determined by the councell.' He appreciated that Norton and Sackville were recommending a mirror image of the circumstances in the play whereby a dynasty was destroyed and a country devastated by Gorboduc's failure to listen to his Council:

> Hereto it comes, when kings will not consent
> To grave advice, but follow wilful will.

Their moral therefore was that the queen's marriage should be settled by the Privy Council, and only if the councillors failed to carry out their responsibility or if the queen refused to follow their advice should a parliament be called to lay down the succession.

The masques played in the evening of Twelfth Night were more direct in their presentation of Dudley's matrimonial suit. In her reconstruction and interpretation of the masques, Marie Axton has shown that in the 'Prince of Pallaphilos' the lawyers created for Dudley, their Christmas prince, a fictitious classical genealogy which elevated him to a rank worthy of marriage to a queen, and that the story of Pallas, Perseus and Medusa presented him as the royal champion ridding England of the many-headed dangers to its safety. This was not the first or last time that Dudley concocted a spectacular pedigree for himself. Richard McCoy has found at Longleat a lavishly illustrated 'Book of Petegrees' which traces Dudley's descent back through more than fifty-seven pages to the legendary Guy of Warwick; another document at the College of Arms traces back Dudley's and Elizabeth's genealogy to a common ancestor, obviously with the intention of proving them a suitable match.[75]

The masque of 'Beauty and Desire', which ended the proceedings, was a wooing allegory in which Lady Beauty (signifying Elizabeth) was successfully courted by Desire (Dudley), and wed in the Temple of Pallas after the goddess had expressed her approval of the match. The wedding was then celebrated by the masquers who took the ladies in the audience as partners in a dance, which itself conventionally signified a wedding. The Christmas Prince was naturally expected to invite the queen to dance and the masque thus concluded with the fiction of Dudley wooing Elizabeth twice: by offering himself as her dancing or marital partner at the fictional wedding of the couple who symbolised themselves.

As the Christmas Prince, Dudley was the active patron of these entertainments and he used them in a renewed campaign of courtship later in January 1562. Barely a week after he had told de Quadra that his matrimonial affairs were 'at a very good point', he brought the play and masques to court to be played before the queen.[76] Within ten days of their performance he approached the Spanish ambassador again and requested Philip II's help in persuading the queen to accept him as a husband. This time, however, he offered little or nothing in return, and explained that Philip should not make any conditions 'en cosas de religion', since it was out of his power to deliver anything.[77] In a re-run of the events of the previous year, Dudley's name was proposed as a royal consort during the celebrations of the Knights of the Garter for St George's Day – but with a major difference. This time, the duke of Norfolk petitioned the queen to marry 'firste generally and at leingth of the L[ord] R[obert]', and he was supported by Sussex, Pembroke, Montague, Clinton, Howard of Effingham and Hunsdon. Only Arundel and Northampton stood apart from this scene and, according to two separate accounts, showed their dissent by walking out. Elizabeth, however, replied more cautiously to the supplication than Dudley had hoped. Although she expressed pleasure at her knights' words and agreement with their judgement of Lord Robert 'who she believed deserved the rule of the world', she declared that she still needed to give the matter further consideration.[78] Also at the St George's Day meeting, Dudley's heraldic crest was altered to allow him to use his family emblem, a bear with a ragged staff, which signified that he would not have to wait long before being raised to the peerage.[79] All in all, Dudley's campaign seemed to be working, and he urged Philip to write in support of the match in time for Easter.[80] The disappearance of the other royal suitors had left him a clear field, and at the same time growing apprehension about the succession was dulling opposition to his marital ambitions. After all, the queen's marriage to Dudley was better than no marriage at all, which was beginning to seem the most likely alternative and would end in an inevitable disputed succession and possible civil war on her death. The Britain of *Gorboduc* seemed not that far away.

Elizabeth revealed little about her intentions towards Dudley at this point. She told de Quadra that she was free from any betrothal, 'notwithstanding what the world might think or say', but that 'she thought she could find no person with better qualities than Lord Robert', if she were obliged to marry in England, which seemed likely because 'she had quite made up her mind to marry nobody whom she had not seen or known'.[81] Perhaps she was hoping that the momentum for the marriage would overwhelm its remaining opponents, and was waiting to see if the scandals of the past could be forgotten. If so, she had reckoned without Cecil. Although the details are obscure, his hand can be detected behind a relatively minor political incident which caused a major reverse in the progress of Dudley's matrimonial plans at the end of April 1562, shortly after the meeting of the Knights of the Garter.

For some time, Cecil had been bribing de Quadra's secretary, Borghese Venturini, to spy on his master and betray the contents of his correspondence. According to de Quadra when he later discovered his servant's treachery, Cecil had been hoping to ferret out information which would discredit him with the queen and put an end to his dealings with Dudley over the marriage and religion.[82] On 28 April 1562, Venturini made a statement which disclosed the extent of his master's communications with Dudley, relations with the English Catholics, and his unflattering descriptions of Elizabeth's indiscretions with her favourite.[83] The effect was devastating. Up till then, both Elizabeth and Dudley had believed that de Quadra was sympathetic to their relationship and wished to see them married, but they now learned the contrary: first that he had been passing on gossip which dishonoured them; and second how he had advised Philip II to do nothing concrete in favour of the match on the grounds that it would alienate the English Catholics who wanted to see religious concessions as a *quid pro quo*. Both were deeply offended and neither took the ambassador into their confidence again.[84] Furthermore, the episode once more brought home to Elizabeth that a Dudley marriage would seriously damage her reputation abroad by seeming to confirm the stories of her loose conduct with her favourite. At the same time, the revelations about Dudley's intrigues with Catholic Spain rekindled suspicions amongst some Protestants that he was prepared to betray the true religion for the sake of worldly ambition.

After this setback, Dudley directed his energies towards foreign affairs, and during the late spring and summer of 1562 he became a leading advocate of armed intervention in the French Religious Wars to help the Huguenots, break the power of the Guise relations of Mary Stuart and to secure the return of Calais for the queen. In November 1561 he had sent his secretary on a secret mission to the Huguenot leaders, Gaspard de Coligny and the young Henry of Navarre, and thereafter he supported a policy of intervention in France.[85] When he first showed interest in French politics, de Quadra believed that he was largely motivated by thoughts of winning Huguenot support for his matrimonial plans, and initially he may well have been looking to France for further international voices to speak out in his favour.[86] But very soon he became both genuinely attracted to an aggressive military policy on the continent as well as conscious of the broader political benefits that could accrue to him from promoting this particular line of action. By influencing foreign policy he could carve out a new role as the queen's adviser which was less constricting for a man of ability and ambition than that of court favourite; by standing out as the most ardent spokesman for the international Protestant cause he could rehabilitate himself with English zealots who favoured giving military aid to their co-religionists abroad. With this in mind, he made friendly overtures to his political opponent, Sir Nicholas Throckmorton, still ambassador at the French court, who was known to support intervention in France, and he successfully convinced him of his sincerity in working for the 'prosperity of true religion'.[87]

During the period of negotiations with the Huguenots and the organisation of the French campaign, the issue of the queen's marriage slipped into the political background, but it came to the fore again at the end of the year as a result of Elizabeth's close encounter with death from the smallpox in October 1562. The most alarming aspect of this traumatic event was the total inability of the Council to reach agreement on a successor. De Quadra painted a picture of near paralysis at court with councillors divided between the rival claimants of the queen of Scotland, Lady Catherine Grey, Lady Margaret Lennox and the earl of Huntingdon.[88] The anonymous mid-Tudor chronicler recorded the 'grete lamentacon made', at the time of the queen's illness; 'no man knoweth the certenty for the succession, every man asketh what parte shall we take'.[89] For this reason councillors planned to raise the question of the succession and the queen's marriage to Dudley in the parliament due to meet in January 1563.[90] No sooner had it been summoned the previous November than de Quadra had heard that its business would include a petition supplicating the queen to marry Dudley.[91]

All historians have recognised the importance of the succession issue in the 1563 parliament. Their accounts of its proceedings, however, have usually concentrated too heavily on the attempts of the MPs to resolve the succession question by petitioning the queen to name an heir, and have failed to appreciate that the main concern of both Houses was to persuade the queen to marry. According to Sir John Neale, for example, 'As politeness and tact – hope also – demanded, there was a humble request to Elizabeth to marry. It was brief, and quite subordinated to the main theme of the succession.' [92] Here Neale was wrong; the marriage issue in fact dominated the proceedings. When looking back at the events of 1563, Cecil made no mention of a bill in the parliament to limit or nominate the succession but noted: 'In Parlement Petition made both by the Lords and Commons, that hir Majesty would marry.' [93] Similarly, before the session began, de Quadra noted that the House would deal with three issues: the queen's marriage to Dudley, money and religion; but he was less sure that a bill would be introduced to designate her successor.[94]

The royal marriage was raised first in the official sermon given before the queen at the opening of parliament on 12 January. The preacher who delivered the address was Alexander Nowell, the dean of St Paul's, whom Sir Geoffrey Elton identified on rather slim evidence as belonging to the clientage of the Dudley family.[95] After outlining some of the 'sharper laws' which he hoped parliament would introduce to erect a godly commonwealth, Nowell praised Elizabeth for entering the wars in Scotland and France 'for the surety of the realm', and exhorted her to provide for its greater security by marrying, producing an heir of her own body, and ending the uncertainties of the succession. Just as the marriage of her predecessor, Mary, had been 'a terrible plague to all England, ... so now for want of your marriage and issue is like to prove as great a plague', he continued. Her recent illness, he said, had been a warning of her mortality and the chaos which would likely follow her demise, for everywhere voices could be heard saying, 'Alas what trouble shall we be in, even as great or greater than France.' With the summoning of this parliament, he concluded, he felt encouraged to hope that all might be resolved: 'there should be such order taken, and good laws established which would again erect up the decay of the same'.[96]

There is much left uncertain about Nowell's sermon. Was he encouraging MPs to introduce a petition on the queen's marriage and the succession, or did he know of plans to introduce one? Was he acting independently or as a mouth-piece for Robert Dudley, William Cecil, or the Privy Council? Conyers Read believed that Cecil might have had a hand in choosing the preacher and the theme of his sermon, but Elton suggested that Nowell was being used by the Dudley faction on the Council 'to work up steam for the general hope that Elizabeth might act'.[97] It certainly seems that the 'coincidental' timing of Nowell's exhortation with the introduction of a petition on the queen's marriage and succession less than a week afterwards is too great to allow for the possibility of Nowell acting independently. His sermon, moreover, referred obliquely to several matters raised in the Lord Keeper's opening speech to the session: a 'sharper' law against papists; godly legislation, and 'defence against the forreyne enemye abroade'.[98] The strong likelihood, therefore, is that Nowell had been informed in advance of the conciliar programme for the parliament and knew also that there was an intention to raise the question of the queen's marriage and succession. The source of his information is unknown, but it seems probable that he was articulating a general conciliar concern rather than acting as the mouth-piece of any particular group of councillors. There was certainly an expectation that the issues of marriage and succession would be raised in the House well before a burgess introduced a motion for the succession to the Commons on 16 January 1563. As already seen, the previous November de Quadra had thought that the queen's marriage with Dudley would be discussed in the forthcoming parliament, while on 14 January 1563 Cecil wrote to Sir Thomas Smith in France that 'I think somewhat will be attempted to ascertain the realm of a successor to this Crown'.[99]

The MP who initiated the debate on the succession on 16 January 1563 was unnamed in the *Commons' Journal* but may have been Richard Gallys, one of Dudley's 'men of business'.[100] His motion was followed up two days later with a debate on the queen's marriage and succession of the crown 'by diverse wise personages', and on 18 January 1563 a committee was appointed to draw up articles for a petition to the queen. The draft petition was read to the House on 26 January by Thomas Norton, one of the authors of *Gorboduc* who had sat on the parliamentary committee, and was delivered to the queen two days later.[101] Its wording echoed the sentiments of the play. Were Elizabeth to die 'without knowen heire', there would follow:

> the great daungers, the unspeakeable miseries of civill warres, the perillous intermedlinges of forreyne princes with seditious, ambicious and factious subiectes at home, the wast of noble howses, the slawghter of people, subvercion of townes, intermission of all thinges perteyning to the maintenance of the realme, unsurety of all men's possessions, lives and estates, dayly interchang of atteindors and treasons.

The queen was urged, therefore, to ensure that the succession would fall to the 'most undowted and best heires of your crowne', by taking a husband and marrying 'whomsoever it be that your Majestie shall choose'. In the meantime, they requested, she should designate her successor, since her name was the last to be mentioned as an heir in the 1543/4 Act of Succession and there was also some uncertainty about the validity of Henry VIII's will (which had given the junior Grey line precedence over the Stuarts in the succession), as the original copy seemed to be missing.[102]

The emphasis on the royal marriage in the Commons' petition was highlighted at the end of the parliamentary session, when the Speaker was brought into the House of Lords to give his final oration. There, Speaker Williams said nothing about defining the succession but rather reminded the queen of the Lower House's desire 'that some happie marriage to your contentacion might shortlie be brought to passe', and beseeched 'God to encline your Majestie's hart to marriage, and that he will so blesse, and send such good successe therunto that we may see the fruit and children, that may come thereof'.[103]

Although there is no mention of any debate on marriage and succession in the *Lords' Journal*, other sources show that the Upper House approved the Commons' petition, before it was presented to the queen, and introduced one of its own on 1 February 1563. The Lords' petition insisted that the marriage and succession should be handled together and 'not sonderly nor th'one without the other'. Their first request was that the queen should marry 'where it shall please you, with whom it shall please yow, and assone as it shall please you'; and their second was that she should name a successor at once in case 'God calls your Highnes without any heire of your body'. Two peers felt sufficiently strongly about the matter to take up pen to write to the queen privately in support of the petition, one of them because he had been too ill to attend the debates.[104] In March, the Lords dropped their consideration of the succession and channelled their efforts into the question of the queen's marriage in the hope that they could make more headway on this issue. Lord Keeper Bacon delivered a speech on behalf of the whole House to the queen, urging her 'to dispose your selfe to marrye, where you will, with whom you will, and as shortlye as you will'.[105]

Elizabeth's answers to the parliamentary petitions were on the whole gracious but non-committal. She did not leap to the defence of her royal prerogative, but thanked the Commons courteously for their petition of 28 January and claimed, perhaps rather unconvincingly, that its contents did not anger her, as 'some restles heades' in the House believed. She refused, however, to give any immediate answer and prevaricated with the words: 'I am determined in this so great and weighty a matter to differ myne answer till some other time, because I will not in so depe a matter wade with so shallowe a witt.' Nearly three weeks later, however, when two councillors speaking on behalf of the Commons reminded her that they had not yet received her answer, there was a note of distinct irritation in her reply, as she told the 'young heads' in the House to 'take example of the ancients' who knew very well that she had not forgotten their suit.[106] Still more tetchiness was expressed in her speech to the Lords, after they presented their original petition; according to de Quadra she told them that the marks on her face were the pits of smallpox and not the wrinkles of old-age, so she still had time to bear an heir and need not name a successor.[107] Elizabeth kept silent on all the petitions until the closing ceremony on 10 April 1563 when in a prepared statement read out by the Lord Keeper, she offered some hope of a future marriage in declaring that whatever her preferences as a private woman for a life of celibacy, 'yet doe I strive with my selfe to thinke it not meete for a prince. And if I can bende my liking to your neede I will not resiste suche a minde'. As for naming her successors, however, she would give no positive answer at that time.[108]

The emphasis on marriage in the parliamentary petitions of 1563 was only in part because it was seen as a better solution to have an heir of the queen's own body than one designated by parliament, which was the argument presented by the MPs. The most important factor was that the question of the queen's marriage was less contentious than that of determining the next in line to the throne. On the succession, the Council and parliament were hopelessly divided between the supporters of the Scottish queen and the various English claimants.[109] What is more, Elizabeth herself was unwilling to exclude Mary Stuart from the throne, which was the aim of many Protestants sitting in parliament. The House of Lords acknowledged the intractability of the succession issue in March, when the Lord Keeper ignored the peers' original insistence that the matrimonial and succession questions should not be separated and instead introduced a new petition which focused only on the marriage. Similarly, Cecil admitted the difficulty of reaching an agreement about a designated heir in that parliamentary session, when he drafted a bill to cut through the Gordian knot of the succession by allowing the Privy Council to exercise power as a regency council on the queen's death until a new monarch was chosen by parliament.

By contrast, the Lords and Commons could unite behind requests that Elizabeth marry. Like motherhood and apple pie, the principle behind the marriage petition could hardly be less controversial, especially as Elizabeth was not urged to select any specific candidate nor even an Englishman in preference to a foreigner, as Mary had been in 1553. None the less, by begging the queen to marry whatever man she wanted, the wording of both the Commons' and Lords' petitions, implicitly acknowledged and accepted the strong probability that Dudley would be her choice and emerge as the royal consort. By 1563, a number of peers and councillors had become reconciled to this less than ideal marriage for Elizabeth. In the absence of any other candidates for her hand, they preferred a Dudley match to her continuing a life of celibacy and to the threat of civil war on her death. In addition there was a sizeable Dudley following in the House of Commons and, although there is no evidence that the MPs were acting together as a coherent faction, some of their number, including Norton and Gallys, took a lead in the debates about marriage and the succession.[110]

This evidence of parliamentary approval for a marriage to her favourite came too late for Elizabeth. By 1563 she had apparently little desire and certainly no intention of taking Dudley as her husband. In late March 1563, while parliament was still pressing her to marry a man of her own choice, she suggested to Scottish commissioners at her court that Dudley would make an excellent husband for their queen.[111] Even if she were not sincere in her offer of Dudley, which she probably was, this was a clear public hint that she no longer thought of marrying him herself. By this time, it appears that she was giving serious consideration to thoughts of marrying a foreign prince rather than one of her own subjects.[112]

The reasons for Elizabeth's decision are nowhere recorded and her state of mind can only be surmised. At the emotional level, it is not unreasonable to speculate that the passionate element in her relationship with Dudley had either waned with time or been extinguished by necessity, so that she felt herself to love but no longer to be 'in love' with her favourite. Perhaps, too, she recognised and resented the element of personal ambition in his feelings towards her, and was seeking to test his affections or even punish him by rejecting his matrimonial suit and offering him another royal bride.[113] At the same time, however, political considerations undoubtedly influenced her conduct. As the Scottish queen had refused to sign the 1560 Treaty of Edinburgh, by which she would have effectively renounced her claim to the English throne, it was vital to see her married to a man whom Elizabeth could trust rather than to a Catholic prince. In addition, Elizabeth was well aware that her own relationship with Dudley was still provoking scandal and realised that her good name could only be restored if they both married elsewhere. This was brought home to her in January 1563 when her Council was informed that Lady Willoughby and others in Suffolk had called Elizabeth 'a naughty woman' and said that during her recent visit to Ipswich 'she looked very pale, as one lately come out of child-birth'.[114] Furthermore, Cecil, who had never been won round to a Dudley marriage, was still using his influence to dissuade her from it by emphasising the attractions of a foreign match. Although no other matrimonial contender was actually on the scene, he had hopes of re-activating the negotiations with the Habsburgs for a marriage with the Archduke Charles of Austria.[115] The Secretary was in contact with the duke of Württemberg who, he hoped, might act as a mediator with the emperor. During the course of 1563 he made considerable progress in convincing Elizabeth that she should marry the archduke, and in January 1564, she wrote to Württemberg:

> in consideration of the leave that her subjects had given her in ample manner to make her owne choise [of husband], then they did to any prince afore, she was ever in curtesie bound to make that choise so as should be for the best of her state and subjects, and for that he offereth therein his assistance she gratiously acknowledged the same, promising to deserve it hereafter.[116]

The parliamentary action of 1563, therefore, had not been in vain, even though it did not move the queen in the direction that Dudley and his supporters had hoped and expected.

Close as he was to Elizabeth, Dudley could not fail to realise after 1563 that he had little chance of achieving his marital ambitions. He seems to have admitted as much to Lady Margaret Lennox in August or September 1564, and in May 1565 he told Don Diego Guzmán de Silva, de Quadra's replacement as Spanish ambassador, that Elizabeth would never marry him 'as she had made up her mind to marry some great prince'. He also confessed to the ambassador that he would find it very hard to bear if the queen married another.[117] In addition to the cost in emotional terms, he appreciated that Elizabeth's husband was unlikely to tolerate their continuing intimacy and he would lose his position as royal favourite. Despite his admittance to the Council in 1562, the extension of his landed base and patronage network, and his elevation to the peerage as earl of Leicester in September 1564, he evidently did not feel confident that his political position was sufficiently strong to survive such a blow.

Consequently, during the middle years of the 1560s Leicester worked to sabotage Elizabeth's negotiations with the Archduke Charles of Austria, who remained her most promising matrimonial prospect. During the early phase of the negotiations in 1564 and early 1565, he secretly encouraged the French ambassador to put forward their young king Charles IX as a rival candidate, mistakenly anticipating that this new suit might divide the Council and take support away from the Habsburg match. Possibly he also hoped that the French would come to back his own suit once that of their king had failed, since they had long viewed the Dudleys as pro-French as a result of the duke of Northumberland's treaty with France in January 1550.[118] Certainly, not long after it had become obvious that Charles IX was completely out of the running, the French ambassador, Paul de Foix, told Elizabeth that she could do no better than marry her favourite; and a French envoy, Michel de Castelnau sieur de Mauvissière, made the same recommendation while on a short visit to the English court.[119] At the same time, Leicester did not neglect to maintain his good relations with the Spaniards in order to stop them favouring an Imperial marriage in preference to his own.[120]

By the summer of 1565, however, it was clear that these tactics had been ineffective. Charles IX's suit had won very little backing in the Council; de Silva had grown suspicious of Leicester's dealings with the French; and Elizabeth had again made it plain that she would marry only a foreign prince. Thereafter, Leicester opposed the archduke match on religious grounds, and at the same time nurtured his links with committed Protestants in the court and country. Increasingly, from late 1564 onwards he presented himself to the zealous Protestants as one of their number, and also offered himself as a protector of the Protestant ministers who were in trouble with the government for refusing to conform to the 'popish' elements in the Prayer Book.[121] As will be seen, it was Protestant opposition to the religious demands of Archduke Charles in 1567 that ultimately influenced Elizabeth against the match.

It is possible that one of Leicester's main motives in acting as the patron of 'godly' ministers in the mid-1560s was his recognition of their potential value as allies in stopping a royal marriage to a Catholic prince. The coincidence of timing is certainly suggestive. Before 1565 Leicester had been noted as a patron of *both* advanced Protestants and crypto-Catholics. He and his brother were the heirs to their father's Protestant following, and many in England regarded him as a Protestant activist especially after his espousal of the war in France as an ally of the Huguenots. At the same time, however, he was using his influence on behalf of religious conservatives like his chaplains, Francis Babbington and John Bridgewater, protecting individual Catholics from the ecclesiastical authorities, and offering them places within his household.[122] Until 1565, important figures in Spain and the Roman Curia thought that he was, at the very least, posing as a friend of Catholicism. Some in the Curia believed that he genuinely favoured the English Catholics and would re-establish the old religion, were he ever to become king; whilst others, doubting his sincerity, believed that he was pretending to be a supporter of Catholicism to win over the ancient nobility to his matrimonial cause.[123] It was only from

1565 that Leicester's Catholic contacts began to fall away, and he came to be viewed as the patron of Protestant radicals.[124] At the beginning of 1565 de Silva observed that the earl used to be seen in England as 'more Catholic than Protestant' but that his recent help to the ministers who were resisting wearing the surplice was leading men to think otherwise. By the end of the following year, the ambassador was convinced that he had gone over entirely to the heretics and was a 'Lutheran'.[125] Although de Silva was inexact about the precise nature of Leicester's religious position, he recognised that the earl could no longer be considered sympathetic to the Catholic cause.

Leicester's playing of the Protestant card proved successful in 1567 in bringing an end to the Habsburg matrimonial negotiations on grounds of religion. Yet he was no nearer to winning the queen's hand for himself. The Howards were now ranged against him for his role in opposing the archduke match, and would not be reconciled to his rise to royal consort, whilst at the same time many at court still believed that a foreign and Catholic match could be arranged if the terms were right. There is some evidence that over the next few years Leicester grew frustrated at this state of affairs and felt increasingly emasculated by his position as royal favourite. In the late 1560s he began an affair with Douglass Lady Sheffield, the daughter of Lord Howard of Effingham, and in 1571 he may even have participated in a secret ceremony during which they exchanged vows, although he denied this afterwards and refused to accept their son as legitimate.[126] Increasingly, too, he came to dream of winning military glory on behalf of international Protestantism and to embrace the cause of Calvinist rebels in the Netherlands, as well as the Huguenots in France. It seems clear that Leicester wanted either to marry the queen and have power as her consort, or else to be given the freedom to pursue a military role abroad and even to marry another. In 1575 he presented Elizabeth with this choice in two allegorical entertainments written and produced under his patronage: the first at Kenilworth in July and the second at Woodstock in September.

During her summer progress in 1575 Elizabeth spent two weeks at Leicester's castle of Kenilworth, and was entertained with a number of 'happenings' designed to put forward the matrimonial suit of her host.[127] On her arrival she was greeted first by a dumbshow, which purported to show the Arthurian pedigree of Leicester, and then by the Lady of the Lake (another Arthurian reference) who in her speech of welcome hinted at a possible marriage with the earl:

> Pass on, Madame, you need no longer stand;
> The Lake, the Lodge, the Lord are yours for to command.

The hint was made more explicit two days later during the episode of the Savage man when, in a poetic exchange with the nymph Echo, the figure of the Savage man described the gifts given to the queen at Kenilworth as 'tokens of true love' and explained their source:

> And who gave all those gifts? I pray thee (Eccho) say;
> Was it not he who (but of late) this building here did lay?
> Eccho   Dudley
> O, Dudley, so methought: he gave himselfe and all
> A worthy gift to be received, and so I trust it shall
> Eccho   It shall

Leicester intended the theme of his suit to be expressed more fully in the masque of the nymph Zabeta, but the show had to be cancelled, ostensibly because of rain. The story of the masque concerned Zabeta (clearly a truncated version of the name 'Elizabeth'), who had been lost to Diana (the goddess of chastity) for 'neere seventeene years past' (the number of years since Elizabeth's accession) and during this time had resisted the entreaties of Juno (the goddess of marriage) that she marry. Juno found Zabeta, who was then restored to Diana, and a debate ensued about whether the nymph should continue in her chastity. The masque ended with the goddess Iris extolling the virtues of marriage in a direct appeal to the queen.

> How necessarie were
> for worthy Queenes to wed
> That know you wel, whose life alwayes
> in learning hath beene led
> The Country craves consent,
> your vertues vaunt themselfe
> And Jove in heaven would smile to see
> Diana set on shelfe . . .
> Then geve consent, O Quene
> To Juno's just desire
> Who for your wealth would have you wed
> and for your further hire.

Because the performance of this masque was cancelled, another attempt was made to ensure that the queen heard Leicester's proposal of marriage within the tale of Zabeta. As Elizabeth rode away on the last day of her stay, the author of the unperformed masque, George Gascoigne, ran along-side the departing guest and told her the story of the nymph who had 'cruelly rejected' all her noble and wealthy suitors and metamorphosed them into the trees and rocks around them. One of these suitors, Deep Desire, he said, had been turned into a Holly Bush, with prickes 'to prove the restlesse prickes of his private thoughts' and, as the queen passed by the bush, Deep Desire delivered his own speech, which told of his continuing love for the virgin Zabeta and pleaded with the queen to stay and live at Kenilworth 'to commaunde againe' the owner of the castle. It is clear that Zabeta was Elizabeth, Deep Desire represented Leicester, and the pricks of the Holly bush symbolised his undiminished sexual desires.

At the same time as Leicester was making his elaborate allegorical proposal of marriage, he was also hinting at the alternative approach of his disengagement from the queen by using both the imagery of courtly love and the recurrent theme of the queen as liberator which ran through the Kenilworth entertainment. The imagery of courtly love was evident in the setting of the pastimes in an imaginary world of chivalric romance, as well as in the Arthurian allusions and the frequent references to the 'beldame', an unobtainable object of desire. Elizabeth's power to liberate was seen most significantly in the tale of the Lady of the Lake whom Elizabeth was requested to liberate from the thrall of the rapacious Sir Bruse sans Pitié. Through these devices, Leicester appeared to be saying that if Elizabeth chose to remain chaste and unattainable, then she should free him from her 'thrall' and his own desires, so that he could act as a liberator in her name in defence of the Protestants abroad.

There is some evidence that Elizabeth was displeased with the Kenilworth entertainments, and even censored them in places.[128] Her reaction may well have convinced Leicester that there was no point in continuing to press his suit. Consequently, only weeks later he prepared for her a second entertainment which conveyed the message that he accepted her rejection but desired another role in political life. In the Woodstock entertainment of September 1575, which was supervised by Leicester's client, Sir Henry Lee, the story was told of two lovers, Princess Gandina and the knight Contarenus, who were forced to part for reasons of state.[129] Although there was not a direct parallel between their lives and those of Leicester and the queen, there were clearly intentional allegorical references. Elizabeth had multiple roles in the masque-drama: she was herself as spectator, and as Queen of the Fairies she was also a participant in the drama; she represented the princess, prevented from marrying her lover, and Contarenus, the passive object of Gandina's desire, who had the strength to renounce their love. Leicester too appeared in more than one guise. He was like both Gandina, the active and passionate lover who had refused to accept objections to an unequal match, and Contarenus, a knight noble in character but 'beneath her in birth' and thus rejected as a suitable husband by Gandina's father. It was through the words of Contarenus, too, that Leicester put across his message at the end of the entertainment: now that he had given up his beloved for the sake of his country, he pleaded that he might leave her presence and go on knightly quests overseas.

Two matching full-length portraits of the queen and Leicester commissioned by the earl in 1575 may have been intended to convey a similar

1 1575 chalk drawing of Elizabeth I by Federico Zuccaro. Reproduced by
courtesy of the Board of Trustees of the British Museum.

2 1575 chalk drawing of the earl of Leicester by Federico Zuccaro. Reproduced
by courtesy of the Board of Trustees of the British Museum.

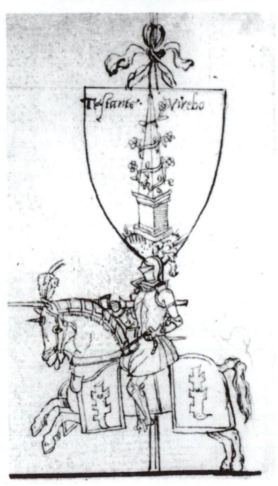

3 A detail of MS M.6, folio 56, verso, showing the impresa shield of Robert Dudley. Reproduced by courtesy of the College of Arms, London.

idea through their iconography (plates 1 and 2).[130] In the sketch for her portrait, Elizabeth is portrayed in what looks to be one of the most naturalistic representations of the queen. In the background stands a column around which a snake is coiled. This calls to mind the earlier emblem of Dudley: an obelisk entwined by a vine leaf which he used to symbolise his constancy, devotion, and dependency on Elizabeth (plate 3).[131] Here, the column, like the obelisk, represents the queen and her Imperial power, while the snake, like the vine, can probably be taken as a symbol for Dudley, her wise, prudent and protective councillor. Unlike a clinging vine, however, a serpent can take independent action in his

71

sovereign's defence. In this painting, then, Leicester is no longer the lover and subject who is dependent on the support of his beloved and sovereign, but is symbolically represented as a royal councillor and soldier ready to take up arms for his monarch. In the matching portrait, this theme is reinforced by the depiction of Leicester in heavy armour, not in the fictitious mediaeval garments of the chivalric tournament, but ready for battle.

Both the Kenilworth and Woodstock entertainments demonstrated that Leicester could come to terms with Elizabeth's rejection of his suit, if only she would allow him to go and fight abroad as her general on the side of the Protestants in the Netherlands in their struggle against Spain. Leicester, however, was thwarted in this direction too, for over the next few years Elizabeth consistently turned down their appeals for a military alliance, and it was not until ten years later that he had an opportunity to realise his military ambitions. No wonder then that the earl grew tired of his bondage to the queen, and in 1578 kicked loose when he underwent a secret ceremony of marriage in the presence of witnesses to Lettice Knollys, the widowed countess of Essex.

During the early years of the reign, the Dudley courtship provided an unstable element in Elizabethan political life, creating divisions and encouraging intrigue at court. Furthermore, for years afterwards it sullied Elizabeth's reputation both at home – where as late as 1590 two Essex peasants alleged that the queen had children by Leicester who had stuffed them up a chimney – and abroad – where a papal nuncio referred to her illegitimate children by Leicester in 1578.[132] Elizabeth's fondness for Dudley, moreover, made her disinclined to accept one of the foreign suitors who came forward at the beginning of the reign and who shared her religion if not her royal blood. By the time that she had finally decided not to marry her favourite, these men had disappeared from the marital scene, leaving only Catholic princes as eligible candidates. The difficulties involved in forging an agreement with one of them, which would allow him to practise his religion in Protestant England, were to dominate and finally doom all succeeding matrimonial negotiations.

4

THE ARCHDUKE CHARLES
MATRIMONIAL PROJECT[1]

During the earliest years of Elizabeth's reign Cecil emerged as the
Protestant champion at the English court by acting as a keen advocate
of intervention in Scotland as an ally of the Protestant Lords of the
Congregation, a determined opponent of the papal Council of Trent, and
a committed enemy of the Spanish ambassador. Yet from early 1563 until
late 1567 he was one of the leading promoters of a matrimonial alliance
with the Catholic Archduke Charles of Austria, the third son of the Holy
Roman Emperor. It was a project that was increasingly to arouse anxieties
amongst the most ardent Protestants in England and the Calvinists in
Europe. For Cecil, however, there seemed no contradiction or inconsistency in his political behaviour. He wanted Elizabeth to marry to produce
an unchallenged Protestant heir, and the archduke was his candidate
because in his view Charles was preferable in every way to Robert Dudley.
The archduke's religion was admittedly an inconvenience but to Cecil's
mind it posed much less of a threat to the security of the realm or the
Protestant settlement than Elizabeth's unmarried state. At the outset of
the negotiations Cecil seemed unaware of any major religious incompatibilities or difficulties with the projected marriage. Emperor Ferdinand's
decision not to enforce all the Tridentine reforms, his eldest son
Maximilian's sympathy towards Lutheranism and Charles's known toleration of Lutherans within his own territories caused him to believe that
the Habsburgs were far more flexible in religion than was really the case.[2]
His mistake was all the more understandable given that the Imperial
ambassador, Baron Breuner, had deliberately misrepresented Charles's
religious convictions during the 1559 negotiations. As Breuner explained
to Ferdinand: 'Had I expressly averred that my gracious master, the
Archduke Charles, was still devoted to the Catholic religion and would
ever remain so, the whole affair would have been abruptly terminated
and all hopes cut off.' Instead, he told the English that Charles 'was born
and brought up in the Catholic faith' but he could not comment what his
future intentions might be.[3] Consequently until mid-1565 there was a
strong belief in England that Charles would convert to Protestantism

immediately upon his marriage to the queen.[4] Even after Cecil realised the strength of the archduke's Catholicism, he still thought that the marriage would not endanger the English Church provided that Charles would agree to conform outwardly to the laws of the realm.[5]

Even without the religious problem, no-one was in any doubt in 1563 that it was going to be extremely difficult to re-open matrimonial negotiations with the Emperor Ferdinand for a marriage between Elizabeth and his son. In the first place, Charles was looking elsewhere for a wife and throughout the year rumours were reaching England of plans to wed him to Mary Queen of Scots.[6] In August 1563 her uncle, the cardinal of Lorraine, travelled from the Council of Trent to Innsbruck in order to discuss the match with Ferdinand, who seemed keen to go ahead with it as long as Philip II was not proposing to betroth Mary to his own son.[7] In the event, it was Mary's rejection of the archduke rather than the rival attractions of Elizabeth that drew the Austrians to look more favourably at an English marriage. Secondly, in the absence of any permanent diplomatic links between Vienna and London it was necessary to use an intermediary to put the case for renewing the courtship before the emperor and the archduke. The Spanish diplomatic network would normally have operated as an effective medium in this connection, but de Quadra was once again in disgrace at the English court and was virtually ostracised by Elizabeth and Cecil until his death in August 1563. It took until June the following year for his replacement to arrive in England and several more months for him to establish a position of trust with the queen and her principal secretary. In the meantime, the duke of Württemberg had offered his services as mediator, and Cecil and Elizabeth had agreed to allow him to intervene on their behalf, but it was nevertheless a slow process to kick-start the negotiations.[8] Everyone involved knew that there would be strong resistance at the Austrian court to a resumption of the matrimonial project, in part because of bad feeling about the failure of the 1559 attempt at an alliance. Even if Ferdinand could overcome his suspicions of the queen, it was felt that 'the Emperor who had already once made the attempt and been refused seemed to be debarred from trying again, as it would lower his dignity'.[9] In addition, Ferdinand had no wish to marry his son to a Protestant.

As a result of these difficulties, no direct talks between the two main protagonists took place in the earliest stage of the negotiations from 1563 until the death of Emperor Ferdinand on 25 July 1564. During this time Cecil's task was to convince Württemberg that it was worthwhile for the emperor to re-open discussions with the queen. In the early autumn of 1563 both he and his agent in Germany, Christopher Mundt, gave the duke 'the cheering assurance that the work would be crowned with success', with the result that the duke raised the marriage with the emperor and sent his servant to England to discuss the match in general terms with the queen.[10] During the ducal envoy's stay at court in January 1564 both Cecil and Elizabeth were keen to express their willingness to re-enter matrimonial negotiations with the emperor. The Secretary explained that English attitudes to the match had changed since 1559, mainly because the nobility no longer wanted the queen to marry an Englishman as 'the *novus homo* who rose to kingship from their midst would favour his own family and oppress the others and therefore it is that they now desire to have a foreigner'. Elizabeth told the ducal envoy that she might have to take a husband out of necessity, yet had resolved not to marry an Englishman, and 'will accept neither France, nor Spain, nor yet Sweden or Denmark', which left only the Archduke Charles as an acceptable prospective husband.[11] Armed with these positive signs of Elizabeth's readiness to arrange a Habsburg marriage, the duke advised the emperor and archduke to write 'a friendly note' to the queen as a first step. No letter, however, was sent, perhaps because Ferdinand fell seriously ill soon afterwards.[12]

The duke of Württemberg's enthusiasm for an Anglo-Habsburg matrimonial alliance owed much to his own religious and political aims in Germany and Europe. In the religious disputes among the German Protestants he represented the Lutheran wing which followed the theological teachings of John Brenz on the ubiquitous presence of Christ in the Eucharist, and he was eager to bring Elizabeth unequivocally into this camp and prevent her allying with Philip of Hesse or Frederick III of the Palatinate, the leaders of the Reformed position.[13] With this in mind, his envoy to England in January 1564 delivered some theological works on the Mass to both Elizabeth and Cecil, and privately entered a disputation with Edmund Grindal, the bishop of London, on Brenz's doctrine on the Eucharist.[14] At the same time, the duke was seeking to extend the principles of toleration laid down in the German Peace of 1555 (*cuius regio, eius religio*) to Europe as a whole, so that the Catholic powers would be at peace with all rulers who had adopted the Lutheran confession of faith. A dynastic alliance between Austria and England would be a first step and a major breakthrough in this policy.

Elizabeth and Cecil were well aware of Württemberg's agenda, as on several occasions the duke had tried to form a Protestant alliance between England and the German princes based on their mutual adherence to the Lutheran Confession of Augsburg. Both were evidently in agreement with it. Elizabeth's religious instincts were naturally conservative, but for political reasons too she was keen to preserve a traditional outward form for her Church. If it appeared to be closer to the Lutheran than the Reformed position, she might be able to hold off the Catholic threat from abroad and keep open the possibility of a matrimonial alliance with a Catholic power. During the protracted Habsburg negotiations, therefore, in her spoken statements to the Spanish and Imperial ambassadors,

Elizabeth often associated her Church with the Augsburg Confession and played down its radical nature. On one occasion, for example, she told the Spanish ambassador that 'they did not live here as Turks, that they had the Holy Sacrament and followed the Confession of Augsburg, as she had understood the archduke did'.[15] On another, she said that people in England did not differ greatly in their religion from Catholics 'except in things of little importance'.[16]

For the same reason, during this period, Elizabeth frequently made ostentatious gestures to display the traditionalism of the English Church. On Ash Wednesday 1565, when Dean Nowell of St Paul's preached against images, she protested loudly and walked out.[17] On Maundy Thursday of the same year, she performed the customary royal ceremony of washing the feet of the poor with great pomp and seeming devotion, even tracing the sign of a very large and well-defined cross which she then kissed.[18] Not long afterwards, just a few weeks before the expected arrival of an Imperial envoy to negotiate the marriage, her almoner, the Lutheran Bishop Guest of Rochester gave a sermon presumably with her knowledge and consent, on the text '*Hoc est corpus meum quod pro vobis tradetur*', in the course of which he asserted the real presence in the Eucharist.[19] To demonstrate the traditionalism of the Prayer Book liturgy to the Austrians, Elizabeth invited the Imperial envoy to attend prayers in her chapel, where he was treated to a special choral service with hymns and anthems in the company of the earl of Sussex, who would be expected to interpret them for him along conservative lines.[20] He was also given a Prayer Book to peruse and send home, so that the Austrians could take note of the retention of Catholic prayers, the traditional ornaments rubric, and the wording of the minister in the communion service which could imply a belief in the real presence in the bread and wine. It is probable that Elizabeth's refusal to allow the 1566 parliament to publish and confirm the Thirty-nine Articles of Faith, with their Swiss reformed doctrines on the Eucharist and predestination, as well as the vigorous governmental drive to enforce conformity on clerical dress after 1565 were intended to serve the same purpose. A printed copy of Parker's *Advertisements* was certainly sent to Spain as an official statement of her archbishop and bishops on the place of Catholic ceremonials in the English Church.[21]

The death of Emperor Ferdinand in July 1564 opened up the opportunity for formal diplomatic contact between London and Vienna. Under the pretext of sending a courtesy embassy to offer both condolences and congratulations to the new emperor, Maximilian II, Elizabeth planned to discuss the question of a matrimonial alliance directly with the Habsburgs. The embassy, however, was never appointed for reasons that are not altogether clear. It is possible that the queen, who was in no hurry to forward the marriage, let it fall by the wayside when disagreements arose over who would lead it. Cecil was initially suggested but pleaded ill health, in part because he did not want to leave the court and allow Dudley to influence the queen against the marriage in his absence.[22]

With this opportunity lost, Cecil suggested through Württemberg that Maximilian should send an envoy to England, ostensibly to return Ferdinand's insignia of the Order of the Garter to the queen but with instructions to discuss the marriage too.[23] In the spring of 1565 the emperor agreed to this device and appointed his councillor and gentleman of his chamber, Adam von Zwetkowich, baron von Mitterburg, to go to London.[24]

By the time of Zwetkowich's arrival at the English court, the Habsburg matrimonial project was no longer an undercover operation but receiving much publicity. News of it had leaked to the Spanish ambassador just before the emperor's death and to the French the following November, and both their governments were forced to formulate policies to deal with this new situation.[25] The French response was to present their fourteen-year-old king as a rival candidate for the queen's hand; their expectations were possibly raised by hints from Elizabeth that she wished to ally herself with Charles IX, and certainly by Leicester who wanted to see the collapse of the Imperial scheme.[26] When the French made their proposal on 14 February 1565, however, Elizabeth practically dismissed the suggestion out of hand and wryly told Paul de Foix, the French ambassador, that she would need to be ten years younger to marry his master who, she feared, would find her 'vieille et partant mal agréable'.[27] Ever more circumspect, Cecil drafted a reply which expressed her reservations but avoided announcing an immediate and final decision. Thus, de Foix was informed in March 1565 that because of the importance of the matter the queen intended to consult with her nobility before giving her reply, and that she promised to stay free from any engagement until that time.[28] The French were then kept in suspense for several more months as deliberations continued at the two courts. Elizabeth did in fact discuss the French matrimonial proposal with several of her noblemen and councillors and found them to be on the whole hostile to it, not least because it would not solve the urgent problem of the succession, as the king was thought too young to sire a child for several more years.[29]

As Cecil appreciated, there were distinct advantages to be gained from keeping alive the French courtship. It could be used as a goad to stimulate the Austrians into action, as an Anglo-French matrimonial alliance would be clearly against Habsburg interests, and it could provide a way of forestalling another Franco-Habsburg dynastic marriage. Cecil and Elizabeth were suspicious about the Franco-Spanish meeting which was planned to take place at Bayonne that summer and concerned that arrangements would be made there to wed Charles IX to a Spanish or Portuguese princess.[30]

Don Diego Guzmán de Silva, the new Spanish ambassador, was at first flabbergasted by news of the plans to re-open discussions with the emperor. Up until then he had believed that Dudley was the only man Elizabeth would wed, and for some time afterwards he thought that the negotiations might be just a ruse to prevent the archduke from marrying Mary Queen of Scots.[31] Increasingly, however, he was forced to take the Habsburg project more seriously as Elizabeth herself told him that 'she wanted to marry but not with him [Dudley]' and explained with apparent sincerity that although her preference was to remain single, she had been forced to negotiate a marriage since the succession issue was so thorny.[32] Uncertain of the best course to follow in these circumstances, de Silva decided to feign support for a marriage with the archduke while at the same time assuring Leicester of continuing Spanish approval of his suit.[33] It was only after Zwetkowich's arrival, when Philip II told de Silva that he would be glad to see the negotiations succeed and ordered him to bring the affair to 'buen efecto', that de Silva gave more wholehearted support to the matrimonial project.[34]

When Zwetkowich arrived in London in early May 1565, the court was preoccupied with the alarming news that Mary Queen of Scots had decided to marry Lord Henry Darnley, the English son of the Catholic Lady Margaret Lennox who herself had a claim to the succession of the English throne. All in the Council agreed that this betrothal spelled great danger to the realm. They also unanimously concluded that 'the only thyng of most moment and efficacy to remedy all these perills and many others ... and that was to obteyne that the Queen Majesty wold marry and use therin no long delaye'.[35] During his stay, therefore, Zwetkowich, found 'so generall a lyking amongst the great Lordes here that he is in great hope to spede'; the French ambassador also noted that most men of importance supported the match.[36]

The most ardent promoters of the matrimonial project were members of the Howard family, especially the earl of Sussex and his kinsman the duke of Norfolk; both had in fact spoken out in favour of a Dudley marriage on several occasions in the past but had recently quarrelled with the earl independently. Sussex, who had left royal service in Ireland under a cloud in 1564, felt betrayed by Leicester's support for his critics there; while Norfolk, always jealous of the favourite, had lost his temper when Leicester flaunted his intimacy with the queen before him during a tennis match in the spring of 1565.[37] The Howard approval of the Habsburg project, therefore, was seen by some as an anti-Leicester ploy, but in truth both men were long-time friends of the Habsburgs and looked to Elizabeth's marriage with the archduke as a way of resolving the succession and improving relations with both Spain and Austria, as well as checking Leicester's pretensions.[38] Other identified supporters included the earls of Derby and Huntingdon, Lords Hunsdon, Clinton, and Howard of Effingham, and Sir Nicholas Bacon. This group encompassed a wide spectrum of religious opinion in England; at one end stood Bacon and Huntingdon, both godly Protestants, at the other were Norfolk and Derby, both noted conservatives.[39]

While Elizabeth showed no enthusiasm for matrimony during Zwetkowich's sojourn at the English court, she did announce her intention to marry, telling him that:

> she had formerly purposed by all means to remain single, but in consequence of the insistent pressure that was brought to bear upon her by the Estates of her realm, she was now resolved to marry, and that I might report as much to your Imperial Majesty in her name.[40]

In contrast with 1559, she was prepared to open serious negotiations with the Austrians and did not fob off the Imperial envoy with evasive diplomatic niceties but rather permitted him to discuss the project with her inner ring of councillors, Cecil, Norfolk and Leicester. She also gave him her terms for inclusion in a matrimonial treaty so that they could be sent to the emperor for his consideration and agreement. These followed closely the clauses in Mary I's matrimonial treaty with Philip: the rights and laws of England relating to both the state and religion could not be changed; all offices and benefices were to be filled by native-born English people; neither the queen nor her children could be conveyed out of the realm; the queen was to to receive an 'adequate' dowry (£25,000 was proposed informally); nothing of any value, whether ships or jewels, was to leave the country; the realm would not participate in any foreign wars 'except under stress of evident compulsion'; and the queen's future consort would be maintained by his own family.[41]

While the court awaited Maximilian's response to these articles, Elizabeth found herself bombarded with conflicting advice: Sussex and the other 'adherents of the Archduke Charles' pressed her to accept the Habsburg suit; Leicester and his following tried to persuade her to reject it; and the French ambassador urged her to marry Leicester if she would not take Charles IX.[42] The discussions at court centred on the relative merits of the Habsburg and French candidates, since the battle over whether Elizabeth should marry an Englishman or a foreigner, which had dominated the debate on the queen's marriage in the early years of the reign, was now irrelevant in the face of her determination not to marry one of her own subjects but to choose instead some great prince.

Marriage to Charles, argued the supporters of the match, would avoid the disadvantages usually associated with a foreign match: the country would not be ruled by a viceroy, since the archduke would live in England; the queen would not have to grow accustomed to her husband's alien behaviour, as the Germans and English were similar in their customs; and the court need have no fear that the Habsburgs would seize the throne if Elizabeth died childless, for 'they remembered that when Queen Mary died, the King of Spain went home'.[43] The pro-Habsburg lobby also pointed to Charles's age, dignity and descent as compatible with those of the queen. Born in 1540, the archduke was only seven years younger than Elizabeth in contrast to the king of France who was seventeen years her junior.Though not a king himself, Charles was the son of an emperor and, they claimed, he might one day reach an even higher status and be elected Holy Roman Emperor, as his elder brother Ferdinand's marriage to Anne of Hungary had made him unpopular with the German princes.[44] In addition, they emphasised the political advantages of an alliance with the House of Austria: an alliance with the emperor, they argued, would ensure the friendship of Spain which was essential for England's commercial and political interests: 'No Prince of England', wrote Cecil in a private memorandum, 'ever remayned without good Amyty with the Houss of Burgundy; and no Prince ever had less Allyance, than the Q. of England hath; nor any Prince ever had more cause to have Friendship and Power to assist her estate.'[45]

The French ambassador, meanwhile, tried to counter these claims for the superiority of the Habsburg match by presenting the archduke as an unattractive suitor and by playing down the advantages that the match was supposed to bring. Archduke Charles, he maintained, was deformed, impoverished, lacked the status of the king of France, and had little chance of ever becoming a future emperor, since his eldest brother Maximilian was still young and likely to leave an adult son as his heir. Rather than enrich the queen, an Austrian marriage would drain the resources of England, because the archduke would be expected to contribute to the costs of his brother's wars against the Turks yet had little income of his own. De Foix also spread rumours that the match would fail to bring the desired alliance with Spain: 'there were certain people who asserted as a fact that the King of Spain was against the marriage, fearing that the Archduke Charles might become too great, strong and mighty and in time mayhap wrest the Netherlands from him'.[46] In the heat of the debate, tempers soon became frayed and in June 1565, both Sussex and Leicester and their respective followers carried arms to court, 'as it were to try their utmost'; this was the first of several hostile encounters over the next two and a half years.[47]

Maximilian's reply to Elizabeth's demand arrived in mid-July 1565 and greatly disappointed the supporters of the match. His response to the matrimonial terms which the English had laid down was extremely discouraging and exposed vital areas of disagreement between the two courts. The most important concerned religion; in answer to Elizabeth's requirement that the archduke should introduce no religious change to England, he insisted that:

this condition must in no way hinder our beloved brother and his Courtiers in the free exercise of their religion. On the contrary, in his palace Divine Service must be celebrated for him and his Courtiers by his Catholic priests according to Catholic ritual without let or hindrance.

A second difficulty related to financial arrangements. Maximilian rejected outright Elizabeth's demand for a dowry; ignoring the precedent laid down in Mary's matrimonial contract, he declared that 'it is the future wife who promises the husband a dowry'. In addition, he disagreed with Elizabeth's proposal that her consort 'shall be maintained by his own family', and argued that the archduke's household expenses should be paid out of the revenues of the English crown.[48] Finally, Maximilian wanted his brother to be given a royal title during Elizabeth's lifetime and the right of succession if she predeceased him without issue. Until these difficulties were ironed out, Maximilian saw no point in allowing his brother to visit the queen.[49]

On receipt of this letter, Zwetkowich went immediately to Sussex's house, where the two of them discussed its contents with Cecil, and tried to devise a strategy for informing the queen of Maximilian's uncompromising demands. They were all in no doubt that the queen would take the letter badly and feared that she would call off the negotiations immediately.[50] Their alarm was justified. In her interview with the ambassador in late July 1565, Elizabeth told him bluntly that she had decided to bring the discussions to a close since 'she most certainly would not marry anybody who was not of her faith', as 'two persons of different faiths could not live peaceably in one house'.[51] Soon afterwards, Cecil wrote out for the emperor the English attitude to the areas of dispute. On religion, the English demanded that 'no-one in this realm shall publicly or privately practise or confess religious rites that are contrary to the laws of this land'. On the expenses of the archduke's household, he intimated that the Austrians should pay up; and on the archduke's title, status and powers after the wedding, the emperor was told that all the terms would have to remain exactly as those that had been concluded between Philip and Queen Mary.[52]

Elizabeth's hard-line stand on religion throughout the negotiations of 1565 is not difficult to understand. Whatever her personal feelings, at that time it was politically impossible for her to allow any future husband private access to the Mass. Since the spring, Archbishop Parker had been engaged in disciplining Lawrence Humphrey and Thomas Sampson at the University of Oxford for refusing to obey the laws on ceremonies and clerical dress, and in May Sampson was deprived of his deanery of Christ Church Cathedral at the queen's command.[53] Elizabeth could hardly then grant an exemption from the law to Catholics at the same time as she was demanding total conformity from committed Protestants. To do so might well raise a political storm amongst not only the radicals, but also the bishops who were only reluctantly following the queen's orders, and the important friends of the non-conforming ministers at court, notably Leicester. She was therefore in a double bind. On the one hand, she had had to impose conformity on radical Protestants in order to keep alive the marriage negotiations with the Austrians; on the other, this refusal to tolerate non-conformity among Protestants prevented any compromise on religious worship with the Habsburgs.

Despite this serious setback, the supporters of the Habsburg marriage in England did not give up all hope for eventual success. For Cecil the main obstacle to the marriage had already been overcome in that 'the Queen's Majestie, thanks be to God, is well disposed towards marriage'.[54] Furthermore, Elizabeth was signalling publicly that her mind was set on the archduke rather than the French king or Leicester. The special favour she ostentatiously showed to a new courtier, Thomas Heneage, demonstrated that Leicester did not hold a monopoly on her affections, leading the earl to lose hope that he would win her hand if the Habsburg suit foundered on the rock of religion.[55] Cecil was therefore inclined to believe that 'we shall see some success', if only the archduke could be persuaded to come to England and agree to the queen's terms – admittedly a big 'if' to gloss over! Sussex more realistically recognised that the archduke would never accept the queen's terms on religion unconditionally, but he thought that a compromise could be devised once the archduke had visited England, whereby Charles would attend English church services 'so that the people would see him', yet be allowed to hear the Mass in private.[56]

Their optimism, however, proved groundless, since the Austrians proved unwilling to compromise. The archduke insisted that he and his entire household should openly hear the Mass, while Maximilian refused to allow his brother to visit the queen before all the outstanding difficulties were settled. Both suspected that Elizabeth was not serious about the marriage but was merely drawing out the negotiations to satisfy her parliament and to defer naming a successor.[57] Charles, therefore, lost all interest in the project and thought 'there was nothing to be done but to abandon the matter'; initially Maximilian concurred and considered withdrawing entirely from the negotiations. After consultations with the Spanish ambassador at his court, however, he decided to make one last effort to secure the match, albeit with some reservations and no intention of making any substantial concessions: 'we do not believe we can go so far as to alienate our brother from his religion against his conscience, or require him to take upon himself a burden which would not be worth the trouble'.[58] He, therefore, asked Philip to continue using his diplomacy on the archduke's behalf, and on 27 November 1565 he wrote to Elizabeth. His letter to the queen was conciliatory, toning down his earlier demands, but firm in requesting assurances that his brother would be allowed to practise his religion without disturbance and would not have to live entirely off his own resources.[59] For his part, Philip II told his ambassador in Vienna to do what was necessary to support the matrimonial scheme provided that Elizabeth dropped her conditions about religion.[60]

At the English court, Elizabeth was unimpressed by the emperor's letter, since she had no intention of giving any assurance that Charles would be allowed to follow his religion without restraint. Cecil, Norfolk, Sussex, Huntingdon and Winchester, however, kept pressing on her their anxieties about the succession and the need to preserve good relations with Spain, while at the same time they pestered her to send an envoy to Vienna to investigate opportunities for some compromise and encourage the archduke to visit England.[61] Unable to ignore the force of their arguments, Elizabeth caved in and in February 1566 agreed to send an ambassador to the emperor. The previous month she had heard the news of Mary Stuart's pregnancy, which intensified the problem of the succession, and she therefore anticipated that the imminent next session of her prorogued 1563 parliament would see a renewal of agitation over the issues of marriage and succession, particularly if the MPs did not see her taking action on the matrimonial front. At the same time, she was dismayed at the failure of a conference held at Bruges with the aim of settling outstanding commercial grievances between England and the Netherlands, and hoped that her willingness to keep open the matrimonial negotiations might encourage Philip II to listen more sympathetically to her personal appeal for agreement to be reached on the commercial question.[62]

The original choice of envoy for the mission to Vienna was Richard Bertie, the husband of the duchess of Suffolk, but de Silva thought him totally unsuitable and communicated his reservations to Cecil; as 'a great heretic' and also a good friend of Leicester, Bertie could not be expected to pursue the negotiations with vigour or present the right image to the Austrians.[63] He was therefore quickly dropped while Leicester was absent from court, and his place was taken by Thomas Sackville, probably on Cecil's advice.[64] Sackville, one of the authors of *Gorboduc*, had earlier supported a Dudley marriage but was now prepared to work for the Habsburg project as the matrimonial proposal which had the most chance of success.[65] His credentials for the mission were excellent. As a cousin of the queen and the son of the privy councillor, Sir Richard Sackville, his appointment would signal to the Austrians the importance which the English placed on the mission and Elizabeth's sincere intention of concluding the marriage. He was also a noted conservative in religion, who had incurred the displeasure of Elizabeth and Cecil in early 1564 for trying to effect a reconciliation between the papacy and England; they could thus count on him to underplay the problem of religion and emphasise the traditionalism of the English Church.[66] But, although instructions were drawn up for Sackville on 25 February 1566, he asked to be replaced because his father was close to death.[67] The man who eventually went to Vienna in May 1566 was the more nondescript Thomas Dannett, an experienced royal servant and a kinsman of Cecil, but according to de Silva another 'great heretic'.[68]

The official purpose of Dannett's embassy was to offer the Order of the Garter to the emperor, but its more important objectives were to discuss the areas of disagreement between the two sides on the terms of the marriage-treaty and to encourage the journey of the archduke to England. Elizabeth was prepared to make one small change to her original terms by consenting to pay for any extra costs to the archduke's household expenses which might arise as a result of their marriage. On religion, however, she would make no concessions; insisting again that a husband and wife could not follow different religions since it would divide the realm into two parts, she repeated her requirement that the archduke attend Protestant services. Dannett was told to reassure the Habsburgs that there was nothing in the English Church or religion to offend him, as he could see for himself from a close scrutiny of the English Prayer Book, which she had already supplied to the Imperial ambassador.[69]

Not surprisingly, Dannett's mission was a failure. Maximilian continued to insist that the archduke and his household should openly practise their religion and that the queen should pay the total cost of her husband's expenses.[70] To make matters worse, Dannett's impression of the archduke dampened any remaining hopes of his immediate conversion to Protestantism; to the envoy's surprise, he discovered that Charles attended Mass every day and was devoted to the Catholic faith; Dannett was also informed that Charles would 'never stirr one foote onelesse he maye have one whole Chirche for him and his'. Agreement on the question of religion, therefore, could only be reached if 'th'emperor will moderat the matter so as with the Quene's Majestie winkinge at sumthinge th'archduke will come into Inglande'. After exposure to the Protestant faith and form of worship, thought Dannett, a conversion might possibly take place: Charles was known to be a reasonable man, and with persuasion 'he maye be broughte (hearinge that he never harde) to yealde to the truthe'.[71] The only really positive note in the report from Vienna concerned Charles's physical appearance. Dannett could personally attest that Charles was not deformed – a matter of no mean importance to the queen – for the Englishman discerned 'he was as straight of hys bodye as any man ys alyve' when they rode together and the archduke's cloak blew free from his shoulders.[72]

Despite the clear evidence of irreconcilable differences between the two sides, the leading English proponents of the match remained undaunted and continued their efforts on its behalf. Their immediate aim was to persuade the queen to send a man of importance to Vienna to take charge of the negotiations.[73] In addition, Cecil hinted to de Silva that Philip II should write in favour of the marriage, while Sussex took the opportunity of his sister's wedding in July 1566 to entertain Elizabeth with a masque which celebrated in verse the superiority of marriage over chastity.[74] In this piece, the goddesses Venus, Pallas and Juno presented the bride, a nymph of Diana, with gifts as rewards for fulfilling her destiny of marriage, while Diana conceded their victory and admitted that the bride 'was borne' for matrimony. The masque ended with Juno proclaiming the benefits of married life.

It was, however, the parliamentary session which opened on 30 September 1566 that provided the supporters of the marriage with the best opportunity to exert pressure on Elizabeth to continue the negotiations with the emperor. Cecil for one intended to use parliament in that way. In a private note to himself written before the session, he concluded that the 1566 parliament should discuss the issue of the queen's marriage, which was 'most natural, most easy, most plausible to the Queen's Majestie', but 'if it succeed not, then proceed to discussion of the right of succession'.[75] Leicester, however, had different priorities in mind. If the reports of de Silva are to be believed, he wanted the parliament to concentrate on naming a successor so that the marriage would no longer be necessary.[76]

The issue of the succession was, in any event, bound to be discussed in the 1566 parliament. To the alarm of most Protestants, Mary Stuart had given birth to a son in June 1566, thereby strengthening the claim of the Catholic Scottish line over the Protestant Grey sisters who were both still in disgrace as a result of their unwise and clandestine marriages. A pamphlet debate on the succession had been raging for more than a year, with the most recent tract appearing in October 1566 while parliament was in session. Entitled 'The Common Cry of Englishmen', it exhorted the queen to resolve the problem of the succession by naming an heir rather than by marrying. Its author, most probably the deprived Oxford don Thomas Sampson, certainly believed that as a woman and a monarch Elizabeth had a Christian duty to marry, and he cited numerous biblical references to prove his point. He also urged her to marry and 'suffer not willingely the royall race so many years contynewed by discente nowe to be cutte of in you'. But he considered that she might have left it too late to conceive, and cautioned her that God might deny her children, as he had other monarchs as punishment for their sins. Consequently he concluded:

> yt is not your marriage, moste noble Quene, which can helpe this mischief for a certene ruine cannot be steyed by an uncertene meanes. It is uncertene whether ever you shall marrye. It is uncertene whether you shall have issue in your mariage. It is uncertene whether your issue shall lyve to succede you, yf you have one.

He then went on to address his cry towards parliament and urged the Lords and Commons to seek an answer to their 1563 petition or, if the queen did not listen, to decide the succession themselves.[77]

There may have been some attempt by the parliament to raise the succession in the first week of the session, because Cecil noted in his diary on 6 October 1566: 'Certain lewd Bills [leaflets] throwne abroade against the Queen's Majesty for not assenting to have the Matter of Succession procede in Parliament'.[78] In a Council meeting on 12 October, Norfolk tried to persuade Elizabeth to change her mind and permit some discussion of the marriage and succession. The queen, however, would not be moved; she angrily retorted that naming a successor would endanger her throne while negotiations for her marriage were already on hand.[79] On 18 October, a debate on the succession was initiated in the Lower House, when John Molyneux, the member for Nottinghamshire, introduced a petition for establishing the succession to the crown. Sir Geoffrey Elton conjectured that Molyneux was acting on behalf of Cecil, but it is more likely that he was working in the interests of Leicester. The MP had no known links with Cecil (as Elton admitted himself), whereas his brother was secretary to Sir Henry Sidney, Leicester's brother-in-law, and Cecil named a 'Mollynex' in a list he drew up of Leicester's 'owne particular Frends' in 1566.[80] Besides, it was Leicester, not Cecil, who wanted to proceed with the question of the succession before the marriage. Moreover, John Molyneux had Catholic sympathies (at least two of his children became recusants) and he may, therefore, have shared the earl's viewpoint on the succession, for Leicester was thought to favour the claims of Mary Stuart at this time.[81]

During the 'long debate' in the Commons which followed the introduction of Molyneux's petition, several privy councillors advised the House against accepting it on the grounds that the queen was already planning to marry. Sir Ralph Sadler told them that it was not an appropriate time to raise the succession, because he had heard the queen say to the nobility that she intended marriage, while Cecil and Sir Francis Knollys announced that 'the Queen's Majesty is by God's special providence moved to marriage and that she mindeth, for the wealth of her Commons to prosecute the same'.[82] The majority in the Commons, however, refused to follow the lead of these councillors and proposed to the Lords that they send a joint delegation to the queen to press their suit. According to de Silva, they debated the issue until very late, with some members insisting that a decision be reached that night and even threatening to close the gates of the chamber to prevent others from leaving for their beds.[83]

Although the sources are unclear about the actual course of events in late October 1566, most historians agree that the queen, hearing that both Houses were preparing a joint delegation, summoned to her presence twenty-one peers, led by Norfolk and Lord Treasurer Winchester, 'to know her pleasure'. At this meeting on 21 October, Elizabeth furiously upbraided the Lords for their temerity in discussing the succession, and then turned her rage on Norfolk, Pembroke, Leicester and Northampton individually.[84] According to Cecil, she was so angry with Leicester and Pembroke 'for furderyng the Proposit. of the Succession to be declared by Parlement' that she excluded them from her Presence Chamber.[85] Elizabeth felt especially aggrieved with her aristocratic councillors because at a Council meeting in September 1566 she had asked for their help in preventing the discussion of the succession in parliament.[86] Meanwhile, the Commons, who had not yet suffered the effects of Elizabeth's sharp tongue, continued to push on with their proposal for a joint delegation to the queen, and on 25 October the Lords agreed to send representatives from both Houses to her with a petition which would request satisfaction on the marriage question as well as the succession.[87] Who was responsible for deciding that the petition should be extended to include the marriage is unknown, but it was clearly in the interests of the pro-Habsburg group in the Council and Lords, as well as in line with the tactics preferred by Cecil.

Given the impasse in the matrimonial negotiations up to that point, Elizabeth was no more willing to receive a petition on the marriage than on the succession. Consequently, on 5 November 1566, she pre-empted further parliamentary moves by summoning thirty members of each House to her presence in order to relay her views on their proceedings. On the question of the succession to the crown, she forbade any further discussion; but as far as the marriage was concerned, after reproaching both Houses for their lack of trust in her promise to marry made during the last parliamentary session, she made an implicit commitment to continue the negotiations with the archduke:

> I wyll never breke the worde of a prynce spoken in publyke place, for my honour sake. And therefore I saye ageyn, I wyll marrye assone as I can convenyentlye, yf God take not hym awaye with whom I mynde to marrye, or my self, or els sum othere great lette happen.

Perhaps just for effect but more likely in the knowledge of Charles's Catholicism, Elizabeth also warned the representatives that 'theye (I thinke) that movythe the same wylbe as redy to myslyke hym with whom I shall marrie as theye are nowe to move yt'.[88]

The pro-Habsburg group had won a minor victory. Despite her serious doubts about the project in hand, Elizabeth had been forced to make a promise on the marriage, albeit with a let-out clause, in order to stave off a debate on the succession. Victory, however, was by no means complete, for Cecil and the other keen supporters of the Habsburg match were unable to put into place mechanisms which would prevent Elizabeth from sliding out of her commitment to marry. Both he and Sussex had hoped that they could persuade the queen to prorogue the parliament for six months, during which time 'it may be sene what God will dispose of hir mariadg'. Another session would then be called to discuss the succession, 'Which may with more satisfaction be done to hir majesty if she shall than be marryed'.[89] In other words, they wanted Elizabeth to continue negotiations with the emperor in the knowledge that this same parliament would monitor their progress after six months and under the threat that it would demand a settlement of the succession if the marriage was not concluded. At the end of the session, however, instead of proroguing the parliament Elizabeth decided to dissolve it. Furthermore, Cecil's attempts to draft a preamble to the subsidy bill, incorporating both the queen's promise to marry and parliamentary hopes for the establishment of the succession, had to be modified in the light of Elizabeth's objection that:

> I knowe no reason whi any my privat answers to the realm shuld serve for a prologue to a subsides boke. Nether not do I understand why such audacitie shuld be used to make without my licence an acte of my wordes.[90]

Elizabeth did not renege on her promise to continue her matrimonial negotiations and four weeks after the parliament's dissolution on 2 January 1567 the Council drafted instructions for an embassy headed by Sussex to go to Vienna.[91] Over the next months Elizabeth postponed its departure several times and inevitably the supporters of the match began to despair of Sussex ever leaving. They believed with some justification that the projected embassy was a mere public relations device intended to silence demands that the queen marry or name her successor. While it was true that Elizabeth was in no hurry for Sussex to leave on a mission which had little chance of success, she also had other reasons for postponing it. First, she knew that the emperor was distracted by the Turks, and second she was waiting to see if an Austrian delegation which had been sent to London to request her aid against the Turks had brought some commission or message related to the marriage.[92]

On 20 June 1567 Elizabeth gave Sussex his final instructions. The earl's first task was to bestow the Order of the Garter on the emperor; his second was to try and conclude the marriage negotiations successfully. Elizabeth offered no new compromise to resolve the disagreement over religion but simply reiterated her demand that the archduke had to observe the laws of the country by accompanying her to divine service and forgoing the Mass. She refused categorically to use her dispensing power to allow any exception to the law, on the grounds that it might set an example of disobedience and encourage her Catholic subjects to expect changes in her religious settlement. Her only hope was that the archduke might conform if he understood the true nature of the English Church, for she feared that he had been given a false account of it. Sussex shared her concern that the Austrians might have gained an unfavourable impression of the religion practised in England but thought the responsibility for this lay elsewhere. As he told de Silva, although 'he believed that her Majesty and the rest of them held by the Augsburg confession', he could see that 'Calvinism was being preached and taught nearly everywhere'. He therefore thought it necessary that the queen make explicit to the Austrians exactly what form of Protestantism was practised in England and 'wished the Council to decide about this as it was a point of the highest importance, those who adopted the Augsburg confession being further removed from Calvinists than from those who professed the ancient religion'.[93] Sussex no doubt knew that within the Holy Roman Empire Lutheran states were recognised and tolerated, unlike those adhering to Calvinism. He may also have been aware of the growing feeling among Catholics and Lutherans that the Calvinists were the trouble-makers of Europe, especially after the iconoclastic riots in the Netherlands during the summer of 1566. Indeed he quite probably shared this perception.[94]

The Privy Council heeded his advice, and instructed Sussex to assure the emperor that the English Church was such:

> as in dede no quyet Catholick may neede to forbeare to resorte to our churches and common prayers, for that ther is nothing redd or spoken other in praiers, or in ministration of the sacramente but only the very wordes of the scripture.

He was told to explain that, where the English Church departed from the scriptures, the prayers said had once been used in the Catholic or early Church; the only difference was that the prayers were now usually related in English, although they were still spoken in Latin in some colleges and churches of the realm where the company was learned.[95] Elizabeth's official instructions made the same point, but with less good grace. The archduke, she wrote, could attend English services with a clear conscience as, unlike those of the Church of Rome, 'there is nothing in our law which is contrary to the scriptures', and as long as he obeyed the laws he could hold whatever opinions he liked on religious matters. If, however, Maximilian continued to insist on a public place of Catholic worship for Charles and his retinue, Sussex was to suggest that the discussions be 'suspended untill his coming hither', saying that the queen and archduke were sure to reach some agreement if they liked each other. Elizabeth also offered no concessions on the questions of the archduke's future title and status, and no further compromise about his household expenses.[96]

Sussex left England on 29 June 1567 and reached Vienna on 5 August. On his outward journey he visited the duke of Württemberg, with whom he held discussions about the marriage negotiations as well as the religious situation in Germany.[97] As instructed by the queen, Sussex informed him that the queen intended to stay faithful to the Augsburg Confession, and was told in return that if this were true the negotiations would not fail over the religious issue. According to the duke, the emperor did not consider the differences in religion between the Lutherans and Catholics to be too great, but was concerned that Elizabeth was being seduced into the Calvinist camp.[98]

Although Sussex was treated very well at the emperor's court, the negotiations made little progress at first, since Charles refused to meet him so that they could discuss the outstanding difficulties face to face.[99] An interview with Sussex, he retorted, 'would not be seeming at present where the whole affair is still so indefinite'; after all, the conditions brought over by the earl 'have been worded exactly as they were before', and he himself would also make no compromise over religion 'not alone for the sake of my Christian conscience, but also because of the marked contemptuous attitude adopted towards the true Catholic and Apostolic religion'.[100] On hearing this reply, Sussex did his best to convince Maximilian that there was far more certainty than the archduke supposed by expressing his own conviction that the queen intended marriage seriously and would accept Charles once she had seen him and discussed with him in person the question of religion. He explained that Charles's demand for an appropriate place for Catholic worship was contrary to the laws of England, but tried to reassure the archduke that the queen had every wish to accommodate his conscience. Going well beyond his commission, Sussex told the emperor that, as long as Charles made a display of obeying the laws, the queen, who 'was not so rigid in religion', would undoubtedly permit him to take the Holy Sacraments within the privacy of his own chamber, after she had met and agreed to marry him.[101] Favourably impressed with Sussex's words and approach, Maximilian advised his brother to come to Vienna and hold discussions with the earl. Swayed by this advice, Charles arrived at his brother's court on 24 September to hold several conferences with Sussex over the next month.[102]

At last, on 23 October 1567 Sussex and Maximilian hammered out their own compromise arrangement. This was based on the agreed principle that the archduke should be allowed to follow his conscience in religious practices but also had to accept restrictions on its exercise in order to provide for the security of the English realm. Sussex then suggested five conditions which Charles would have to accept as limitations on his freedom of worship. First, the Mass and other sacraments would be celebrated only in his own private chamber from which all Englishmen would be excluded. Second, he would accompany the queen to Protestant church services. Third, the Austrians would refrain from criticising English religious practices and discussing religion with any Englishman. Fourth,

Charles would suspend holding his Catholic services for a period of time if any disturbance arose from the toleration. Finally he would agree to accept the advice of the English Council on all matters relating to religion.[103]

In reporting this arrangement to the queen, Sussex expressed confidence that the religious problem had been resolved. Maximilian, he wrote, had secretly agreed to four of the five restrictions and was prepared to reconsider the fifth once he knew her attitude to the compromise. As for the difficulties concerning the title and status of the queen's future husband, Maximilian now accepted her terms: 'yf ye wyll satisfye the Archduke's request for his conscyence, they wyll bothe accorde to eny thing you wyll requyre in eny other matter'.[104] In reality not all the difficulties had been cleared up. Charles had not yet reached any final decision on the first two proposals, which were the most important, and he considered the fifth – the suspension of the Mass in the event of any disturbances – 'too exorbitant and exacting'. There was also some confusion about exactly what the second condition required. While Sussex believed that he was requesting the archduke to attend Protestant services at all times, Maximilian thought that the request was for attendance 'from time to time'.[105] It was the earl's interpretation of the agreement that was sent for Elizabeth's approval by way of his messenger, Henry Cobham. In the meantime, Sussex remained in Vienna to await her answer and had to content himself with sending off the arguments in favour of the compromise to Cecil for his use in the debate at home.

Cobham arrived in England on 7 November 1567 but it took a month for the queen to decide on what answer to send Sussex, as her Council was deeply divided on the issue. According to George Stanley, a friend of Sussex, the opposition to the marriage came from Leicester, Pembroke, Northampton and Sir Francis Knollys, whilst its supporters were Cecil, Clinton, Howard of Effingham and the Controller of the Household, Sir James Croft.[106] Unfortunately for the supporters of the marriage, Norfolk had been absent from court since September on account of a depressive illness brought on by the death of his wife in child-birth and he felt too sick to obey the queen's summons to the Council meeting convened to discuss the terms negotiated in Vienna. Despite Sussex's entreaties that he attend, Norfolk would only write her a letter in favour of the compromise and marriage.[107] At the meeting, the opponents of the match were able to take advantage of his absence to press home the case for refusing the concessions on religion and rejecting the marriage.

The arguments against allowing a private Mass to be celebrated in the archduke's chambers were both ideological and political. For zealous Protestants the Mass was against the law of God and an evil which should never be sanctioned in a godly commonwealth.[108] This belief was not only expressed in the Council but also preached from the pulpit. In a sermon at St Paul's Cross, Bishop Jewel took as his text, 'Cursed be he that goeth about to build the walls of Jericho', to deliver a chilling warning to his listeners of the consequences of ignoring or side-stepping God's curse on the Catholic Church by allowing the limited use of the Mass. The biblical passages both immediately before and after the text told how God had punished the children of Israel with a military defeat merely because one family had committed 'a trespass in the accursed thing' and taken spoil from the city of Jericho into their home.[109] Like some other bishops, Jewel had been prepared to accept the Habsburg marriage only on condition that Charles renounced popery.[110] With Charles's commitment to 'popery' now manifest, Jewel spoke out, possibly at the prompting of Leicester, to rouse public opinion against royal acceptance of a Catholic husband.[111]

The political argument against the terms negotiated by Sussex was that permission of a private Mass would imperil the security of the realm. On the one hand, Catholics might be encouraged to attend the archduke's services or break the law by hearing the Mass in the privacy of their own houses or even to work for future changes in the Church Settlement. On the other hand, Protestants might use violence to attack the ungodliness in their midst, thereby inciting religious disturbances within the realm; only recently a Protestant extremist had vandalised the ornaments in the queen's own chapel. More seriously the danger of political disturbance over religion could be seen all over Europe, especially in France where civil war had broken out for a second time in September 1567. Again, these arguments were raised in the Council, but to demonstrate their legitimacy the opponents of the match kindled an anti-Catholic scare in a manner not dissimilar to that used by Cecil in 1561. In November some councillors accused the Spanish ambassador of encouraging English Catholics to attend his private Mass, presumably as a warning of what might happen if the queen accepted the emperor's terms. De Silva's house was then raided during his Mass in a search for English participants who were hearing it in defiance of the law, and a number of Englishmen attending the service were arrested. On 21 December 1567 de Silva reported that four or five of them were still in prison.[112] At the same time, a commission went to work in London to root out those who were not attending church regularly.[113] In addition, judges were summoned before Star Chamber and ordered to enforce the laws against the possessors of Catholic books, while the Lord Keeper in Star Chamber denounced papists who denied the Royal Supremacy and called for the queen to be more diligent in executing the laws against Catholics.[114]

Elizabeth was therefore left in no doubt that marriage to the archduke on the terms he required would be extremely unpopular with her most zealously Protestant subjects. The dangers of contracting a controversial marriage were all too evident in the recent fate of Mary Stuart whose marital history had been largely responsible for her forced abdication and custody at Lochleven barely six months earlier. It was in these circumstances that Elizabeth decided that she was unable to permit the archduke the right to hear a private Mass within his chamber.

On 10 December the queen wrote to Sussex of her decision. First she explained that her conscience balked at the idea of allowing a private Mass, as it could not be done 'without manifest offence of God'. Given her psychosomatic illnesses when forced by her sister to attend Mass and her hostility to the elevation of the host at the beginning of her reign before the law was changed, Elizabeth's objection on grounds of conscience may not have been the 'nonsense' sometimes supposed, even though it was by no means the the sole determining factor.[115] Second, and more importantly, Elizabeth pointed out to the earl that the laws of the country forbade the Mass, which meant that she would either have to use her dispensing power or gain parliamentary consent before agreeing to the archduke's demand. Given the anti-Catholic sentiment of the Commons, their approval was unlikely to be forthcoming, and she herself balked at allowing exceptions to the law for fear that it would lead to the kinds of political unrest then being experienced in Scotland, France and Flanders. In any event, she explained, the time was not right to consent to a compromise on religion, for if she disliked the archduke on meeting him she would be unable to give religion as the excuse for breaking off the negotiations. She maintained that she was still keen for the negotiations to continue and hoped that Charles would visit her in England. Sussex, therefore, was instructed to measure his words carefully in his reply to Charles and neither to grant nor refuse him the right to hold the Mass in his chamber.[116]

Two days later, however, Elizabeth adopted a more negative line. Perhaps after further consultations with some of her councillors she saw no point in pursuing the negotiations any longer. She consequently told Sussex that it was unwise for the archduke to come to England with the hope of persuading her to grant him toleration, in case 'upon conference to be had by us in this matter, we cannot accord to his request'.[117] This letter dealt the death-blow to the Habsburg matrimonial project, despite Sussex's attempts to salvage the negotiations. In February 1568 he left for home empty-handed and bitter against Leicester and his friends.[118] To his mind, they had used the cloak of religion to cover their own self-interested motives to the detriment of the realm: 'when subiects begin to deny princes titells for privat respects, it semeth to me good reson and councell that the Queen's Majestie should loke to her awne surty and make her self strong ageynst such as be so cold in her mariage'.[119]

Despite its ultimate failure, this second phase of the Habsburg negotiations was taken very seriously at the English court between 1565 and the end of 1567. Both its supporters and opponents struggled hard to win the day, and political divisions soon developed over the issue, which threatened at times to end in open violence. Fuelled by personal grievances against Leicester, neither Norfolk nor Sussex accepted lightly his opposition to a scheme which they believed to be in the best interests of the queen and realm. Their fury at his self-interested conduct led to serious tension and the menace of violence at court, especially when it looked as if he might be successful in sabotaging the project. June 1565 saw the first 'Variance betwixt the Erles of Sussex and Leicester', when the supporters of both men carried arms to court. Things settled down only when the queen summoned the two earls to her presence and forced them to make peace.[120] In January 1566, there followed an equally ominous development when all the Howard adherents at court wore yellow ribbons and Leicester's friends wore purple.[121] Five months later 'hard words and challenges to fight were exchanged' between Sussex and Leicester, and the queen again felt compelled to intervene to patch up their quarrel. On this occasion their dispute was thought to be so public and violent that the show of reconciliation had to be prominently displayed. Hence the two earls rode through the streets of London together in order to reassure and calm down 'the people who had become excited about their dispute'.[122] In the spring of 1567, the promoters of the Habsburg match probably tried to discredit Leicester by encouraging John Appleyard, Amy Dudley's half-brother, to state publicly his suspicions that the earl had not done enough to discover the truth about her death way back in 1560. This attempt, however, was foiled when Appleyard eventually retracted his accusation.[123] These political antagonisms and divisions at court were not insignificant. They were serious enough to attract the attention of observers, to necessitate Elizabeth's personal intervention to keep the peace, and to lead some contemporaries to fear that they might develop into factional conflict on a grand scale. Cecil, for example, wrote to Sidney of the conflict between Leicester and Sussex in June 1566 in these terms: 'I wish that God wold direct the hartes of these two Erles to behold the harme that ensueth of small sparkes of dissension betwixt noble houses, specially such as have allyances and followers.'[124]

The Habsburg negotiations contributed to domestic religious uncertainties as well as political tensions. During the 1560s few believed that the 1559 settlement would be permanent, since it satisfied almost no-one other than the queen. Protestants were disappointed with the conservative features of the Prayer Book and expected a further instalment of reform once the acute danger from the Catholics at home and abroad was over. At the same time, English Catholics were waiting for better times to come, either as a result of Elizabeth's marriage to a Catholic or of Mary Stuart's accession on her death. The matrimonial negotiations, therefore, raised Catholic hopes and aroused Protestant fears that further changes in religion were imminent, especially as they were accompanied by Elizabeth's campaign to impose conformity over clerical dress and conservative ceremonials on radical

94

Protestant ministers. In the spring of 1566, for example, the archdeacon of Essex had become alarmed by rumours that the papists were expecting to hear the Mass again, and he felt compelled to preach a sermon rebuking those who said that the queen intended to restore popery.[125] At the end of the same year, Elizabeth told de Silva that her MPs were seeking to introduce religious bills into parliament, probably in order to be forearmed against the return of the old religion which they feared would follow her marriage to the archduke.[126] While some Protestants were fairly confident that religion was safe in Elizabeth's hands, others were concerned that the queen already seemed too addicted to 'popish' ceremonies. For them, there existed the danger that she might be tempted by a Catholic husband either to restore Roman Catholicism or to shift the Elizabethan Church in a more Lutheran direction and subscribe to the Confession of Augsburg, which for most English Protestants, whether Bishop Grindal of London or the non-conforming Thomas Sampson, was hardly better than Catholicism.[127]

Although there was no likelihood at all that Elizabeth would ever return to the papal fold, Protestant anxieties that the matrimonial project was leading her away from a thorough reformation of the English Church were not entirely unjustified. The negotiations coincided with the queen's adamant refusal both to sanction further reform or religious change, as promoted by her bishops, or to permit deviations from the Prayer Book. The timing of the clamp-down on Protestant non-conformity, in particular, seems to be connected with their progress. Elizabeth's letter of 25 January 1565 to Archbishop Parker, which ordered him to impose uniformity, was but a few months before the expected arrival of Zwetkowich. And it is surely significant that Cecil, previously the Protestant champion and later a protector of non-conforming ministers, was behind this attack on diversity in religion. It was he who drafted Elizabeth's letter to Parker, and contemporary rumours also held him responsible for the Lambeth proceedings of March 1566 which attempted to force the London clergy to conform.[128] As already seen, Sussex was alarmed that Calvinist preaching and practice put the negotiations at risk, and it is understandable that Cecil, sharing his anxieties, would take action and let the Habsburgs know of Elizabeth's determination to retain traditional ceremonials and clerical dress.[129]

As well as affecting politics and religion at home, the matrimonial negotiations were also a key element in early Elizabethan foreign policy. Many of the supporters of the match, who like the Howards had long been pro-Spanish and suspicious of the French, viewed a Habsburg marriage as the best means of preserving and bolstering England's traditional alliance with the House of Burgundy (at that time the Spanish branch of the Habsburg family who ruled the Netherlands). For well over a century Anglo-Burgundian amity had been thought essential for England's commercial interests and political security against the 'Auld

Alliance' of France and Scotland, which threatened to encircle the realm. Thus, Sussex could remind Philip II of this ancient friendship as well as of England's and Spain's equally ancient hostility towards France, and point out that 'nothing proves more the usefulness of this marriage with the house of Austria than that the French our enemies detest it'.[130] In the mid-1560s, however, England's traditional alliance with the Spanish Habsburgs seemed close to collapse under the strain of religious differences, commercial disputes, and mutual suspicions. Although Elizabeth and many of her ministers had been confident that Philip II would not try to incite a Catholic rebellion in England while Mary Stuart was queen of France, after her return to Scotland and marriage to an Englishman they did begin to fear that Philip might now take action against Elizabeth. The 1563 ban on English exports to the Netherlands, the meeting of the Spanish king with the French at Bayonne in 1565, and the raising of a huge army in 1567 to suppress the relatively small-scale religious disturbances in the Netherlands, all appeared to be ominous signs of Philip's hostility towards England and plans to form an international league to suppress European Protestantism. England's traditional friend looked about to become Elizabeth's most dangerous enemy. Knowing that an Anglo-Spanish match was out of the question because of religious differences, Cecil and the Howards promoted a marriage alliance with Philip II's first cousin as an effective way of dispelling the danger and restoring the old relationship.[131] As de Silva pointed out in June 1565, though admittedly with some exaggeration, the queen saw the match as 'her only means of surviving in her state and acquiring both the king of Spain and emperor as her protectors'.[132]

For this reason, the supporters of the match needed to be assured that Philip II favoured the marriage and would extend his friendship to Elizabeth if it went ahead.[133] The Spanish king, however, was less committed to the negotiations during this second phase than he had been in 1559, when he had seen the matrimonial project as the only way to rescue Elizabeth from the heretics and save England for the Habsburg interest. By 1565, he was not convinced that Elizabeth was sincere in her overtures towards the archduke or would be won over to the Catholic faith, and unlike Maximilian he saw little benefit in a marriage which was not designed to bring about the reconversion of England. He was also rather suspicious of the fact that the Austrians had not kept him notified about the negotiations at their inception and well briefed on their progress.[134] His approach, therefore, tended to be cautious; while he encouraged de Silva to use his influence to further the marriage he had no intention of committing himself publicly to the talks in case they failed, and he was totally opposed to the emperor agreeing to any concessions over religion. During Sussex's visit to Vienna, the Spanish ambassador at the Imperial court strongly advised Maximilian against continuing the matrimonial negotiations; in his opinion the archduke would be made to look ridiculous if he went to England, especially as 'that queen has no inclination to marry'; of even more importance, the ambassador considered that a marriage which did not allow Charles the public and full worship of his religion would be 'prejudicial and a bad example' for Catholicism.[135]

The collapse of the negotiations did considerable harm to Anglo-Habsburg relations. The Austrians felt betrayed and humiliated by Elizabeth's rebuff, while in Spain there ended the last remaining hope that heresy in England could be eradicated peacefully. The Spaniards were irritated by the new drive against Catholics which accompanied and followed the break-down in the negotiations, and also concerned that Calvinists were gaining ascendancy at the English court for fear that they might aid their rebellious subjects in the Netherlands.[136] As far as England was concerned, the failure of the negotiations meant that Elizabeth and Cecil had to find a new policy to protect the realm against the perceived Catholic threat from abroad, which in early 1568 had suddenly become more acute. The presence of a Spanish army in the Netherlands under the command of the duke of Alva after August 1567, together with the rumours that it would be used on behalf of the pope against England, were causes for some alarm. As a result, Cecil began to reconsider prospects of an international Protestant league. First he looked to the German princes as allies, and in 1569 he also considered a defensive alliance with Denmark, Sweden and the Protestant states of Germany. Elsewhere, the cooling of Anglo-Habsburg relations also gave rise to new hopes of a general Protestant alliance under Elizabeth's presidency, and in early 1568 the Elector Palatine Frederick III sent Emmanuel Tremellius to England for this purpose.[137]

To sum up, for a long time it looked to many contemporaries as if the Habsburg matrimonial scheme had a good chance of success. The queen had declared her intention to marry a great prince and the archduke's suit had many obvious advantages. At the outset, moreover, religious differences did not appear to be too problematic. Many at the English court believed that the Emperor Ferdinand 'was not so addicted to the Roman religion', that Maximilian was a crypto-Lutheran, and Charles was moderate in his religious beliefs.[138] In these circumstances, both Elizabeth and Cecil thought that it would be possible to gloss over the differences between the liturgy used in England and the Empire to the satisfaction of both sides. Only as it became apparent that the toleration of a Mass in the royal household was a prerequisite of a Catholic marriage did the project run into difficulties and support for it die away. Leicester, who had consistently been unhappy with the idea of the queen taking a husband elsewhere, exploited Protestant fears and helped to direct a campaign against the emperor's terms; at least, Sussex and his friends, who were admittedly biased, saw his hand behind the displays of opposition to the match. But Elizabeth, too, had her doubts about allowing a limited toleration, as she disliked its constitutional implications and feared its political consequences. Faced with a divided Council and some outspoken opposition from Bishop Jewel (and possibly others) in the autumn of 1567, she was not prepared to risk putting aside her reservations. By contrast, Cecil continued to give his support to the marriage, even on the emperor's terms, right to the very end. In his view, an uncertain succession and an international Catholic league were far greater threats to the Protestant Settlement than the private celebration of a Mass by a foreign prince in rooms from which all Englishmen would be excluded. It was in this belief that he was to lend his support to the various schemes to marry Elizabeth to a French prince in the next decade. The failure of the Archduke project because of religious incompatibilities, however, meant that the precise nature of the religious difficulties were brought out into the open, for it was clear that no practising Catholic would consent to live in England without a Mass even if he might agree to attend some Protestant services. In this way the discussions of the mid-1560s had helped define, or at least publicise, the differences between the English and Catholic Churches and were to influence future matrimonial negotiations.

5

HENRY DUKE OF ANJOU
1570–1

During the first decade of Elizabeth's reign the main obstacles in the way of an Anglo-French matrimonial alliance had nothing to do with religion. From the English point of view, a French dynastic marriage was unwelcome since it would mean a re-orientation of foreign policy away from friendship with the rulers of the Netherlands which was still thought essential for the realm's prosperity and security. Despite tensions over commerce and religion, the value of close relations with the Spanish Habsburgs dominated thinking in the 1560s and was a major influence on marriage considerations. On practical grounds, too, it was difficult to arrange a suitable royal marriage in France because of the disparity in age between Elizabeth and the three unmarried sons of Henry II and Catherine de Medici. The extreme youth of the Valois princes made it impossible to seal the Treaty of Câteau-Cambrésis with a dynastic alliance as was the custom, despite the attempts of the treaty-negotiators to find some formula to make it possible.[1] One imaginative scheme proposed by the French was for a future marriage to be agreed between the as yet unborn daughter of the *dauphin* and the eldest son born of the so far unmarried Elizabeth, with Calais to be the dowry.[2] Even later on, in 1565 when Charles IX was of marriageable age, the French king seemed far too young to marry Elizabeth, who commented that she would look like a mother leading her child to the altar.

The initiative for a marriage between Elizabeth and Charles IX's younger brother, Henry duke of Anjou, came from the Huguenot leaders and their allies, Francis duke of Montmorency and his brothers, who, though Catholic, were great rivals of the ultra-Catholic Guise faction at the French court. They first promoted the idea in June 1568 in an attempt to wean Anjou away from the influence of the cardinal of Lorraine, the senior member of the Guise family. Elizabeth, they thought, would be interested in opening the courtship for the same purpose, since she had consistently tried to prevent the Guises from dominating the French court and using their power to assist the pretensions of their kinswoman, Mary Stuart (the cardinal's niece).

To attract Elizabeth to the matrimonial scheme her ambassador in France, Sir Henry Norris, was told that the Guises were enticing Anjou into an enterprise for rescuing Mary Stuart from her recent captivity in England by promising him marriage to the Scottish queen or a grant of her pretended rights to both the English and Scottish thrones. The opening of matrimonial talks with Elizabeth, it was suggested, would prevent an assault on England, or Ireland, block a Marian-Anjou match and undermine the power of the cardinal of Lorraine; the proposers of the marriage had every hope that Francis of Montmorency 'taking in hande to deale herein shall in suche sorte crepe in creditt withe Monsieur, as in the ende he hopithe to worke the Cardinal of Lorayne owt of favor with him'.[3] Alarmed by this report of Guise intentions, Cecil, Leicester and Pembroke immediately told Norris to respond positively to the overture:

> for the dyvertyng of the enterprise intended by the Cardinal of Lorrayne and, although ther is no lykhood of the sequele of this overture for sondry respects, yet we allow so well therof as we wish you wold make such answer to the sayd party, as it may procede.[4]

No more, however, was heard of the matrimonial scheme, presumably because Anjou, 'who thoughe yonge yet a most ernest and cruell enemy' of the Huguenots, would not hear of a match with a heretical queen and especially with one who was more than twice his age.[5] In any event, civil war again broke out in France in October 1568, and the proposal could be pursued no further.

Two years later the Anjou match was raised again. In October 1570 Odet, cardinal of Châtillon, the brother of the Huguenot leader Gaspard Admiral Coligny, spoke about it to both Elizabeth and Catherine de Medici. At about the same time Jean de Ferrières, seigneur de Chartres, another Huguenot leader exiled in England, broached the subject with some English councillors and urged Francis of Montmorency to use his influence in its favour.[6] By this time the aim was not simply to draw Anjou away from the influence of the Guise family but part of a more ambitious project. After the signing of the edict of St Germain on 8 August 1570 which ended the Third French Civil War, the Guises had lost political power at court and the Protestants were hoping for a permanent reconciliation with the French crown. At the same time, the Montmorencys and some of the younger Huguenots led by Charles de Teligny were planning to attack the Spanish army in the Netherlands; they intended to mount a joint campaign with Count Louis of Nassau and the Calvinist exiles from the Low Countries who had taken refuge in France after the duke of Alva had suppressed their revolt and defeated the forces of William of Orange, Nassau's brother. This project required the support of Charles IX but, although the French king was attracted to it as a method of enhancing his own military reputation and uniting France against its traditional Habsburg enemy, he was also understandably reluctant to risk war with Spain without powerful foreign allies. For these Huguenots, therefore, Anjou's marriage to Elizabeth was thought desirable both to cement a Protestant-Catholic accord within France and as a first stage in building up an anti-Spanish alliance in Europe.[7]

Yet even before Charles IX had been persuaded into the Netherlands campaign, he had begun to show interest in a marriage which would remove Anjou from the French political scene. The king resented his brother, who had been unjustifiably feted as the victor of the battles of Jarnac in March 1569 and Moncontour the following October. He was also apprehensive about Anjou's association with the Guises, who were leading ultra-Catholic opposition to the edict of St Germain which had given the Huguenots a considerable degree of toleration.

Otherwise, however, there was little enthusiasm for the match at the French court. Catherine did not believe that Elizabeth seriously intended marriage and anyway thought her far too old for the nineteen-year-old duke.[8] On the other hand, she was attracted to the prospect of her favourite son securing a royal crown and becoming detached from the Guises. Thus, in October 1570 she queried with her ambassador in England, Bertrand de Salignac de La Mothe-Fénélon, whether Elizabeth might be persuaded to name Catherine Grey or some other female relation as her successor and marry her to Anjou.[9] Such ignorance of English affairs must have taken the ambassador's breath away. As he informed the queen-mother, Catherine Grey had died in 1568 and no other unmarried Englishwoman was in line for the throne; besides, Elizabeth had consistently refused to designate an heir and seemed unlikely to change her mind.[10] Catherine de Medici was forced to think again. She thereupon decided that little would be lost and much might be gained by pursuing the matrimonial discussions with Elizabeth further. Anjou, however, encouraged by the Guises and the papal nuncio, was adamant that marriage to a bastard heretic would dishonour him and initially refused to co-operate.[11] Also opposed to the matrimonial project was Admiral Coligny, who preferred to see a marriage between Elizabeth and the titular head of the Huguenots, Henry of Navarre, in order to bring England into a pan-Protestant war against Spain.[12]

From the English point of view, there remained strong arguments that could be voiced against a French marriage. Anjou's age, religion and nationality made him a less than ideal candidate for the queen's hand. He was eighteen years younger than the queen, a Catholic who had taken up arms against Protestants, and as a Frenchman 'hee shalbee comonly misliked of the nation of England'. To make matters worse, he was the heir presumptive to the French throne and, since Charles IX was physically frail, he or his son might well one day become king of France, thereby uniting the two crowns and leaving England to be ruled by a viceroy.

There was also the danger that a marriage alliance with France, would 'ensewe coldnes of amytie with Spayne and Burgondye', and might draw England into a foreign war 'as Q. Marye was with Kinge Phillipp againste Fraunce, wheareby Callys was loste'.[13]

By 1570, however, these arguments were less persuasive than they had been previously. Most important of all, there was no great danger that a marriage with Anjou would have a deleterious effect on relations with the Habsburgs, as 'coldness of amity' had already developed mainly as a result of tensions arising from the Spanish suppression of the revolt in the Netherlands. After 1568, Alva's ruthless reprisals against Calvinist rebels marked Spain out as the enemy of Protestantism everywhere. Many in England feared that Philip II would follow up his success in extirpating heresy in his own territories with an invasion of England. The outbreak of the Northern Rebellion in late 1569, the papal bull of excommunication in 1570, together with Spanish intrigues in Ireland, all seemed convincing pieces of evidence that an international conspiracy led by the Spanish king was operating against Protestant England. Elizabeth was well aware that Don Guerau de Spes, the resident Spanish ambassador, had encouraged and abetted the northern rebels, and that the earls of Northumberland and Westmorland had sent appeals for help to Alva and Philip. In October 1570, moreover, she learned that rebel leaders, including Westmorland and Lord Dacres, had taken refuge in Antwerp, where they were well received by the Spanish authorities.[14] Nor could Elizabeth protect herself by arranging a marriage to a Habsburg, for when in desperation she had sent an envoy to Vienna at the end of August 1570 to enquire if the Archduke Charles might be interested in resuming matrimonial negotiations, she heard that he was planning to wed the Catholic daughter of the duke of Bavaria, while Maximilian was hoping to strengthen his relationship with Spain by marrying his son to Philip II's daughter.[15] At the same time, England's profitable trade connections with Antwerp and her second-best market Spain had been severed in December 1568 when Alva had seized the goods of English merchants and imposed an embargo on English trade in retaliation for Elizabeth's seizure of treasure destined for his army in the Netherlands.[16]

With hindsight, the danger from Spain was less immediately menacing than Elizabethans feared. Philip II lacked the financial resources to attack England while he was preoccupied with the Morisco Revolt of 1568 to 1570 and the Turkish threat in the Mediterranean. Furthermore, Alva wanted to restore relations with England as soon as possible and acted as a restraining hand on the king. None the less, in the long term Elizabethans had reason to worry, for Philip II was beginning to consider an enterprise against England when the time was right.[17]

In these circumstances of international danger and commercial disruption, a French matrimonial alliance began to look more attractive to the queen and her inner group of councillors. Elizabeth, Cecil and Lord Keeper Bacon, however, were not seeking a diplomatic revolution whereby the traditional Burgundian amity would be exchanged for an offensive French alliance along the lines sought by some of the Huguenots; rather they were hoping that an Anglo-French matrimonial alliance would empower and protect the realm against the hostility of Spain. Philip II, they believed, would be encouraged to restore trade, 'kepe both the amity and the treatyes of th'entercourse with the Q[ueen] Majesty', and 'more curteously use the Queene and here subjectes'.[18]

In addition, new problems surrounding Mary Stuart encouraged both Elizabeth and her inner ring of councillors to view an Anjou match positively. In May 1568 Mary had fled over the border after her deposition from the Scottish throne in favour of her son James, who was still a baby, and in January 1569 she was confined in Tutbury Castle in Staffordshire. Her presence in England at once intensified the succession question and destabilised political life, sparking off a series of grave internal crises: the court conspiracy of Norfolk to marry her, the 1569 rebellion of the northern earls, and the 1571 Ridolfi plot. Though all unsuccessful, these events highlighted Mary's menace as a focus of conspiracy and revolt.[19]

To make matters worse, there also existed the danger that the French king or the Guises would actively take up Mary Stuart's cause. From the time of his sister-in-law's arrival in England, Charles IX had been agitating for her release and restoration. During the spring of 1570, moreover, he had threatened to send troops to help the Marian party in Scotland, which had taken up arms against the regent and his supporters, who were themselves receiving English military assistance.[20] In the autumn and winter of 1570, the Guises were again looking at plans to rescue Mary and backing proposals to marry her to Anjou.[21] Unwilling to risk a confrontation with the French at a time when she could not count on the neutrality of Spain, Elizabeth decided to start up negotiations for Mary's return to Scotland. These talks lasted from May 1570 until June 1571 but made no progress, since the Scottish regent tried to block his queen's restoration by creating innumerable difficulties. In these circumstances, opening matrimonial negotiations with the French might bring at the very least short-term political advantages: Charles IX, it was hoped, would cease to exert pressure for Mary's release and the Guises would be unable to tempt Anjou into becoming her protector. Furthermore, according to the thinking of Cecil and Bacon, the successful conclusion of the negotiations would contain the problem of Mary Stuart, as she would be permanently denied French aid, and lose her claim to be heiress presumptive if Elizabeth were to produce an heir. Thus, in the words of Bacon:

By this mariage the Q[ueen] shalbe delyvered of the continuall feare of the practizes withe the Queene of Scottes, on whome dependeth almoste the onlye prosperitie of the Q[ueen's] hole liffe and raygne; so as here Ma[jes]tie may delyver if shee please, and permitte hir to marrye whome shee liste: and indeede it weare convenient shee weare also maried after that the Q[ueen] shalbee married.[22]

Once the political advantages of the Anjou match were recognised as significant, the remaining arguments against the match were easily reasoned away. The discrepancy in age between Elizabeth and the prince seemed to matter less now, since Anjou was a mature adult who had apparently proved his military prowess at the battle of Jarnac the previous year and Elizabeth was not yet too old to bear a child. Anjou's Catholicism remained a problem, but there was some doubt about the strength of his beliefs, especially as the English ambassador to France had at times expressed the view that he had taken up arms against the Huguenots out of political rather than religious motives. Moreover, even if Anjou were a Catholic by conviction, it seemed possible that some accommodation could be reached over religion. Charles IX had just granted a more extensive toleration to the Huguenots in the Treaty of St Germain and, besides, the French kings had never been strong papists. Although French representatives had been sent to the papal Council of Trent, their instructions had been to resist attempts at papal ascendancy and the *parlement* of Paris had subsequently refused to confirm the Tridentine decrees.[23] It therefore seemed unlikely that they would insist on Elizabeth returning to the papal fold or even require a papal dispensation for Anjou to marry a heretic.[24] Similarly, Anjou's royal blood also appeared a less important obstacle in 1570 since Charles was just about to be married and might well soon have a son of his own. In any case, it was Anjou's royal blood that made him so attractive as a candidate. Not only did Elizabeth prefer to marry within the rank of princes, but also if the marriage were effected Anjou would bring with him the defensive alliance with France that could provide the necessary protection against Spain. Bacon believed, moreover, that arrangements could be made to avoid a union of the two realms if Charles died leaving no son.[25]

For these reasons, Elizabeth showed interest when the matrimonial project was put to her by Châtillon in October and the French ambassador in December 1570. In addition, she saw advantages in opening up matrimonial negotiations which would coincide with the session of parliament due to meet in April 1571, for it seemed highly likely that this new parliament would return to the themes of marriage and succession which had so annoyed her in 1566. She therefore told the French that she was free to marry and was determined to marry a foreign prince rather than a subject.[26] In January 1571 she brought the matrimonial project directly to the attention of her Council, where at least one member voiced qualms about the match both on grounds of the duke's youth and 'that it would be well to consider deeply before they broke entirely with the House of Burgundy'. Although she too had privately expressed her concern about the disparity in age to La Mothe-Fénélon, Elizabeth evidently brushed these objections aside and recommended that her councillors listen to and consider carefully the detailed proposals made by the French.[27] In this she had the clear backing of Cecil, Bacon and Leicester.

Catherine de Medici, however, responded only tentatively to these encouraging signs from the English court. She could not press ahead with the match until they had secured Anjou's assent, which she was not able to extract from the reluctant duke until mid-February 1571.[28] Even then Catherine wanted to proceed cautiously, since she was anxious to avoid protracted and public negotiations. As any mention of the match would arouse the suspicions and antagonism of the Spaniards and the ultra-Catholics, secrecy was necessary 'obvier des empeschementz que plusieurs, tant de dedans que dehors nos royaulmes, y voudroient donner'.[29] In addition, she wanted to avoid her son being humiliated in the event of the negotiations ending unsuccessfully. In the words of Sir Francis Walsingham, Elizabeth's new ambassador in France, 'here they stand uppon their reputation, and therefore would be loath to move speech unlesse they were in full hope of speed. The experience of others that have heretofore attempted the like matter maketh them more doubt-full how to proceed.'[30] The way forward agreed implicitly by both courts was for Catherine to take advantage of Charles IX's impending wedding to talk about the Anjou match secretly and informally with members of an English embassy sent to France to congratulate the king on his marriage.

The embassy was headed by Thomas Sackville,.one-time co-author of *Gorboduc* and now Lord Buckhurst, and it included as a member of the entourage Guido Cavalcanti, a semi-official Italian diplomat, who was often used as an intermediary between England and France and had already been involved in discussions about the marriage with Cecil and La Mothe-Fénélon.[31] Before his departure in February 1571, Buckhurst was instructed how to act if the subject of the marriage was raised with him. As a result he was not at all surprised when Catherine spoke first with Cavalcanti on five separate occasions about Elizabeth's attitude to marriage with her son, and then arranged to meet him 'by chance' in the Tuileries Gardens to discuss the match. At this meeting on 12 March, Buckhurst repeated Cavalcanti's assurances that Elizabeth was sincere in seeking a marriage for the good of the realm. Apparently satisfied, the queen-mother agreed to open negotiations on condition that they were conducted in secret. On the next day her servant gave Buckhurst 'notes and writings' containing her thoughts on the marriage. In the interests of total secrecy he was told to make his own notes from them, return the originals and present the points to Elizabeth personally.[32]

Reflecting her fear that Elizabeth did not intend to marry, Catherine's points focused on the diplomatic processes of negotiating a marriage, with the aim of ensuring that the French court could keep control of discussions and prevent them from becoming bogged down in courtly conventions, as had happened in 1565. Catherine therefore asked Elizabeth to declare her intentions before a formal offer were made, requested that all future negotiations should initially take place secretly in France between Walsingham and Paul de Foix, and in another attempt to pin Elizabeth down, asked her to propose her own terms for a marriage-treaty.

According to her closest councillors, Elizabeth was 'more bent to marry then heretofore she hath been', yet she responded very cautiously to Catherine's 'notes and writings'.[33] Although she affirmed her 'resolute determination' to marry, she refused to commit herself to marry Anjou in advance of negotiations. Aware of the difficulties there might be in reaching a settlement over religion, she was determined to hear what kind of terms were on offer before she agreed to accept his proposal. She therefore begged 'the Queen Mother not to be over curious in requiring so precise an answer, until the matter may be further treated upon and explained'. In addition, she was unwilling to submit formally her own terms as the basis for discussion, as this would imply a resolution to marry Anjou. If, however, Walsingham were asked what articles Elizabeth would look for, he was to tell Catherine informally what she expected so that the French could decide whether it was worth pursuing the match. The terms that Elizabeth had in mind were very similar to those offered to the Archduke Charles in 1565:

> no lesse can be offered for conditions, then was by the Emperour Charles, with King Philip to Queen Mary. And that further, of necessity it must be specially prejudged, that Monsieur shall not have Authority to exercise the form of Religion in England, that is prohibited by the Laws of our Realm. And though you be not instructed hereof, yet would we that you should specially open this matter secretly to the Q. Mother; and though we mean not to urge her Son to any change of conscience, otherwise then we wish him to be directed to the best, yet surely we cannot, nor may not give him any authority to have any exercise in facts of such rites as are prohibited by our Laws. And as for his allowance of our religion, although we wish he might in conscience like it (and if he did understand the form thereof, truly we do not mistrust, but he would not mislike it) yet we shall onely require his presence in our Oratories and Churches.[34]

Despite her reluctance to make the running, therefore, Elizabeth wanted her conditions to be clear from the outset, especially those concerning religion.[35] There was to be no prevarication or equivocation; nor was there at this point any talk of meeting her suitor first and settling religious differences afterwards, as there had been during the Habsburg negotiations. On the contrary, Elizabeth was prepared to risk the immediate rupture of the negotiations by stating her position straightaway, and made no attempt to spin out the talks for as long as possible by avoiding the issue. It is therefore difficult to see why so many historians have accused her of diplomatic dalliance.

Elizabeth's hard-line policy on her future husband's religion was not shared by Cecil (created Lord Burghley in February 1571). One of the few to recognise the strength of Anjou's present commitment to Catholicism and to remember the minimum demands of the Archduke Charles, Burghley had decided as early as 1570 that some concessions would have to be made to Anjou's conscience if the matrimonial negotiations were to proceed. Whilst he agreed with Elizabeth that the duke would have to accompany her to Divine Service, he was prepared to allow him a limited use of the Mass:

> as long as he shall observe the premises, and untill he may by instruction [be] induced to thynk the use of the English Service in the chirch sufficient for hym without usage of any other, he may for three dayes in the weke use his own relligion.

Mass could only be heard, however, in his private chamber and with only six or seven of his own attendants present.[36] For this reason, Burghley advised Walsingham to avoid initiating discussions on religion along the lines suggested by the queen.[37]

Walsingham was ready to comply. Although he was in total agreement with Elizabeth's firm stand, he did not think the time was right for such direct speech. With the Guises intriguing against the marriage and the king and queen-mother unhappy with Elizabeth's refusal to make a firm commitment to wed Anjou, he feared that her demands on religion would be construed 'for a quarrel of breach'. As a result he 'somewhat swarved from the precise course of her Majestie's instructions' and decided to say nothing about these terms.[38] It was therefore left to the French to put forward articles for negotiation without any knowledge of Elizabeth's conditions. On 12 April 1571 La Mothe-Fénélon presented to Elizabeth their demands. Burghley and Leicester, the only councillors who were made privy to them, then discussed them with the ambassador in three separate conferences and gave him a formal reply several days afterwards.[39]

The French demanded such impossible terms that it has been suggested that Anjou and his friends designed them with the deliberate intention of sabotaging the talks and throwing the blame for their breakdown onto England.[40] This, however, seems unlikely. In the first place, Don Francisco de Alava, the Spanish ambassador at the French court, commented at the time that Anjou had only become 'converted' to the match in the belief that it would be for the good of Christendom as well as for his own personal benefit; these terms would guarantee both.[41] Furthermore, Catherine was to insist on making very similar demands for her youngest son, Francis, during the matrimonial negotiations of 1578 and 1579; evidently, they seemed perfectly reasonable to the French, at the very least as a starting-point for discussion, even if they were totally unacceptable to Elizabeth and her councillors.

Most of the French proposals concerning Anjou's future status and income went far beyond the terms stipulated in the treaty between Mary and Philip, and inevitably Elizabeth would have none of them. Like the Archduke Charles before him, Anjou wanted to be crowned king imme-diately after the wedding, to participate in government and receive a substantial allowance (£60,000 per annum) to meet his household expenses. If Elizabeth died leaving a child, he expected to keep his title and powers until the child was old enough to rule alone; and were Elizabeth to die childless, he asked to retain his pension for the remainder of his lifetime and enjoy the title 'Rex Dotalis'. Two of these conditions the English rejected outright. While Anjou would enjoy by virtue of the marriage the 'stile, honneur et nom de roy', his powers would be circum-scribed as in the treaty of Mary and Philip, and he certainly could not be crowned king as this might endanger the succession. As for the pension, Elizabeth was willing to make some contribution to the expenses of his household but not to cover the total cost; and she thought that its continuance after her death was better discussed later by parliament after he had become better known in the kingdom.[42]

The French articles concerning religion were equally uncompromising, in line with Anjou's statements that he would never 'enter farther into the matter', unless his conscience were fully satisfied.[43] The French made two general demands: first that the wedding ceremony should exclude any rites which were 'not conformable' to the Catholic religion; and second that Anjou and his servants should have the 'free exercise' of their religion. In response Elizabeth tried to be as amenable as she could in safety. While she insisted that the English marriage service contained nothing contrary to the Church of Rome, she nevertheless gave an assurance that Anjou need not take the sacrament of communion if it offended his conscience, and that he could have his priests present at the wedding ceremony to act as witnesses. Similarly, Elizabeth accepted that Anjou and any of his servants who were not subjects of the crown of England would not be compelled 'against his or their conscience to exercise any ecclesiastical rites according to the customs of the English Church' if they were repugnant and contrary to the religion 'qu'on appelle catholique'. What she meant by this statement is not entirely clear, but she was evidently not permitting their absence from all English services, as she demanded that Anjou 'ne recuzera point' to accompany her to the church or oratory at suitable and accustomed times.[44] It is probable that she was offering the more limited concession that he might abstain from communion until he felt ready to participate.[45] On his request for a private Mass, however, Elizabeth would brook no compromise: 'being specially forbidden by our Laws, we cannot without manifest offence and perill to our State accord thereto'.[46]

Understandably, the French expressed strong dissatisfaction with Elizabeth's response to their terms. La Mothe-Fénélon for one thought that they were so tough because the English were either playing for time or losing interest in the marriage. Others at the French court were aggrieved that her conditions denied Anjou any benefit from the marriage; not only would his powers be limited as king during the queen's lifetime but after her death he would have no lands, titles or income in England. Thus, he would have 'employé bonne partye de sa jeunesse avec une femme plus aagé que luy de bien XVII ans, et refusant par ce moien une noble, sage et vertueuse Princesse qui ne luy peult manquer', yet if they were childless, he would be sent back to France on Elizabeth's death 'sans aucun recompanse ne gratifficaçon'.[47] But it was the English response to Anjou's demand for the free exercise of his religion that caused greatest discontent. Catherine complained to Walsingham that the English statement on religion was 'very hard, and neerly toucheth the honour' of her son.[48] As far as the French were concerned, by denying Anjou access to the Mass, Elizabeth was asking her suitor to change his religion immediately on their marriage: 'the not having the exercise, was as much as to change his Religion'. And, as de Foix told Walsingham, a sudden change in religion was out of the question:

> Monsieur hath either Religion, or no Religion. If he have Religion, then Religion being a constant perswasion, confirmed by time, cannot but in time be removed, and not upon the sudden: if he have no Religion, then he is unworthy of your Mistress, and the place and degree he beareth.

In the future, argued the French negotiators, Anjou might convert to Protestantism through the influence of his wife, but in the meantime he must be allowed to practise his religion.[49]

When confronted with these arguments at the French court, Walsingham took an uncompromising stance. A zealous Protestant, he was unable to disguise his hostility to Catholicism and readily admitted his hope that Anjou would speedily be converted to the 'true religion'. Like his queen, he tried to maintain the distinction between religious belief and practice, but seeing that this argument made no impression on Catherine or Paul de Foix, he took another tack and strongly denied that the queen was in any way impugning Anjou's honour by denying him the Mass, as there were sound hopes for a swift conversion:

if it were true that I had heard, Monsieur was not so far from our Religion, having had some introduction therein ... if it please him to water those seeds, that he had already received by some conference, he should be able easily to discern that the change of his Religion, should breed unto him no dishonour at all, it being no less fault to continue in error, then commendable to come from error to truth.

In the meantime, continued Walsingham, the Mass could not be heard in England, for otherwise the queen's laws would be flouted, her 'good Subjects' would be offended, and her 'evil Subjects' encouraged. Furthermore, he said, Anjou's own position would be untenable as a Catholic king; he would be unable to stand aside from religious disputes and would ultimately become unpopular with both sides of the religious divide, for his religious faith would alienate him from his Protestant subjects and his loyalty to the queen and her laws would lose him the support of the Catholics.[50] Of course, Walsingham's real fear was that Anjou would not be impartial in religious matters or even loyal to the laws of the kingdom, but on the contrary would seek toleration for his co-religionists and encourage their disobedience to existing statutes.

The French negotiators, however, knew that Anjou as a pious Catholic could not live without the Mass and they explained to Walsingham that the match would have to be called off unless Elizabeth changed her conditions. On 27 April 1571 Catherine gave her ten days to decide whether or not she still intended to proceed with the marriage and to send them a statement of her own terms if she wanted the negotiations to continue. Elizabeth disliked this ultimatum, but Burghley and La Mothe-Fénélon persuaded her not to take offence, arguing that the French genuinely wanted the marriage to go ahead and were not seeking an excuse to pull out of the project.[51]

In her reply on 11 May 1571 Elizabeth declared her continuing interest in the matrimonial proposal but refused to put forward her own terms for negotiation until agreement had been reached on religion. She also rebutted the French claim that by denying Anjou the free exercise of Catholicism she was asking him to convert immediately or to live without his religion. As a believer in the doctrine of solafideism, to her it made perfectly good sense to emphasise belief and doctrines over sacraments and worship, and to draw a distinction between religious belief and the exercise of religion. She either could not or would not see that for Catholics the Mass was the supreme sacrament, regular attendance at which was indispensable to their spirituality and salvation. Therefore, as far as she was concerned, she was not compelling the duke to act against his conscience nor demanding his instant conversion, since he could believe what he liked as long as he obeyed the law. Nor, she claimed, was she forcing him to live without religion for as her husband he would be accompanying her to church and hearing Christian prayers. Her Book of Common Prayer, she argued, contained nothing 'that hath been yea that is not at this day used in the Church of Rome', as even Catholics admitted, and Anjou could thus use it in accordance with his conscience. If he objected to an English liturgy, there was also no problem. A Latin Prayer Book was already in use in the universities and available for him, or if he preferred he could have a French translation like the one printed in Guernsey. All in all, therefore, she claimed not to see how her demands required the duke to make any sudden change in religion:

> mean we not to prescribe to him, or any person, that they should at our motion, or in respect of us, change their Religion in matters of faith. Neither doth the usage of the divine Service of England properly compell any man to alter his opinion in the great matters now in controversie in the Church.

Only communion with its implicit denial of transubstantiation might offend his conscience, but she was prepared to offer him exemption from it, 'until he might better consider thereof'. For the rest, she could appreciate that a Catholic who did not know the English liturgy might at first balk at participating in the unfamiliar rites and ceremonies, but she was convinced that her Book of Common Prayer was based on the Scriptures and therefore could offend no Christian conscience. For this reason, she would send a copy to the French royal family so that they might see for themselves its liturgical conservatism.[52]

At the same time as Elizabeth was insisting that her demands did not impair Anjou's conscience, she found that granting him the free exercise of his religion would touch both her conscience and political security. Although she did not go as far as Walsingham or her Protestant clergy in seeing the Mass as an evil which would pollute the realm, she did view it as an irrelevant superstition and its celebration offended her religious sensibilities. For this reason, she had originally planned to tell the French that its use touched her own conscience, even though Burghley had advised her against it. Only when she learned from La Mothe-Fénélon that an appeal to her conscience would lead Anjou to withdraw entirely from the project, was she persuaded to emphasise exclusively the political and constitutional objections to its use.[53] Consequently, she only made a fleeting reference to her conscience and went on to focus on the 'inward troubles within our realm' which would surely follow the introduction of the Mass and to explain the constitutional objections to meeting their demand. Permitting her husband the Mass, she argued, was quite different from allowing her Spanish and French ambassadors to hear it. In their cases she had not had to use her dispensing powers to grant them exemption from the law but had merely suffered them to be left unmolested when a Mass was held in their homes. She could not turn a blind eye, however, to her husband's religious practices. After all, he would be the joint governor of the realm, and as such he had a responsibility to assist in the maintenance of law and order and to provide a good example to their subjects. How could she then suffer him to break the law? In his case she would have to use her dispensing power and allow an exception to the law, which would be dangerous and unpopular. Her parliament and clergy would certainly object to any such proposal, yet parliamentary approval would be required for ratification of the marriage-treaty.

Were Elizabeth to allow Anjou 'the free exercise of his religion', she would effectively be undermining her own arguments, and probable conviction, that her Prayer Book could not offend any Christian conscience, a position which justified and helps to explain her attitude towards not only her matrimonial suitors but also her Puritan and Catholic subjects. It was particularly necessary to hold firm to this position in 1571 as it was then being challenged by both extremes of the religious spectrum. Elizabeth's Protestant clergy had always felt uneasy about the retention of popish ceremonies and ornaments in her Church, and increasingly some ministers and their congregations were unwilling to conform to those parts of the Prayer Book which they considered to be 'more superstitious or erronious then in soe highe mattrers bee tollerable'. In April 1571 William Strickland had even introduced a bill into parliament for the introduction of a reformed prayer book.[54] Catholics, too, were ceasing to view the Prayer Book in Elizabeth's ecumenical way. At the beginning of the reign very few English Catholics had refused to attend weekly services, even when they abstained from annual communion. De Quadra, the Spanish ambassador, had maintained in 1562 that the Common Prayer 'contained no false doctrine nor anything impious', composed as it was of extracts from the Bible and of Devotions which had been adapted from Catholic models, and he had asked the pope for instruction on its use in the hope that the pontiff would authorise the attendance of English Catholics at these services.[55] Pope Pius IV, however, had referred the question to a committee of the Council of Trent and the congregation of the Inquisition, which pronounced that Catholics would risk eternal damnation by attending English church services. In 1566 Pius V formally forbade their attendance and sent his envoy, Lawrence Vaux, to England to inform Catholics of his decision, while the following year the Inquisition confirmed the necessity of recusancy. Thereafter, many English Catholics had begun to drift away from their parish churches, and the ecclesiastical and secular authorities became seriously alarmed by the increase in recusancy, especially after the publication of the 1570 papal bull of excommunication which absolved the queen's subjects from obedience to her laws.[56] In the parliament which sat from 2 April to 29 May 1571, some MPs had introduced a bill to fine those who did not take communion once a year; however, Elizabeth had vetoed this not only because she disliked its principle but also because she was preparing to offer a Catholic husband that very concession. With the problem of recusancy so high on the political agenda, royal use of the dispensing power to allow Anjou to stay away from church altogether and hear his own Mass would be especially provocative; Protestants who were pressing for harsher penalties against recusants would be outraged, while Catholics would treat Anjou as a role-model and a potential protector for recusants in trouble with the authorities. On the other hand, if Elizabeth could persuade the French to accept her interpretation of the Prayer Book and agree to Anjou's attendance at divine service alongside her in public, it would be a major propaganda coup against the pope and encourage her Catholic subjects to obey her laws.

Although Elizabeth made no further concessions on religion in her letter of 11 May 1571, Charles IX and Catherine did not break off negotiations as they had threatened. Instead they claimed to find her reasons for denying the Mass 'of great moment' and asked her to forward her other terms so that the negotiations could advance.[57] Since Elizabeth had not made her conscience the grounds for her decision, they were hopeful that she might in fact overlook a private Mass if no mention was made of religion in the marriage-treaty and political safeguards were agreed unofficially. This expectation was also founded on the impression of La Mothe-Fénélon who believed that Burghley and Leicester had said as much to him.[58] Both the king and queen-mother were now determined that the marriage should go ahead because a matrimonial alliance with England had become a linchpin in each of their separate political projects. Catherine's plan was for a double marriage to bring peace to France: she wanted Elizabeth for her son to secure an Anglo-French entente, satisfy his dynastic ambitions and detach him from the extreme Catholic party; at the same time she was also trying to wed Henry of Navarre to her daughter Marguerite de Valois in order to weaken the Huguenots and bind one of their leaders to the crown.[59] Both marriages, however, would be at risk if the Anjou project fell through, as Elizabeth might then be persuaded to marry Navarre in his place. This had been the matrimonial alliance originally proposed by the Huguenot leaders and it was still favoured by Coligny as part of a broader English–Huguenot–Dutch coalition.[60] For his part, Charles IX saw the Anjou marriage as a way of obtaining English military help for a campaign in the Netherlands in pursuit of glory and dynastic territorial claims. Some time towards the end of April 1571 he had assented to embark on a military enterprise which would bring him Hainaut and Artois.[61] His fear now was that if the negotiations failed, Elizabeth might make her peace with Spain, especially as she had been holding discussions with an envoy from Alva since March 1571 and had recently sent a deputation to Philip II with the intention of settling their differences.[62]

In England, Elizabeth was reluctant to hand over her terms before the religious question was resolved, but Burghley and La Mothe-Fénélon 'with some long laborious perswasions' were able to convince her that this was necessary if negotiations were to proceed. Burghley then had to struggle to persuade her against including the restoration of Calais as one of the articles, which he managed only to do by bringing in several other councillors, Northampton, Sussex and Leicester, to advise her 'to forbeare that Toy of Calais'.[63] At last on 4 June 1571, the terms were delivered to La Mothe-Fénélon. There were nine points in all, nearly all of them reiterating a clause in the marriage-treaty between Philip and Mary. None was controversial as the problematic issues – religion, Anjou's pension and his rights to a coronation – were omitted.[64] With this evidence of Elizabeth's willingness to carry on with the matrimonial project in their hands and in the expectation that she would not stop Anjou practising his religion in private, Catherine and Charles IX felt ready to bring the negotiations into the open. They therefore dispatched an envoy to the English court with instructions to promote the marriage and announce the imminent arrival of a formal embassy to conclude a marriage-treaty. Grimonville de l'Archant, Anjou's captain of the guard, was the man chosen for this mission.

De l'Archant's visit in early July 1571 was not a success. The issue of religion dominated the discussions and proved again to be an intractable problem. As Leicester wrote to Walsingham, the religious scruple was so great that it 'will utterly break off the matter'.[65] Burghley blamed the Frenchman for the reverse: 'he was so earnest for the cause of religion that he did little good', he wrote in his diary of the Anjou negotiations.[66] Yet in truth it was Elizabeth who first raised the question of religion and then discussed it in an entirely uncompromising way.[67] As soon as de l'Archant announced his king's intention to send over ambassadors to arrange the marriage-treaty, Elizabeth put forward objections. There was no point in their coming, she said, before the difficulty over religion had been settled, and

> except the King would declare his contentation and his Brother's, agreeable to her Majestie's minde already declared in the matter of Religion (that is, that she could not grant unto Monsieur liberty to exercise the Roman Religion in any matter contrary to her Laws) she saw it but labor lost to send any Ambassadors.

Burghley and Leicester tried to repair the damage by suggesting that the French should refrain from including religion in their points for discussion and even in the final treaty. As they pointed out, if Anjou requested the free exercise of religion Elizabeth would have to turn him down, but

> if Monsieur should forbear to require it, and thereby her Majesty should not grant it, but that the matter should be forborn, and pass

in silence, it might be, that Monsieur's friends might retain their good opinions of him, as of one that had not changed his Religion: and likewise the Q. Majestie's good subjects should continue their opinions of her Maj. as of a Prince that would not assent to any thing against her Religion.

The French negotiators saw some merit in this arrangement, provided that it meant that toleration would be permitted in practice, and de l'Archant left England with that hope intact.[68]

In reality, however, Elizabeth was unhappy with this compromise and unwilling for it to go forward in such an ambiguous way. Thus, soon after de l'Archant's departure, she told Walsingham that if anyone at the French court mentioned religion, he should explain that its omission from further discussions was intended only as a face-saving formula for Anjou, and that 'the forbearing of it [the Mass] by way of Treaty shall not content us only, but also the forbearing of the use of it':

> And so we require you to express the same plainly, where you shall see cause; for we cannot esteem it a plain dealing to pass it [religion] over with silence in the Treaty, and yet to be in doubt whether the same [the Mass] shall be used indeed, and thereby move a new controversie between him and us, of more danger then is meet to be suffered, to follow for lack of plain dealing with them.[69]

Burghley's compromise was anyway as unacceptable to Anjou as it was to Elizabeth. Although Walsingham kept sending home optimistic reports about the likelihood of his conversion to Protestantism, the duke was in fact coming increasingly under the control of the extreme Catholic party in France led by the cardinal of Lorraine. As early as April 1571 Charles IX had complained that his brother was influenced by 'certain superstitious Fryers, that seek to nourish this new holiness in him'. On 25 July Catherine reported to La Mothe-Fénélon that her son was plotting with the papal nuncio about ways of restoring Catholicism throughout France.[70] Also in July, Anjou told his mother that he refused to go to England 'sans avoir une publique asseurance pour l'exercisse de sa religion', while Walsingham and the Spanish ambassador both heard that he was saying that marriage to a heretic was completely out of the question, even if she granted him toleration.[71] Despite his usual malleability in the face of his mother, Anjou was holding firm against the combined pressure from Catherine and Charles: 'Nyther the King's threatenyng nor the Queen Mother's perswatyons can draw Monsieur to proceade in this mariage', wrote Walsingham on 27 July.[72] To break down his opposition, the bishop of Dax, one of the royal councillors, wrote the duke a letter in early August, explaining that passages in St Paul permitted a mixed marriage and telling him that a Catholic king could do no more for his religion than win over a Protestant princess and her realm to the true Church. It may be that it was with these thoughts in mind that Anjou reluctantly allowed negotiations to continue on his behalf.[73]

In any event, the king was determined to continue negotiations with Elizabeth. On 12 July 1571 he had attended a secret meeting with the Huguenots at the château of Lumigny and between 28 and 30 July participated in another at Fontainebleau, where plans were drawn up with Count Louis of Nassau for a war against Spain and the partitioning of the Netherlands.[74] These war plans depended on the co-operation of England; consequently, despite Anjou's obduracy and the opposition of some of his councillors, Charles decided to send Paul de Foix to the English court to salvage what he could of the marriage negotiations. As Anjou would not agree to a verbal commitment along the lines discussed between Burghley, Leicester and de l'Archant, de Foix was told to obtain from Elizabeth an explicit acceptance of Anjou's demand for freedom of worship and 'en faire passer l'article, comme le reste de ce qui sera accordé du traité par le Parlement et Estats du pais'.[75]

French plans for the enterprise of Flanders were a badly kept secret. By the end of July 1571, news of it had leaked to the Spaniards, who believed incorrectly that Elizabeth was one of the instigators behind a campaign in the Netherlands. Walsingham too knew in general terms that some kind of design against Spain was under discussion at the French court and believed that Elizabeth might be offered an alliance with Charles IX if the marriage project collapsed.[76] In early August 1571 he was more fully informed of the war plans by Louis of Nassau, and on 12 August he let Burghley and Leicester know that the count had offered Zealand and some other islands to Elizabeth in return for her participation in a league against Spain.[77] As a result of Walsingham's information, Elizabeth and Burghley fully expected de Foix to speak to them about an alliance if the matrimonial negotiations broke down during his visit to England. Charles IX, however, gave de Foix no instructions of this kind; on the contrary, the envoy was told to withdraw 'prudemment', offering only 'grande affection et bonne volonté' if the religious difficulties remained unresolved.[78]

De Foix's stay in England from mid-August until mid-September 1571 coincided with acute governmental anxieties about Catholic conspiracies and Spanish hostilities. From April 1571 onwards, Burghley had been uncovering evidence of the Ridolfi plot involving agents of Mary Stuart, an unknown English nobleman, Pope Pius V, Philip II and the duke of Alva. Although the extent and details of the intrigue had yet to be revealed, it was known by the time of de Foix's arrival that a widespread conspiracy existed to depose Elizabeth and enthrone Mary by means of a Catholic rebellion and Spanish invasion. In early September, just before de Foix's departure, Norfolk was implicated in the plot while Arundel and

Lord Lumley also fell under suspicion of involvement. In this political emergency, Elizabeth desperately needed a defensive alliance with the French to cut off their support for Mary Stuart and end her own perilous isolation. Consequently de Foix found her far more flexible in trying to meet the French demands.

De Foix had his first audience with Elizabeth on 15 August 1571 and met formally with her councillors, Burghley, Leicester, Bacon and Lord Howard of Effingham a few days afterwards.[79] Initially their discussions focused on three of the original French demands: that Anjou be crowned king, that he share in the administration of the realm, and be allowed the free exercise of his religion. The first two issues were settled quickly with Elizabeth making compromises acceptable to the French. Although Anjou could not be crowned immediately after the wedding as this required the consent of her parliament, she agreed that he would be accounted king by right matrimonial and would be allowed to have some share in the administration of government.[80]

The question of religion posed more problems, and de Foix held some seven or eight special conferences with the queen and her Council in search of an agreement. First, the two sides went over the same old ground; de Foix requested toleration for Anjou, which Elizabeth refused; then he asked her 'to agree secretly that he [Anjou] should not be impeached in the secret use of his Religion', which she also rejected. Eventually, however, Elizabeth offered a new concession on the advice of Burghley: on three occasions a week, she said, Anjou could practise the forms of his own religion 'Verbo Dei non aperte repugnantius' (which were not repugnant to the word of God) in a secret and private place, until such time as he had been properly instructed in the English religion and on condition that she could suspend her permission if 'public offence has arisen or may possibly grow to the disturbance of the public peace'.[81] Relieved that a formula of words had been proposed that did not seem to rule out the use of the Mass, de Foix initially agreed to this new suggestion. On seeing it in writing, however, he took exception to the words 'Verbo Dei', recognising that the English would obviously argue that the Mass was contrary to the word of God. He requested, therefore, that the form of words be changed.

Elizabeth's initial reaction was to refuse this request but Burghley advised her otherwise; if she did not want the talks to fail and if she, 'for such urgent, necessary, honorable and proffitable causes, as have bene by your counsell at many tymes playnly ernestly and at good length delyvered unto you . . . [you] shall yeld your self to marry with Monsieur D'Aniou', then, suggested Burghley, she should propose to amend the words to 'non repugnantius Ecclesia Dei' (not abhorrent to the Church of God) and leave to a later interview the question of 'how his conscience may be satisfyed'.[82] Following this recommendation, Elizabeth consented to

'*Ecclesia Dei*' claiming that the two different phrases shared the same meaning. For this reason de Foix again objected and asked that the words be changed to '*Ecclesia Catholica*' (not abhorrent to the Catholic Church). This would unambiguously have granted Anjou the use of the Mass and consequently Elizabeth would not agree to them.[83]

By the end of August 1571, Elizabeth had made as many concessions to the French as she dared on the issue of religion. She had agreed that Anjou and his household would not be compelled by law to use any rites, sacraments or prayers in the Prayer Book 'which is not contained in the holy Scriptures, nor made use of in the Gallican Church', and had promised to allow them the exercise of their own religious ceremonies which did not offend the Church of God.[84] Both these concessions were vague and would have undoubtedly opened up future debate had they been accepted by the French; but there could be no question about the central issue: Elizabeth was refusing to sanction the use of a private Mass. She proffered her concessions with the aims of demonstrating her good-will to the French royal family and keeping her options open. If Anjou continued to be intransigent about the marriage, Charles IX might be sufficiently impressed by her sincerity and graciousness to offer another form of amity. On the other hand, if Charles and Catherine succeeded in detaching the duke from the cardinal of Lorraine and in persuading him to go ahead with the royal marriage on her terms, Elizabeth and Anjou could sort out the details of permitted and proscribed religious practices at a personal interview later on.[85]

Given the uncertainties and difficulties over religion, why did Elizabeth not abandon the marriage and instead concentrate her efforts on negotiating an alliance with the French? After all, during de Foix's visit of the late summer some of her Protestant councillors, including Leicester, Sir Francis Knollys, Sir Walter Mildmay and possibly Lord Admiral Clinton, had come out against a marriage which would grant a degree of toleration to a Catholic and spoke in favour of making a league with the French.[86] Walsingham from outside the Council had also cooled towards the marriage when he realised that an alliance was under discussion in France. In his view, the marriage looked unlikely 'because it hath so many over-throws both here and there'; whereas an Anglo-French alliance seemed to be on offer and besides had many merits. A league directed against Spain, he believed, would work 'to the advancement of God's glory, and her Majestie's safety', because English intervention in the Netherlands would further the Protestant cause in Europe as well as bring the queen 'honour, profit and surety'.[87]

Elizabeth herself, however, had several reservations about a league. In the first place, she had no evidence that the French wanted her to join one: 'upon indirect speeches used by some of our trusty Ministers to de Foix in that purpose: he hath earnestly declared, that without prosecution of the marriage, he had no Commission to deal in any other matter at all'.[88] Second, the kind of league described by Walsingham on 12 August 1571 had no appeal to Elizabeth. As she was to show time and again over the next few years, the possibility of French expansionism in the Netherlands filled her with dread. At the same time, she was not attracted to the prospect of acquiring Zealand and other islands. The English crown had never ruled territories in the Netherlands, and they would be difficult to capture and hold. In addition, Burghley had strong doubts about the value of any league without marriage and his views might well have carried weight with the queen.

In Burghley's opinion, 'a strayght amity' without marriage was a far more hazardous policy than a matrimonial alliance. Without the marriage, he asserted, 'the French Amity shall serve to small purpose, but to make us ministers of their appetites, and those fulfilled, to cast us off'.[89] An offensive alliance directed towards an enterprise in the Netherlands, of the kind desired by the French king, could end in a costly and dangerous war against Spain; it would also destroy the Burgundian commercial relationship, which was still thought to be capable of repair and in England's best interests. Furthermore, judging from past experience, in the event of war with Spain Charles IX might make a separate peace and leave Elizabeth to foot the bill and continue the fight alone. These perils could be avoided if the alliance with France were purely defensive, but amity without marriage would anyway last only as long as 'it shall be proffitable to France to kepe it', argued Burghley. Charles IX could easily mend his relationship with Spain and break with England, thereby leaving Elizabeth once again isolated and vulnerable to attack.[90]

Despite Elizabeth's and Burghley's reservations about a league, by early autumn 1571 there seemed to be little other choice, as the prospects for the marriage were daily growing gloomier. In September de Foix declared that Elizabeth's concessions on religion were insufficient to satisfy Anjou's conscience, and he also turned down her request for a personal meeting with the duke, at which they could try to work out an agreement together to settle the religious difficulty. Instead, he

> hath very earnestly moved her Majestie to send some one person of credit to the French King, to affirm and justifie the reasons for her answer or rather, if the Marriage shall not take place, to enter into the Treaty of some straiter allyance and confederacy.[91]

On leaving England, de Foix admitted to Cobham that he was returning to France 'with smayll hope'.[92]

By early October 1571, Anjou was refusing to marry Elizabeth under any circumstances whatsoever, and as a result Walsingham found that all support for the match at the French court had fallen away.[93] Charles IX gave up all thoughts of a marriage and concentrated on setting up a league as a preliminary to war in the Netherlands. Consequently, he echoed de Foix's advice and asked that the English gentleman who was sent to explain the queen's answers should also be given a commission to negotiate other matters 'that may tende to encrease of further amytye'.[94] Catherine too recognised that Anjou was beyond her influence in the matter of the marriage, but in her anxiety to avoid war against Spain she put forward her youngest son, Francis duke of Alençon, as a substitute candidate in preference to talks of a league.[95] On the other hand, the Huguenot leaders, especially Coligny and possibly also the prince of Condé, began to think in terms of Henry of Navarre as an alternative bridegroom in order to keep Elizabeth within the international Protestant fold and committed to the enterprise in the Netherlands. Although their negotiations are obscure since Walsingham's dispatches made no mention of them, it appears that plans were laid at La Rochelle in September 1571 for Louis of Nassau to intercede with Jeanne d'Albret, Navarre's mother, to win her support for a match with Elizabeth.[96] D'Albret, however, was vehement in her opposition to the proposal. Her dynastic ambitions for her son as well as her religious interests were centred exclusively on France, and in her view a marriage to Elizabeth would do nothing to assure Navarre's position as sovereign of Béarn nor to strengthen the Huguenot cause as a whole within France.[97]

Elizabeth, too, did not want a Navarre match, which would offer her no security but instead embroil her in French factional politics and place her unwillingly at the head of an international Protestant league. By contrast, the need for a matrimonial alliance with the French crown seemed more pressing than ever in the autumn of 1571. The full revelations of the Ridolfi plot had exposed Elizabeth's political vulnerability, while news of the Habsburg–papal naval victory at the battle of Lepanto which reached her in early November raised alarms that Philip II, apparently freed from the Turkish threat in the Mediterranean, might mobilise his resources against England.[98] In September 1571 the assassination of the philo-English regent, Lennox, in Scotland by one of Mary Stuart's supporters propelled that country into civil war, thereby awakening anxieties that the French would send military aid to help the Marian party gain control there.[99] It was in these circumstances that Burghley believed that Elizabeth had not relinquished hopes of the marriage and was even prepared 'to yealde in tolleration'.[100] In fact, however, Elizabeth's doubts about the marriage were increasing with the news of Anjou's intransigence and she decided to wait upon the French response to the terms given to de Foix rather than make another overture and risk a humiliating rejection at her suitor's hands. At the same time, she was in no hurry to conclude a league with France for fear of encouraging Spanish reprisals. Therefore, despite Walsingham's entreaties that she act swiftly, Elizabeth delayed sending an envoy to France with a commission to negotiate a treaty. When in October 1571 she dispatched Sir Henry Killigrew to cover for Walsingham during an illness, she instructed him only to relay the details of the Ridolfi plot and excuse her tardiness in sending the commissioner.[101]

By December 1571, Elizabeth could wait no longer for a French initiative. She sent Sir Thomas Smith to France to conclude discussions on the marriage and investigate the possibilities for forming a defensive alliance if the matrimonial negotiations failed. Almost certainly, Elizabeth recognised that marriage with the Catholic Anjou was by then beyond resuscitation but decided to complete the formalities before broaching the question of a league. She had no intention of making any further concessions and yielding toleration to Anjou, as Burghley had expected and many historians have since presumed.[102] Her instructions to Smith make clear that he was told to refuse the Mass on the grounds that it was 'nott only danngerous but also absurd yea allmost impossible' for 'the Head of the people' and her husband to have different religions.[103] Elizabeth's interest in a league, on the other hand, can be seen by her insistence that Coligny be present at court during Smith's visit and that he assist in the negotiations.

By the time of Smith's arrival at the French court in early January 1572, the marriage was no longer on the agenda. Within the first few days of his visit, Smith had learned that Anjou was in the midst of an affair with a Mademoiselle de Châteauneuf, and was so 'assottied' in religion that he was hearing Mass twice or three times a day and fasting regularly. In addition, his Catholic servants and Guise friends were warning him of the dishonour such a marriage would bring him and feeding his ambition with promises that he might replace Don John as head of the Holy League against the Turks.[104]

At the first opportunity, Smith tried to clarify how the land lay with Anjou and discover whether the marriage was at all viable. In an interview with Catherine de Medici on 6 January 1572, he spoke of his commission 'eyther to knot it [the marriage] up, if reasonable condicons be offred, or to plainly cut it of' and told her that he needed to have Anjou's position made plain. When Catherine answered that the problem lay with her son's religion, Smith began exploring exactly what terms Anjou would accept. Would he agree to the marriage 'if we should yelde to him in religion'? How would he react 'yf he be suffred for a tyme to have his mas private in some litle oratory or chappell to hym and a few of his'?[105] Had Catherine replied in the affirmative, it is difficult to see what Smith could have done next as he had been given no authority to offer these concessions, but he was probably expecting a negative response. Even so, Catherine's reply appears to have shocked him: by the free exercise of his religion, she said, Anjou was making the same demands that the Huguenots had made of the French government: 'preaching, christening, burying, not in cashete but open and fre, that thei should not seme to be ashamed to serve god after ther maner'. For his part, therefore, Anjou was insisting upon

> an highe mas, and all the ceremonies therof according to the tyme, and in song, and after all solempne fashion of the Romayne church, and a church or a chapell appointed wher he may openly have his preestes and singers and use all their ceremonies.[106]

These demands were of course totally out of the question. As a horrified Smith pointed out:

> my mistress will never agree to eny mas, not so miche as private and in a small chambre or oratory. Now the Queene here, when I ax the question, whither it wolde suffice, if the Queen my mistres wold graunt him for a tyme a private masse, untill he were better instructed or god had torned his heart, demanded of me not that onely, but an open churche consecrate for those maters, and great high mas, with all ceremonies of Roome according to the season, prest, deacon, subdeacon, chalice, aulther, belles, candlestickes, patene, singing men. . . .[107]

Anjou's unrealistic demands killed the matrimonial project stone-dead, no doubt just as he had intended. Although Catherine again suggested her youngest son as a substitute, Elizabeth showed no interest in his suit and diplomacy shifted towards negotiations for the formation of an Anglo-French league. The outcome was the Treaty of Blois concluded on 19 April 1572 which provided for common action in case of attack and contained the promise that neither party would assist the enemy of the other.

Unlike previous matrimonial negotiations, the Henry of Anjou project provoked scarcely any controversy or division in the English court or Council. According to La Mothe-Fénélon, some of the queen's ladies spoke out against the match several times during the negotiations, and he also reported in January 1571 that there had been 'une merveilleuse contention' at the first mention of the matrimonial project in the Council, when it had aroused the opposition of the 'Catholic lords' who feared its repercussions on Mary Stuart's future and were suspicious of the intentions of the Huguenots in promoting it.[108] None the less, there is little evidence to substantiate the view of Professor R. B. Wernham that the Anjou negotiations drove the already dispirited English Catholic noblemen into desperation, leading Norfolk to agree, albeit half-heartedly, to the treasonable plans of Ridolfi.[109] It is true that dislike of the Anjou match was one of the reasons given by Norfolk to the Catholic powers in March 1571 as an explanation for his involvement with Ridolfi, but the marriage came third on his list, placed after his concern about the treatment of English Catholics and worries about the succession.[110] Furthermore its inclusion may have been meant either for the purpose of emphasising his pro-Habsburg credentials to Philip II and the duke of Alva or in order to persuade the Spaniards to act swiftly against Elizabeth. It hardly seems credible that he was genuinely exercised about the match in early March 1571, when the Anglo-French talks were only at a preliminary stage and there was no reason to believe that they would be any more successful than previous abortive matrimonial plans. In the testimonies of the conspirators made in the autumn of 1571, there is no indication that the Anjou negotiations played any part in Norfolk's grievances or those of Arundel and Lumley; the Catholic lords, said the bishop of Ross, were disturbed by the 'certane extreme and rigorous Lawes' passed against the Catholics in the 1571 parliament, while Norfolk was offended by his continuing house-arrest and exclusion from political life.[111]

After the early questioning of the wisdom of opening the Anjou matrimonial negotiations, there was no significant conciliar opposition to the marriage until July 1571, and in the meantime the inner group of councillors who were responsible for the negotiations worked together harmoniously in an attempt to produce terms agreeable to both sides. Leicester for once seemed to be acting positively to arrange a foreign marriage for his queen. He often acted as a constructive intermediary between the French and Elizabeth and earned the thanks of Charles IX and Catherine for his help in promoting the match. Burghley found that he 'doth by all good means, to my knowledge, further the mariage', while in his letters to Walsingham, Leicester frequently expressed his support for it.[112] Either Leicester was dissembling most effectively, or else he had decided that the queen's marriage to Anjou would benefit the realm without harming his own interests.

In truth Leicester's deepest feelings about the match are impenetrable and can only be surmised. It is certainly possible that he felt that he had to feign support for a matrimonial alliance, which Elizabeth was considering and much Protestant opinion at home and abroad favoured, for fear of otherwise laying himself open to the accusation that he was behaving out of self-interest and against the security of the realm. To avoid such charges, he may have decided to hold his fire, especially as there was every chance that the match would self-destruct on the issue of religion without any intervention from him. His frequent emphasis on the religious difficulty and his approval for Elizabeth holding a firm line on religion, as declared in his letters to Walsingham, can be construed as evidence that he was hoping and working surreptitiously for the ultimate failure of the matrimonial talks over this issue.[113] On the other hand, Leicester did not have to work quite so hard to forward the match if he were secretly hoping for its collapse. Rather than using religion as a wedge to separate the two sides, Leicester on several occasions encouraged the French to think that the queen might allow Anjou to practise his religion in private.[114] Similarly, instead of exploiting the differences that emerged during de l'Archant's visit, Leicester co-operated with Burghley to find a formula to reconcile the two sides and save the negotiations. Perhaps then his support for the match was genuine. There were, after all, important advantages to be gained from the queen's marriage to Anjou. Like the other councillors, he could appreciate that a dynastic alliance would strengthen Elizabeth against the Guises, the pope and Philip II; and like Walsingham he believed that the match would assist his Huguenot friends and the Protestant cause in Europe. Furthermore, until the summer of 1571 there appeared to be no alternative policy which Leicester or anyone else for that matter could devise to overcome the perceived dangers to the realm. As Walsingham explained:

> when I particularly consider her Majestie's state, both at home and abroad ... and how she is beset with Forraign peril, the execution whereof stayeth onely upon the event of this match, I do not see how she can stand if this matter break off.[115]

Additionally, at a personal level the queen's marriage would free Leicester to re-marry and father an heir. Leicester may have been thinking in terms of Douglass, Lady Sheffield, the daughter of Lord Howard of Effingham with whom he was rumoured to be having an affair in August 1571, but Catherine de Medici was investigating the possibilities of him marrying the duchesse de Nevers de Montpensier.[116] An Anjou match might also provide him with the opportunity of leading an English army in the Netherlands and satisfying his thirst for military action. Finally, he had good reason to hope that as a royal consort Anjou would have little influence with the queen or involvement in political life, for the young duke was thought to be immature and easily manipulated. All in all, therefore, the queen's marriage to Anjou might have seemed for a time politically desirable and personally unthreatening.

Whatever the truth of Leicester's original feelings about the marriage, it is clear that he came to oppose it once the matrimonial negotiations were deadlocked over religion and a French alliance without marriage seemed to be on offer. As early as July 1571 he welcomed Walsingham's news of Charles IX's plans to forge a league against Spain in the Netherlands, and expressed his hope that 'some other amity may be accepted'. In August, he promised Walsingham that he would 'do all that is possible' to promote a league with France, and there are hints that during de Foix's embassy to England he was trying to influence the queen against the marriage and in favour of the league.[117] This policy brought Leicester into open disagreement with Burghley who wanted talk of a league to be put aside until there was no chance at all of marriage, in case 'the offers of so great Amitie will diminish or divert the former intention of the marriage'.[118] According to the Spanish ambassador, at the meeting of the Council to discuss the marriage Lord Keeper Bacon and Sussex sided with Burghley while Leicester had the support of Knollys and Clinton. Mildmay, unmentioned by de Spes, was also an opponent of the marriage, believing that 'yelding in that point of religion will offend God and surely perill her Majestie'.[119] No bitter dispute, however, developed over the issue, since it was obvious to everyone that Anjou was sabotaging the negotiations and that the future of the marriage was dependent on his attitude rather than Elizabeth's policy.

Outside the court and Council there appears to have been little interest in the Anjou match. The parliament which met in April 1571 mounted no campaign to persuade the queen to marry or name a successor as it had in 1563 and 1566. With the councillors at this stage united behind the Anjou marriage and Elizabeth pursuing the French negotiations energetically, councillors did not need to encourage a parliamentary initative to 'augment the pressure on her'.[120] There is also no evidence of a Protestant public relations campaign in the form of ballads, sermons, drama or printed books against a Catholic marriage, as there had been in 1567 and was to be again in 1578 and 1579. With men like Walsingham, Leicester and Bacon backing the match, Protestants had no cause to fear it on religious grounds nor any incentive to speak out against it. When informing Heinrich Bullinger at Zurich of Anjou's suit on 8 August 1571, Bishop Horne of Winchester claimed that he found it difficult to be a judge in the affairs of princes and was leaving the matter to be disposed of by God; his view may have been widespread.[121]

The Henry of Anjou matrimonial project, therefore, had less impact on political life than most of Elizabeth's other courtships. The political temperature was not raised by disputes at court, debates in parliament or the appeal to anti-Catholic public opinion. Like the dogs that did not bark in the Sherlock Holmes story, this absence of noise is significant. It suggests that the lack of debate was the result of both the unity of the Privy Council and the readiness of Elizabeth to follow its lead. In other words there is a clear impression that the councillors were the orchestrators of parliamentary business and the initiators of so-called popular political action in early Elizabethan England.

Elizabeth's attitude to the marriage remains as always an enigma. Can we really be as certain as Wallace MacCaffrey that 'she had no intention of taking the Duke of Anjou or anyone else as her husband'? [122] If she was interested in the negotiations to contain the French rather than in the marriage itself, why did she not seek to spin them out rather than risk their rupture by stating clearly and unambiguously her position on the issues in dispute? Walsingham, Burghley and Leicester all preferred some degree of obfuscation especially in the spring of 1571 for the purpose of keeping the discussions alive, and despite their Protestant zeal they were prepared to fudge the extent of religious freedom Anjou would be allowed. Does this mean, then, that Elizabeth was opposed to the negotiations with the French and had only agreed to talks under pressure from her inner ring of councillors? Again this explanation is unsatisfactory. It fails to explain why Elizabeth was prepared from the start to offer Anjou better conditions than the Archduke Charles over the exercise of his religion and why she tried so hard to reach a compromise with de Foix in August 1571. Furthermore, whenever Elizabeth was told by Burghley that her attitude would be thought unreasonable and cause the project to collapse, she retracted her demands and changed her approach: thus with extreme reluctance she dropped Calais from the terms to be included in the treaty; she avoided an appeal to her conscience as an explanation for her refusal to permit Anjou the Mass; and she came back to de Foix with a formula of words that Burghley thought might be sufficient to satisfy the French.

On balance, therefore, it looks as if Elizabeth had resolved to marry if the terms were right. Badly shaken by the political crises of 1569 to 1570 and the breach with Spain, it seems that she turned to a French dynastic alliance for the purpose of obtaining personal and political security. Marriage to Anjou, however, was not a course of action she relished and she was aware it would bring her little prospect of personal happiness. Apart from his religion, it was the age disparity that bothered her most and she needed frequent reassurance from her ladies and councillors that it did not matter. Not all her ladies, however, would oblige her, concerned as they were that the eighteen years between prospective husband and wife were too great. Again and again Elizabeth confessed her anxieties about Anjou's youth: she would look ridiculous walking to church alongside a youthful bridegroom; the duke would despise and spurn her as she grew older, especially if she could not have a child.[123] Such worries would have been unnecessary had she not seriously considered marriage. There was also the fear, which was mentioned by some of her councillors, that 'it mighte be a daunger to the shorteninge of here Majestie's life, lest some insinuation might lighte into the harte of the Duke to attaine to the mariage of the Q[ueen] of Scottes'.[124] Anjou's own behaviour did not lessen her anxieties. Although he was occasionally prepared to mouth conventional compliments about her to Walsingham, he also made unflattering observations about his intended bride, which were relayed back to her, and he demonstrated a strong reluctance to wed her which was also impossible to hide. It is difficult to believe that this was a courtship that Elizabeth enjoyed!

In the short term the negotiations had little success in achieving their aims. Anjou remained close to the Guises and the extreme Catholic party in France throughout 1571 and was more attracted to their promises to make him commander of the papal Holy League against the Turks or leader of an invasion force in Ireland than he was to the acquisition of an English crown. At the same time, Charles IX continued in his attempts to protect Mary Stuart and her party in Scotland by diplomatic means right up until the signing of the Treaty of Blois in April 1572. As Burghley himself realised, Charles could not give up Mary's cause for fear of the damage to his reputation, the loss of French influence in Scotland, the irritation it would cause to the Guises and the danger that Mary and her faction would turn towards Spain for assistance. On the other hand, there was little practical help that the king could give her, since the dispatch of a French force to Scotland was out of the question, with the French navy under the charge of Admiral Coligny who would not allow a fleet to be used to help the Marian party. Besides, while there was hope of English participation in the enterprise of Flanders, Charles wanted to avoid military confrontation in Scotland. Whether or not Anjou became Elizabeth's husband was essentially irrelevant to these considerations.

The negotiations, moreover, did nothing to restore Anglo-Spanish relations as Elizabeth and Burghley had hoped. Although Alva's readiness to enter into further talks to reinstate commerce in early 1572 may have been somewhat influenced by fears that an Anglo-French accord would lead to the establishment of a cloth staple in France, the duke had long been keen to end the embargo which was damaging Antwerp's commerce. Indeed, overall, the Anglo-French negotiations exacerbated the mutual fear and distrust between Elizabeth and Philip II. Although they were supposed to be secret, news of the matrimonial talks filtered through to the Spaniards from the very beginning.[125] On several occasions, particularly in the spring of 1571, de Spes was sure that 'the marriage will be effected, notwithstanding the ancient enmity between the two nations', while Alva reported of the high hopes in France that the marriage would take place.[126] Neither Philip II nor Alva, however, could believe 'there is anything in it' except an indication of Elizabeth's hostile intentions towards Spain, and by late spring 1571 the king began to think that the negotiations were a cover for an Anglo-French enterprise in the Netherlands.[127] It was in this conviction that he gave his conditional approval to the plots of Roberto Ridolfi in June 1571, which in turn fuelled English suspicions of the Spaniards.[128] In June 1572 the arrival of the French commissioners to ratify the Treaty of Blois also alarmed the Spaniards who feared that it would lead to further negotiations for an enterprise in Flanders.

The Anjou matrimonial project certainly marked an important stage in England's changing relationship with France and Spain. Indeed, some historians have seen the negotiations with France that began in 1570 and ultimately led to the Treaty of Blois as a 'diplomatic revolution' and a turning-point in Elizabethan foreign policy. During those years, it has been argued, the queen turned away from her traditional partnership with the rulers of the Low Countries towards an entente with France, which had

127

been regarded until then as her most troublesome neighbour.[129] They corrrectly point out that a number of Elizabethan statesmen, including Walsingham, saw the negotiations with France as a much-needed opportunity for a new alignment in European politics. In Walsingham's view, the ancient friendship with the rulers of the Netherlands was an anachronism now that 'the house of Austria is become the Pope's Champion, and professed enemy unto the Gospel'.[130] Speaking the rhetoric of religion, he expressed his hopes in the summer of 1571 for an Anglo-French league fighting on behalf of the Protestant cause in the Netherlands against Spain: 'The proud Spaniard (whom God hath long used for the rod of his wrath) I see great hope that he will now cast him into the fire, that he may know what it is to serve against God.'[131] At one level, therefore, the negotiations with France between late 1570 and early 1572 did represent a break with the past and point to a future when Elizabeth would stand side by side with the French crown and Huguenots against Catholic Spain and the Guises.

On the other hand, neither Elizabeth nor Burghley saw the negotiations in this light. In the first place they entered into them with the intention of containing France as much as protecting the realm against Spain. As has already been shown, important initial objectives of the negotiations were to cut off Guise support for Mary Stuart and allow Elizabeth to intervene in Scotland without the threat of Charles IX's retaliation. At the end of 1571 Elizabeth and Burghley were also beginning to be alarmed by French expansionist aims in Flanders, a consideration which influenced them in rejecting Charles IX's scheme for an offensive league and led them to draw closer to Philip II. At no time did Elizabeth or Burghley have any intention of engaging in military conflict with Spain. Far from seeking an end to the ancient 'amity' with the House of Burgundy, they hoped that an Anglo-French dynastic alliance would deter Philip II from an enterprise against Elizabeth in Ireland or England, and force him to lift the trade embargo, restore the confiscated goods of English merchants and renew the ancient treaties of the Intercursus. Even the Treaty of Blois was not intended to cause or mark a breach with Spain. It contained no offensive clauses and was far removed from the godly league envisaged by Walsingham. As Sir Thomas Smith commented, the treaty was intended to act 'as great an assurance and defence of your Majesty as ever was or can' so that 'if Spain will now threaten or shew evil Offices, as it hath done of late against your Highness' surety, it will be afraid hereafter, seeing such a wall'; on the other hand, if Spain wanted friendship with England, 'nothing is done on your Majestie's part to break the amity'.[132] Just before the treaty was signed, Elizabeth and Burghley made conciliatory overtures towards Philip II and indicated their readiness to reach an agreement over the restoration of commerce.[133] Their attempts to curb the activities of the Calvinist privateers, known as the 'Sea Beggars', who were exiles from the Netherlands, and their decision to expel them from English ports in early 1572 were also intended as a concessionary move towards Spain and a way of removing a major cause of friction between the two monarchs.[134] Therefore, although the negotiations were born out of England's deteriorating relations with Spain, they did not indicate a decisive change in Elizabeth's foreign policy. This was recognised by the French king and queen-mother who wanted to tie Elizabeth more closely to their tails. It was for this reason that they pursued their attempts to arrange a dynastic alliance and opened the suit of the youngest Valois prince, Francis duke of Alençon.

6

MATRIMONIAL DIPLOMACY: THE ALENÇON MATCH 1572–8

Before 1572 Elizabeth was on the whole straightforward with her suitors. On only two occasions did she simulate interest in a match which she had no intention at all of entering: first when she and her councillors had deliberately, though briefly, encouraged false hopes during the suits of Archduke Charles of Austria in the autumn of 1559; and then with Charles IX of France in mid-1565. By contrast, Elizabeth's handling of the suit of Francis duke of Alençon between mid-1572 and late 1578 was a master-piece of protracted dalliance. Under pressure from some of her councillors she gave it serious consideration in the early summer of 1572, but between the massacre of St Bartholomew in August 1572 and the arrival of Jean de Simier at her court in January 1579, she used matrimony simply as a diplomatic tool. The French were rarely if ever deceived, but then they too were more interested in the benefits to be gained from the negotiations than in the marriage itself. It was for this reason that the courtship could go on for so long without making any progress. Both sides were following the same rules in the game of diplomacy.

The failure of the Anjou matrimonial negotiations in January 1572 had greatly disappointed Charles IX and Catherine de Medici who blamed Henry for their collapse. Both recognised the limitations of the Treaty of Blois and feared that accord between the two realms would have little bite without a dynastic marriage to hold it together. Catherine was anxious about the capacity of the Guises, the pope and Philip II of Spain to damage Anglo-French relations, whilst Charles considered that only a French husband could tempt Elizabeth into an enterprise in the Netherlands. In search of a closer amity, therefore, Catherine put forward Alençon's suit as soon as Henry had announced his refusal to marry Elizabeth, and Charles supported the proposal once he realised that the English were interested only in negotiating a defensive treaty with him.[1] Believing that the groundwork of the matrimonial negotiations had already been completed, they were both hopeful that Alençon could be fairly easily exchanged for his brother and a marriage-contract speedily drawn up and ratified. Erroneously they presumed that the religious difficulty had disappeared when Sir Thomas Smith had asked Catherine in January 1572 if Anjou would be satisfied with a private Mass. This they had misunderstood to be a definite offer from the queen, and they were sure that Alençon would 'make no scruple' in accepting it. Alençon's youth also did not seem to them an important impediment to the match, since Elizabeth had already accepted the principle of marrying a much younger man in taking the Anjou negotiations so far.[2]

Sir Thomas Smith, Elizabeth's special envoy to France, received the Alençon proposal with some eagerness, although he had no authority to treat of it. As a general principle, he agreed with Catherine that 'it was true, the knot of blood and marriage was a stronger seal than that which was printed in wax and lasted longer, if God gave good success'. The new candidate, moreover, he found to be an improvement on his brother:

> D'Alanson is as riche in lands and moveables as D'Angiou, th'other is th'elder and higher, this is the more moderate, more flexible and the better fellow. . . . Yndede D'Alanson is no so tall and so fayer as his brother but that is fantasied. Then he is not so obstinate and froward, so papisticall and (if I may say so) so foolish and restyve like a mule as his brother is.[3]

Following Anjou's complete defection to the ultra-Catholics, who were bent on destroying the Peace of St Germain, Alençon had become the 'refuge and succour' of the Huguenots, who had flocked to his service from his brother's household: 'so that these two brethern as I can lerne be allmoste become *Capi de Guelphi et Gibellini*'.[4] Smith was not alone among Elizabeth's servants to be content with the substitution. Both Burghley and Lord Keeper Bacon judged Alençon to be preferable to Anjou in part because of his religion but also because he was less likely to inherit the French throne.[5]

Elizabeth, however, had already suffered enough humiliation in her dealings with Anjou and she saw no reason to expect better treatment from his brother; nor did she feel any attraction to the suit of a sixteen-year-old youth. Thus, when Burghley broached the Alençon proposal with her, her response was so negative that La Mothe-Fénélon was told that for the time being he would do better to refrain from speaking to the queen about the match.[6] In her reply to Smith on 26 January 1572, Elizabeth pointedly dismissed the suit as not worthy of her attention or comment: she made no specific reference to Alençon but merely told her ambassador to complain to the French royal family about his elder brother's 'contrary dealyng', concluding with the words:

> we ar in no wise miscontent in our own mynd that the matter [the Anjou marriage] proceedeth not, for now may we satisfy our subiects that we have delt herin playnly, and hav gon and yelded as farr therin

as God's cause may move us ... and so by God's assistance we
shall now determyne with advice of our good Consellors to enioye
our own naturall desyre that is to lyve unmaryed, and yet provyde
remedyes for the quetness of our realme, both in our own tyme and
for our posteryte.[7]

Similarly, during the winter and spring months of 1572 Elizabeth gave her
ambassadors in France, Smith and Walsingham, no directions about how
to reply to the Alençon proposal and made no move to resume matrimonial discussions with either Catherine or Charles IX.[8] By March 1572,
Smith had become impatient with her silence on the subject, protesting
to Burghley that he and Walsingham 'can say nothing, whereof we are
more sorry and do lament in our hearts, to see such uncertain, so negligent
and irresolute provision' for the queen's safety.[9]

At the end of April 1572, however, Elizabeth somewhat modified her
stance. A parliament was due to meet on 8 May and the queen needed
no reminding that her MPs would very likely call for the naming of
a successor if there were no prospect of a marriage in view. Despite
her words to Smith on 26 January she had no intention of resolving the
succession question. Furthermore, events in the Netherlands during April
had further unsettled international relations. On the first day of that month
the Calvinist 'Sea Beggars' had unexpectedly captured Brill and three
weeks afterwards they occupied Flushing. With these two Zealand towns
in open revolt against the authority of the duke of Alva, Elizabeth and
Burghley had reason to fear that the French would seize the opportunity
to invade the Netherlands as allies of Louis of Nassau and William of
Orange.[10] One governmental response to this danger, probably initiated
by Burghley, was to allow English volunteers to go to Flushing with the
aims of preventing the French taking over the town and of aiding
the rebels; another was to keep on the closest terms with the French king
in order to influence him against armed intervention. Some time towards
the end of April, therefore, Burghley informed La Mothe-Fénélon that
the queen had listened to him 'plus volunteries' than usual about Alençon's
suit and was now ready to hear a formal proposal of marriage.[11] This
statement was a long way from the truth, but it indicated Elizabeth's
and Burghley's wariness about offending Charles IX and his mother at
this important time. The queen's instructions of 25 May 1572 to the earl
of Lincoln, who was to lead an embassy to France for the purpose of
ratifying the Treaty of Blois, reflected the same concern. Although she
told Lincoln to complain of Anjou's ill-use of her if the French king or
queen-mother spoke to him about Alençon's suit, she insisted that his
speech should be carefully worded to avoid causing offence. In addition,
while the earl was to say that 'he hath no charge to speak' of the match
at that time, he was also to thank the French king for his 'sundry offers

... of daily increase of this Amity now newly established between them' and tell him that 'though her Majestie doth not percase so often answer these his kindnesses in words or writing, yet he shall be assured that, whensoever occasion shall be given to shew the like affection in deeds, she will not be behind them'.[12] In a postscript Burghley instructed Lincoln to explain to the French that the difficulties in the way of the match related to the duke's age and religion.

Notwithstanding this luke-warm response from England, Charles IX decided to open formal matrimonial negotiations. Taking advantage of the embassy due to be sent to England for the purpose of ratifying the Treaty of Blois, he empowered his deputies, Francis duke of Montmorency and Paul de Foix, 'faire l'ouverture du mariage', to start negotiations and 'adviser les bons moyens et expediens pour parvenir a la conclusion et effet'.[13] Before their arrival Catherine wrote to known supporters of the previous Anjou match in the English Council to ask for their support in this new venture.[14] Burghley, in fact, needed no prompting, and together with Leicester he promised to help Montmorency find the right time, place and arguments to promote the marriage.[15]

When the French embassy led by the duke of Montmorency arrived at the English court in June 1572, they found that Elizabeth was still touchy about Anjou's rebuff and 'usa plusieurs parolles pour monstrer qu'elle se ressentoit des empeschemens qui avoient esté mis au mariage'.[16] During their first interview, she also gently mocked this new matrimonial proposal in a short speech in which she made much of her obligation to the queen-mother 'pour luy avoir presenté tous ses enfans l'un après l'autre'. Above all else, Elizabeth made clear that she considered marriage to a man twenty-two years younger than herself to be ridiculous. Throughout the visit she could not be persuaded otherwise by the ambassadors who insisted that inequalities of age were common amongst princes, as their numbers were too few to allow for age-compatibility in every case. Nor was she convinced by their argument that it was far better for her to marry someone so much younger if she wanted to continue to rule her realm: 'parcequ'elle estoit accoustumée à commander seulle et que sy elle prenoit mary de plus grand aage indubitablement il voudroit commander au lieu'.

None the less, after individual deliberations with some of her councillors Elizabeth was prepared to continue matrimonial negotiations with Montmorency and de Foix. As she was facing unwelcome parliamentary calls at that time for the execution of Mary Stuart or at the very least her exclusion from the throne, the queen could not ignore the urgent need to settle the succession by producing an heir of her own body. Consequently, she allowed the French ambassadors to talk privately with Burghley and Leicester, and on several occasions brought their offer and terms to the whole Council for its opinion. During the course of these subsequent discussions, which lasted for nearly two weeks, Elizabeth was prepared to admit to the ambassadors that it was in her interests to marry. Not only would marriage assist her security at the present time, they were told, but it would also satisfy her loyal subjects who justly feared that 'si elle decedoit en l'estat qu'elle est, elle les laisseroit en extreme calamité et misère'. She also admitted that there was much to recommend Alençon as a husband: his royal birth, the proximity of his apanage to England, and of course his personal merits, though the latter was hardly the truth as she had heard disturbing rumours about his short height, pock-marked face and sexual prowess. In all the talks, however, she returned again and again to the difficulties surrounding his age and religion.

Although Elizabeth made more of the age difficulty when speaking to the ambassadors, she viewed the religious demands of the duke with at least equal concern. She and Burghley individually quizzed the ambassadors about the exact concessions required by Alençon to satisfy his conscience and tried to move the discussions away from the generalities preferred by the ambassadors to specifics: in particular they wanted to find out if the duke was demanding the Mass. As the precise nature of his conditions began to emerge, they were brought to the Council for discussion.

Alençon was indeed more flexible in religion than his brother had been, but not flexible enough for the queen and some of her councillors. The duke demanded access to the Mass for reasons of conscience and reputation, but was prepared to make some concessions as he did not want to bring 'aucun scandale ne troubler le royaume'. Consequently he agreed to: a ban on the public exercise of his religion, the exclusion of all the queen's subjects from the chamber where the Mass would be celebrated, and his own attendance at English church services. In addition, so as to avoid any rumours or anxieties among Protestants in England, the French did not insist that a free exercise of religion would be written into the marriage-treaty but declared that the duke would be satisfied with the queen's private promise to permit it in practice.

When Elizabeth first heard that Alençon was demanding the Mass, she consulted 'tous ceux qu'elle peult' of her Council. Soon afterwards Burghley told the ambassadors that a majority of her councillors had advised that she could not 'endurer' its use and that the marriage would have to fall on these grounds. Once Alençon's precise proposals emerged, however, Elizabeth consulted her Council again, and this time it was decided that the duke's conditions were 'tollerable' and that the talks should continue. But several of her councillors were absent from the meeting, being occupied with the parliament then in session. The names of those who attended are not mentioned in the sources but they probably included Burghley, Sussex and Lord Howard of Effingham, and it seems likely that among the absentees were the most uncompromising

Protestants, Sir Francis Knollys and Sir Walter Mildmay, both of whom were busy in the Commons.[17] Elizabeth herself obviously did not agree with the view expressed at the council meeting; she told the French ambassadors that she was not satisfied that Alençon's conditions could do her no harm, relayed to them the dangers already posed by the Catholics at home and abroad, and pointed out the importance of denying to her enemies opportunities to 's'enfler et enorgueillir'. She then called another meeting of her whole Council to discuss Alençon's terms as well as some further political safeguards promised by the ambassadors. With the presence of the more radical group, she could expect a different response, one more in line with her own preferences.

On the following morning, 25 June 1572, the full Council met but, because of strong disagreements amongst the members, failed to reach a decision. Besides Burghley, Sussex and Howard of Effingham, Leicester may also have spoken in favour of the marriage. In early June the earl had expressed to Walsingham his support for the match, which in his view promised to bring security to the realm and 'unyversal good to the cause of Relygion', since it would be followed by English help to William of Orange who was at war with the Spaniards in the Netherlands.[18] On the other hand, Knollys and Mildmay most certainly opposed it. With her Council divided but her leading ministers wanting the marriage, Elizabeth prevaricated and asked the French for a waiting period of a month during which time she could give it further serious consideration.

Elizabeth used this breathing space to make enquiries about the duke. Walsingham was instructed to discover Alençon's exact age and 'inclination to Religion', and to report on his appearance and character. She also told him to investigate the possibility of the French offering to compensate her for the unsuitability of Alençon's age by ceding Calais to her or to any child born from the union.[19] Walsingham's report did little to allay Elizabeth's doubts. On religion, he learned from the Huguenot leaders that there was every hope that Alençon 'is easely to be reduced to the knowledge of the trewthe' and might cease hearing Mass after his marriage to the queen; but similar assurances had of course been made without foundation about the fervently Catholic duke of Anjou, and in the meantime the French king and queen-mother were still sticking to their demand for a private Mass. As for Alençon's appearance, the news was no better. In the knowledge that the duke was considerably shorter than the queen, Walsingham wrote little about his size; he also made no precise comments about his looks, but Elizabeth had heard elsewhere of 'his great blemish in his face' as a result of the smallpox.[20]

Walsingham had also learnt that there was no possibility at all of Charles IX agreeing to the cession of Calais; indeed the French seemed affronted by any suggestion that compensation was needed for their prince. They said openly that Alençon was bringing to the marriage his own personal power and the power of his brother; at the same time, they might well have been thinking privately that the duke would be the one making the sacrifice in marrying an ageing woman who might be unable to bear him children and who refused to allow him to share in her rule. Besides, Charles and his Huguenot allies hoped that the marriage would be a first stage on the way to a war in the Netherlands in which Elizabeth could make other territorial gains. Hence, Paul de Foix suggested to Walsingham that instead of offering the return of Calais the king could include in the marriage-contract a commitment to help Elizabeth hold and conquer the rest of the island of Flushing in the Netherlands, where companies of English volunteers had landed in June and July 1572.[21] This suggestion, however, was completely unsatisfactory to the queen who had no expansionist aims in the Low Countries, no intention of joining a war against Spain but plenty of suspicions about the 'Flanders enterprise' planned by the French.[22] Indeed she and Burghley were so alarmed about the possibility of Charles IX gaining a foothold in the Netherlands, 'specyally the marytyme partes', that in June 1572 they even considered giving help to Alva to repulse the French 'if he is not habell to defend his mastere's contryes' by himself.[23]

Towards the end of the agreed waiting period, Elizabeth gave a form of answer to the proposal of marriage. On 23 July 1572, she told Walsingham that because of Alençon's age and the reports of his misshapen face:

> we cannot indeed bring our mind to like of this offer, specially findyng no other great commodity offered to us with him, whereby the absurdity that in general opinion of the world might grow to commend this our choice after so many refusals of others of great worthiness might be counterprised or in some manner recompenced.[24]

Four days later, however, under pressure from Burghley and the French ambassador, she softened her approach and suggested that a personal meeting might remove her doubts about the appropriateness of the match.[25] Not surprisingly, these mixed messages created some confusion in France since no-one was clear why Elizabeth should be offering Alençon an interview if she were rejecting his suit.[26] The ambiguity of the response was almost certainly not by design but the result of Elizabeth's own perplexity and irresolution about the best course to follow. Her instinct warned her against marriage to Alençon; its cost to her personal happiness seemed too high; there were incalculable political risks arising from his religion; and the presence at court of a deformed husband who was young enough to be her son would diminish her dignity. On the other hand, it was important to nurture the Anglo-French entente, which was already under strain because of divergent policies towards the Netherlands and the civil war in Scotland where the Regent Mar had not yet subdued the adherents of Mary Stuart. Elizabeth could also see that the marriage offered her other political advantages and probably the last opportunity to produce a child. Setting up a meeting with Alençon would allow her to postpone making an irrevocable decision, whilst the interview itself would provide her with the information which would help her come to a resolution. Only by seeing and talking to the duke would she be able to judge whether she liked him sufficiently to risk marriage, whether he would be likely to drop his demand for a private Mass, and whether his short height, scarred face and youthful looks would make them look an absurd couple in the eyes of the world and thereby demean her.

Though confused, Charles IX and Catherine de Medici appeared to be neither too disappointed nor discouraged by Elizabeth's response, since the queen had avoided specific mention of Alençon's religious demands as a cause of her dislike of the match. Catherine had already dispatched the sieur de la Mole, one of Alençon's household servants, to England with letters from the duke; during late July and August 1572 he charmed Elizabeth into showing a more favourable disposition towards the duke's suit, although she still expressed worries about his religion.[27] As a result of his encouraging reports from England, Catherine began to change her mind about an interview. Initially she had been most reluctant to agree to one unless assurances were given beforehand that 'upon the enterview, there might grow a liking' and that the queen had an earnest intention to marry. On 21 August 1572, however, the queen-mother wrote to La Mothe-Fénélon about the possibility of setting up a secret meeting on a ship somewhere in the Channel without such conditions.[28] Thus, on the eve of the assassination attempt on the Huguenot leader Admiral Coligny on 22 August 1572 and just before the St Bartholomew's Day Massacre on 24 August there was some optimism at the French court that the interview would take place, while in England Burghley even expressed some hope that the marriage might go ahead if the duke pleased the queen.[29]

On St Bartholomew's Day 1572 the Huguenot leaders (including Coligny), who had gathered in Paris for the wedding of Henry of Navarre and Marguerite de Valois, were murdered on the king's orders. The violence soon spread out of control and over the next three days there followed an indiscriminate slaughter of Huguenots in Paris. As word of this massacre travelled throughout the kingdom, Catholics struck out against the Protestants in almost every important French city. The news of these events stunned the English court and swept away all thoughts of a dynastic marriage and closer ties with the French king. Protestants in England experienced a natural revulsion at the 'barbarous treacherie' of the French Catholics in murdering their Protestant 'brethren' and breaking the edict of toleration signed in 1570.[30] At the same time, Elizabeth's councillors were acutely alarmed at the political implications of the attack on the Huguenots. In Burghley's judgement the mass murders indicated that the French king had fallen in with the duke of Guise and 'the faction of the papists' and would now seek to extirpate heresy in England and Scotland.[31] Furthermore, the formal alliance between England and France as embodied in the Treaty of Blois had been made possible only by the apparent removal of Guise influence from the French court and the reconciliation between Charles IX and the Huguenot leadership. With the destruction of the Huguenots and the return to ascendancy of the duke of Guise the treaty was thought to be fairly worthless and Elizabeth's security once more under threat.

It would not have been surprising if all discussions of an Anglo-French marriage had ended in the immediate aftermath of St Bartholomew. Elizabeth expressed her repugnance that the very same king who was seeking her marriage to his brother found her religion so odious that he was working to 'roote owt of his realme' all those Frenchmen who shared it.[32] Furthermore, although Alençon was in no way responsible for any of the violence in August 1572, as a member of the French royal family he was held guilty by association: thus, when Philip Sidney wrote his famous letter against the Anjou marriage in late 1579, he reminded Elizabeth that 'the very common people well know this: that he is the son of the Jezebel of our age; that his brother made oblation of his own sister's marriage, the easier to make massacres of all sexes.'[33] Alençon's participation in the royal army's siege of the Huguenot stronghold at La Rochelle soon after the massacre was also viewed as a mark against him, even though it was understood that he was 'then very young and acting at the direction of the king and queen-mother'.[34]

Even though marriage was now completely out of the question, the matrimonial negotiations were not completely broken off in the autumn of 1572, but rather used by both sides as a basis for a diplomatic link during this period of suspicion and tension. Neither Elizabeth nor Charles IX wanted to abandon the policy of rapprochement and they found that the Alençon match could serve a useful diplomatic function in encouraging courtesies and keeping open lines of communication despite the French court's policy of waging war against Elizabeth's co-religionists.

Charles IX and Catherine de Medici took the initiative in keeping the matrimonial project alive in the hope that it would demonstrate to Elizabeth their continuing amity. At one level, they used the marriage talks as part of their more general propaganda campaign aimed at Protestant Europe, which was designed to show that the crown's quarrel was with rebels and traitors not members of the Reformed Church. In addition, they wanted to dissuade the queen from giving asylum to Huguenot refugees and sending assistance to La Rochelle, which had been in effective rebellion since September 1572.[35] For her part, Elizabeth allowed the matrimonial talks to continue in order to salvage something of the friendship accorded at Blois. Although she now had no intention at all of marrying Alençon, she had no wish to drive the French into the arms of Spain by displaying a lack of goodwill and severing relations; nor did she want the French to send troops to Scotland, where the Marian party was holding Edinburgh Castle and the pro-English king's party was in disarray after the death of Regent Mar at the end of October 1572. In addition, Elizabeth used the discussions about her marriage as occasions to put pressure on the French king to reach an accommodation with the Huguenots which would grant them security and a degree of toleration. Historians usually describe Elizabeth's policy between 1572 and 1576 as swinging between seeking friendship with the French court and giving aid to the Huguenots; in reality the matrimonial negotiations provided frequent opportunities for her to do both at the same time.[36]

Charles IX and Alençon each sent separate envoys to England in the autumn of 1572 with instructions to assure the queen of their master's fidelity and continuing interest in the marriage. In November, Michel de Castelnau, sieur de Mauvissière, arrived on a formal embassy from Charles and Catherine.[37] The same month a member of Alençon's household, Jerome de l'Huillier, seigneur de Maisonfleur, delivered to Elizabeth a message from the duke, denying any complicity in the massacre and proposing a secret meeting.[38] Meanwhile, La Mothe-Fénélon passed on Catherine's offer that an interview could be arranged at sea, or if preferred in Guernsey or Jersey, and regularly raised the marriage issue with the queen and councillors.[39] The match was again urged upon the queen when the earl of Worcester attended the baptism of Charles IX's infant daughter in February 1573.

During all these overtures Elizabeth remained courteous but 'refroidie'.[40] She did not rule out marriage with Alençon but returned to the themes of his youth and religion as major obstacles. The former, she claimed, could be removed at a personal meeting which would settle whether there was sufficient liking to overcome the great inequality in age, but an interview at sea in the autumn or winter was out of the question, while the Channel Islands were too far distant at any time of the year.[41] As for the obstacle of religion, this had grown in importance after the murder of her co-religionists and the outbreak of the the fourth religious war in France. Alençon had to realise, she said, that after the betrayal at St Bartholomew she could not trust his guarantees about religion which had been delivered by Montmorency and de Foix in June 1572. Consequently, she was determined to 'suffer noo permission' to any other religion within her realm; in practice this meant that she was refusing Alençon not only a private Mass but also any other ceremony 'trop contraire à la sainte parolle de Dieu et aux loix establies pour la religion reçue en Angleterre'.[42] As Walsingham told Catherine: 'that thinge which is tollerable at one tyme is not tollerable in an other'.[43] Naturally Charles and the queen-mother complained bitterly about

Elizabeth's uncompromising position and were unwilling to arrange an interview on mainland England while there was so little likelihood of a successful outcome.[44] On the other hand, Alençon, who was perhaps the only person to take this round of negotiations seriously, declared his intention in April 1573 to go to England and woo the queen as soon as the fortress of La Rochelle had fallen to the royal army.[45]

Elizabeth was aghast by Alençon calling her bluff in this way and withdrew her invitation as quickly as she decently could. Although she put on a brave face to La Mothe-Fénélon, who thought that she 'had a good disposition' to it, she soon tried to call off the interview, making the excuse that the French would take offence if she did not like the duke sufficiently to accept his hand in marriage.[46] When this did not deter him, she told Charles and Catherine the truth. In June 1573 she sent a special ambassador, Edward Horsey, to France with both an explanation for her refusal to grant Alençon a safe-conduct and a critique of French policy towards the Huguenots.

Horsey told Charles IX that the royal family's persecution of the Huguenots was leading to the belief in England that they were determined, 'as farr as they may, to roote up' all the French Protestants, and in these circumstances it was impossible for her to receive the duke. If he came either during or after the subjugation of La Rochelle, 'he will com to sue for marryage with an arme or a sword inbrued with the blud of them that professe the same religion that heere he shall fynd generally receaved and favoured'; her Council, therefore, would only allow a personal meeting to take place when the policy of persecution ended. Exploiting the opportunity presented by Alençon's evident desire for the marriage, Elizabeth then offered through Horsey to mediate between the king and his subjects and help bring a swift conclusion to the war with a peace-treaty that would guarantee the security and religious freedom of the Huguenots in accordance with former edicts; once this was achieved the interview could go ahead at a later date.[47] The same point was made formally to the French ambassador in London by Elizabeth's councillors, with an even stronger warning that if the siege of La Rochelle were not lifted soon Elizabeth would be forced to supply its inhabitants with military aid.[48] Having just signed an agreement with Spain to restore trade and mindful of the recent fall of Edinburgh Castle to James VI's party, Elizabeth and her Council felt confident about taking this tougher line with the French king.

Elizabeth's tactics appeared on the surface to have succeeded. At any rate on 2 July 1573, soon after Horsey's arrival, Charles IX signed the edict of Boulogne, making a limited peace with the Huguenots. Elizabeth was led to believe that this development was the direct result of her intervention and the French court's desire to see Alençon *en route* for England.[49] The reality however was very different. Henry of Anjou who was officially at the head of the Catholic forces against La Rochelle had been elected king of Poland in May 1573 on condition that he would establish religious toleration in France. For a variety of reasons, Charles and Catherine were eager for Anjou to obtain the Polish crown, and consequently they submitted to the pressure from the Poles, lifted the siege of La Rochelle, ended the war and packed off Anjou to his new kingdom.[50] None the less, the peace allowed the French to maintain that they had fulfilled Elizabeth's conditions and to demand a personal interview.

Elizabeth agreed to a meeting, in part because she had run out of excuses but also in order to extract some further political advantages from the negotiations.[51] Arrangements were quickly made for an interview to be held with the duke at Dover at the beginning of September. This time, however, the French court backed off. Catherine claimed that Alençon was ill and appointed the comte de Retz to go in his place.[52] The choice of de Retz is interesting. On the one hand, his appointment signalled that the French were treating the visit as a high-level mission, for the count was of exalted rank, close to Catherine and a long-serving royal councillor; on the other, he was widely considered to be one of the ringleaders behind the St Bartholomew's Day Massacre and was thus an insensitive choice for special envoy. Elizabeth decided to concentrate on de Retz's importance and forget his reputation; she interrupted a royal progress in order to greet him at Canterbury and entertained him with lavish pomp during his short stay.[53]

The de Retz visit in September 1573 did nothing, however, to further the negotiations or improve relations between the two courts. As the French were making all the running, the English councillors tried to exploit their evident desire for the marriage and obtain concessions over a range of political fronts, but without success. The count was informed that because of the recent events in France the matrimonial proposal was now generating such a 'generall feare and mislyking' among the people, especially 'the nombre of such as ar zealous to the Queen's Majesty for the favor of relligion', that Elizabeth, whose only motive for taking a husband had been to satisfy her subjects, was fast losing interest in the project. In these circumstances, explained the councillors, they did not see how the match could be concluded unless some way was found 'to mak this marriadg appere beneficiall or at the lest not hurtfull to the state of hir realme'.[54] One way, of course, was for Alençon to drop his religious demands; another was for some tangible commodity, such as Calais, to be offered to the queen. In the meantime, suggested the councillors, the French king should recognise the government of Mary Stuart's son in Scotland and do more for the Huguenots in France. De Retz appeared oblivious to these hints and tried to counter the councillors' lack of enthusiasm for the match by stressing the size of the duke's patrimony and by promising that he would 'use his religion very privately and should avow the religion of England by accompanying the Queen's Majesty to church', but this made no impression on them at all.

Throughout the talks, Elizabeth was careful not to cut off all hope. She agreed to give Alençon a safe-conduct to visit her, recommended that he should come with a small retinue composed of Huguenots or others 'that had never been persecutors', and asked that he should forbear hearing the Mass during his stay. She also took up de Retz's suggestion that a trusted agent be sent to interview the duke and bring back a portrait, and a month later dispatched Thomas Randolph to France for this purpose.[55] No doubt she anticipated that the continuing courtship would provide her with the means to exert influence on the internal affairs of France and protect the Huguenots, just as it had appeared to yield benefits the previous June. By this time, however, Catherine was losing interest in matrimonial diplomacy, and saw no point in wasting time and risking a loss of face by setting up a royal interview. The answers to de Retz had confirmed that a dynastic alliance with Elizabeth was a mirage, and with the respite in the civil wars there was less need for immediate concern about England's links with the Huguenots.[56]

With all hope of securing the throne of England dashed, Alençon's restless ambition began to be directed towards internal French politics. During the winter of 1573-4 he became increasingly alienated from the Guises, whom he saw as his main political rivals, and grew correspondingly closer to the malcontent noblemen who wanted to see the end of Guise influence at court. After a cousin of the duke of Guise had been offered the office of lieutenant-general of France, a position he himself coveted, Alençon began conspiring with Henry of Navarre who had been detained at court since the Massacre of St Bartholomew.[57] Not surprisingly, Alençon's political antics were viewed with increasing suspicion by his mother, especially during early 1574 when she thought he was plotting to prevent the accession of Anjou to the throne in the event of Charles IX's death, which was regarded as imminent. As a consequence, Alençon and Navarre were kept under close surveillance and, after an abortive attempt to free them by force of arms, they were placed at Easter 1574 under a heavy guard in the fortress of Vincennes. Elizabeth and Burghley looked on these events with some anxiety, since the imprisonment of Alençon and Navarre left the Guise faction in control of policy. They were therefore inclined to view Alençon's predicament with sympathy and his requests for English aid favourably. Elizabeth tried to obtain his release from captivity by using the subterfuge of the proposed marriage to grant him a safe-conduct to come to England for an interview. But Catherine was not fooled and refused to permit his departure. Burghley then arranged to send money to France to help the prisoners bribe their guards to allow their escape, a manoeuvre which was equally unsuccessful.[58]

The death of Charles IX on 31 May 1574 and the return of Henry III from Poland in September 1574 launched France into another bout of civil war. Henry was too closely associated with the Guise faction and the ultra-Catholics for either the Montmorencys or Huguenots to feel secure under his rule. His extravagant gestures of personal piety in the first months of his reign – such as his participation in a penitential procession alongside the cardinal of Lorraine and some five hundred other penitents – intensified Protestant fears that he would not wait long before renewing war on the Huguenots.[59] Even before he was crowned, Huguenot leaders and the Montmorencys moved towards open rebellion, and over the next year sought the help of Protestants abroad. Frederick III of the Rhenish Palatinate contributed money, his youngest son John Casimir offered to head an army of 16,000 men, while Elizabeth agreed to a secret loan of 50,000 thalers (some £15,000).[60]

Meanwhile Alençon, who remained a virtual prisoner at court, was uncertain which way to turn. Although still jealous of the Guises, he had also quarrelled with Henry of Navarre, and he might well have abandoned the Huguenots altogether had his brother shown him favour and granted him the office of lieutenant-general of the kingdom. Henry III, however, was unwilling to raise his brother's status and power in this way. Alençon, therefore, continued to plot with disaffected noblemen and to plan his escape. Fearing the two-fold danger of a Protestant league and Alençon's intrigues, Catherine and Henry III decided that one way out of their difficulty might be to revive the matrimonial project in the hope that it would neutralise Elizabeth and remove the disruptive prince from the factional unrest in France. With this in mind, Mauvissière was sent over to England in early September 1575 with a formal offer of marriage from the duke.[61] It was a policy born of desperation; as Villeroy, one of the French Secretaries of State, pointed out, Elizabeth's marriage to Alençon would be 'plus dommageable que utile' since it would unite the two against the crown.[62]

Once again Elizabeth saw in the negotiations an opportunity to free Alençon from his imprisonment at court, and she consequently tried to persuade the French of the value of a personal meeting with the duke. Assuring Mauvissière of her resolution to marry and her desire for an alliance with France, she argued that all outstanding difficulties over religion should be negotiated at an interiew and she refused to discuss any articles except in the presence of Alençon.[63] The duke, however, was not content to sit in captivity and await the outcome of the matrimonial negotiations. On 15 September 1575 he escaped from Vincennes, headed towards Dreux in his apanage and, following a time-honoured course of action for French princes of the blood, proclaimed himself the protector of the common weal. Likewise, he appealed to England's monarch for support, as had his late mediaeval predecessors. Seriously alarmed by the prospect of English intervention in France's internal politics, Henry III and Catherine alternated between issuing warnings and offering friendship in the form of the matrimonial alliance to ward off Elizabeth.[64] At the same time, they attempted to make terms with Alençon; short of funds, he signed a six-month truce of Champigny with his mother in November 1575 but he had no intention of keeping it and on the pretext of arranging an interview with Elizabeth to further the marriage he sent his agents to England for the purpose of persuading her to join a league with him and the Elector Palatine.[65]

Elizabeth's response was cautious but encouraging. Initially she offered to mediate between the king and his brother, but by March 1576 she seemed to favour joining a league of foreign princes, French nobles and Huguenot leaders. Deeply suspicious of Henry III, she could see merit in the plan to set up a broadly based coalition of princes and nobility who would act together in France with the aim of removing the king's 'evil councillors' and forcing his acceptance of an edict of toleration.[66] Not all her Council, however, agreed with this policy; Sussex in particular wanted her to avoid a war which would be costly and dangerous, and advised her instead to 'procure the peace in France' and look again at the matrimonial proposal.[67] In the event Elizabeth did not have to make a final decision and her vague promises of help were not put to the test, for Catherine and Henry III were powerless to confront the opposition forces already mounted and consequently agreed to a general edict of pacification on 6 May 1576. This edict of Beaulieu, which came to be known as the Peace of Monsieur, met the demands of all the participating members of the coalition against them. Elizabeth, however, disapproved of the peace, which she rightly believed would not last, and was disgusted with Alençon and the rest for signing it.[68]

For two years after the Peace of Monsieur there was little communication between Elizabeth and the duke of Alençon (now properly called Anjou as he was given the more important apanage and title as his spoils from the peace to add to that of Alençon) and no further talks of marriage. During this time Anjou abandoned his Protestant allies and supported his brother in the sixth civil war which broke out in the spring of 1577. In particular, he was the nominal head of the royal army which successfully besieged the Huguenot towns of La Charité in April and Issoire in May.[69] In these circumstances, neither Henry III, Elizabeth nor Anjou saw any point in renewing negotiations, and it was not until the duke was contemplating helping the rebels in the Netherlands against Spain that it became advantageous to all three to re-open the project.

The provinces of Holland and Zealand in the Netherlands had been in arms against their ruler, Philip II, since 1572 when the 'Sea Beggars' had unexpectedly seized the towns of Brill and Flushing. By the summer of 1575, after the failure of peace talks with the Spaniards at Breda, William of Orange, the leader of the rebels, had become convinced that the revolt would be successful only if fully supported by a foreign prince. In November 1575, therefore, the States of the two provinces had offered their sovereignty to Elizabeth, but she had declined to accept it since she preferred to see them return to the allegiance of their legitimate ruler on terms that would guarantee their political liberties. As a result, Orange resorted to Anjou, and in May 1576 the States made him a formal offer which he in turn rejected. But, after the peace of Bergerac, which ended the sixth civil war in France in September 1577, the duke displayed a new interest in events in the Netherlands and intimated that he would be prepared to give the States military assistance.

By this time the revolt had spread to the southern provinces of the Netherlands, whose Catholic nobility had used their influence in the States-General (the representative body of all the provinces) to secure the election of Archduke Matthias, brother of the Austrian emperor, as governor-general in place of the unpopular Spaniard Don John.[70] This development was clearly a setback for Anjou but he continued to offer his aid, and his opportunity arose the following February after the disastrous military defeat of the States at the battle of Gembloux on 31 January 1578. During March, Anjou negotiated with the States-General and separately with the provincial States of Hainaut, whose Catholic nobility looked to him as a potential leader of their revolt. At the same time he began raising troops in his apanage for use in the Netherlands.[71]

Elizabeth and many of her councillors had long been worried about the prospect of French involvement and expansion in the Netherlands. As Sussex succinctly commented in August 1578: 'the case wylbe harde bothe with the Queen and with Ingland yf ether the Frenche possesse or the Spanyardes tyranyse in the Low Contryes'.[72] For this reason, as far back as 1572, Elizabeth had refused to support French plans to assist Louis of Nassau and she now came to view with increasing concern Anjou's plans to put himself at the head of the revolt. The perceived danger was so great that it led to a significant shift in policy. Until then, despite the pleas of councillors like Leicester that she provide the States with military assistance, Elizabeth had been more or less content to remain aloof from the struggle, merely offering to mediate between Philip II and his rebellious subjects and allowing volunteers to fight on the rebel side. In September 1577, however, fearful that the States might accept Anjou as their protector in default of any other foreign aid, she offered them financial assistance and soldiers too should the need occur. On 7 January 1578 she made good this offer by signing an agreement which promised the States a loan of £20,000 and some troops. Even after the battle of Gembloux, when Elizabeth reconsidered this proposal out of fear that her direct intervention would provoke the wrath of the victorious Spanish general, Don John, and might also encourage Henry III to send a royal army to assist him in an act of religious solidarity, she decided in the end to offer to organise a Protestant league and hire Duke John Casimir of the Palatinate to raise and lead an army to help the States on her behalf.[73]

Elizabeth's promises of assistance were insufficient to turn the States away from Anjou, and in April 1578 they informed William Davison, her agent in the Netherlands, of their plans to sign a treaty with the duke. Elizabeth was both furious and alarmed. It was outrageous and a betrayal of her past friendship, she railed, that the States would open negotiations with a foreign prince without first consulting her and obtaining her consent. It was also a threat to English interests, especially if the duke were to be rewarded for his assistance with some territorial gain in Flanders or title of importance in the whole Netherlands. To make matters worse, given his record of changing sides in France, Anjou could not be trusted to remain faithful to the States and might well betray them (as he had previously turned against his Huguenot allies) by joining up with Don John and using his army to help crush their revolt.[74] For these reasons, virtually all of Elizabeth's advisers, even those most devoted to the Dutch cause, were dismayed at the prospect of French intervention in the Netherlands and agreed that Anjou had to be stopped. The one exception was Sir Nicholas Bacon who thought that the States' need for military assistance was so desperate that their supporters in England should not oppose any offer of aid on their behalf.[75]

During the late spring of 1578, Elizabeth was trying desperately to devise some means to prevent the conclusion of an agreement between Anjou and the States. Those councillors who had long wanted to furnish the rebels with substantial aid now saw their chance to press her once again to send an English army to the Netherlands or increase her loans significantly to the States, so that they would look to her as their saviour rather than to Anjou. Elizabeth, however, preferred if possible to avoid further military commitment to allies whom she viewed as untrustworthy, and to avert a policy which would lead to direct confrontation with Spain. Overall, she preferred to see a truce between the two sides which would remove the necessity or opportunity for French intervention. She tried, therefore, to persuade Don John to agree to a cease-fire, and sent Lord Cobham and Walsingham to the Netherlands in June 1578 with directions 'to travell for a peace' by all possible means as their primary task. The most she would do to help the States was to hasten the delivery of her original loan to Casimir, but at the same time she threatened them with its immediate withdrawal if a treaty were concluded with Anjou.[76]

Meanwhile, the earl of Sussex had another plan to draw the duke away from the Netherlands. Sometime in May 1578, he contacted the resident French ambassador, Michel de Castelnau, sieur de Mauvissière, and suggested a re-opening of the matrimonial negotiations with Anjou. Evidently, his overture was made with the approval of Elizabeth, for she too spoke with Mauvissière and around the same time instructed her envoy, Sir Edward Stafford, to raise the possiblity of reviving the match with Catherine de Medici.[77] Surprisingly, Sussex's interview with Mauvissière went ahead without the knowledge of Burghley. He was kept in the dark about the informal talks until later in the summer when Anjou dispatched his own envoys to England to discuss the match with Elizabeth: 'I heare, the french ambassador here hath bene the cause [of the new matrimonial talks], upon some conference lately had with Hir Majesty, to me unknowen', Burghley confessed to Walsingham and Cobham in late July 1578.[78] In fact, throughout this early stage of the revived Anjou project it was Sussex not Burghley who was viewed by the French (and the queen) as 'notre guide et conducteur en cest affaire', and it was only in early 1579 that the latter emerged as the leading champion of the match.[79] This was the first time in the history of Elizabeth's matrimonial negotiations that Burghley was excluded from policy-making. As his foreign-policy priority in the spring and summer of 1578 was to persuade Elizabeth to commit herself to military aid for the States, Elizabeth may have felt with some justification that he would be out of sympathy with Sussex's scheme, seeing it as at best a distraction and at worst an alternative strategy to his own.

The logic behind the matrimonial project was that it looked to be the best way of dealing with the dangers arising from Anjou's planned enterprise in Flanders. Once Elizabeth and Sussex learned that the duke was acting on his own initiative and not as an agent of the king of France, they planned to use the offer of an English crown as bait to entice him away from military adventures and satisfy his search for glory. While Elizabeth probably hoped that the negotiations themselves would be sufficient to make Anjou do her bidding and defuse the immediate crisis, Sussex was certain that only a marriage would win the duke for the queen and that without it she could do nothing to 'hynder his gretenese any wayes and specyally in this enterprise'.[80] In Sussex's opinion, the danger from the duke would continue as long as his ambitions remained unsatisfied; thus, if he were prevented from helping the States his need for greatness would probably lead him to offer his services to Don John. Furthermore, thought Sussex, matrimonial diplomacy by itself would not resolve the longer-term problem of the Netherlands. Even if Elizabeth were successful in diverting the duke from intervention in the war, this still left the problem of the States' vulnerability in the face of the Spanish army. To Sussex's mind, only the combined pressure of the French and English would be sufficient to bring both sides to a peace which would safeguard the liberties of the States. No other policy would work, he argued. The States at the present time would not sign a peace except on terms 'so farre owt of reason' that they would be unacceptable to the Spaniards; while Philip II would not agree to grant any concessions to his

147

rebellious subjects unless he had to. The only other option available to Elizabeth was that she made herself 'the head of the warre' and this would prove too financially onerous for her subjects.[81]

Sussex was certainly right about Anjou's maverick qualities, but like practically all other observers he overestimated the duke's military power and ability. In reality, Anjou's forces were few and his funds insufficient to keep them in the field for long, while his military experience was slight despite his presence at a few key sieges during the French religious wars. Sussex's diagnosis of the foreign-policy options open to Elizabeth was also sound, while his dread of direct intervention in the Netherlands was sensible. None the less, his solution to the problems of foreign policy seems with hindsight naïve, and he was woefully unaware of the hostility which the match would arouse at home.

On receiving the news of Elizabeth's interest in a matrimonial alliance, the French were understandably suspicious. Henry III was sure that there was 'plus d'artifice que de volunté' in the English initiative and Catherine believed that 'il n'y ait aulcune affection'.[82] Anjou seemed to share their doubts; although he claimed to be pleased to receive the offer and ready to marry the queen, he urged that the affair be dealt with promptly 'sans tirer les choses à la longue' as it had always been in the past.[83] Whatever their reservations, however, they all made encouraging noises to Elizabeth – but for different reasons. While Anjou probably saw Elizabeth as a potential source of income for his military enterprise, Henry and Catherine disapproved of his negotiations with the States and welcomed any initiative which might distract him from embarking on an anti-Spanish campaign in the Netherlands and which would remove him from France where his intrigues were becoming dangerous.

As a result of the favourable French response to the marriage suggestion and Anjou's promises to heed her wishes in the Netherlands, Elizabeth began to soften towards the duke. On 7 June 1578 she instructed her ambassador in France to inform him that 'in some sort her Majesty would be content that he should deal in the Low Countries'. In addition, the final draft of her instructions to Cobham and Walsingham on 12 June toned down considerably the clauses highlighting the danger posed by France which had dominated an earlier draft.[84] Soon afterwards she went even further, telling Jacques de Vray, one of Anjou's financial secretaries, that as long as the duke had no expansionist aims in Flanders and wanted only to help the people of the Netherlands gain 'their liberties by force of armes agaynst the spanyshe tyrannie', she 'woulde gladly joyne with him in assistance to doe so good a deede'.[85] Throughout June and most of July 1578 she discounted all warnings about Anjou, and instead put her trust in the duke's promises to use moderation in his dealings with the States and in his assurances that he had no intention of self-aggrandisement.[86]

Elizabeth's matrimonial diplomacy at best mystified and at worst horrified many of her councillors, especially as it was accompanied by a determination to withdraw her financial help from the States. In June 1578 Walsingham expressed his grief to Hatton that Elizabeth seemed 'so strangely affected as she is' and also his fear that 'if Her Majesty do not look unto it in time, yea and that out of hand, I see no remedy but the French will be masters of the country'.[87] In late July, he confided to Leicester that he had no idea why Elizabeth had so 'merveilous opinion of his [Anjou's] synceritie' and that he could not understand her attitude to the marriage project, 'seing yt apparent yt [that] he interteynethe her at this present only to abbuse her, therby to wyn her the better to disjeast his proceadynges heere'.[88] Together with Cobham he advised the queen that her 'good opinion' of the duke might be mistaken. Elizabeth, however, was unwilling to heed their warnings. Only after she heard of Anjou's unexpected arrival with his army at Mons in the province of Hainaut on 12 July 1578 and also learned that plans were afoot to wed the duke to the daughter of William of Orange were her suspicions again aroused.[89] Only then did she begin to accept her councillors' advice that she should boost her financial assistance to the States.

Just at this time when Elizabeth was beginning to share her councillors' doubts about Anjou, he sent two envoys, M. de Bacqueville and M. de Quissy, to England for the purpose of re-opening his matrimonial suit. They were also told to reassure her that the duke was 'at her Majesty's devotion' and would follow her directions in the Netherlands.[90] Shortly afterwards, Henry III, who disliked his brother's independent behaviour, sent over his own envoy, M. de Rambouillet, to keep an eye on the negotiations in England.[91] During their stay in August and early September 1578, Elizabeth treated these French ambassadors with great favour, often spoke of her desire to marry a prince 'de bonne maison', and made light of the age difference which had caused her so much unease in the previous negotiations; Anjou, she said with apparent contentment, would be a son to her as well as a husband.[92] Nor did she make difficulties about religion; at an audience with the ambassadors in the presence of some of her councillors, Burghley speaking on behalf of the queen said that the couple could settle the outstanding disagreements privately when they met. The only problem which Elizabeth raised with the ambassadors concerned Anjou's sincerity. As she had already been let down several times in the past during her courtship with the duke and had previously been jilted by his brother, she insisted that he prove his many protestations of affection in person during a visit to her court. Although she could not guarantee that an interview would lead to marriage, she could assure the duke that no marriage would take place without one.[93]

No-one was quite sure whether Elizabeth herself was sincere in this matter. The French ambassadors found her performance convincing and believed that she wanted the marriage, although Mauvissière admitted that he was always 'plein de doubte et d'incertitude' in the affairs of princes.[94] She certainly seemed to be listening to the advice of Sussex, whereas her conferences with Leicester were but 'seldome and slender'.[95] On the other hand, both Burghley and Leicester found it hard to believe that Elizabeth really meant to marry the duke.[96] Further afield, Mary Stuart suspected that both Elizabeth and her councillors 's'en mocquent soubz main'. At the same time, Philip II claimed that he was in no doubt that the marriage would never take place, although he still tried to sabotage the proposal by offering Anjou his second daughter with a substantial dowry, including parts of the Netherlands.[97] As far as most of her councillors were concerned, however, whatever Elizabeth ultimately decided, the matrimonial negotiations were a problem in themselves, since they represented an alternative policy to the war-strategy favoured by the majority.

The opponents of the Anjou matrimonial negotiations kept a low profile at court during the visit of the French envoys, and Mauvissière had no notion at all that Leicester was hostile to it. At this stage, the rumblings against the match provided a background chorus to the visit but as yet no individual voices were distinguished and no coherent arguments heard. Although some mention was made of the dangers arising from Anjou's Catholicism, most of the criticisms of the suitor heard by Mauvissière concerned personal matters which were presumably thought to carry some weight with the queen; including the accusations that the duke was deformed and had bad breath.[98]

The most outspoken and explicit criticism of Elizabeth's matrimonial diplomacy during 1578 came not from inside the court but in the form of dramatic entertainments performed before the queen and de Bacqueville in Norwich where the court stayed for about a week during her summer progress to East Anglia. There, the playwright Thomas Churchyard put on a number of pageants and masques which had been commissioned by the strongly Protestant Lord Mayor and aldermen of the city. There is some evidence that Leicester was involved in the planning of the progress and he certainly had political links with Norwich. It is therefore possible that he kept the godly magistrates abreast of the matrimonial plans and foreign policy debates at court and encouraged the inclusion of the political themes in the entertainments.[99]

On the first day of Elizabeth's visit to the town, she was greeted by a pageant in which Old Testament figures urged her to act as the 'finger of the Lord' and 'his mighty hand' in defending the Protestants abroad against the forces of the Anti-Christ. Deborah reminded her how Israel in her time had been at the mercy of King Jabin of Canaan who 'ment by force of furious rage to overrun us' and used 'cruell Captain Sisera by force to make us yeelde'. Yet God

> Appointed me Debora for the Judge of his elect:
> And did deliver Sisera into a Woman's hande.

Elizabeth, Deborah advised, should follow this model and 'weede out the wicked route' and 'pull downe the proud and stoute' so that she could reign in peace, please God and defend her state and subjects. Judith re-iterated the message in her speech: reminding Elizabeth that God had appointed her, a poor widow, to slay Holofernes, she uttered the words:

> If this his grace were given to me poore wight,
> If Widowes hand could vanquish such a Foe:
> Then to a Prince of thy surpassing might,
> What Tirant lives but thou mayest overthrow?

Then the figure of Esther, who had herself saved the children of Israel from the persecuting Hamon, called on Elizabeth to protect her co-religionists:

> No fraude, nor force, nor foraine Foe may stand
> Againste the strength of thy moste puyssaunt hand.

During an indoor masque on 21 August, Mars the god of war picked up the theme and offered his services to the queen, who had been known up to then as a 'Prince of Peace':

> To conquer, kill, to vanquish, and subdue,
> Such fayned folke, as loves to live untrue.

To reinforce his message, he gave the queen a set of knives, blunt on one side and sharp on the other, on which were engraved the words:

> To hurt your foe, and helpe your friend,
> These knyves are made unto that end.

At the same time as exhorting a war-policy, the Norwich entertainments implicitly criticised the renewal of the Anjou marriage negotiations and urged Elizabeth to remain single, laying stress on her special status as a Virgin Queen. In the masque of the 21 August, for example, when other Roman deities besides Mars gave Elizabeth gifts and laudations, the goddess Diana idealised her chastity in a way that invited comparison with the Virgin Mary:

> Who ever found on earth a constant friend,
> That may compare with this my Virgin Queene?
> Whoever found a body and a mynde
> So free from staine, so perfect to be seene.

In other theatrical devices too, Elizabeth's unmarried state was referred to as a supernatural quality; she was an 'unspoused Pallas', 'a Virgine pure', and 'a sacred Queene'. Although not yet portrayed as Astraea, the goddess who ushered in a Golden Age, she was described as possessing the virtues of all the Roman deities: the wisdom of Pallas, the grace of Venus, the eloquence of Mercury and more besides. Hence

This Lady mayst thou goddesse call for she deserves the same:
Although she will not undertake a title of such fame.

The queen's chastity was also celebrated in one of the few pageants which had a plot. In the device *Cupid's Fall from Heaven*, vain Venus and blind Cupid, expelled from heaven, were forced to wander on the earth where they met a philosopher and Chastity who tried to teach them the error of their ways. After the philosopher had condemned them both as 'the drosse, the scumme of earth and skyes', Chastity handed over Cupid's bow and arrows to the queen with the message that she could do with them 'what she pleased' and 'learne to shoote at whome she pleased', since she was impervious to carnal lusts and had chosen 'the best life' of celibacy. The political point should have been obvious both to Elizabeth and the Frenchmen in the audience: Elizabeth might send out overtures of marriage to Anjou but her true destiny was celibacy. In fact, the point seems to have been lost on the diplomats, as no mention of the entertainments appears in the French sources, while Elizabeth herself probably chose to ignore it.

The message that reached Anjou, therefore, was that Elizabeth was open to the idea of a match but would not marry anyone whom she had not met. Seeing that his Flanders enterprise was in danger of collapse owing to his disagreements with the States and the desertions of his troops, Anjou decided to take Elizabeth at her word and pursue his courtship more vigorously. None the less he still held back from making a personal visit to the queen. Henry III had warned him against entering such a commitment until the terms for a marriage-contract had been agreed, and besides he was needed in France because of the breakdown in the religious peace there.[100] Consequently, he first sent his intimate councillor, Bussy d'Amboise, to the English court and then dispatched his trusted household servant Jean de Simier, baron de Saint-Marc, to woo Elizabeth in his place and negotiate a matrimonial treaty based on the demands put forward on behalf of his brother in 1571.

By the time Simier was due to arrive, Elizabeth had already begun to blow hot and cold about the visit and marriage. In early October 1578, she had sent Anjou her portrait and presents, but a month later she was beginning to prevaricate.[101] According to Mauvissière, there had been 'grands factions' attempting to persuade the queen against receiving him, and rumours had been spread that Anjou was secretly planning to marry a Spanish princess.[102] She was also concerned that Simier would want to negotiate a treaty which she was not prepared to consider before an interview with the duke took place.[103] None the less, she decided to go ahead with the meeting but refused to discuss articles to be included in a matrimonial treaty until after Anjou's visit.

Simier's visit was a turning-point in the long Anjou courtship. Because of new dangers at home and on the international horizon, particularly Philip II's designs on Portugal, Elizabeth began to favour a marriage-alliance; and once Anjou had finally made an appearance in England and courted her assiduously, she even began to savour the prospect of married life. The effect on court politics was devastating; divisions which emerged in the Council spilled out into the country, threatening to paralyse policy-making and revolutionise political life. Only with the abandonment of the matrimonial scheme did the crisis pass and normality return to Elizabethan political life.

7

THE WOOING OF FRANCIS DUKE OF ANJOU 1579–81

By the time that Jean de Simier arrived in England in January 1579 to negotiate a marriage between Anjou and Elizabeth both the protagonists were ready to treat the project as a serious proposition and not simply as a piece of matrimonial diplomacy. As far as Anjou was concerned, his fortunes in the Netherlands were at a very low ebb at the beginning of 1579, since his troops had deserted from lack of pay and his Catholic supporters in the southern provinces were defecting to Alexander Farnese, the prince of Parma, Don John's able replacement as commander of the Spanish army.[1] Henry III, moreover, showed no sign of backing his brother's venture. It was only by marrying Elizabeth and involving her in the Dutch war that Anjou might obtain much-needed resources to finance a new army and regain his credibility with William of Orange and the northern provinces who were continuing the fight against Spain. It was therefore vital for his military and political ambitions that Simier's mission was a success.[2] Consequently, Anjou gave his envoy a large expense-account to cover his trip and costly presents of jewels to bestow upon the queen.[3] For his part, Simier admirably rose to the occasion. As William Camden remarked, he was 'a choice Courtier, a man throughly versed in Love-fancies, pleasant Conceits and Court-dalliance', and Elizabeth was soon won over by his charm.[4] By February 1579 he had become her 'ape', a nickname arising from a Latin pun on his name.[5]

Fundamentally, however, it was developments in the international scene rather than the wooing of the wily Frenchman that accounted for the shift in Elizabeth's attitude to the marriage. Most immediately, she had to contend with the new situation in the Netherlands, where the fragile unity of the States in their struggle against Spain was on the point of disintegration. On 6 January 1579, the day after Simier's arrival at her court, the States of Hainaut and Artois seceded from the States-General and formed the Union of Arras which on 21 February 1579 agreed to open talks with Parma. Walloon Flanders soon joined them and they became formally 'reconciled' to Philip II in May 1579. In these circumstances it was difficult to see how the remaining provinces in the States-General could hold out against the Spanish army without substantial foreign aid. Thus, although the fiasco of the duke's military intervention in the Low Countries had temporarily removed the danger of French expansionism in Flanders, it had also raised the spectre of a total Spanish military victory and the extirpation of Calvinism in the rebellious provinces.

Whatever her feelings for her co-religionists, Elizabeth was in no doubt that their defeat and possible extermination would leave her vulnerable to a Spanish invasion. It was with this threat in mind that she began to think again in terms of a French dynastic alliance which could be used to force Philip II to make peace with his rebellious subjects on terms to guarantee their liberties. As Walsingham commented:

> The negotyacion of Monsieur here taketh greater foote then was at the first lookid for and receaveth no smaule furtheraunce upper [sic] occasion of the decayed state of things in the Low Countryes, for that Her Majesty, foreseeing that yf the King of Spayne come once to have his will there he will prove no very good neytbour to her, thinccketh this [the Anjou match] the best meane to provide for her safety that can be offerid, in which respect yt is to be thought she will in th'end consent to the matche, though otherwyes not greatlie to her liking.[6]

At the same time, an Anglo-French matrimonial alliance seemed the best route to safety in the face of a new and unexpected danger from Spain. In early January 1579 Elizabeth was hearing rumours that Philip II was planning to assert his claim to the Portuguese throne on the death of its recently crowned king, an elderly Roman Catholic cardinal who was likely to die soon without issue.[7] If these scare-stories were true (which in fact they were) and Philip did inherit the Atlantic state and overseas empire of Portugal, he would drastically increase his power and acquire the resources needed to re-conquer the Netherlands and launch an armada against England. Only joint action by England and France could thwart Philip's plans and counteract Spanish power.

For these political reasons Elizabeth greeted Simier with a courtesy and coquetry that surprised most contemporaries. For more than two months she held regular, lengthy and intimate interviews with the Frenchman – sometimes three times a week, sometimes every day – where the talk was of love rather than alliance or the terms of a matrimonial treaty. She also entertained him at feasts, dances, masques and jousts, and presented him with gifts of gloves, handkerchiefs, flowers crafted in gold and a miniature portrait of herself as love-tokens for the duke.[8] Some historians have suggested that these attentions were a genuine expression of Elizabeth's feelings and a sign of an emotional instability possibly caused by the onset of the menopause.[9] On the other hand, this was not the first time in the history of her courtships that her behaviour had been flirtatious and her speech full of marriage. When the French seemed to be losing interest in the suit of Henry, Francis of Anjou's elder brother, just when Elizabeth most needed it in the summer of 1571, La Mothe-Fénélon had reported several conversations in which the queen had spoken coquettishly of her suitor for the purpose of re-activating the courtship.[10] In 1579, Elizabeth had equally good reason to put aside the maidenly modesty expected of a sixteenth-century woman; she needed to make an impressive outward show of a romantic interest in Francis and a serious intent to marry him in order to convince the French of her sincerity and to prevent a return to the sterile rituals of their past relationship. Above all else, Elizabeth wanted to cajole Simier into agreeing to the duke's visit to her court before the terms of a marriage-contract were negotiated.[11] Presumably she still wanted reassurance about the duke's appearance, and a personal interview in which liking and mutual trust might develop was also the only way to break through the deadlock over religion. Anjou was still insisting upon freedom of worship and, when asked to reconsider his position, he refused, declaring: 'je me tiens ferme en set article, que c'est pour le devoyr de ma conscience'.[12] Furthermore, a visit by the duke would be the clearest indication that he too was serious about the match, and would dispel remaining suspicions that he might well jilt the queen at the last minute in a repeat performance of the events of January 1572. There were, after all, still rumours circulating the English court that a marriage was being arranged between Anjou and a princess of Spain.

In order to secure an early interview, Elizabeth conscripted Leicester and other councillors to persuade Simier and Mauvissière that, in contrast to the situation in the mid-1570s, the whole Council was in favour of an Anjou marriage, and that Elizabeth was therefore only awaiting the duke's visit before formally accepting his suit.[13] In his discussions with the French ambassadors, however, Leicester did not put up an entirely convincing performance. Reading between the lines of their reported conversation, it would seem that Leicester obeyed the queen only reluctantly and attempted to inform Anjou and Henry III in an underhand way that the path of courtship would be considerably less smooth than she was leading them to believe. Although he showed 'ung [sic] visage allegre' and 'plein d'esperance' at the mention of the marriage, he also made it plain that there was, or at least had been, strong opposition to a French match among some of the nobility. Staunch Protestants like Huntingdon and Bedford, he said, worried lest the duke would help the English Catholics, and also feared a repetition of the St Bartholomew's Day Massacre within their own shores, whilst other lords who were more conservative in religion, including Shrewsbury, Pembroke, Rutland and Arundel, also had their doubts about the wisdom of the match. Leicester reported that he himself had been instrumental in changing the minds of all these men and had done so from a willingness to serve Anjou, his future king and master.[14]

Simier and Mauvissière were delighted with Elizabeth's evident enthusiasm for the match, but equally determined to finalise the clauses of a matrimonial treaty before Anjou embarked on a journey to England. Simier had brought with him the terms proposed by the king and queen-mother as a basis of negotiation; these were very similar to the original articles put forward in April 1571 during the attempts to arrange a marriage between Elizabeth and Henry, and did not reflect any of the compromises that had been subsequently hammered out.[15] Clearly, neither Henry III nor Catherine was inclined to be accommodating; indeed, they were less keen on a marriage at this stage than either Elizabeth or Anjou. With the danger of Anjou's intervention in the Netherlands receding, they saw less need of an English marriage to absorb the duke's energies and ambitions. They were also concerned that the heir presumptive's marriage to a woman of forty-five seemed unlikely to produce a male heir to carry on the Valois line. Nor were Henry III and his mother yet persuaded of Elizabeth's sincerity or her willingness to agree to the freedom of worship which they regarded as a *sine qua non* of any marriage.[16] Consequently in mid-February 1579 Catherine begged her youngest son to resist going to England before the contractual articles had been agreed and other assurances delivered.[17]

In these circumstances Elizabeth decided to give way and allow formal negotiations on the marriage-treaty to commence. At the end of March 1579, selected councillors began attending a series of meetings at Westminster to discuss the matrimonial project. At this stage most, if not all, of them were fully conscious that Elizabeth was serious about the marriage. As Leicester had written to Davison in late February 1579:

And if the person adventure without condition an assurance to come hither, if she then like him, it is like she will have him ... by that I newly hear and find in her deep consideration of her estate and that she is persuaded nothing can more assure it than marriage, I may be of mind she will marry if the party like her.[18]

Consequently the Council devoted long hours and many weeks to the matrimonial issue; their debates lasted more than a month from 27 March until early May 1579, and at their most intense they started at 8.00 a.m. and continued until supper-time.[19] The discussions did not just centre on the clauses to be part of the matrimonial treaty but also examined the domestic implications of the marriage and spanned the whole area of foreign policy. On all these issues the Council was divided, with Burghley and Sussex acting as the main spokesmen on one side and Walsingham and Mildmay on the other.[20]

As far as the marriage-treaty was concerned, all the Council agreed that four of the articles proposed by the French were unacceptable as they stood: Anjou's demands for the free exercise of his religion, a coronation, joint authority with the queen over patronage, and a pension. There was also unanimity that the question of religion should be left for discussion until after the duke's visit and that his terms concerning royal patronage should be 'utterly rejected and denyed'. A minority of the Council also wanted the remaining two articles – the demands for a coronation and pension – to be rejected out of hand, 'being Matters partly dangeroose, partly hurtfull, and partly over-chargeable'. The majority, however, proposed that they should be discussed in a parliament following the duke's visit. After a long deliberation the Council agreed that these too should 'be held in abeyance until the Duke's coming over'.[21]

Those councillors who wanted all the contentious articles to be rejected straight away opposed the Anjou marriage on principle. As in the past, men like Walsingham and Mildmay disliked the duke's religion and were uneasy about his nationality for fear that they spelled danger to the Church and state; but now they found two new, equally compelling objections to a match. First, they believed that Elizabeth was too old to contemplate marriage. If she conceived, she ran the risk of dying in child-birth and, if the child died too, there was the danger of a disputed succession or a French seizure of the English throne, either on Anjou's behalf or that of Mary Stuart. On the other hand, if Elizabeth failed to conceive, her husband might 'seeke by treason to be delyvered of her' in the hope of having children by another wife.[22] Second, after four years of a barren marriage Henry III was not expected to produce a son. There existed, therefore, the possibility that the duke might succeed to his brother's throne during Elizabeth's lifetime. Even worse, if Elizabeth did produce a surviving son, there was a strong likelihood that the two realms would be permanently united under one king and England left under the governorship of a viceroy.[23]

These objections to the queen's marriage expressed legitimate concerns and were very hard to answer; indeed, it is difficult to understand why men like Sussex and Burghley were not swayed by them, but were instead prepared to take such risks with the queen's life and the stability of the realm. Although there were a few contemporary examples of successful late pregnancies and deliveries (such as the late duchess of Savoy and the present queen of Sweden, who was said to have given birth to a child at the age of forty-eight), there were far more cases that had ended in the death of mother and child, including those of Elizabeth's grandmother, Elizabeth of York, and step-mother, Catherine Parr.[24] One possibility is that the chief supporters of the match were prepared to put their trust in God for a happy outcome, but this seems somewhat implausible as they were not usually inclined to leave the fate of the realm in the hands of divine providence alone.[25] Another is that they believed that Elizabeth was already past the point where conception was likely; after all, even apart from her age, neither the Tudors nor the Valois kings had a good record in procreation. Admittedly, in memoranda prepared for the Council meetings Burghley wrote frequently of Elizabeth's capacity to bear children without danger to her life or health; however, neither he nor his mistress would want it to be publicly admitted if they had any doubts on that score or even knowledge to the contrary. It was not until nearly two years later when she was seeking to negotiate an alliance without the marriage that Elizabeth acknowledged to the French court the possibility that she might be unable to conceive.[26]

The purpose of this projected marriage, however, was not to resolve the question of the succession, but to deal with the international dangers confronting the realm.[27] It had been originally proposed by Sussex as the best way of countering the menace of French intervention in the Netherlands, while Elizabeth had also come to see its value as a method for dealing with the threat of a Spanish victory there.[28] In the spring of 1579 Burghley promoted it as the only realistic and safe remedy for all the foreign perils that afflicted the realm. Without the marriage, he claimed, 'her Majesty shall stand alone, withowt ayd of any myghtye prynce ... and weakened at home'. The danger as he saw it came from the 'joyning of the King's [sic] of Spayne & Fraunce together with the Pope, the Emperor & others'. Together they made up a formidable Catholic threat in that they were, he believed, conspiring to stir up rebellion in England and Ireland, aid the Marian faction in Scotland, and to attempt 'a common warr by ther own joynt forces' against England. Furthermore, if Elizabeth refused Anjou, he might well wed a Spanish princess and thereby strengthen the Franco-Spanish axis. On the other hand, by marrying the duke, argued Burghley, Elizabeth would forge an alliance with the crown of France that would drive a wedge in the Catholic coalition, strengthen the Huguenots and 'compell the King of Spayne to agre with his subyects upon reasonabell condytyens'.[29]

Burghley had then clearly changed his position from that of mid-1578 when he had wanted Elizabeth to subsidise the States-General as the answer to French intervention and Spanish power, and had shown little or no interest in the Anjou match.[30] The change might have come with his recognition that the queen was determined to avoid financial commitments to the States despite the deteriorating international situation, since he certainly judged that the only alternative to the marriage was 'to contynew the inward troobles of the French Kyng and Kyng of Spayn' by supporting the Huguenots and Dutch rebels.[31] In addition, however, personal political considerations might have possibly influenced him, for his espousal of the policy of marriage unquestionably strengthened his own position with the queen and at court. Following his appointment as Lord Treasurer (in July 1572) and that of Walsingham as joint Secretary (in December 1573), Burghley had been steadily losing political ground; unlike his rivals Leicester and Sir Christopher Hatton, he no longer attended daily upon the queen, whilst compared to Walsingham he also began to play a back-seat role in the formulation of foreign policy.[32] By his advocacy of the Anjou marriage, however, he once more came into the limelight, regaining the initiative at court. As his old friend Sussex was only too happy to allow him to act as the senior partner in Council meetings, the queen treated him as her main ally in policy-making, and for a time his political rivals lost favour and influence.

Whatever his motives, Burghley's arguments did not go unchallenged during the Council debates in the spring of 1579, for Walsingham presented an alternative scenario and recommended a different strategy.[33] He criticised Burghley's view of England's international position as unnecessarily alarmist. The danger from France, claimed Walsingham, was exaggerated; Anjou's abortive campaign in the Netherlands had demonstrated that he was hardly a dangerous adversary, while the power of the king and the Guises was being held in check by the Huguenots who were gaining strength under Henry of Navarre. Similarly the peril from Philip II could be contained as long as the forces of the States continued to pin down the Spanish forces. Indeed, argued Walsingham, the international Catholic threat was considerably less serious at that time than it had been in the past, when Elizabeth had been weak and her neighbours untroubled by domestic difficulties. He, therefore, expressed confidence that England could count on its own strength to provide for its safety, especially if Elizabeth would lend the Huguenots money and give military assistance to the States, both of whom would be more trustworthy allies than the royal house of France. The marriage, he claimed, could only make existing problems worse: it would alienate James VI of Scotland by threatening an end to his hopes of inheriting the English crown, and it might well provoke God's anger against England for making an unholy accommodation with Catholics.

Nor was opposition to the marriage confined to the Council chamber. During the spring of 1579, strong criticisms were expressed both at court and in the country, especially by the Protestant clergy who opposed a royal marriage to a Roman Catholic. Bishop Cox of Ely sent a Latin treatise to the queen to dissuade her from wedding Anjou. On the first Sunday of Lent the queen was treated to a sermon, prophesying that the marriage would bring the destruction of the kingdom and reminding her of the many martyrs burnt as a result of Mary I's union with a foreigner.[34] Indeed, so many London ministers were railing against the match that according to George Talbot, son of the earl of Shrewsbury, Elizabeth prohibited ministers from preaching on any text which might be construed as relevant to the question.[35] Some contemporary observers had their suspicions that important men at court were orchestrating the sermons and protecting their authors, since the queen was taking no action to punish the preachers responsible.[36] There may even have been an assassination attempt against Simier; on 17 July 1579 a passing boat-man fired a shot at the barge in which the Frenchman and the queen were travelling, although Elizabeth refused to believe that the shooting was anything other than an accident and pardoned the man responsible.[37]

The match also attracted some support outside the Council, but this seems to have been confined to a coterie of crypto-Catholics at court, many of whom had been denied preferment by the queen. These included some of Sussex's kinsmen, who were part of the Howard connection: Philip Howard, the son of the attainted duke of Norfolk; Lord Henry Howard, the late duke's younger brother; and Sir Edward Stafford who had married Leicester's cast-off mistress, Lady Douglass Sheffield, the daughter of the late Howard of Effingham. Other members of this group were Edward de Vere, seventeenth earl of Oxford, who was Burghley's estranged son-in-law and also related to the Howards, Charles Arundell, one of Oxford's close friends, the duke of Northumberland, brother of the attainted rebel of 1569, and the earl of Arundel who had been implicated in the Ridolfi plot. Some of them had friends and relations among the queen's ladies, such as Stafford's mother and sister, who used their influence where possible with their mistress.[38] Not surprisingly, relations between this group and the opponents of the marriage soon began to sour. Conflict had only just been avoided in November 1578, after Roger Lord North, one of Leicester's political allies, had deliberately and publicly insulted Sussex; and the following August the Spanish ambassador heard that Leicester and his friends were 'greatly incensed against Sussex'.[39] The 'tennis court quarrel' in 1579 that nearly led to the fighting of a duel between Oxford and Philip Sidney, Leicester's nephew, also had its roots in the power struggle that was emerging as a result of the Anjou marriage deliberations.[40]

For a time during the late spring and summer of 1579, it looked as if those in favour of the match had gained the upper hand. Although Simier professed to be 'greatly grieved' with the Council's response to Anjou's demands, the decision to postpone discussion of the contentious articles had amounted to a victory for Burghley and Sussex, as they had carried with them sufficient councillors to enable the negotiations to proceed. They scored another success a little later, when Elizabeth learned that Leicester had secretly married her cousin Lettice, the widowed countess of Essex, in September 1578. Apparently Lord Henry Howard and Charles Arundell revealed the secret to Simier who then told Elizabeth. A storm was immediately unleashed and Elizabeth 'grew into such a Chafe' that Leicester left court for a short period under a cloud.[41] It may have been her angry reaction to his deceit and perceived disloyalty that prompted Elizabeth to agree under pressure from Sussex and Burghley to issue the duke with a safe-conduct to come to England, despite the vocal opposition against the marriage. At any rate, Mary Stuart seems to have gained this impression from her informers, who no doubt included the resident French ambassador. In a letter of 4 July 1579 she reported that the news of Leicester's marriage

> Hath so offended this Queen, that it is thocht she hath bene led, upon such miscontentment, to agre unto the sicht of the duke d'Alençon, notwithstanding she had diferred thre whol dayis, with an extreme regrete, and many teares, before she would subscribe the passport, being induced therunto, and almost forced by those that have led this negotiation.[42]

On 16 June 1579, the Council granted the duke a safe-conduct to visit the queen and soon afterwards sent it to France.[43]

Anjou, of course, could not travel to England without the permission of the French king, and Henry III was still ambivalent about the match and suspicious about his brother's intentions. Despite her own doubts, Catherine had tried to convince the king in the spring of 1579 that it would be safest to placate Anjou and agree to the marriage, for otherwise he might begin intriguing with the Huguenots again.[44] Eventually, Henry complied and gave Anjou a grant to facilitate his trip to England, but he was still so nervous about the potential results of an alliance between his brother and Elizabeth that he took the precaution of writing to the governor of Calais to say that on no account should he allow the duke to enter the town without an express order from the king.[45]

On 3 August 1579 Anjou slipped away from the French court, and after a brief delay at Boulogne due to bad weather he sailed for England, reaching Greenwich on 17 August. As Elizabeth wanted the visit to be kept secret in order to avoid popular demonstrations against the marriage, the duke travelled incognito, as the seigneur du Pont-de-Sé, with only a small retinue, despite the fact that some of his supporters would have preferred to have seen him go in great pomp as a prince about to ratify a matrimonial treaty rather than as a suitor in disguise and on approval.[46] The secret, however, was very badly kept. News of it soon reached Antwerp and Spain, and was carried to Italy by way of the papal nuncio and the Tuscan and Venetian ambassadors at Paris.[47] In England too, news of it leaked to the court, forcing Elizabeth to forbid all gossip among her ladies and gentlemen and to take measures to prevent attacks on Anjou's person.[48] According to a report at Mons, the queen issued an edict which forbade anyone from speaking of the visit and carrying a firearm within a certain distance from the court. This rumour had substance; on 26 July 1579 a proclamation was indeed issued 'against the common use of Dagges, Handgunnes, Harquebuzes, Callivers and Cotes of defence' and this may have been intended as a security measure to protect the duke.[49]

There is very little comment about Anjou's short visit in English documents and the most detailed accounts appear in the dispatches of the

French and Spanish ambassadors.[50] In fact the duke's stay was uneventful. He met with no open or obvious hostility, and believed that the interview 'a esté trouvée bonne par tous les peuples de delà'.[51] He did not enter into any discussions with the queen's councillors, many of whom were deliberately absent from court for most of the ten days that he spent at Greenwich and Richmond. Instead, his days and nights were spent at balls, parties and banquets, and his conversation was more amorous than political. None the less, the queen did discuss with him his religion and plans in the Netherlands: on religion it was agreed that he should have some liberty of conscience, although 'not exactly in such form as he would have liked'; as for the Netherlands, the queen no longer tried to prevent his venture but wanted assurances that Henry III would financially support it and not expect her to pay its costs.[52] From the point of view of the match's supporters, the visit was a great success. Elizabeth found her suitor so attentive and gallant that the age difference between them did not seem to matter. His looks and personality pleased her and she appeared quite smitten with her 'frog', the nickname she gave him, maybe because of his deep gravelly voice or his bandy legs and pockmarked complexion. Anjou too appeared genuinely impressed by Elizabeth. On his return to France, comments were made that: 'Quelques-uns pensoient du commencement qu'il fust plus amoureux du Royaume que de la personne, mais il fait bien paroistre maintenant le contraire.'[53] Although no doubt an inaccurate assessment of Anjou's true feelings, this comment and others like it indicate that he found the queen more agreeable than he had expected.

During his visit and beyond Elizabeth played the role of a woman in love, carrying around with her Anjou's miniature in her prayer-book and writing him a poetic lament on his departure.[54] How much was real and how much simulated is unknown, and her true emotional state has to remain a mystery. Was she frighteningly aware of her biological time-clock ticking away and desperate to grab at this – her last – chance of marriage? Was she thrown off-balance by Leicester's marriage to a younger woman and propelled towards Anjou on the rebound? Or was she still in control of her emotions and at least as anxious about the growing might of Spain as excited by the opportunity of marrying an attractive man?

The likelihood is that Elizabeth was influenced by her head first and her heart second. After all, political considerations had led her to initiate the courtship and the events of the summer and autumn of 1579 gave her strong reason to continue it. In the Netherlands, the Spaniards looked set to bring the rebels under their control: Parma had captured the great fortress of Maastricht in June and Mechelen in July. Even while Elizabeth was entertaining Anjou at court, James FitzMaurice's Spanish and papal-backed expedition had landed in Munster to stir up rebellion throughout Ireland. Soon after Anjou's departure, Esmé Stuart d'Aubigny, who was an agent of the duke of Guise, arrived at the court of James VI with the intention of converting the thirteen-year-old king to Catholicism and encouraging him to throw off the tutelage of his Anglophile regent, the earl of Morton.[55] In these circumstances it was no wonder that Elizabeth was seeking to end her isolation by looking for a French marriage, just as she and her councillors had done in 1571. Yet at the same time, a marriage to Anjou may well have personally appealed to the queen. He was a first prince of the blood of the oldest of the great dynasties and a man sexually attractive to women. For the second time in her reign, Elizabeth could contemplate marriage not with distaste but pleasurable anticipation. As a bonus, she could retrieve her pride after the 'desertion' by Leicester.

Elizabeth's positive feelings about the match were not shared by most of her Protestant subjects. On the contrary, from August 1579 onwards pamphlets, popular ballads and Latin verses vehemently opposed to the marriage poured forth.[56] Two pasquins were posted on the Lord Mayor's door, both containing 'very harsh words' about a French match and threatening armed resistance to it. As one of them declared:

The kinge of ffrance shall not advance his shippes in English sande
Ne shall his brother ffrancis have the Ruleng of the lande:
Wee subiects trwe untill oure queene, the forraine yoke defie,
Where too we plight oure faithefull hartts, *our* lymes, *our* lyves
& all
thereby to have *our* honor rize, or tak *our* fatall fall.
Therefore, good ffrancis, Rule at home, resist not *our* desire;
for here is nothing else for thee, but onely sworde and fyer.[57]

In London preachers took to the pulpits to denounce the marriage and express their horror that Elizabeth had invited a Catholic prince to court. Some were also organising public prayers and fasting 'for her Majesty's good estate, which they feared was now like to be in great peril'.[58] The most famous polemic against the match came from the pen of John Stubbs, a lawyer originally from Norfolk, who was the brother-in-law of the Presbyterian Thomas Cartwright and had friends among the radical Protestants as well as connections at court. His *Discoverie of a Gaping Gulf whereinto England is like to be swallowed by an other French mariage, if the Lord forbid not the banes, by letting her Majestie see the sin and punishment thereof* was published in early August 1579 and appears to have been widely distributed. Evidently thousands of pamphlets were printed, while fifty copies were sent to Sir Richard Grenville in Cornwall for him to hand out among his friends.[59]

When pared down, Stubbs's arguments against the marriage were very similar to those presented in the Council during the previous spring – the duke's religion, his nationality, Elizabeth's age, and the dangers of a

164

marriage to 'the brother of childless France' – so similar in fact that suspicions were raised that one of the councillors had given him detailed information about the conciliar discussions.[60] He also came up with answers to the points made by Burghley at the same meetings. The tone of the pamphlet, however, was far different and its language was 'unashamedly Puritan', conventionally sexist, deeply anti-foreign and politically factious.[61]

The arguments against a Catholic marriage in the *Gaping Gulf* drew upon Puritan hermeneutics. England was likened to the kingdom of Israel, whereas France was condemned as 'a kingdom of darkness' and 'a principal prop of the tottering house of Antichrist'; Anjou himself was dismissed as 'as yet no enrolled citizen in the outward kingdom of heaven'. Parallels were similarly drawn between contemporary religious conflicts and the Old Testament struggles of the children of Israel against the forces of idolatry. Texts and stories were taken from the Bible, mainly the Old Testament, to provide evidence for the sin of a Catholic marriage and to threaten divine retribution on Protestant England for breaking God's covenant. A deep pessimism also imbued the work: 'everywhere it is set down how the wicked perverted the good, but nowhere that the better part converted the wicked', and Anjou was cast as the serpent at the Fall 'whose sting is in his mouth, and who doth his endeavor to seduce our Eve, that she and we may lose this English paradise'.

Like Eve, Elizabeth as a woman was thought particularly vulnerable to the forces of Satan. In addition, like all women, she was deemed 'subject by the law of God and oweth both awe and obedience' to her husband, 'howsoever the laws by prerogative or her place by pre-eminence may privilege her'. For Stubbs, therefore, there was no likelihood of Anjou's conversion to Protestantism, but only Elizabeth's to Catholicism. Indeed throughout the work the author described Elizabeth in phrases which drew attention to the weakness of this particular vessel: she was being 'led blindfold as a poor lamb to the slaughter' by the councillors advocating marriage, and was left 'helpless in her choice of the person'; she was 'mild' in her temperament and had a 'honey-sweet mouth'; all a far cry from the real Elizabeth who was a main driving-force behind the marriage.

While the *Gaping Gulf* attacked the French marriage primarily on religious grounds, it also expressed a more general xenophobic sentiment. Some of its arguments were similar to those expressed by Sir Thomas Smith nearly twenty years earlier, but its tone was more populist and Puritan. 'It is natural to all men to abhor foreign rule as a burden of Egypt, and to us of England if to any other nation under the sun', wrote its author. Elizabeth had redeemed England from the foreign yoke of Spain and it was now inconceivable that she should foist on her subjects 'a more dangerous foreigner'. For no matter how bad Spanish rule had been, a French king would be worse. The French, thought Stubbs, were 'the scum of Europe'; French papists were 'irreligious, haughty and faithless'; while Anjou himself, he implied, was guilty of 'vile sins of the body' and was of a 'foul, vicious and irreligious' mind.

As Stubbs did not stop at criticising and answering the arguments of supporters of the match but went on to impugn their motives and urge their replacement, the pamphlet can legitimately be labelled 'factional'. Burghley came under fire when Stubbs told Elizabeth to test the sincerity of her advisers by questioning if 'they have continually been thus earnest and taken every good occasion to persuade you to marriage'. They clearly could not be trusted if they had hitherto been 'either dumb or slow speakers in this cause, when all good men wished it, and whose parliaments humbly besought it', claimed Stubbs, no doubt remembering Burghley's opposition to the Dudley marriage between 1560 and 1563. The Howards and the Oxford group were attacked as self-seeking political adventurers using the marriage as a means for obtaining power in Stubbs's comment: 'Those, therefore, that persuade this band of strange alliance must needs be such Englishmen as find themselves not advanced in this state according to that desert which they conceive in themselves and therefore disdain at others' good estate.' Elizabeth, urged the author, should turn away from councillors such as these; she should stop her ears 'against such sorcerers and their enchanting counsels', 'put out of heart all flatterers' and return to the 'plain, honest speakers' who opposed the marriage for the good of the queen and her realm.

Elizabeth's response to the pamphlet was immediate and merciless. She issued a proclamation on 27 September 1579 to call in the 'lewde seditious booke' and ordered the Lord Mayor of London to collect and burn all copies. Bishops were told to root out the book and prevent preachers in their dioceses from giving sermons which echoed its views – even Archbishop Grindal of Canterbury was brought out of his enforced semi-retirement to carry out the task. Bishop Aylmer of London immediately summoned some forty ministers to his palace 'to admonish them about Stubb's book', urged them to speak out against 'the seditious libeller' and warned them against any meddling in the queen's affairs.[62] Stubbs, his printer Hugh Singleton and William Page who had helped to distribute the pamphlets were arrested, swiftly put on trial, and found guilty under a statute of Philip and Mary against publishers of seditious writings. On 3 November 1579 the three were led to the scaffold, where Singleton received a last minute reprieve on account of his age but the other two had their right hand chopped off with a cleaver.[63] Stubbs and Page remained in the Tower for many months afterwards. In addition, two lawyers, James Dalton and Robert Monson, were imprisoned in the Fleet for protesting that the convictions of the three men were wrong in law on the grounds that the statute under which they had been prosecuted had expired on the death of Mary.

All these victims of the queen's fury had powerful patrons and friends in the Council who were opponents of the marriage. According to Mauvissière, it was generally thought that they had encouraged the publication of the pamphlet: 'estimoit l'on qu'il [Stubbs] ne l'avait faict sans le consentiment de quelques ungs de ce conseil', he reported on one occasion, and 'Il ce trouve que la chose vient de plus longue source que des petiz escrivains', he wrote on another.[64] De Villiers, William of Orange's secretary in Antwerp, also believed that Stubbs had not been acting alone; he suspected that his friend William Davison, Elizabeth's agent in the Netherlands between 1576 and the spring of 1579, was implicated in the affair. But although Davison was certainly a good friend of Stubbs and an enemy of the marriage, he was not a member of the Council and therefore would not have been fully conversant with the arguments presented there.[65] Walsingham is a far more likely suspect for Stubbs's informant; according to the Venetian ambassador in Paris, Elizabeth banished him from court in October 1579 because he 'had knowledge of this affair'.[66] Leicester, meanwhile, was one of Singleton's patrons, while Page, Dalton and Monson have all been identified recently as protégés of the earl of Bedford.[67] It is a measure of the queen's rage and resolution to marry Anjou that she meted out such severe punishments to men who had such powerful friends on the Council. Nor were Stubbs and his confederates the only critics of the match to be punished. In January 1580 the Privy Council ordered a man from Marlborough to be pilloried and whipped for 'utteringe of lewde, unreverende and seditiouse speaches againste the duke of Anjou'.[68]

The prosecution and punishment of Stubbs and his accomplices were undoubtedly unpopular in London and some other towns. The city of London's ministers 'utterly bent their brows' both at their queen's proclamation and Bishop Aylmer's speech against the author of the pamphlet, on the grounds that 'they conceive and report that he is one that feareth God, dearly loveth her Majesty, entered into this course being carried with suspicion and jealousy of her person and safety'.[69] In Norwich the town magistrates debated whether or not to obey the queen's orders and publicise the royal proclamation.[70] An eyewitness of the execution of the sentence against Stubbs recounted later that 'the Multitude standing about was deeply silent', either out of horror at the form of punishment and pity for the man, or out of hatred for the marriage.[71] Anjou judged correctly that it would have been better had the queen pardoned the offenders.[72]

The strength of the opposition to the marriage seems to have taken Elizabeth and Burghley by surprise, and they proved ineffective in silencing it or winning the argument. Elizabeth hoped that censorship and the deterrent value of Stubbs's public punishment would bring the opponents of the match to heel. Burghley for his part tried to organise a counter-propaganda campaign. Extrapolating the main points from the *Gaping Gulf*, he handed them over to colleagues to produce a riposte; but, although a couple of pamphlets were written, they remained unpublished and evidently had only a limited circulation. Lord Henry Howard's 'Answer to Stubbs's Book' appeared in several manuscript copies in 1580, and there is only one manuscript copy extant of another book addressed to Elizabeth from an anonymous author which also answers Stubbs.[73] In fact, the only widely disseminated governmental propaganda was Elizabeth's proclamation calling in Stubbs's book; most unusually for a royal proclamation against printed books it not merely ordered the book's suppression but attempted to refute its argument.[74]

Although it was increasingly expressed more cautiously, the open hostility to the match continued unabated. According to a Spanish ambassador's report of 16 October 1579, even after the proclamation against Stubbs, 'many writings have been sent to her [Elizabeth] lately dissuading her from this business. This has been managed by Leicester and Hatton', who were adept at channelling evidence of hostile public opinion in the queen's direction.[75] A letter written from England on 29 November 1579 informed the Venetian ambassador in France that defamatory libels against Anjou were still appearing every day and that Leicester's chaplain had presented the queen with a petition against the marriage.[76]

Another piece of writing which reached the queen through Leicester's influence was *A Letter to Queen Elizabeth* by Philip Sidney, his nephew. Asked, probably by the earl, to take up his pen against the marriage, Sidney tried to avoid the queen's displeasure by constructing an elegant and courteous appeal which was not printed but delivered into the hands of the queen and distributed privately among courtiers.[77] Although his arguments followed the line of Stubbs, Sidney was careful to moderate his attack on Anjou and avoid too many 'unreverent disgracings of him in particular', instead concentrating on describing the dangers to the realm if the marriage went ahead. He was equally assiduous in flattering the queen, and ended his letter by calling her 'the example of princes, the ornament of this age, the comfort of the afflicted, the delight of your people, the most excellent fruit of all your progenitors, and the perfect mirror to your posterity'. Probably for these reasons, Sidney escaped punishment.[78]

Fear of punishment led the opponents of the match to express their sentiments ever more cryptically. Although at court frog jewellery became popular gifts for the queen, at a popular level pejorative references to 'frogs' or 'toads' proliferated in all kinds of published works from 1579 to 1581, acting as a coded form for hostility to the match.[79] The song *The Moste Strange Wedding of the Frogge and the Mouse* was one such example; another was the Latin poem *The Battle of the Frogs and Mice* which was licensed for publication in January 1580. This reworking of the familiar tale in which a frog (Anjou) drowned a mouse (Elizabeth) which he was supposed to be helping, and so provoked a war between the frogs and the mice (Catholics and Protestants) which was unfairly won by the frogs, was an easily interpreted political allegory which could avoid suppression by the authorities.

Other writers expressed their opposition to the match still more obliquely in sophisticated allegorical poems which could be interpreted in various ways. One such work was *Prosopoia or The Mother Hubberd's Tale* which was written by the poet Edmund Spenser, a member of Leicester's household from the spring of 1579 until mid-1580. Although not published until 1591, when its author described it as a work 'long sithens composed in the raw conceit of my youth', it was probably written while Spenser was working for Leicester and circulated at that time in manuscript amongst sympathetic courtiers within the earl's circle.[80] At one level the poem was a satirical allegory of court life but at another it was a biting attack on the Anjou marriage. Written as a beast fable, a genre which was used during the Renaissance to signal a political meaning, the poem told the story of an ape, abetted by a fox, seizing the crown from the sleeping lion, who was the monarch of the forest. The ape represented both Simier (Elizabeth's 'ape') and Anjou; the lion stood for Elizabeth, while the fox was Burghley. The purpose of the allegory was to show how an alliance between Burghley and the French threatened the queen, who was unconscious of the danger because of her infatuation for the duke, and would prove disastrous for the realm. The ape was portrayed as a cowardly and ungodly beast, but in a clear reference to Simier was also described as an accomplished courtier, 'with gallant showe' and 'fine feates and Courtly complement':

> And with the sugrie sweete thereof allure
> Chast Ladies eares to fantasies impure.

Once king, however, the ape became an oppressive ruler, appointing 'a warlike equipage of forreine beasts, not in the forest bred' and subjugating 'the wilde beasts', who until then had held 'the greatest sway' at court:

> All wylde beastes made vassals of his pleasures,
> And with their spoyles enlarg'd his private treasures.

The fox too oppressed the creatures of the forest. He had allowed the ape to become king 'upon condition, that ye ruled bee in all affaires, and counselled by mee', and once the ape had the crown, the fox seized control of patronage:

> Nought suffered he the Ape to give or graunt,
> But through his hand must pass the Fiaunt.

Rescue from this oppression only came when Jove slew the ape, woke up the queen and restored the natural order in the forest. Interestingly little was made of the danger to the Protestant Church in the poem; the emphasis was rather on the oppressive nature of foreign rule and the perniciousness of factional government.

Spenser's beast fable was adapted for a similar purpose by Philip Sidney in *Philisides's Song*, in the Third Eclogue of *Arcadia*, 'As I my little flock on Ister bank . . .' which was probably circulating in manuscript in early 1580. The song told of the process by which a monarchy began and was later transformed into a tyranny, but, through its resonance with both Spenser's *Mother Hubberd's Tale* and the popular fable of the frogs who wanted a king and were given a stork who ate them up, it could also be interpreted as an allegory of England's fate were Anjou to marry Elizabeth and become king.[81] It began by setting the scene on an August night when a shepherd, Philisides, beset with unnamed fears for himself and his flock, sang for comfort the song taught to him by 'old Lanquet'. As August was the month of Anjou's visit to the queen and Lanquet an allusion to Hubert Languet, Sidney's political mentor who advocated Protestant interventionist policies abroad, the poet was evidently signalling that the song would contain advice about the threats posed by the French marriage.

The song first drew a picture of idyllic life on earth where 'the beasts with courage clad, Like senators, a harmless empire had'. It then described the disaster that befell the animal kingdom after they asked Jove for a king. Reluctantly yielding to their entreaties, Jove gave them a man who shared many of their own characteristics to become their lord. Predictably, his rule soon became tyrannical; first the wild beasts, those who had previously held power in the kingdom, were destroyed: 'Then 'gan the factions in the beasts to breed', then 'murders done, which never erst was seen'. The exploitation of the weaker animals soon followed for, once the nobility who had held power was destroyed, the whole commonwealth was at risk, even the 'meanest herd' of smallest birds:

> At length for glutton taste he did them kill:
> At last for sport their silly lives did spill.

That factionalism, civil war, and oppression would be England's fate if Anjou were set up as king could certainly be read as one message of the song.

Still more obscure in its political meaning was Edmund Spenser's *Shepheardes Calendar*, which was significantly published anonymously in December 1579 by Hugh Singleton, the printer of the *Gaping Gulf*. Its imagery is so subtle that literary critics have disagreed about the work's relationship to the Anjou marriage; none the less, most of them agree that in at least three Eclogues, those of February, April and November, Spenser does seem to be making references to contemporary events at court.[82] The November Eclogue, which lamented the death of Dido, seems to be a more general lament for the death of Protestant England and the eclipse of Leicester, which Spenser and his circle believed would follow the marriage of Anjou and Elizabeth. Similarly, the February Eclogue appears as a warning of the dangers to the state and political life if Elizabeth's elder statesmen, men like Leicester and Walsingham, were to lose royal favour and be removed from power. This moral was implicit in the fable of the Oak and Briar, a tale which its narrator claimed had a pointed meaning, or in other words was a political allegory. The simple story of the spiteful and jealous briar attacking the sound but aged oak until the tree was felled by the husbandman seems an easily recognisable allusion to the factional conflicts at court during 1579, with the oak representing Leicester and the briar one of the new breed of courtiers who were seeking power on the back of the Anjou marriage. The Latin name for oak, 'robur', recalls Robert while the oak was also one of Leicester's personal symbols. The descriptions of the oak as 'Thoroughly rooted and of wonderous hight' and one who 'had bene the King of the field' were appropriate for the earl. The description of the briar brings to mind the earl of Oxford: the 'bragging brere', 'embellisht with blossoms fayre', popular with maidens, and so arrogant and bold that he 'scold, And snebbe the good Oake, for he was old'. The husbandman was clearly the queen, called in the poem 'my liege lord', 'my Soveraigne Lord of creatures all', who mistakenly cut down her trusted oak thereby leaving the land and briar exposed to winter's storms.[83]

Finally, in the April Eclogue, Spenser followed the lead of Thomas Churchyard in the Norwich Entertainments of 1578 and expressed opposition to the Anjou marriage by cultivating an image for Elizabeth as a Virgin Queen.[84] Using the imagery associated with the Virgin Mary, he lauded 'Fayre Eliza' as 'the flowre of Virgins', 'without spotte', 'no mortal blemish may her blotte'. In addition, he represented Elizabeth as the chaste Moon goddess: 'her angelick face like *Phoebe* fayre' and also a *Cynthia* 'with thy silver rayes'. All in all, Elizabeth was a 'goddesse plaine', far out of the reach of mere mortals and destined for a life of chastity.

The idea of Elizabeth as the Virgin Queen was given pictorial representation for the first time during the debate on the Anjou marriage in the series of some seven 'Sieve' portraits painted between 1579 and about 1583. These paintings showed Elizabeth holding a sieve, which served as a symbol of virginity through its reference to Tuccia, a Vestal Virgin, who, when accused of breaking her vestal vows, proved her virginity by filling a sieve with water from the River Tiber and carrying it back to the Temple of Vesta without spilling a drop. This imagery was deployed to show that Elizabeth's virginity was her strength, providing her with the magical power to make the sieve (the state) impenetrable and thus invulnerable. Her virginity, it was also implied, was inextricably linked to the foundation of an English empire destined to rival that of Spain, for icons of empire were included in the portraits. The version by George Gowers (see frontis-piece) shows part of a luminous globe, a visual representation of empire, behind the queen's right shoulder. A more elaborate portrait, which is attributed to Cornelius Ketel and was painted sometime between late 1579 and early 1581, also has a globe behind the queen, this time to her left, with the light falling on England from which ships are departing. To her right stands an Imperial column, decorated with medallions depicting the story of Dido and Aeneas from Virgil's *Aeneid*. The allusion could not be clearer: just as Aeneas was destined to abandon his lover in order to go on to found Rome, so Elizabeth would have to renounce Anjou and establish an empire of her own by pursuing an ambitious and aggressive foreign policy. Almost certainly the patron of this device was Sir Christopher Hatton, who has been identified as one of the gentlemen in the background from the heraldic device of a white hind on his sleeve, and who had emerged in late 1579 as a leading opponent of the match and a supporter of an interventionist foreign policy.[85]

It was in early October 1579 that members of the Council openly voiced their objections to the French marriage. Initially Elizabeth commissioned a small group of councillors to debate the marriage, and on 4 October Burghley, Sussex, Hunsdon, Hatton, Leicester, Dr Thomas Wilson and possibly Walsingham met at Westminster to consider its pros and cons and offer her their advice.[86] A few days later, on 6 October there was a meeting of the whole Council at Greenwich with one or two notable absentees, including Walsingham, presumably because of his known opposition to the marriage. At this meeting, Burghley reiterated the points he had made in the debates of the previous spring, though he put more emphasis on the dangers from Scotland and Ireland as a result of the developments there over the summer and early autumn.[87] The opponents of the match, however, made their case more fully and persuasively than they had previously with the result that Burghley had to concede some of their arguments. Thus, he admitted that 'ther is no Benefitt such by this Mariadg, but except ther be also Provisions accorded, and wisely established to withstand certen apparent Perrils, no wise Man can make'. Among those 'provisions' he proposed: 'Penalties [be] increased upon Recusants', aid be given to James VI of Scotland, and certain conditions imposed to restrict Anjou's freedom of worship. As far as the latter was concerned, Burghley recommended that

> he shall accompany hir Majesty at hir publyc Repayring to the Church to common Prayers, and shall order that no Favor be gyven to any Recusant; and also shall publyckly kepe some Nombre of Gentillmen of the Relligion reformed, and shall direct them to be of the French Church, then ther will be less Cause of Comfort gyven by hym to the obstinat Papists.[88]

Even offering these safeguards, Burghley could not carry the majority of the councillors with him. Leicester, Sidney, Knollys and Mildmay had always disliked the marriage, but they now won over to their side councillors who had either previously registered their approval of it or who had never before been consulted as to their opinion. Sir Christopher Hatton admitted a change of mind, as did Lord Admiral Lincoln, who felt that Burghley was exaggerating the dangers facing the realm and 'thought it not Reason, to mak her afraid of any Perils, but that she might be suer ynough without marriage'. Sir Ralph Sadler, participating in the debates for the first time, found himself influenced by Mildmay's arguments concerning Anjou's religion, his closeness to the French throne, and the queen's age. The former two concerns, he believed, posed a danger to the state while the latter endangered the life and happiness of the queen. In Sadler's opinion, not only was Elizabeth too old to bear a child safely but would also suffer her husband's scorn and neglect, since she would be well past her prime in a few years time just when Anjou would be 'in his best lust and flourysshing age'.[89] Only Sussex, Hunsdon and Wilson followed Burghley in giving the marriage their approval.[90]

The next day, 7 October 1579, Burghley made a final plea to his fellow-councillors. They should assent to the marriage, he urged, because Elizabeth wanted it and would take 'sufficient provisions and conditions' to avoid 'all inconveniences voydable by man's wisdom'. The majority, however, still refused to advise the queen to accept Anjou; but, as it was unwilling to expose its disunity, the Council decided to adopt a common and bland formula for presentation to the queen. Later the same day, four of their number delivered the 'message accorded in full Counsell' to Elizabeth, which basically handed her back the burden of decision-making:

> we do humbly desyre to pardon us of our stey, and if she will shew to us any Inclination of hir Mynd, we will so procede as all hir Honor shall be preserved, and whatsoever may seme burdenoose, we will bear it with common Consent.[91]

This failure to deliver a firm resolution on the marriage infuriated and distressed Elizabeth, since she realised that the form of words in their message to her was a mere cover for conciliar opposition. She upbraided her councillors, 'not without sheddying of manny Teares', for their refusal to petition her to marry and rebuked them for their fears over religion, which implied that she was indifferent to God's cause and her own security. On hearing her angry reaction, the whole Council decided on the following day, 8 October 1579, to offer the queen 'all our Services in Furderance of this Mariadg, if so it shold lyk her', but this luke-warm and grudging endorsement of the marriage did not satisfy her either, and she was 'very sharp in reprehendyng of all such as she thought wold mak Arguments ageynst hir Mariadg'. It must have been at about this time that Elizabeth considered admitting to her Council four influential Catholics: Viscount Montague and Sir William Cordell, one-time councillors under Mary, together with the earl of Northumberland and one other.[92] It is possible that she also considered dismissing Walsingham, with whom she was still very angry and who had not yet returned to court.[93] It looked as if a palace revolution might well be in the offing.

Elizabeth, however, drew back from the brink of a policy which would have gravely threatened the stability of political and religious life. To change the balance of her Council by appointing known Catholics would have alienated her clergy and practically all her present councillors, even those who supported the marriage, since they too were committed Protestants. At the same time she would have raised the hopes of all Catholics for either some form of toleration or a change in the Church Settlement. A major rebellion, even civil war, might well have resulted from this disturbance to the *status quo*. Yet she could hardly go ahead with the marriage policy without having her Council's full backing for the project. Not only would this exacerbate the factionalism which was already rocking the court, but there was no hope of securing parliamentary ratification of the matrimonial treaty if she could not rely on total conciliar support. On the other hand, Elizabeth did not want to be seen to be caving in before the pressure of public opinion, especially as she felt very angry with those who seemed to be orchestrating it. The councillors suspected of involvement in the public relations campaign were, therefore, given strong evidence of her displeasure. Hatton was excluded from her presence for a short while after the fatal Council meetings in October; more seriously in early November 1579 Leicester was confined first to Greenwich and then his own property; neither he nor Walsingham returned to court until the beginning of 1580.[94]

For most of the autumn Elizabeth could not make up her mind about what course of action to follow. On 20 November 1579, however, she took the decision to commission Burghley, Lincoln, Sussex, Hunsdon and Wilson (all but one of them supporters of the match) to negotiate a matrimonial treaty with Simier.[95] The preliminary treaty was drawn up within four days and Simier immediately left the court to take it back to France. As Anjou had already dropped his demand for joint authority with the queen on matters of patronage, the articles in the treaty concerning his political power followed closely the terms in the marriage-contract of Mary and Philip: after the marriage Anjou would bear the name and title of king but the disposition of all patronage would be in the hands of the queen, who would bestow benefices and offices only on Englishmen. The question of Anjou's coronation was to be left to parliament; yet even if he were to be crowned king before the marriage this would in no way prejudice Elizabeth's rights and power but be 'seulement pour communion et particippacion de l'honneur Royal'. Only on financial arrangements did Anjou gain substantially better terms than Philip; the treaty accepted the principle that he should be paid the expenses incidental to his marriage, although the exact sum of his pension was to be determined later by parliament.[96] On religion, however, the French made fewer concessions; although the queen's deputies still raised objections to Anjou's religious demands, the relevant article was agreed in a form which allowed the duke and his French entourage 'the exercise of their religion' in a private place.

The signing of this treaty did not mean, however, that Elizabeth had finally decided to marry Anjou. On the contrary, two uncertainties in the treaty arrangements indicate that she had determined to call off the marriage unless Anjou could be persuaded to change his hard-line demand for religious freedom and to forswear the Mass. First, several articles, including the one concerning the form of the wedding ceremony, were not entirely resolved but were to be left for their final wording until the arrival of a French embassy to ratify the treaty. Second, Elizabeth agreed to sign the contract only on the understanding that it could be set aside at any time during the next two months if she could not obtain her people's consent to the marriage.[97] At the end of January 1580, in tones of deep regret Elizabeth duly informed Anjou that her subjects' objections to the match had not been overcome, and asked him to reconsider his demand for freedom of worship. In the meantime, she told him, he was to postpone sending over the French commission, while she herself would prorogue the parliament which was supposed to be summoned for the purpose of ratifying the matrimonial treaty.[98]

The French had no doubts that Elizabeth was telling the truth about her subjects' opposition to the match and was not simply trying to slip out of her commitment to marry Anjou. Mauvissière was keeping Henry III and Catherine well-informed about its unpopularity with 'les puritins' while a French copy of Stubbs's book had turned up at Paris.[99] The king was, therefore, fully cognisant that the hostility towards Anjou was mainly on account of his religion. None the less, he was totally unsympathetic to Elizabeth's request that Anjou modify his demand for religious freedom, and he would allow no change to the articles brought back by Simier: his brother was resolved 'de se tenir au contenu desdictz articles sans ne rien diminuer', he told Elizabeth's envoy, Sir Edward Stafford, in early February 1580.[100] Neither Henry nor Catherine was too upset at the prospect of the match falling through; on the contrary they both hoped that Anjou would now look elsewhere for a more suitable bride. Catherine spoke to the duke of a marriage with the sister of Henry's wife, Queen Louise of Lorraine, while Henry was talking to the papal nuncio about arranging a match with a daughter of Philip II.[101]

Anjou himself, however, had no intention of pulling out of the English marriage, and was anxious to prevent Elizabeth jilting him because of the article on religion. Although he would not modify his demand for a private Mass, in April 1580 he sent Jacques de Vray to speak to the queen privately and frankly with a new proposal, which was intended to enable her to meet his demands and at the same time satisfy her subjects. The offending article, he suggested, could be deleted from the treaty to be presented to parliament and some vague clause, which would seem to limit his religious freedom, be put in its stead. Then, in a separate and secret written statement, Elizabeth could promise to follow the original article.[102] What Elizabeth thought of this proposal is nowhere recorded but she must have recognised it as thoroughly impracticable, for her husband's religious observances could hardly be kept a secret from the Council. She might well have rejected it out of hand, as the French never raised it again. She certainly ignored Anjou's plea that she invite over as soon as possible the French commissioners to ratify the treaty.[103]

Elizabeth's policy on all fronts remained in a state of limbo for most of 1580, and she took little action in response to the international Catholic threat that was growing ever more serious almost month by month. At the end of January 1580, the king of Portugal died and Philip II was rumoured to be planning a military campaign to assert his claim to the throne. The same month, Pope Gregory XIII re-issued the bull of excommunication against Elizabeth, and was known to be plotting some new enterprise against her in Ireland. During the spring in Scotland, James VI accused Regent Morton of treason and was falling completely under the spell of the 'very Catholic' D'Aubigny, whom he created earl of Lennox and put in charge of the key fortress of Dumbarton Castle. In April, some councillors even feared that James might 'be conveyed into France, and so governed and directed by the Guysians'.[104] In the summer, Philip II sent his troops over the Portuguese border to take possession of his new throne, and in August they captured Lisbon. In September, Spanish troops landed in the West of Ireland and occupied Smerwick. Throughout the year seminary priests and Jesuits were trickling into England from the Continent.

Elizabeth would dearly have liked an alliance with France to rescue her from these menacing developments. A matrimonial alliance still appeared to be her preferred option, as it would also have given her a certain amount of control over Anjou, who was again dabbling in Flemish politics and trying to re-negotiate a treaty with the States-General of the Netherlands. Conciliar opposition, however, had checkmated the policy of marriage. At the same time, a renewal of the civil wars in France which had been brewing since February 1580 and developing into open warfare in May removed for the time being any chance of or point to opening talks for a direct alliance with Henry III; not only was he preoccupied with internal problems, but a France in turmoil would prove no effective ally against the might of Spain. The only other policy available to the queen, until such time as Henry III restored order in his realm, was active military intervention abroad: helping Morton in Scotland, the rebels in the Netherlands, and the Huguenot leaders in France. This was the policy favoured by Leicester and Walsingham, who returned to court in early 1580, but was equally strongly opposed by Sussex and to a lesser extent Burghley. Elizabeth herself held back from an interventionist policy which would be expensive, provocative, and close the door on any future alliance with Henry III.[105] All she could do, therefore, was wait upon events. Consequently, she continued to offer hope to Anjou, and to cultivate good relations with Henry III by turning down the prince of Condé's requests for aid in June 1580 and staying out of the troubles in Scotland.

Only when news arrived at the English court in late June 1580 that the States-General was about to offer Anjou the sovereignty of the Netherlands, did Elizabeth's policy move – at least briefly – into a higher gear. Stafford was immediately sent to France for the purpose of binding the duke fast to the queen. Following instructions, he expressed Elizabeth's eagerness for the marriage and agreed to the dispatch of the French commissioners to conclude the matrimonial treaty. In a clue to her thinking, however, Stafford asked that the commissioners be sent with powers 'regarder et arrester et estendre la paix et amityé' if God would not allow of the marriage.[106] Impatient with the slow progress of negotiations with the States, Anjou was delighted with Elizabeth's unexpected readiness to receive the embassy. He, therefore, asked his brother to arrange for the French commissioners to arrive in England at the beginning of August 1580 in time for a parliamentary session to be held on the 15th. At the same time, however, he was determined to dispel further obfuscation and explained to Stafford that the matrimonial treaty would be the only item on their agenda. To reassure Elizabeth about his role in the Netherlands, he promised not to conclude an agreement with the States before first informing her.[107]

Henry III and Catherine de Medici, who had been in the process of negotiating a Spanish marriage for Anjou, were horrified by this development and immediately made it clear that commissioners could not possibly be sent so soon.[108] None the less, they realised that Anjou was resolved on both the Flanders enterprise and the English marriage, and they consequently agreed to send over the embassy as soon as it was practicable.[109] With no prospect of the commissioners discussing an Anglo-French alliance, however, it was Elizabeth's turn to prevaricate and she demanded a delay in their departure until internal peace had been restored to France.[110]

Catherine de Medici soon picked up Elizabeth's hints about an alliance, and in August 1580 she asked Sir Henry Cobham, the English ambassador at the French court, for a clarification of the queen's intentions:

that in case her Majestye have no lykyng to deale in the mariage they myght here proceade to treat some forther degree of amytye, being a thing most necessarye for bothe crownes to be well varysed in respect of the greatness that the crowne of Spayne is growing unto.[111]

Elizabeth, however, was in no hurry to respond. As she well knew, Henry III would have little value as an ally while his realm was tearing itself apart in another civil war. Furthermore, she did not have to take any immediate decision about what to do when Anjou took up arms in the Netherlands, since his expedition there had been postponed to allow him to mediate a peace in France. Only when a French peace seemed close in mid-September 1580, did Elizabeth direct Cobham to raise the question of the league with Catherine and Henry III.[112] Following his mistress's instructions, Cobham spoke to Henry III of her concerns about Philip II's conquest of Portugal and her desire to conclude a treaty 'pour s'opposer au dit Roy d'Espagne et sa grandeur'.[113]

Initially, Henry III and Catherine de Medici were ready to negotiate an alliance separate from the marriage.[114] They too were perturbed by the growth in Spanish power resulting from Philip II's annexation of Portugal, especially as Anjou looked set to lock horns with the prince of Parma in the Netherlands. On 29 September 1580 Anjou had signed an agreement, the Treaty of Plessis-les-Tours, with the States, and on 23 January 1581 he took the title 'prince and lord of the Netherlands'. Accordingly, Henry allowed some of his ministers to discuss terms for a league with Cobham and planned for a treaty of alliance to be drawn up in France, which could then be concluded and ratified in England by the commissioners sent over to finalise the matrimonial contract.[115] Before the end of the year, in a draft commission, the king empowered his envoys, who were as yet unnamed, 'confirmer, asseurer, estreindre et fortiffier' the peace that already existed between the two realms, 'si tant est que le dit Mariage ne pusse avoir lieu'.[116] Thus, at this time he was prepared to enter a league without marriage.

Soon afterwards, however, Henry III began to have second thoughts, as talks with the English ambassador about a league began to reveal the different priorities of each side.[117] While Elizabeth was primarily interested in securing French financial support for an enterprise on behalf of Don Antonio, a pretender to the Portuguese throne, Henry thought that it was too late to overturn Philip II's conquest of Portugal. For his part, Henry wanted Elizabeth to aid his brother in the Netherlands, whereas she was still suspicious of French ambitions there and unwilling to pursue a policy which could lead her into an expensive and open war against Spain. In addition, the French were keen that a treaty should include commercial clauses for the benefit of their merchants, whilst Elizabeth was equally determined not to relinquish any commercial advantage. Thus, when three of Henry's ministers conferred with Cobham about the terms to be negotiated, they were disconcerted to find that he had no powers to discuss the matters most dear to them: the establishment of a staple at Rouen, piracy, and help for Anjou's campaign in the Netherlands.[118] As these differences became manifest, Henry decided to work for the marriage first and to negotiate an alliance with England only after its consummation. Once married to Anjou, he believed, Elizabeth could not fail to give her husband financial assistance nor be associated with his war against Spain. Henry was still hopeful that a marriage could take place, because Mauvissière was sending him dispatch after dispatch containing optimistic accounts of the support for it at the English court.[119] He and Catherine were also impressed by Elizabeth's offer that she would free the duke to marry elsewhere, presumably by means of an annulment, if after their own marriage she found herself barren.[120] Consequently, in the final commission signed on the last day of February 1581, Henry's deputies were given no powers to discuss either a defensive alliance or an offensive league, but could only 'rediger en forme de contract ensemble resouldre et conclure certain poinct de contenu des articles'.[121]

Although arrangements for appointing and instructing the commission began in early January 1581, it took until mid-April for the embassy to arrive eventually in England. The delays were almost all on the French side, as Henry III and Anjou bickered over its composition and problems arose over the ill-health of three of its members.[122] Possibly too, Henry was in no hurry to dispatch the commissioners while he was still deciding whether or not to authorise them to negotiate an alliance if the marriage fell through. The embassy which arrived in England included some five hundred people, led by an impressive body of noblemen, experienced royal councillors, and close household servants of the duke of Anjou: François de Bourbon (the *prince dauphin* of Auvergne), the marshal de Cossé, Barnabé Brisson (a president in the *parlement* of Paris), Claude Pinart (a Secretary of State), the sieur de Lansac, the sieur de Carrouges, La Mothe-Fénélon and Mauvissière (past and present ambassadors to England), and two members of Anjou's household, de Vray and the sieur de Marchaumont.[123] Even so, the two most distinguished members of the delegation were unable to participate; the comte de Soissons (only twelve or thirteen years old but included because of his status as a prince of the blood) and the duc de Montpensier (uncle of the king) proved too delicate in health to travel.[124]

There was, however, no possibility at all of Elizabeth concluding the marriage in the spring of 1581. Discounting her own preferences, the opposition to the match from the 'Puretains fort passionez' was as strong as ever.[125] Indeed the queen was so apprehensive of anti-French disturbances in London that she issued a proclamation on 18 April 1581 commanding honour to be shown to the ambassadors on pain of death.[126] In addition, the parliament which met from 16 January to 18 March 1581 sent out clear signals that there should be no tolerance for Catholics. Although the marriage was not actually raised within the Houses of Commons or Lords, the parliamentary attempt to introduce more stringent laws against English Catholics who either heard the Mass illegally or did not attend communion in their parish church showed an uncompromising anti-papal sentiment.[127] Members of parliament in this mood would never approve a matrimonial treaty with Anjou which allowed him the private use of the Mass. It is also possible that a few of the MPs advised Elizabeth against the match in a private consultation. At any rate, Elizabeth told the French embassy in April 1581 that some of them had confided to her their concerns 'that for two reasons the seyd mariag woold not be grateful' and that the match 'coold not but be greatly to the dyscontentment of the subiectes of this realm'. According to her account, the MPs warned that the English Catholics would take advantage of Anjou's presence in England to follow the Jesuits' call for disobedience to her laws and expressed their anxieties that she and her new husband might draw the realm into a long and burdensome war against Spain.[128]

At the same time, the erstwhile supporters of the match were in political disarray and in no position to promote it. During 1580, the earl of Oxford had quarrelled with Lord Henry Howard over the married earl's seduction of Anne Vavasour, a fifteen-year-old gentlewoman of the queen's Bedchamber, whose family were kin and close friends of the Howards. Over the Christmas season of 1580-1 Oxford broke entirely with his former friends and, at the instigation of Leicester, confessed to the queen his own Catholicism and accused Howard and Charles Arundell of signing a declaration 'that they would do all they could for the advancement of the Catholic religion'. Although at this time Elizabeth was disinclined to believe that the two men were traitors, she none the less put Howard into the custody of Lord Chancellor Bromley and Arundell in Hatton's charge.[129] In addition Oxford was sent to the Tower of London in late March 1581 on account of Vavasour's pregnancy and confinement. Not only did the episode remove some of the keenest supporters of the match from court, but Oxford's revelations also discredited the matrimonial cause, since the champions of the match were exposed as Catholics hoping for religious change.

With marriage out of the question, Elizabeth planned to use the presence of the prestigious French embassy to negotiate and sign a treaty of alliance; like other observers she was under the mistaken impression that the commissioners would have authority to conclude a league apart from the marriage.[130] In the spirit of the Field of Cloth of Gold, she entertained the French magnificently during their stay in London from 21 April until 14 June 1581, and treated them to feasts, tournaments, the ceremony of the Knights of the Garter, and a spectacular two-day Triumph staged over Whitsun, entitled 'The Four Foster Children of Desire'.[131] This elaborate tilt was originally intended to take place on 24 April, as the first entertainment to greet the French, but was postponed until later in their stay. It was designed not only to impress them but also to convey the political message that the English court stood united against the Anjou marriage. The subject of the allegory was the siege of the Fortress of Perfect Beauty (signifying Elizabeth and her chastity) by four knights, the 'Children of Desire' (representing Anjou). The Triumph concluded with the knights admitting their defeat at the end of the second day: 'They acknowledge this fortresse to be reserved for the eie of the whole world. . . . They acknowledge the least determination of Vertue (which stands for the gard of this fortresse) to be too strong for the strongest Desire.' Playing the parts of the four knights were Philip Sidney and Fulke Grenville, who had opposed the match, and Philip Howard, earl of Arundel, and Lord Windsor, who had favoured it. The more obvious allegorical touches of the entertainment included the representation of Elizabeth as the sun whose rays blessed her subjects and the pelting of the fortress with the weapons of roses (the flowers of Venus as well as Elizabeth). Overall, the allegory portrayed the queen as both an unobtainable object of desire in the chivalric tradition and a neo-Platonic celestial being; the clear message was that her chastity was part of her special mystique and that her marriage to the French prince was therefore out of the question.[132]

In the political discussions, too, Elizabeth and her leading councillors (again both supporters and opponents of the match) made it plain to the commissioners that an alliance rather than a marriage was their desired outcome of the visit. At their first conference on 24 April 1581, Burghley invited the French to deliver 'what you had to say on behalf of the Christian king' in the clear expectation that they would mention a league as well as the marriage.[133] To the surprise of the queen and her councillors, the commissioners stated that they only had the power to settle the outstanding articles and ratify the matrimonial treaty. But all hope of a pact was not lost, explained Barnabé Brisson, for the marriage would bring the assurance of an alliance and tie an indissoluble Gordian knot to 'fortifier, corroborer, et perpetuer' the friendship between the two realms.[134] Unfortunately, this was not the kind of alliance that Elizabeth and her councillors either wanted or had anticipated. Consequently, in an audience with the French commissioners on 28 April, Elizabeth gave them a warning that she might not be able to marry Anjou, because the previous difficulties obstructing the marriage not only remained but had intensified with the passing of time: at her age child-birth was undoubtedly more perilous; the arrival of the missionary priests to England had exacerbated the dangers arising from Anjou's Catholicism; and his activities in the Netherlands threatened war against Spain. Until she had heard the duke's comments on these problems, she pronounced herself unable to reach any final decision about the marriage.[135] In the circumstances, however, Elizabeth could hardly send back the commissioners empty-handed without offending their king. On the following day, therefore, Walsingham told them to carry out their task of drawing up a marriage-contract, 'because personages of their qualyte sent from so great a Prynse, shood no seem to come hither to no purpose'. At the same time, however, he reiterated the obstacles mentioned by the queen.[136]

On 11 May 1581 Burghley, Lincoln, Sussex, Bedford, Hatton, Leicester and Walsingham were appointed to conclude the marriage-treaty with the French.[137] The English commissioners knew very well that the contract would never be implemented; if nothing else, the queen stipulated from the first that it would not be binding on her until she had discussed it with Anjou.[138] Yet they nevertheless solemnly debated the contentious issue of the queen's dowry and drew up a contract which was detailed even to the point of specifying the inheritance of each of several children born of the couple.[139] During this time they were almost certainly drawing out the negotiations while they awaited word from Anjou. They might well have been expecting another visit, for he had intimated to Elizabeth that he would be coming over to England during the stay of the commissioners. Indeed Anjou began his journey in late May 1581 but storms in the Channel beat him back to Dieppe. A few days after the news that he would not be coming reached the English court, the matrimonial treaty was signed.[140]

Because the treaty would never be implemented, the English commissioners all agreed without demur to the French proposals on the outstanding matters concerning religion and the wedding ceremony. On religion, the article stood as it had been in Simier's version: that the duke and his servants who were not subjects of the queen would be given a private place to exercise freely their Catholic religion but would do nothing to disturb the religious peace or encourage the violation of English law. As for the wedding ceremony, the relevant clause described in great detail the form it would take. To avoid its celebration in a Protestant church, the French planned that a dais or theatre be erected at Westminster where the queen and duke would exchange vows in the presence of two bishops, one of each religion. The exact words to be spoken by bride and groom were laid down, including Elizabeth's promise to 'porteray obeissance coniugalle'. After the exchange of vows the queen would be taken by the duke to the door of a chapel where she would hear prayers, then he would withdraw to a place 'a part separé' where 'il aura exercise libre de sa religion'.[141] This format was modelled on the wedding of Henry of Navarre to Marguerite de Valois. As soon as the treaty was concluded on 11 June 1581, Elizabeth took steps to ensure that it had no real status. Together with its ratification, the commissioners were made to sign a statement which effectively nullified the contract. Elizabeth, it read, was under no obligation to marry Anjou until they were mutually satisfied about all matters, and she had six weeks to reach a decision before the treaty would come into operation.[142]

Even before the commissioners had left England, Elizabeth had decided to use Anjou's involvement in the Netherlands as the cause of her final withdrawal from the marriage. Just before his departure, she told de Vray privately: 'De Vray, I wold not mary Monsieur being intanglid in a warre. But if the King wold assist him in his actions to oppose him self against the King of Spain's greatness: she [sic] saw no cause why this mariage shuld not be made.'[143] This de Vray took to mean that Elizabeth wanted confirmation that Henry III would share the costs of Anjou's enterprise, but in reality Elizabeth was hinting at something else altogether. Although she was by now reconciled to giving some financial help to Anjou, she planned to argue, in perfect truth, that her subjects would not allow her to fund her husband's wars, and that without the marriage she would be freer to provide him with money in secret, either unofficially or as part of an Anglo-French alliance negotiated to protect their joint interests against Spain.

On 20 June 1581, therefore, Elizabeth instructed Sir Henry Cobham and John Somers, a minor but experienced diplomat, to explain to Anjou and Henry III that her subjects would never agree to make *any* contribution towards a war which had been started by her husband without the Privy Council's consent. If Henry would not promise to provide all the sums necessary to support his brother's campaign in the Netherlands, they were to tell him that she would have to retire from the marriage. They were then to suggest that in this circumstance both monarchs would do better to join together in a confederacy 'to stay the growing greatness' of the king of Spain by giving underhand aid to Don Antonio and the duke of Anjou. This league, she insisted, must not lead to open war against Spain, as this would adversely affect the commercial interests of English merchants who 'have always great quantity of goods remaining in Spain'. She also stipulated that her contribution to the covert war in the Netherlands would be only one quarter of the total costs, although she would also 'cause something to be attempted by sea' to help Don Antonio.[144]

Not surprisingly, Henry III was annoyed with Elizabeth's message: 'nothing com content heere [here] but the confirmating of the mater contracted', wrote Somers to Burghley on 11 July 1581, 'And how offensyve it is to moove any other thinge'.[145] As far as the king was concerned, the only communication he had expected to receive from Elizabeth was an official notification of her final resolution about the marriage within the allotted six weeks. Irked by her demand to be told his exact contribution to the war effort in the Netherlands, he initially prevaricated although he made clear that Elizabeth would have to pay her full share (preferably in providing men and ships) and not 'to bee a looker on'. Only when pressed hard by the English diplomats did he put forward the proposal that Elizabeth should contribute one-third of the total cost, leaving him, Anjou and the States of the Netherlands to find the rest and to supply men, artillery and munitions. Elizabeth's insistence that the aid to Anjou should be secret Henry dismissed outright: his ministers 'answered directly that the king would do nothing underhand' even if it were possible, and demanded that England come out in open war so that France would not have to face Spain alone.[146] Henry and his mother correctly assessed that Elizabeth was trying to avoid the marriage; more importantly they also suspected that she did not want to be personally 'meslée' in Anjou's enterprise in Flanders, but aimed to land the French with the total charge and sole danger of the war against Spain.[147] As a result, the king insisted that there could be no league between the two countries before the celebration of the marriage, which he demanded should take place before September 1581. A league would then take two forms: the first an open one similar to the 1572 Treaty of Blois; the second a secret treaty which would lay down the assistance to be given by each side to Anjou's campaign in the Netherlands, as well as to Don Antonio in Portugal if the English so wished. Although the treaty was to be secret, the aid was to be open.[148]

Henry III's specification of the assistance expected from Elizabeth provided her with the excuse she was seeking to escape from the marriage-contract, and in July 1581 she told Mauvissière that there was little point in pursuing the marriage any further and that Henry should now look to 'une bonne amytié' instead.[149] Immediately afterwards, Walsingham was dispatched to France, first to Anjou and then to Henry III, for the purpose of reaching some accord without the marriage.

A scrutiny of Walsingham's instructions of 22 July 1581 demonstrates that Elizabeth wanted to keep various policy-options open, but that a key element in all of them was her readiness to provide some under-cover assistance for Anjou's campaign against Spain in the Netherlands.[150] Her Secretary's primary task was to offer the duke secret subsidies: she would 'joyn with the French King to ayd Monsieur with a reasonable portion, so as it may not be so overtly, as thereby to provoke a war upon us and our realm'. If, however, this proposal did not satisfy the French, which seemed probable, and it also looked as though Anjou would be forced 'to leave his enterprize for lack of our further yielding', Walsingham was to say that the queen was prepared to enter a formal 'League and Contract' with the French king both to aid Anjou and 'also some other way to impeach the King of Spain's greatness'. If that overture failed as well, Walsingham was to continue discussing the marriage with Henry, for otherwise we shall be left alone without any aid from the King, subject to the malice of Spain, and not free from the evil neighbourhood of Scotland and lastly uncertain of the good will of the French King or his brother or of both.

A little later, Burghley explained Elizabeth's thinking behind these instructions:

if she should make a league, whereby a war might follow, she said, she had rather be at the charges of a war with the marriage, then without a marriage. But, saieth she, let Walsingham know my minde to be this, that I would gladly enter a league with the French King, onely with these conditions, that if I were invaded, he should help me, and if he were invaded, I would help him, and so to abate the King of Spain's greatness. She said she would concur with the French King to do that, by aiding of Monsieur, and also the King of Portugal underhand.[151]

In his enthusiasm for a league against Spain, however, Walsingham did not carry out the queen's instructions precisely as they were laid down in the final version. Instead of offering Anjou and Henry informal aid first and a league only as a second-string substitute for the marriage, he spoke to them of a league but said nothing about informal aid. Perhaps too he thought it would be a complete waste of time to discuss secret aid in the light of Henry III's earlier responses to Cobham and Somers.

When Walsingham met Anjou on 2 and 3 August 1581, the duke was with his army at La Fère-en-Tard on his way to besiege the fortress of Cambrai on the frontier between France and the Netherlands. Although Anjou presented an appearance of feeling very disappointed, even discontented, that the marriage was to be postponed indefinitely, there were signs that he needed money so badly that he would forgo Elizabeth's hand in return for her financial support. In a private interview with Walsingham, the vicomte de Turenne, one of Anjou's military captains, requested an immediate English loan in order to keep his army in the field. A couple of weeks later, Anjou informed his brother that he 'was contented that the treaty should go forward', whether or not it was followed by the marriage.[152]

Henry III, on the other hand, refused to negotiate a league without a marriage. As previously, he expressed the fear that Elizabeth would prove an unreliable ally, who would 'not resolutely imbarque her self into any such certain proportion of charges (as both this action of the Low-Countryes, and other charges, which in time may be found necessary) will require'.[153] This suspicion was bolstered by Elizabeth's present reluctance to commit herself either to open war against Spain or to any precise sums in support of Anjou (save the general statement that the English should contribute no more than a third of the sum paid by the French who would gain the most from Anjou's action in Flanders). At the same time, Henry was not yet convinced that the marriage was impossible and believed that the queen would return to it if she could not obtain French amity any other way. This view was no doubt confirmed when Walsingham asked for an extension of the six-week time limit on the matrimonial contract when it was due to expire on 22 August 1581.[154]

Misreading the situation, Walsingham was for a time inclined to believe that a league was negotiable if only Elizabeth would offer a specific contribution to the war-effort.[155] On the 30 August 1581, however, Catherine de Medici informed him and Cobham that the king had decided that without the marriage there could be 'no sounde Frendship' or league.[156] Shortly afterwards, at a meeting where the ambassadors had expected to discuss the league with Henry's two Secretaries of State, Walsingham found that the Frenchmen had only been commissioned to conclude the marriage.[157] Then, in an audience on 10 September with Henry himself, Walsingham learned that the king had made a 'ferme resolution' to leave aside discussions about a league until after the marriage.[158] Two days later, Henry and Catherine penned separate letters offering Elizabeth their true friendship but denying her the treaty requested by her envoy.[159]

Elizabeth was less disappointed than her minister at the failure of the negotiations. During Walsingham's mission in France, she had been annoyed with him for concentrating too heavily on the league and giving insufficient emphasis to the part of her instructions which concerned the offer of informal aid to Anjou.[160] She was coming round to the view that the provision of secret assistance to the duke on an unofficial basis was potentially less expensive and dangerous than an open league with Henry III. In by-passing the French king, she hoped to retain control of her own purse-strings and to avoid direct confrontation with Spain. Thus, when she heard the news of Anjou's surprisingly easy capture of the fortress of Cambrai on 18 August 1581 and his urgent need for money to continue the campaign against Parma, she approved immediately the first instalment of a £30,000 loan.[161] Elizabeth's loan was most welcome to Anjou, especially as it amounted to more than three times the sum provided at the same time by his brother. By late September 1581, however, the duke was running out of funds again and his army was starting to disband. With the winter drawing near and the campaigning season nearly over, he decided to pay a second visit to the queen in search of further sponsorship and not entirely without hope of marriage.[162]

Anjou landed in England on 31 October 1581 and arrived in London on 1 November where he stayed for three months. This time the visit was public and he received a warm welcome from the queen and her councillors, who were fairly sure that Elizabeth had no intention of marrying him. Elizabeth herself commissioned portraits and musical scores to commemorate his visit.[163] The news of the English court's friendly reception of Anjou soon reached France and once more encouraged Henry III to be optimistic about the marriage.[164] When he had originally heard of his brother's intended trip to England, he had given it no official backing and had adopted a cautious wait-and-see approach.[165] On 14 November 1581, however, he felt sufficiently confident that the marriage was 'si bien acheminé' that he decided to send over Pinart to assist its progress. The Secretary was instructed to express Henry's support for the marriage and his readiness to enter an offensive and defensive league immediately upon its solemnisation. He also carried with him a letter patent which contained the king's promise that as soon as the wedding was over he would enter a league on whatever terms Elizabeth required and would pay half of Anjou's costs in the Netherlands if she would pay the other half, either secretly or openly, whichever she preferred.[166]

Before Pinart's arrival on 29 November 1581, however, Elizabeth had already signed an agreement with Anjou that made no mention of the marriage but pledged her to assist him in the Netherlands. In addition, they had both issued reciprocal declarations of friendship, vowing to defend each other from their enemies.[167] The marriage issue, however, suddenly came alive again on 22 November while the court was assembled at Whitehall to celebrate the Accession Day festivities. According to several different accounts, Elizabeth declared in public that she would marry Anjou, kissed him on the mouth and gave him her ring. All those who either saw or heard of her action interpreted it as a form of espousal and took it to mean that 'a mariage was by reciprocall promise contracted betweene them'.[168] The news spread like wildfire; in Antwerp bonfires were lit in celebration, while in France, Henry announced that his brother was king of England and would soon be 'a nasty thorn' in the leg of the Spanish king.[169]

The celebrations were premature. The night after the incident some of her ladies put pressure on the queen to retract the promise, while opposition to the marriage was strongly expressed by Leicester, Walsingham, Hatton and Thomas Norton, the latter ending up in the Tower immediately afterwards for 'his overmuch and undutiful speaking touching this cause'.[170] The following day Elizabeth spoke to Anjou privately; according to one account she told him that it would be unfair to marry him, as he needed a wife who could bear him children and continue the Valois line, but she promised instead to help him in his campaign in the Netherlands.[171] Camden commented that Anjou displayed some irritation at this news, throwing aside the ring she had given him and 'taxing the Lightness of Women, and the Inconstancy of Islanders with two or three biting and smart Scoffs'; the Spanish ambassador in contrast reported that the duke accepted her decision 'very mildly'.[172] No doubt Anjou was mollified by Elizabeth's promises of a further subsidy.

What did this curious episode mean? Camden claimed that Elizabeth was carried away by 'the Force of modest Love in the midst of amorous Discourse' on the 22nd and was then immediately brought back to cold reality by her councillors and ladies – an interpretation which is hard to take seriously. The Spanish ambassador, on the other hand believed that her performance had been a deliberate device to encourage Anjou to leave England quickly:

> since his arrival he [Anjou] was pressing her [the queen] every day more urgently for a reply [concerning the marriage], without which he declared he would not leave the country, she rather prefers to let it appear that the failure of the negotiations is owing to the country and not to herself, as it is important for her to keep him attached to her, in order to counterbalance his brother, and prevent anything being arranged to her prejudice.[173]

According to this view Elizabeth was expecting and indeed counting upon the negative reaction of her court in order to be rid of the duke who had overstayed his welcome. Although more in keeping with Elizabeth's character, this explanation betrays an ignorance of the exact political situation. Re-opening the matrimonial issue just when Pinart was expected to arrive with some new offer from Henry III was far more likely to prolong discussions on the marriage than send Anjou on his way. Furthermore, despite his flattering attentions to the queen, Anjou's behaviour during his stay suggests that he was more interested in obtaining the promise of a loan than a marriage.

Another possible explanation for Elizabeth's display on November 22nd is suggested by Holt; that it was just 'a ruse, in all probability designed to pressure Henry III into the treaty she had long desired'.[174] It is difficult to see, however, how these antics could have either pressurised or lured Henry into a treaty; after all Elizabeth retracted her promise within a day. If she had been merely play-acting, why did she not warn her councillors in advance and so avoid a political storm and why was she so angry with Norton that he ended up in the Tower? All in all, it seems most likely that Elizabeth meant the exchange of rings before witnesses to stand for an espousal but had to withdraw because of renewed opposition at court.

As already noted, when Walsingham was negotiating a league with the French court Elizabeth had not ruled out marriage with the duke; indeed she often said that there would be no advantage from a league without marriage if she were still to be expected to contribute a substantial proportion of Anjou's expenses in the Low Countries. Besides, Henry III had made it perfectly clear that he would not agree to a league without marriage. Elizabeth was therefore left with the choice of either financing Anjou informally and possibly alone, or concluding the marriage. Judging by the speed with which Anjou had spent her recent 'loan' and come back for more, it appeared that the former policy would prove more expensive than had originally been thought. The marriage, moreover, had considerable advantages: in particular Anjou had assured Elizabeth that the king would make a major contribution to his expenses and defend her against attack from Spain once it was concluded. Furthermore, knowing that Pinart had set out for England, Elizabeth might well have thought that he carried with him an improved offer from the king concerning his financial contribution to Anjou after the marriage.[175]

Elizabeth could have been in no doubt that any attempt to call parliament to ratify the matrimonial contract would have ignited hostile public opinion. There was some hope, though, that Henry III and Anjou would be satisfied with an espousal as a measure of her commitment and sincerity; after all Henry himself had promised Cobham that as soon 'as the mariage shalbe done, *or that Monsieur shall go into England to be maryed*, the King will put his army together with Monsieur's into the feeld'.[176] Elizabeth might also have calculated that few objections would be raised at home to an espousal. During the duke's visit there had been no revival of the popular agitation against him nor any evidence of political factionalism. Leicester was courting Anjou assiduously, while Walsingham viewed him favourably as the 'protector of Cambrai' and a prince 'that yieldeth to a toleration of religion'.[177] Elizabeth might have judged, therefore, that the drama of 22 November 1581 would bounce her councillors into acceptance of the espousal, especially if there was no prospect of a wedding ceremony to follow but only of an Anglo-French league. If this were indeed her thinking Elizabeth badly miscalculated; opposition to the match on religious grounds was still so strong, that she was compelled to retreat the following day.

With the marriage route obviously blocked, Elizabeth returned to the position which she had adopted in July 1581 and made unacceptable demands to Henry III; Pinart was told that the king would have to pay all Anjou's costs before she could assent to the marriage – a condition which he had already rejected. This time, however, she made no further comments about a league.[178] Instead, she made independent arrangements to help Anjou financially. In December 1581 she agreed to provide him with two 'loans' of £30,000 each, the first to be paid within a fortnight of his departure from England and the second to be handed over two months afterwards.[179] Thus within the course of one year, 1581–2, Elizabeth delivered a total of £70,000 to Anjou, a sum which amounted to more than one-quarter of her regular annual income.

For the remainder of his visit in England, Anjou's interest lay only with the campaign in the Netherlands. Hence he drew closer to Leicester, who favoured war but opposed the marriage, and correspondingly became alienated from Sussex, his long-time supporter, who fervently objected to a war against Spain.[180] At last on 1 February 1582 Anjou left London for the Netherlands as a protégé of the queen. She accompanied him as far as Canterbury, and a delegation of some forty or so English gentlemen and nobility, including Lords Hunsdon and Howard, the Vice-Admiral, the earl of Leicester and Philip Sidney, attended him on his way to Antwerp.[181] They were present at his inauguration as ruler of the Netherlands provinces (with the exception of Holland and Zealand and the provinces reconquered by Parma) and his magnificent coronation as duke of Brabant, thereby signifying Elizabeth's approval of the States' formal act of rebellion and French sovereignty over most of the Low Countries. Elizabeth's foreign policy had a moved a long way from its position in 1578.

Elizabeth's matrimonial and foreign policies during the years 1578 to 1581 have earned much criticism from historians.[182] The inconsistencies and vacillations are so striking. In July 1578 the queen was discussing marriage with Anjou to prevent his intervention in the Revolt of the Netherlands; in August of the following year she was thinking of financing his enterprise after the marriage took place; and in August 1581 she actually sent him a loan to keep an army in the field against Parma, although no prospect of marriage was in sight. In 1578 she feared that Henry III would back his brother's venture, whereas in 1581 her ambassador and envoys were trying to persuade him to bear its major cost. During Walsingham's two missions abroad, to the Netherlands in the summer of 1578 and to France in the summer of 1581, his instructions included a range of policy-options and no-one seemed to be certain exactly what were Elizabeth's political objectives; Conyers Read even suggested that in August 1581 Elizabeth herself did not know.[183] Furthermore, while the matrimonial negotiations were drifting on, Elizabeth was failing to take decisive action elsewhere; her stock with William of Orange was falling as she allowed Parma to regain control over Artois and Hainaut and to capture the towns of Mechelin, Maastricht, Kortrijk and Breda; she did nothing effective to stop the French Catholic D'Aubigny gaining ascendance over James VI in Scotland; and until an agreement had been reached with the French she refused to go ahead with the plan put forward in the summer of 1580 to use the Azores as a privateering base from which to attack Spanish shipping. Only when the negotiations for a league and a marriage were over at the end of 1581, did Elizabeth return to a policy of active, though indirect, intervention beginning with the sponsorship of Anjou in the Netherlands.

Elizabeth's stumblings and tergiversations, however, did not signify a total loss of direction, but rather reflected the difficulties in reorienting policy during a period of uncertainty and change. Throughout these years the dominant European problem was the Revolt of the Netherlands with its dual threat of an unconditional victory for Spain and expansionist opportunities for the French. Elizabeth and all her councillors recognised the truth of Sussex's dictum that England's security depended on the freedom of the Netherlands from both Spanish military rule and French aggrandisement.[184] The difficulty lay in establishing ways to prevent both these occurrences. For Walsingham and Leicester, the only sensible course was for the queen to join forces with William of Orange. Even if she refused the sovereignty of the States, she should, they believed, send over troops, or at the very least substantial sums of money to finance an army, in order to prevent both a Spanish conquest of the provinces and French intervention. With good reason Elizabeth harboured doubts about this policy; it would devour fearsome sums of money just when she was having to devote considerable resources to Ireland; the disunited States were likely to prove unreliable allies and, besides, were rebels against their king; and, most dangerous of all, direct aid to the States was likely to lead her into an open war against Spain which would damage trade and leave her exposed to military defeat and invasion. This was, of course, largely what happened when Elizabeth finally embarked upon a policy of direct intervention in 1584.

Instead, Elizabeth decided upon a matrimonial alliance with France. Alarmed at the growing strength of Philip II in 1579, she saw the benefits of a French alliance to 'impeach' his power, safeguard the States and protect her realm; but to her mind it was necessary for two reasons to conclude a *matrimonial* alliance and not just a league. First, Anjou was acting as a free agent, independent of his brother Henry III, and the only possibility for controlling him personally was by accepting his hand in marriage. Initially, she hoped that marriage to a queen would satisfy his restless ambition and lead him to hold back from entry into the Netherlands Revolt, and that after the wedding they could use their joint diplomatic muscle to force Philip II into a negotiated settlement. During Anjou's visit, however, she realised that marriage or no marriage, the duke was bent on military glory. Furthermore, after the failure of peace talks between representatives of Spain and the States at the end of 1579, it had also become obvious that Philip II would never concede guarantees for the liberties of the provinces or for any kind of religious toleration.[185] In these circumstances, French intervention in the Netherlands seemed a necessary evil to prevent Parma's relentless progress towards reconquest. Once Elizabeth decided to use the duke to do the fighting on her behalf in the Netherlands, she had to ensure that he did not pursue his own wayward path which would harm her interests. Mistakenly, she believed that his desire for the marriage made him dependent on her good-will and thus malleable.

Second, from 1579 onwards Elizabeth considered that only a matrimonial alliance with France would provide her with security against Philip II. It was impossible to forget that Henry III had been a close friend of the Guises and had recently taken up arms against the Huguenots. Consequently it was difficult to feel confident that without a marriage to his brother, he would come to her defence or even remain neutral if a Catholic league was formed against her. Only a matrimonial treaty, claimed Burghley and Sussex, 'wyll by all lykelyhod staye the French Kyng and that Realme from attemptyng eny thing that may be prejudycyall to her Majestie and her husband his brother'. Elizabeth probably also hoped that her marriage to Anjou would end French intrigues in Scotland, for Burghley and Sussex both advised her that 'The suspyton and perrell of all ill practyses abrode and at home that may come by Fraunce for popery or competytyen wyll by this marryage be taken awaye.' Although there was the danger that Henry would prove an ineffective ally because of France's civil wars, the supporters of the match held out the hope that the marriage of Anjou to a Protestant could bring internal peace to France. In the words of Burghley:

> The Queen's Majestie & her husband by means of this partye shall be habell to assuer the Protestantes in Fraunce from massacre & to assuer the King of ther servyce, wherby the relygyon ther shall not be subverted and that realme by this meanes shall contynewe in crystyen peace.[186]

These advantages of an Anglo-French dynastic alliance seemed so compelling that Elizabeth still hankered after the policy of marriage, even after her Council had effectively vetoed it. Although she opened talks for an ordinary alliance with Henry III in 1580 and 1581, she still had her doubts about its value. Evidently, she feared that an Anglo-French league would commit her to financing a war in the Netherlands without a corresponding guarantee of French military help if she were attacked directly by Spain. She was also concerned that the French monarchy might absorb any territorial gains made by Anjou in the Netherlands, especially if the duke eventually became king, which was looking increasingly likely. It was for these reasons that Elizabeth was indecisive in the negotiations for a French alliance in 1580 and 1581, and hovered uncertainly over the available options: the marriage, an alliance without marriage, and the role of Anjou's unofficial paymaster. It was only when the first two policies were completely ruled out that she fully embraced the third in late 1581.

Royal policy therefore did have an underlying coherence and rationale which is not always immediately evident. For all that, it was still ill-conceived and ill-executed. In reality, under the influence of Sussex and Burghley, Elizabeth overestimated the benefits of a matrimonial alliance. With so little control over the Guise family, Henry III would have been powerless to secure the cessation of their support for Mary Stuart or the recall of D'Aubigny from Scotland. In addition had there been a full-scale Spanish invasion of England or Ireland in the early 1580s Henry would hardly have had the means to come to Elizabeth's defence, even if the will had been there. In these circumstances a league, without the marriage, which aimed at limited offensive action in the Netherlands and on the high seas, would have been more appropriate and potentially beneficial.

Elizabeth, moreover, seriously overestimated her control over Anjou, who ignored her wishes, took actions without informing her beforehand, as he had promised, and took the military initiative in the Netherlands, while expecting her to pick up the bill. Furthermore, the duke was a poor choice of military commander; his military experience in the French Civil Wars was very limited, while his relationships with his brother and the Huguenots had shown him to be headstrong, double-dealing and disruptive. He began his 1578 campaign in the Netherlands recklessly with an insubstantial army and insufficient resources. During the three years between his occupation of Mons and his second visit to England, his only significant military achievement was the capture of Cambrai, and that he took without a shot being fired, since the Spanish troops retreated as the French forces advanced. Although warned time and again about Anjou's personal shortcomings, Elizabeth chose to disregard them – as it proved to her cost. Anjou's expedition to the Netherlands was catastrophic. He proved unable to build up a working relationship with the States, lost most of his troops in January 1583 in an abortive attempt to capture Antwerp (which was not even held by the Spanish), and returned home ignominiously to France the following June.

In addition, Elizabeth gravely underestimated the domestic opposition to the match. Although signs of it were apparent in the spring of 1579 when the preachers took to their pulpits, she was totally unprepared for the wave of agitation in the following late summer and autumn, and had taken no steps to mobilise a propaganda campaign of her own to counter the opposition. It has been suggested that her 'tone-deafness to religious questions' prevented her from anticipating and understanding the 'deep-rooted Protestant ideology, characterized by an almost reflexive anti-Popery', which caused the unrest.[187] This may be true, but what is more important is that Elizabeth was lulled into miscalculation by her councillors. During the spring, their expressions of hostility to the match had been fairly muted, while the supporters of the match had been in the majority in the council debates. The extent and strength of conciliar opposition in October 1579, therefore, took Burghley as well as Elizabeth by surprise.

Finally, Elizabeth's negotiations with Henry III for an alliance were badly handled. In late 1580, she failed to give the right signals to his ambassador in England and led Mauvissière to conclude that she was still intent on a policy of marriage when she was actually seeking to set up a league. At the same time, she left Cobham in France without sufficient instructions or powers to negotiate the precise terms of an alliance just when Henry was resigned to the idea of a league without marriage. Somers's mission to Henry in July 1581 was equally inept. Her attempt to evade the marriage solely on the grounds of her subjects' unwillingness to pay the cost of his expedition to Flanders was a flimsy excuse bound to encourage doubts in Henry's mind about Elizabeth's trustworthiness and value as an ally. Similarly, her bald refusal to become involved in an open war with Spain confirmed his suspicions that she planned to look on while France took all the risks in the Netherlands' war. Elizabeth's ambivalence towards France largely explains these weaknesses in her diplomacy, but so does her usual reluctance to spend money. Their effect was to cut off the policy-option of a French alliance and leave her isolated against Spain.

Rather than securing protection against Philip II, the Anjou matrimonial project further destabilised Elizabeth's uneasy relations with Spain. From 1579 onwards Philip's ambassadors at the French and English courts regularly passed on to him their suspicions that the marriage was merely a cover for an Anglo-French league against Spain. On 6 August 1579, Juan de Vargas Mexia notified Philip that it was generally believed in Paris that the marriage would not take place and that the negotiations all dealt with Flanders and Portugal; then on 6 January 1580 he advised the king that the marriage project had only one aim: for Anjou to take Flanders with English help.[188] Similarly, on 11 June 1580 Don Bernadino de Mendoza, the ambassador in London, described the matrimonial negotiations as a pretext for making a revolution in the Netherlands and, if possible, impeding the conquest of Portugal; and on 6 April 1581 he informed Philip that the purpose of the French embassy due to be welcomed at the English court was the conclusion of a league.[189] The prospect of Elizabeth giving aid to his rebels greatly alarmed Philip who was convinced that England's neutrality was vital for Spanish interests. On 12 February 1582, barely two weeks after Anjou had left England for Antwerp with a train of English nobles, Philip instructed de Mendoza to warn Elizabeth of the dangers she faced if she antagonised him by intervening in Portugal or the Netherlands.[190] The attendance of her nobles at Anjou's investiture was a provocation Philip and de Mendoza were not to forget. This last phase of the Anjou matrimonial negotiations, therefore, did nothing to halt Parma's advance in the Netherlands, but much to bring England closer to the confrontation with Spain so much dreaded by Elizabeth and the supporters of the match.

8

THE UNDERLYING DEBATE

During the first half of Elizabeth's reign politicians and preachers engaged in lengthy debate on the subject of the queen's marriage. The issues raised were in part pragmatic, concerning for example the perils of child-birth for a middle-aged queen, the expense of maintaining a consort's household and the practical problems arising from marriage to a foreign king. But they were also theoretical, centring on questions with far-reaching theological implications: was marriage a higher state than celibacy? were marriages between Protestants and Catholics against the word of God? was the Mass an evil which could never be sanctioned in a godly common-wealth? To obtain guidance on all these issues Elizabethans automatically turned to the authority of the Bible, which contained a variety of teachings or texts open to conflicting interpretations. In addition, with the benefit of a humanist education behind them, they looked to history to provide examples of the effects of foreign or mixed marriages which they then used to substantiate their arguments. During the years 1570–75 discussions tended to be confined to the Council chamber; usually, however, there was wider public involvement in the debate as councillors and other interested parties encouraged pamphlets and sermons to be written in support of their own particular line.

Few Elizabethans disputed that marriage was not only politically desirable for a reigning monarch but also pleasing in the eyes of God. None the less, because of Elizabeth's continuing rejection of her many suitors as well as her public statements expressing a preference for a life of celibacy, a number of works exhorting the queen to take a husband included detailed theological justifications for matrimony. These drew on the arguments of Protestant reformers who had attacked the practice of clerical celibacy in the Roman Catholic Church as well as the mediaeval veneration of voluntary chastity as the highest ideal of Christian life for the laity.

As Elizabethans saw it, the Catholic case for celibacy had largely rested both on the example of Christ and the Apostles, and on Pauline teachings in the New Testament. For example, in preparatory notes for his

'Discourse on the Queen's Marriage' Sir Thomas Smith included in the list of arguments to be used by Spitewed in presenting the case for a life of chastity:

> Virginitie [is] above matrimonie, because followed by Christ
> Preferred by St Paul, n. [sic] "The virgin hath care to please God, &c"
> John Baptist, and the rest of the Apostles, [were] virgines.
> Virginitie [was] kept in the primitive church as best pleasing to God.
> Virginitie, because it is so hard to be kept, is more laudable in princes.[1]

The importance of Pauline teachings in extolling celibacy and commending marriage only for the weak who were susceptible to fornication was brought out strongly in the *Play of Patient Grissell*, where the main protagonist, Prince Gautier initially rejected marriage on the grounds that:

> ... single life preferred is, in sacred scripture true
> But happie are the married sort which live in perfit love
> Twice happier are the single ones, S. Paull doth plainly prove
> For such as leade a virgin's life, and sinfull lust expell
> In heaven's above the ethrall skies with Christ ther lord shal dwel.[2]

In attacking clerical celibacy, some Protestant reformers on the Continent and in England had challenged these teachings, and instead emphasised the value and sanctity of married life for all individuals. 'Christ aloweth mariage in all men and in all tymes', wrote John Bale in 1543. The marriage bed, claimed John Poynet in 1556, was 'an undefiled bed/ a pure/ a clean/ and an unspotted bede/ as a spirituall manne ... may lie in'.[3] Other Protestants, however, continued to view marriage as a necessary evil, a remedy against the sin of fornication; thus Thomas Becon's *Booke of Matrimonie* of 1560 pronounced chastity to be 'the greate and singulare benefite of God (whiche is so rare a gifte, that it chaunceth to fewe) ... the Wyseman sayth: I knowe, that I can not lyve chaste, except God geveth me the gifte.'[4] This sort of reasoning, however, was inappropriate to set before Elizabeth; there was always the danger that she might seek to emulate the 'fewe' special individuals who were free from sexual temptation and thus on a higher spiritual plane. The writers who were urging the queen to marry, therefore, used different lines of Protestant argument.

First, they attempted to persuade Elizabeth that the Scriptures did not teach that celibacy was the highest estate to which princes and pastors should aspire. Thus, to counter the examples of the holy celibate figures in the Gospels, they pointed to the Patriarchs of the Old Testament who had married and sired children: 'Abraham', asserted Smith was 'as holye in knowing Sara, as Elias in his virginitie'.[5] At the same time, Smith maintained that in the key Pauline text (I Corinthians, 7), 'It *were* good for a man not to touche a woman', St Paul had not in fact been lauding chastity and condemning as sinful all sexual relations, even those which took place within the confines of holy matrimony. On the contrary, St Paul had merely been saying that marriage would inevitably bring earthly toils and difficulties because of the fallen state of humankind: 'Paul prayseth virginitie not for itself, but in itself, as having lesse trowble.' [6] This interpretation followed closely that of the commentator on this text in the *Geneva Bible* of 1560 who in the marginalia added the explanation: 'or *expedient* because mariage through man's corruption, and not by God's institution bringeth cares and troubles.'[7]

Next, writers who were exhorting Elizabeth to marry found scriptural authority for the holiness of marriage in God's very first commandment given to humans in Genesis: 'Bringe forthe frute and multiplie.' Marriage and procreation were therefore, they claimed, divine orders which Elizabeth as a Christian had to obey: 'You which are by grace a christen women shoulde covette issue in mariage', went the 1566 petition entitled 'The Common Cry of Englishmen'.[8] For further evidence of the sanctity of procreation the author of this petition turned to God's covenant with Abraham, also in Genesis: 'Beholde I *make* my covenant with thee and thou shalt be a father of manie nacions.'[9] As he and others pointed out, the words of this covenant were echoed throughout the Old Testament where examples proliferated of children who were born as a mark of divine favour and a special gift to holy parents or good princes: 'Issue is a blessing of God to good princes, as to David and John; but the wante thereof a token of disfavour, as in Saul, Jeroboam, Achab', noted Smith.[10]

As procreation was so important to humankind, women were thought to be biologically programmed for marriage and childbirth, although the danger of death from the latter was also well appreciated. Sir Thomas Smith, therefore, expressed confidence that childbirth would bring the queen an improvement in her physical health: 'I think that bringing forth of children doth not only preserve women from many diseases, and other inconveniences, but it doth also clear their bodies, amend the colour, prolong their youth.'[11] Burghley agreed, and some years later in 1579 opined that marriage, with or without childbirth, would protect the queen from the illnesses and low spirits that commonly afflicted spinsters:

> it may be by good reasons maintained that by forbearing from marriage her Majesty's own person shall daily be subject to such dolours and infirmities as all physicians do usually impute to womankind for lack of marriage, and specially to such women as have their bodies apt to conceive and procreate children. And to this end were to be remembered the likelihood of her Majesty's pains in her cheek and face to come only of lack of the use of marriage'.[12]

No-one was in any doubt that the divine injunction on marriage and procreation applied more rigorously to princes because of their urgent need for heirs. Children born to all men and women of rank and property, wrote Lord Henry Howard in 1580, were 'accounted one of the greatest blessings that can be granted by God to any family for the continual establishing of their private patrimonies', but those born to princes were 'the most wished benefit, the highest treasure'.[13] According to the 'Common Cry', Elizabeth had a duty to bear children and hand down 'the porcon geven of God to you and yours as it was geven to yor progenitors for you'.[14] Scripture and history again came to the aid of these polemicists: the many examples of disputed successions in the stories of ancient Israel, classical Rome and mediaeval England and Europe, which arose from the 'want of a lineal and natural successor in the prince's governing', painted a terrible warning of the dangers to England and the Protestant Church if the royal house of Tudor died in Elizabeth's person.[15]

Though procreation was identified by all writers as the most important purpose of a royal marriage it was not the only one. Just as Protestant preachers emphasised the value of marriage as a comfort and help to ordinary couples, so those who urged Elizabeth to wed explained that marriage could be a 'solace' and 'comfort' to the queen. Statesmen, therefore, not only focused on the queen's duty to marry, but also talked about the personal 'benefits' which she would gain from married life.[16] For this reason, they also favoured her choosing a man who pleased her. The earl of Sussex even expressed the view that affection for a marriage partner might well increase the likelihood of conception; writing in support of the Dudley match in 1560, he suggested that if Elizabeth was allowed 'to follow so much her own affection as by the looking upon him, whom she shuld chuse, *omnes sensus titillarentur* which shall be the nearest wayes with the helpe of God to bring us a blessed Prince'.[17]

Consideration of the value of a companionable married life informed much of the debate over whether Elizabeth should wed an Englishman or a foreigner. Thus, in the opinion of Sir Thomas Smith, the queen would be likely to take more 'comfort, pleasure and joy' from an English husband.[18] Disagreeing strongly some twenty years later, Lord Henry Howard contended that only marriage to a foreign prince of equal status would provide the queen with the 'friendship' expected in a marriage:

> it is of necessity requisite and behooveful that in the alliance of matrimony (which both by the laws of God and all civil constitutions is accounted one of the strictest and most indissoluble bonds of amity) there should be found no dissimilitude, or at the least, antipathy in the qualities of the mind, much less in the estates, of the persons contracting matrimony. For what proportion is there between a poor and rich man in power, an ox and an ass in burden, the brazen pot and the earthern pitcher in force? And shall Her Majesty be able to make choice of any within her realm between

whom and her excellency there shall not be seen a greater dissimilitude than is before spoken of? Are the virtues of her mind to be equaled by any, or is the force and power of her state to be answered by whomsoever her inferior subject?[19]

Although in reality, both writers had more on their minds than the personal happiness of the queen, the lip-service paid to the importance of friendship, pleasure and comfort in a marriage is possibly a sign of the hold that this expectation of married life had on contemporary thinking.

Even more contentious than the nationality of the queen's husband was the question of his religion. This issue was first debated during the Archduke Charles negotiations and further discussed during the French matrimonial projects of 1571 and 1578–81. Throughout this time few doubted that Elizabeth's marriage to a Roman Catholic prince who was permitted access to a Mass within his own household would lead to serious political and legal problems. As already shown in earlier chapters, amongst the political difficulties identified by Elizabeth and her councillors were the dangers that conflict might arise between Protestants and Catholics within England, that the precedent of allowing exceptions to the law would encourage Catholic disobedience to the religious statutes of the realm, and that the royal consort might seek to honour God by converting the queen and restoring England to the obedience of Rome. The legal difficulties were no less problematic. Elizabeth's husband would be the joint Supreme Governor of the Church of England and could therefore hardly practise a religion different from the one established by statute. If his duty was to uphold the established religion, how could he stand apart from the Church and disobey the law by hearing a private Mass? It was mainly for this reason that Elizabeth was unwilling to use her dispensing power on behalf of any potential husband.[20]

While even the supporters of a Catholic husband for Elizabeth admitted the reality of these difficulties, they believed that the dangers to religion and the state had been grossly exaggerated by the opponents of the proposed matches with the Archduke Charles and the Valois princes. In particular, they argued that there was no need for anyone to fear that 'the doctrine of the ghospell shoulde be shadid or eclpsid in this lande' by a Catholic marriage. As one anonymous petitioner explained to the queen at the time of the Francis of Anjou match:

he [the duke] shall not have authority nor powre to alter religion now used and established, he brings no preachers to perswade, and violently to do it wher shallbe his force? Example shall do no hurt, since his chappell dore shall be shutt.[21]

In addition, the supporters of these matches challenged the assumption that Elizabeth might be converted to Catholicism through the influence of her husband. Inverting the contention that women as the weaker vessel were both more susceptible to sin than men and bound to follow their husband even into error, one anonymous writer argued that Protestantism was safe in the queen's hands precisely because she was the daughter of Eve:

> I will deliver by diligent observation, that where the wife is a sister, there is less peril of her revolt, and more hope of the husband's conversion than the contrary. For as every wife retaineth still a natural kind of *rhetoric* and insinuation, from her mother Eve, towards her husband; so every husband abideth firm in the old credulity of his father Adam towards his wife.[22]

Historical examples to support this contention could be found in the conversion to Christianity of the Emperor Constantine by his mother Helena and of King Clovis I of France by his wife Clotilda; a more recent case cited was the king of Navarre's conversion to Protestantism through the influence of his wife Jeanne d'Albret.[23]

This kind of subtle reasoning, however, was not popular and other writers on the subject tended to argue that Protestantism was secure in England because of Elizabeth's resolute faith. Whatever women might do in general, explained Archbishop Parker in 1567 when writing in favour of the Archduke Charles matrimonial project, the queen herself would hardly convert to Catholicism. Had she not amply demonstrated her fidelity to Protestantism during the reign of her sister, when she 'would not yeald to accompany the Queen's Majesty in the place wher the masse was said' until she was persuaded to attend 'by such as were not without zeale of true religeone ... for the preservacon of her lyfe'?[24] Yet, even in the remote circumstance of Elizabeth's seduction into error by her husband, Parker went on, a change in religion within England could only take place with the 'free consent of the three estates'. Thus, 'it is to be well considered with what difficultie it shuld be to compase a generall change of Religeon in this Realme (beinge nowe setled therin by lawe)', since parliament would never agree to see a return to the burnings and exiles which accompanied the restoration of Roman Catholicism in Mary I's reign; wise men were 'now well taughte by experience deerly boughte to make it a harder matter at this day to put the Realme in the hands of the papistes'.[25]

In fact, those who supported a Catholic marriage for the queen declared their conviction that Elizabeth's consort would in time convert to Protestantism. Quoting from St Paul: 'how can a man believe unless he heard?', they argued that after the queen's husband had attended English church services for some time and received instruction in the Protestant religion, he would lose his blind belief in popery. In their view, experience showed that 'whersoever the Papistes permitted it [the Protestant Church]

200

to have place, it did encrease and diminishe the other, and contrary wher the papistycall was tollerated it never increased but diminished'.[26] Although Francis of Anjou's detractors reasoned that his conversion was nigh impossible since he was heir to the throne of France and besides 'from his cradle he hath been bredd and nourished up in papistrie', supporters of the match claimed otherwise.[27] Quoting the teachings of Peter Martyr (the Protestant reformer who had preached in England during part of the reign of Edward VI) one tract in favour of the match pronounced: 'it is not lawfull to dispaire of any man, for he that is to day an Atheist, to morrow perhapps shall not be so.'[28]

In all the debates on the queen's marriage, both sides took it for granted that in time one of the partners would convert to the other's religion. There was a general consensus that a marriage where husband and wife followed different faiths and worshipped in different ways was in the long term untenable. As Elizabeth herself wrote to the Emperor Maximilian in April 1566:

> I confide so greatly in Your Majesty's discernment that I do not think it necessary to enumerate the thousand and one difficulties which would result if husband and wife held different conscientious views. What worse lot could befall a realm than division into two parties, one championing him and the other espousing her cause. That would be like a span of horses with various paces which could never pull together. What should be one will working in harmony would then be converted into a mutual hate.[29]

Fearing the power of idolatry and the weaknesses of women, opponents of Elizabeth's marriage to a Catholic prince were convinced that Elizabeth would eventually be drawn into Catholicism. By contrast the supporters of a Catholic match were optimistic in their belief that truth would triumph over ignorance and error.

The debate on religious intermarriage raised more than just political and legal issues. The question of whether or not it was a sin for a Protestant to marry a Papist was thought to be still more important. Even if it could be proved that the queen's marriage to a Catholic prince would not endanger true religion at home, but on the contrary would bring the realm allies against foreign enemies, the opponents of religious intermarriage were convinced that 'we muste not do evell that good may come thereof.'[30]

Those Protestants who opposed marriages between partners of different faiths tended to appeal to the authority of texts from the Old Testament of the Bible. For them, the elect nation of England was bound to obey God's laws on intermarriage which were laid down in the Mosaic code for the Chosen People of Israel. At the same time, they saw in the history of the patriarchs and Israelites, who had struggled to uphold God's covenant while surrounded and often threatened by idolatrous nations, a parallel for their own experiences; like them, England, 'a region purged from idolatry, a kingdom of light, confessing Christ and serving the living God', was struggling for its survival against its idolatrous neighbours.[31] Thus, God's will for English Protestants, they believed, could be found in the lessons of the Old Testament.

The most important sources for the prohibition of mixed marriages were the divine injunctions in the Mosaic law which unambiguously demanded the separation of the Israelites from heathens and idolaters. Thus, in the Genevan Bible text of Exodus 34 God told Moses: 'Take hede to thy self, that thou make no compact with the inhabitants of the land whither thou goest, lest thei be the cause of ruine among you.' In the same chapter God specifically warned against Israelite sons taking the daughters of the Canaanites in marriage, lest 'their daughters go a whoring after their gods, and make thy sonnes go a whoring after their gods.' Similarly, Deuteronomy 7 stated unambiguously: 'Nether shalt thou make mariages with them. . . . For they wil cause thy sonne to turne away from me and to serve other gods: then wil the wrath of the Lord waxe hote against you, and destroy thee sodenly.'[32]

Further force to these divine injunctions was provided through the example of the patriarchs, Abraham and Isaac, 'those good men of whom we love to be esteemed the children and followers'. Their example was thought especially important because they had followed the spirit of the Mosaic code on mixed marriages even before God's law had been promulgated. Neither Abraham nor Isaac would allow their favoured sons to wed the 'daughters of Canaan', but made them marry 'with their own kind', even though such unions involved long journeys back to the lands whence they originally came.[33] The words of Jacob's sons, when their sister was sought as a wife by a heathen prince, seemed to follow the same principle: 'we cannot do this thing, to give our sister to one that is uncircumcised'.[34] Opponents of mixed marriages also pointed to the re-statement of the Mosaic Law in the later books of the Old Testament as evidence of its importance. In the Book of Ezra, after the children of Israel had intermarried with their heathen neighbours and followed their 'abominations', the prophet Ezra prayed for God's forgiveness and made the men put aside their 'strange wives' and children.[35] Similarly, in the Book of Tobit in the Apocrypha, Tobit told his son Tobias: 'Beware of all whoredome, my sonne, and chiefly take a wife of the sede of thy fathers, and take not a strange woman to wife, which is not of thy father's stocke.'

The opponents of a Catholic marriage for Elizabeth equated contemporary Papists with these heathens or Canaanites of Biblical times and refused to accept the view put forward by some of the supporters of the 1579 Anjou match that the Mosaic injunctions did not apply to marriages between Christians who confessed the same God. If that were the case, reasoned John Stubbs, 'then might we intermarry with Turks, Jews, Muscovites, and divers other paynims'. As far as Stubbs was concerned, Papists differed so greatly in fundamental doctrine from Protestants that 'it will be hard to make them of one faithful household with us'.[36] Papists like heathens were idolatrous in their worship of images and their veneration of the host in the Mass. This was particularly relevant because the main reason given in the Old Testament for the condemnation of intermarriage was that it would lead those who followed the true religion to fall into idolatry. No Biblical figures, believed Stubbs, had been immune from this propensity to sin; thus, when Solomon, the wisest of kings, took heathen women to bed, 'even him did outlandish women cause to sin', behaviour for which he was roundly criticised by the prophet Nehemiah in a later book of the Old Testament.[37] If Solomon, 'a peerless king beloved of God', did so 'foully foul by joining himself in marriage with idolatrous women', what hope was there by implication for Elizabeth?

According to this view, the marriage of Elizabeth to a Catholic was thus clearly unlawful and sinful; such a transgression 'in a Gospel-like land where the law of God is preached' could only result in divine retribution. 'God will not indure any tollerating, temporising or qualyfying for any respect derogatory to his honour', warned Sir Walter Mildmay; 'all blessing is taken away and plague followeth' prophesied Stubbs.[38] Once again, the opponents of a Catholic match dredged up cases in the Old Testament to prove this point, but during the Francis of Anjou negotiations they found additional and compelling evidence closer at hand. The 1572 Massacre of St Bartholomew, which followed the wedding of the Huguenot Henry of Navarre and Catholic Marguerite de Valois, was in their eyes not only the work of wicked Papists but also the will of God and a 'punishment of such wicked willing matches between Christian true Jews and Popish bastard Israelites'.[39]

The counter arguments of those who supported religious intermarriage rested on a mixture of theological principle and alternative Biblical examples. First, the supporters of a Catholic marriage rejected the 'puritan hermeneutics' of writers like Stubbs. Thus, one anonymous tract claimed in 1579 that the Protestants bore no resemblance to the Israelites: 'I am sure yf we should call an Israelite to be umpyre, he will soone conclude both protestant and papist to be as impure as the Chananite, and neither of them to be an Israelite.' In the same way, its author continued, it was not legitimate to compare the Papists to the heathens or Canaanites of the Old Testament. Indeed, he insisted, Protestants and Papists had more in common with each other than either had with the Israelites or Canaanites, as both 'sects' of Christians believed in the Trinity and accepted the New Testament. Just because Papists revered the Mass, he argued, it did not mean that they were idolaters who should be shunned. In the words of another writer who had taken up his pen to point out the 'errors' in Stubbs, 'The Lutherans have ther masse yet none hetherto hathe holden so monstruouse opinion as that the Swinglians [Zwinglians] might not marye with them'; otherwise, he claimed, objections would have been raised when Duke Casimir of the Palatinate wedded the daughter of the duke of Saxony; 'nether was this doctryne hatched when the Kinge of Swedon a Lutheran soughte to match in Englande'.[40]

In the eyes of writers who supported the Archduke and Anjou matches, therefore, the Mosaic Law prohibiting marriage to heathens was deemed irrelevant to the case of intermarriage between Christians: 'that case is not like this, for the papiste and protestant worshippe one and the same godd and differ only in forme and manner.'[41] For them, intermarriage between Christians rather resembled unions between Pharisees and Sadducees or even those between the 'pure Israelite' and 'the idolatrous Israelite'. Such marriages were nowhere forbidden in the Bible. On the contrary, pointed out one writer, the Patriarch Jacob had shown no hesitation in marrying Leah and Rachel who stole away their father's household gods when leaving with their husband for the land of Israel: 'Yf Jacob hade bene so precise as some are in our dayes', he argued, he would not have taken to wife such idolaters.[42] Yet even when the Israelites chose partners from the heathen nations, their marriages were not always accursed nor did they inevitably lead to the sin of idolatry, claimed the defenders of intermarriage. As proof of the validity of such marriages these writers were able to produce numerous examples of Old Testament heroes and heroines who had married heathens: Moses, Joseph and Esther, all saviours of the Israelite nation, had married idolaters, yet 'none of them in all the holye storye reproved'; Saul, one of the conquerors of the Holy Land, was the descendant of Ruben (Jacob's son) and a heathen wife, while Tamar and Ruth, both ancestresses of Christ, originally came from neighbouring tribes and had married into the Israelite nation.[43]

In any event, thought these supporters of a Catholic marriage for the queen, it was questionable how far the Mosaic Law on intermarriage should apply to Christians: 'Concernyng which covenaunte and lawe before recyted owt of Exodus and Deuter., yt is specially to be noted that they were lymitted and circumscribed, with perticularitye of personnes, place and tyme.' For example, argued an anonymous writer who favoured the 1579 Anjou match, Abraham's decision to find a wife for his son amongst his original people was made 'because he knew that the people of Canaan were accursed of the Lord and destined to servile condition'. Ezra's injunction, on the other hand, arose because the Israelite men were using heathen women to satisfy their lust and God condemned all marriages made in lust. That Ezra was condemning lust rather than arguing for a ban on mixed marriages was evident from the fact that he spoke only to the Israelite men and did not order the Israelite women to put aside their heathen husbands.[44] Here the story of Tobias in the Apocrypha was also thought to be instructive. What was important here was not that Tobias, the son of Tobit, took a wife from his own people but that he married her out of love not lust and in order to save her from the devil who had killed all her seven previous husbands. This devil had no power to harm Tobias because in his own words 'I took not this my sister for lust, but in truth.'

In general terms, these writers argued that the Mosaic law laid down in Exodus and Deuteronomy enjoining separation from the heathen nations was intended only for the Israelites who were carrying out God's particular purpose of settling the land and bringing forth Christ the Messiah. Once the Messiah was born, these laws no longer applied, since a new covenant had been made with Christ's followers:

> for Moses is gonne and Christ is come. . . .We are to consider that we have not Aaron but Christe for our high preist; we have a new covenaunte, and have not to do with th'olde; nether Moyses nether Josua are appoynted our leaders into the lande of promysse, but Paule the chosen messenger of the great Jehovah.[45]

All Protestants accepted that some parts of the Mosaic Law were not binding on Christians; they distinguished between the old laws relating to ceremonies which had no place in Christian worship, the judicial parts which remained in force only to the extent that the circumstances they dealt with remained the same, and the moral code which 'is in full strength as ever it was before the coming of our Saviour Christ'.[46] Division, however, arose between the supporters and opponents of religious inter-marriage over which part of the law was relevant to the question. Whilst opponents of the Austrian and French matches believed that Elizabeth's marriage to a Catholic would affront the universal and timeless Mosaic Laws relating to accommodation with idolatry, the supporters of these projects clearly disagreed, seeing the laws concerning separation from non-believers as particular to the Jewish peoples and not applicable to Christians. They consequently turned for advice to the New Testament, especially to the writings of St Paul, for guidance.

Pauline teachings could be interpreted as authorising religious inter-marriage. The relevant text cited by the supporters of the Valois and Habsburg matches was I Corinthians 7: 'And that the woman which hath an husband that believeth not, and if he be pleased to dwell with her, let her not leave him. For the unbelieving husband is sanctified by the wife.' Peter Martyr had apparently interpreted this text as referring to mixed marriages which were undertaken with the hope of converting the unbelieving partner to the true faith: 'the unbeleaving is sanctyfied by the faithe of the beleeving, and the cohabitation lawfull for the hope's sake of conversion.' Writers who favoured the queen's marriage appealed to these authorities and pronounced that a Protestant marriage to a Catholic contracted 'with a hope and desire to win the unbelieving part to the religion' was a godly match and in accordance with holy writ.'[47]

The authority of St Paul was cited to justify religious intermarriage not only in Protestant England, but also among Catholics in both France and Austria where discussions were similarly held on the question of whether or not it was legitimate for a Catholic prince to marry the heretical queen of England. Thus, when in the summer of 1571 Henry of Anjou expressed his horror at the idea of marrying an excommunicated heretic, the bishop of Dax tried to persuade him that a Catholic prince could do nothing better for his Church than marry a Protestant princess in the hope of bringing her realm back to the papal fold. He invoked the authority of St Paul against those who opposed the match on 'a religious scrupule', citing the same text where the apostle defended a believing husband who remained with his unbelieving wife.[48] In 1579, the Venetian ambassador to Paris reported that many of the arguments concerning Francis of Anjou's marriage to Elizabeth focused on the question of religion – in particular whether or not the duke's presence in England might encourage conversions and strengthen Catholicism, thereby justifying the marriage.[49]

Despite the 1579 campaign by English 'puritans' against the Anjou marriage, religious intermarriage was defended in terms that would allow Elizabeth to retain her credentials as a Protestant queen while wedding a Catholic prince. Burghley seems to have been behind these attempts to find scriptural justifications for religious intermarriage; surprisingly, however, he apparently did nothing to publicise the arguments produced under his patronage. There is only one extant manuscript copy of the fullest treatise defending a mixed marriage which is contained within the Lansdowne papers. Perhaps by the time the material was produced he was anxious to dampen down public debate rather than ignite it by offering an intellectual challenge to Stubbs.

It was far more difficult for defenders of a Catholic marriage to justify Elizabeth granting freedom of worship to her consort while at the same time presenting her as a model Protestant queen. None the less, some attempt was made in 1567 to show that a good Christian might allow another Christian to hear the Mass temporarily 'until the party may also be instructed in time to come to understand the error thereof'. The discourse on the subject, probably written by Archbishop Parker, put forward two arguments in favour of such toleration. The first maintained that Protestants in England and abroad generally did not consider such toleration to be a sin; the second appealed to texts in the New Testament.

As far as contemporary attitudes were concerned, Parker claimed that Catholic worship was permitted in some Protestant areas of Europe, notably Frankfurt, Augsburg, Basle and Strasbourg. Furthermore, even in England foreign ambassadors were allowed to hear Mass within their own private apartments. In addition, Parker asked how could it be that toleration for Papists was against divine law if the punishment for hearing a Mass in England was but a mere 100 mark fine, 'wher yf an English merchant doo but custome in his name the goods of a straungere, he looseth all the goods which he hath of what value so ever they bee'?[50]

Turning to the scriptures, Parker argued that the New Testament allowed the toleration of erroneous religious practices for the purpose of encouraging conversions. Thus, instead of separating himself from the Pharisees, 'Christ himself kept company and dined with them, who esteemed their own traditions more than the commandments of God'; furthermore, he stayed so often in Samaria that he was called a Samaritan in Luke 17. Pauline teachings similarly endorsed toleration. In Corinthians 10 the apostle had permitted the Christians of Corinth to dine with their heathen neighbours on the meats dedicated to idols 'with safety of conscience', despite the fact that he had just exhorted them to flee from idolatry. The relevant verse had Paul declaring: 'If any of them that believe not bid you to a feast, and ye are minded to go; eat whatsoever is set before you, asking no question for conscience sake.' From this speech, Parker extrapolated the principle:

> If the meat which was of the infidels dedicated to idols might be used and suffered of the Christian Corinthians with a safe conscience; then the mass which the papists use may be now used and suffered of the right Christians with a safe conscience.

He went on to explain that just as the 'abominable abuse and idolatry' of offering the meat to the Devil did not affect the quality of the meat 'so ungodly abused' so it might always be eaten lawfully, provided that 'no offence be given to the weak'; in the same way, 'the wicked abuse of the mass taketh not away the free and indifferent using of the same without the abuse'.[51]

In addition, Parker pointed out that St Paul had permitted the continuation of Jewish religious practices, including the rite of circumcision, the Mosaic dietary laws and their traditional holy days, even though these rituals embodied theological error: 'the Jews still accounted it so needful that they thought they could not be saved without it, nor please God without it.' This principle of toleration for ceremonials based on error, Parker believed, should be extended to contemporary Papists:

> How then can we rightly condemn them, which for ignorance use the mass with such holiness and opinion, as the papists? For as they judge it necessary for salvation, and for worshiping of God, so did the Jews judge the abolished law of Moses to be. And as the mass is but the ordinance of man, no more was the Levitical and ceremonial law, being before taken away by Christ . . . And therefore as the superstitious users of the abolished law of Moses were born withal, so ought we to do with the superstitious users of the mass.[52]

In comparing the Papists to the Jews in this way Parker was reasserting the superiority of the New Testament over the Old and proclaiming the irrelevance of much of the Mosaic Law to Christian life.

The opponents of allowing a limited toleration for Elizabeth's Catholic husband were unconvinced by this argument. Once again they saw the issue in terms of accommodation with idolatry. In such a case, they believed, the Mosaic laws were binding on Christians and indeed had to be followed precisely, and not circumvented in any way. The lessons of the Old Testament on this issue, similarly, could not be ignored as irrelevant but had to be treated as evidence of God's will.

Throughout the Old Testament there were express divine prohibitions against any compromise with idolatry and countless cases where even minor transgressions had provoked divine retribution. The example of Achan in the Book of Joshua was most frequently cited, as it provided the most terrible warning of all. Achan excited God's wrath for surreptitiously taking away accursed spoil from the idolatrous city of Jericho, even though the stolen objects were not accoutrements of idolatry but merely a goodly garment and some silver and gold. In late 1567 Bishop Jewel drew on this story when preaching against the granting of a limited toleration to the Archduke Charles.[53] In 1579 John Stubbs used the same Biblical example to warn the queen against permitting the celebration of the Mass in London, an act which would dishonour God and menace the Church:

> The sin of Achan, though not in this kind, proves that the sin of one man, and him private, done in secret and buried close under the ground, gave forth such a stench in the Lord's nostrils as was contagious to the whole host, and his garment brought the plague among them. Much more shall the high sin of a highest magistrate, done and avowed in open sun, kindle the wrath of God and set fire on church and commonweal. [54]

It is no wonder that the opponents of the match who adopted this uncompromising position were often labelled 'Puritans' by their opponents.

The debates on the queen's marriage, therefore, exposed important differences within the English Protestant 'consensus'. While both sides appealed to scriptural authority and shared a common hostility to Catholicism, the writers who opposed the Catholic matrimonial projects emphasised the authority of the Old Testament and believed that Papists were outside the pale of the Christian community, whereas the adherents of the matches followed the New Testament teachings of St Paul and viewed Papists as members of a Christian sect which had fallen into error. Although some supporters of the Catholic marriages labelled their opponents as 'precisionists' and 'Puritans', further investigation is required to discover how closely differences over the marriages mirrored the faultlines between Puritans and conformists. Peter Lake has already discussed how different attitudes to popery marked off Puritans from conformists, and J. S. Coolidge has shown interesting distinctions between the two in their approach to St Paul and the concept of edification. Further research, however, is now needed into Protestant attitudes towards the Mosaic codes and use of the Bible in debate.[55]

9

CONCLUSIONS

Why then did Elizabeth I not marry? Eizabeth's personal preferences provide no answer here, for as we have seen there was little room for them to operate in this crucial area of policy. Had her Council ever united behind any one of her suitors, she would have found great difficulty in rejecting his proposal; likewise, without strong conciliar backing Elizabeth would not or could not marry a particular candidate. In the case of those men whom she had no particular wish to wed, opposition from within the Council allowed her to elude their suits. Thus, it had required concerted conciliar pressure to force her into negotiations for a marriage with the Archduke Charles, and it was only when a significant number of council-lors spoke out against accepting Habsburg demands for a private Mass in November 1567 that she felt able to bring the courtship to an end. Similarly, in 1572 she was able to slip out of the negotiations with the duke of Montmorency for a marriage alliance with Francis duke of Alençon on the grounds that her Council was divided over whether or not to accept the French terms on religion. As she herself said on several occasions, she was only thinking of marriage to satisfy her subjects, so there was no point at all in taking a husband who would displease a significant number of them. In part such statements provided a convenient excuse to avoid the responsibility for the failure of particular sets of negotiations, but they also contained more than a grain of truth. Furthermore, on the practical side, she needed full conciliar support for a match so that the matrimonial treaty would not run into difficulties when presented to parliament for ratification.

At other times, however, when Elizabeth appeared to be close to accepting the hand of her favoured suitors, first Robert Dudley and then Francis of Anjou in 1579, the active opposition of some leading councillors convinced her that it would be definitely unwise and perhaps disastrous to proceed with the match. She was all too aware that both Wyatt's Rebellion in Mary I's reign and Mary Stuart's deposition in 1567 had occurred when a queen regnant insisted upon taking a husband against the wishes of her important subjects. Elizabeth was far too cautious and politically adept to make the same mistake. There is every reason to suppose that had her councillors overwhelmingly supported either Dudley in late 1560 or Anjou in 1579, she would have gone ahead with the wedding.

But why could no suitor ever command the overwhelming support of her councillors? As far as most of the early matrimonial candidates were concerned, the answer is that there was little to recommend any of them: Philip II was unacceptable in England as the man held responsible (admittedly most unfairly) for the disastrous French War and the persecution of Protestants during the previous reign; marriage to him, moreover, was clearly incompatible with the radical changes in religion favoured by the queen and her new Council. Charles IX was out of the question because of his age; in 1564 when his suit was first raised he was only fourteen to the queen's thirty-one years. While Elizabeth herself was worried that she would look ridiculous at the wedding, like a mother taking her child to the altar, her councillors were more concerned that the young king would be unable to consummate the marriage for several years and that the match would thus fail to resolve immediately the succession problem.

Almost all the remaining early candidates were simply not thought good enough for a reigning monarch. As the Spanish ambassador in France said of the earl of Arran in 1560, these suitors brought nothing with them but their own person. Although the dukes of Saxony, Holstein, Ferrara and the rest might meet the requirement of siring an heir, the queen would gain no prestige, riches or valuable foreign alliance by wedding them. On the contrary, there was the strong likelihood that as consorts they would prove a drain on the queen's resources and bring her enemies rather than powerful friends. In addition, the disparagement involved in marrying a mercenary, such as Holstein, or even an elected king, such as Eric XIV, was not insignificant for a queen who had been pronounced a bastard and whose title to the throne was challenged by Mary Stuart and her allies. Elizabeth's preference for a husband of royal blood, therefore, was not just snobbery, as is frequently claimed, but a considered means of enhancing her own status and authority.

Robert Dudley, of course, should have been viewed as a candidate in this category, for as Cecil rightly noted: 'Nothing is increased by Marriadg of hym either in Riches, Estimation, Power.'[1] It was frequently said that the nobility despised him as a 'new man', whose father and grand-father had been attainted for treason, and that they considered the queen's marriage to a commoner as disparagement. Again, such thoughts went beyond the social elitism that was undoubtedly present; Elizabeth's child might well have to compete for the throne against Mary Stuart or any son she might have, and would be at a disadvantage with only one grand-parent of royal blood, especially as some Catholics persisted in questioning whether Henry VIII had indeed fathered Elizabeth. The queen's deep affection for Dudley, however, outweighed these obstacles, while his own abilities as a self-publicist and politician helped him gradually to win over many initial opponents of his suit. As a result, he was considered a serious candidate by contemporaries until the mid-1560s and beyond.

Dudley's main handicap in courting the queen was the mysterious death of his wife. Although the coroner's court judged Amy Robsart's fall down the staircase at Cumnor Place to be 'death by misadventure', many clearly believed otherwise. Consequently, Elizabeth had good reason to fear that her marriage to Dudley would confirm the rumours that he had conspired to bring about his first wife's death, that she too was implicated in the murder, and that she and Dudley had long been lovers. Councillors like Cecil and royal servants like Throckmorton who opposed the marriage played on this anxiety by bringing to her attention the scurrilous comments circulating both at home and abroad about her relationship with her favourite.

The single most important reason for their hostility to Dudley's suit, however, was political self-interest. Most of Elizabeth's councillors and nobles distrusted Dudley as a potential faction-leader who would promote his own men and take revenge on the enemies of his father, the late duke of Northumberland. 'He shall study nothing but to enhanss his owne particular Frends to Welthe, to Offices, to Lands, and to offend others', wrote Cecil when listing his reasons against a Dudley marriage.[2] Cecil was also no doubt well aware that his own political power would be most at risk if Dudley became royal consort. Like the favourite and unlike his aristocratic colleagues, Cecil had little power-base of his own in the early 1560s and his position depended entirely on the queen. Thus, in contrast to Dudley's earliest enemies, Arundel, Norfolk and Pembroke, Cecil was never won round to the match or seduced by the belief that it would be preferable for the queen to marry her Master of the Horse than to remain single. He, therefore, worked quietly but consistently behind the scenes to subvert Dudley's Spanish strategy in the springs of 1561 and 1562.

The opposition within the Council to the other strong candidates for Elizabeth's hand was also based to a large extent on political self-interest. Dudley's hostility to the suits of Eric XIV, Archduke Charles and Francis of Anjou owed much to his anxieties that his own political position would be adversely affected by a royal marriage, for his intimacy with Elizabeth, the main source of his political influence and material rewards, could hardly continue once she had a husband. Furthermore, his political rivals, who were promoting these matches, would be likely to benefit if the queen married their favoured candidate. Sussex made this point in late 1567 when he told the Spanish ambassador at the Imperial court that 'if he concluded the marriage it would help him greatly against his political enemies'.[3] For these reasons, Dudley took the lead in opposing these three matrimonial projects. In 1560 and 1561 he encouraged propaganda against a foreign consort in order to foil his Swedish rival. In the mid-1560s he helped the French to present Charles IX as an alternative candidate to the Archduke Charles in an attempt to cloud the issue and divide the Council; when that failed, he opposed the match in the Council on religious grounds, and he may well have been behind the anti-Catholic scare whipped up in late 1567 and early 1568 to warn Elizabeth of the dangers in conceding a measure of religious toleration to the archduke. Between 1578 and 1579, his hand can again be detected behind many of the strategies designed to warn Elizabeth off a marriage to Francis duke of Anjou.

On each occasion Dudley was ultimately able to count on the active support of other councillors because of the nationality and religion of the suitors. For the queen and the supporters of the Habsburg and Anjou matches, marriage to a foreign prince was desirable as a means of placing a protective mantle around the realm. A match with the Archduke Charles was expected to bring with it an informal alliance with both the emperor and king of Spain; while the marriages to Henry of Anjou in 1571 and Francis of Anjou in 1579 were intended to bind England and France in a defensive league against Spain. Yet many at court disliked the prospect of the queen marrying a foreigner. Besides xenophobic prejudices, they shared a genuine apprehension about the practical political problems that seemed likely to arise from any union between Elizabeth and a foreign prince. Her consort, it was feared, might draw the queen into wars of his own making and expect her subjects to pay their cost; he might take his wife abroad to live in his own territories, leaving England to be governed by a viceroy; worse still, the birth of a male child would put at risk England's national independence. Furthermore, if Elizabeth were to die in child-birth, her husband would act as regent with the authority to rule until the child reached maturity. Even though a number of these concerns could be dealt with in a carefully worded marriage-contract, as indeed they had been in Mary I's matrimonial treaty, these alarming prospects influenced many to speak out against Elizabeth's foreign candidates. Anxieties were expressed both in Council meetings and political tracts, such as the discourse of Thomas Smith directed against the Swedish and Habsburg candidates and the pamphlet of John Stubbs attacking the Anjou project.

The greatest objection of all to the Austrian and French candidates, however, was their Catholicism. In each case, the promoters of the marriage believed that in time Elizabeth's consort would change his religion. Thus, when Cecil opened negotiations with the Archduke Charles of Austria in 1563, he was under the mistaken impression that the prince was sufficiently flexible to convert to Protestantism soon after the marriage. Similarly, it was hoped that Henry of Anjou would be educated into accepting the Protestant faith once he was removed from the influence of the Guises, and marriage negotiations with Francis of Alençon were initiated only in 1572 because he was held to be 'more moderate' and 'not so obstinate' in religion. Although some extreme Protestants opposed marriage to a Papist on ideological grounds, the majority view in the Council appears to have been that it would be acceptable provided that there were sound expectations of a conversion to Protestantism.

In the meantime, however, difficulties existed over the terms on which a Catholic consort could live in Protestant England. As already seen, there were three main issues to be resolved. Was the wedding ceremony to follow the Catholic service or the English Prayer Book, and was it to be presided over by a priest or minister? Did Elizabeth's husband have to attend English Protestant services? Would he and his household be allowed to hear the Mass? Attempts to reach agreement on these issues bedevilled all the matrimonial negotiations. Henry of Anjou's refusal to make any concessions at all and his insistence both on non-attendance at Protestant services and freedom to hear public Mass ended his suit. Both the Archduke Charles and Francis of Anjou, however, were more accommodating and after tough negotiations Elizabeth was able to reach a compromise with them on the first two points which was satisfactory to the majority of her councillors. It was on the question of the Mass that the Council divided. On this issue, both suitors were again more flexible than Henry, in that they agreed to forgo public celebrations of the Mass provided that they and their fellow countrymen could hear it privately. But while this demand seemed reasonable to some councillors, it was totally unacceptable to others.

The division in the Council on the issue of the Mass was in part ideological. The councillors who recommended a limited toleration were on the whole conservative in religion: Sussex, Norfolk, Howard of Effingham, Croft and Hunsdon. On the other hand, Protestant zealots and Puritan patrons like Walsingham, Mildmay and Knowles viewed the Mass as extreme idolatry: 'The highest treason that can be against the lord's own person.' For them and many other Protestants outside the Council, it was Elizabeth's religious duty to take up the sword against this 'pagan rite', and not to allow it to be set up 'on the highest hill of the land, in London, which is our Jerusalem'. None the less the Council did not split cleanly along religious lines. Dr Thomas Wilson, a Marian exile and supporter of an interventionist Protestant foreign policy, gave his support to the Anjou match in 1579; whereas Sir Christopher Hatton, Archbishop Whitgift's patron and a noted conservative, came out as a leading opponent. Wilson's fear of an international Catholic league led him to accept the Anjou match as a necessary evil; Hatton, on the other hand, had more faith in England's power to withstand the international threat but feared the internal consequences of allowing Anjou liberty of worship.[4] Cecil, whose deeply ingrained anti-Catholicism reflected an apocalyptic world view, nevertheless consistently promoted Catholic marriages for the queen on terms which would allow her consort a private Mass.[5] As seen in earlier chapters, his promotion of the Archduke match was mainly motivated by his worries about the succession, while in 1571 and 1579 he advocated a French match as a way to protect England against an international Catholic league. Nor were more self-interested political considerations ever entirely absent from his thinking.

In late 1567 Elizabeth did not need much convincing against the Archduke match, for she had her own doubts about agreeing to the Austrian's terms on both legal and political grounds. Conciliar opposition, however, bolstered her resolve and enabled her to reject the Archduke's request for a private Mass, thereby bringing the negotiations to a close. At the time of the Francis of Anjou matrimonial negotiations, however, Elizabeth strongly favoured the duke and was even ready to pass over the issue of the Mass in order to marry him. The overwhelming advantages of the Anglo-French matrimonial alliance seemed to outweigh the dangers of allowing Anjou the restricted exercise of his religion; it is also probable that she believed that, once married and under her influence, he would soon cease to hear Mass. On this occasion, therefore, the conciliar opposition to the match had to move into higher gear to persuade the queen against the marriage on these terms; led by Leicester and Walsingham, councillors against the match helped to mobilise a widespread propaganda campaign which Elizabeth could not ignore.

Elizabeth's gender was of some relevance in these considerations, but not as much as is generally assumed. The marriage of a female ruler obviously exacerbated fears about both 'faction' and foreign influences, but these problems existed even when a king or prince was choosing a bride. On almost every occasion that Henry VIII took an English wife, faction reared its head and the marriage resulted in a shake-up of political groupings at court: according to David Starkey, Henry's choice of Anne Boleyn 'triggered faction'; his marriage to Jane Seymour in 1536 was accompanied by the destruction of 'a whole court faction'; and his decision to wed Katherine Howard helped seal Thomas Cromwell's fate.[6] In the following century, when James I planned to marry his heir to a Spanish princess, he provoked a political storm which 'opened the most dangerous gap between the political "court" and "country"' in his reign. According to Thomas Cogswell, many Jacobean men and women feared that 'a fecund Infanta could well draw England into the "empire" just as earlier Habsburg princes had done in the Netherlands and in Spain itself'.[7] At the same time, anxieties about the Infanta's Catholicism dominated popular concerns and in 1623, when Prince Charles and the duke of Buckingham travelled to Spain, they ignited an anti-Catholic scare which was not dissimilar to that of 1579.

Undoubtedly Elizabeth's marriage was a divisive issue in the Council and at court; but to what extent, if any, did it create, reflect or exacerbate 'factional' struggles involving Cecil, Leicester and the Howards? Simon Adams has consistently argued that faction played no part in the politics of the Elizabethan court before the 1590s. He questions the very existence of faction on three main grounds. First he has found no evidence that either Burghley or Leicester had an exclusive following and operated as faction-leaders: 'In a number of cases – for example those of Walsingham himself, Henry Killigrew, Robert Beale, William Herle – clear lines of allegiance have been very difficult to draw.' Second, he believes that there is little evidence of intense competition over patronage between the leading figures in the court before the last decade or so of the reign. Third, he argues that Cecil and Leicester were 'men from a similar political milieu' who shared the same outlook and who 'had too much in common for permanent antagonisms to be established'. Court politics, he therefore concludes, were less the product of divisions amongst courtiers than of disputes between 'an able, charming yet imperious and idiosyncratic queen and councillors and intimates who generally shared a high degree of social, political and cultural homogeneity'.[8]

Adams is certainly correct in emphasising that the Elizabethan court was not riven in two by the rivalry between Leicester and Cecil. With regard to patronage networks, men seeking favours from the queen solicited help from several important figures at the same time and did not turn to only one for advancement. In the field of policy-making, Cecil, Leicester and Walsingham frequently co-operated, as indeed this study shows was the case during the early stages of the Henry of Anjou matrimonial negotiations. Furthermore, as both Adams and Eric Ives rightly point out, there was never a complete break-down in relations between Leicester and the Howards or Cecil.[9]

None the less, this study has demonstrated that it would be a mistake to conclude that the absence of 'faction' in a narrowly defined sense meant that harmony always prevailed in political life. Between 1558 and 1581 personal antagonisms, political rivalries and policy differences were at least as much a feature of the court scene as co-operation and consensus. As is evident from earlier chapters, disagreements over the question of the queen's marriage and foreign policy exacerbated personal conflicts amongst courtiers and councillors, which could easily get out of hand and disrupt political stability. In late 1560 the threat of armed conflict between Dudley and the earls of Arundel and Pembroke shook the court. In 1562 a meeting of the Knights of the Garter around the time of St George's Day was disrupted when Arundel and Northampton stormed out in protest after a petition in favour of Dudley marrying the queen was approved. In 1566 rival followers of the Howards and Leicester wore distinctive colours to show their group loyalty and the danger of armed violence between Sussex and Leicester was so great that the queen was forced to intercede between them. In 1579 the divisions generated by the Anjou matrimonial project nearly resulted in a 'palace revolution' when Leicester and Walsingham were banished from court and the queen considered bringing some Catholics onto the Council. Nor were these disputes always confined to the court. Both the 1563 and 1566 parliaments were affected by divisions within the Council on the marriage and succession, while in 1579 preachers and polemicists brought a wider public into the debate on the Anjou marriage.

There is little evidence that Elizabeth encouraged these disputes and divisions by pursuing 'a divide and rule' policy which gave her 'freedom of action' and turned her into 'an umpire to whose judgment the contenders would always have to bow'.[10] Too much weight has been placed on the report of the Jacobean Sir Robert Naunton that Elizabeth made and unmade factions 'as her own great judgment advised'.[11] On the contrary she usually encouraged rival politicians to work together to formulate and execute policy, and attempted to calm down passions which arose from their disputes. Thus Cecil was brought into the negotiations with de Quadra and Dudley in 1562 concerning England's representation at the Council of Trent, a move which in the event allowed her Secretary to outmanoeuvre both queen and favourite. In 1571 she left the day-to-day negotiations with the French to be handled by Leicester and Burghley in tandem. In October 1579 she tried to obtain the consent of the whole Council to the Anjou match; only later did she seek out councillors' individual written views as a way of breaking down the opposition to her plans. On the whole, then, Elizabeth preferred 'consensus' politics to 'divide and rule'; and the divisions at her court were a mark of political failure not a means for securing freedom of action. Indeed, as we have seen, it is questionable whether Elizabeth experienced very much 'freedom of action' in the area of matrimonial policy.

The queen who emerges from the pages of this book has less control over politics and policy-making than the Elizabeth of earlier studies. Even when we look at the creation of her public image, we can see that the iconography of chastity was imposed on her by writers, painters and their patrons during the Anjou matrimonial negotiations. Furthermore, in her dealings with foreign powers she appears far less adept at matrimonial diplomacy than her admirers have often asserted: there is little sign of the elusiveness and prevarication with which she is said to have dazzled and bewildered her suitors and their representatives for months, even years, on end. On the contrary, in practically all of her many courtships Elizabeth was straightforward and direct with those who wooed her, so much so that on several notable occasions Cecil intervened to advise a more cautious and evasive approach. In none of her negotiations, moreover, was Elizabeth herself successful in extracting major concessions from foreign courts.

On the other hand, the matrimonial negotiations also reveal Elizabeth's great strength as a ruler. Like all successful heads of state she had a highly developed instinct for survival: a sensitivity to public opinion and an aware-ness of what was politically possible. She listened and acted upon calls to marry; but turned down suits which proved unpopular or divisive. Only briefly during 1579 did her political intuition falter but even then she soon recovered and stepped back from the brink of the disaster which would surely have accompanied the Anjou marriage. She was not the Queenie of the television series *Blackadder* who could chop off heads at will or get her own way by throwing a tantrum. She was not the Glenda Jackson of *Elizabeth R* whose snarl could tame a cast of courtiers. She was not a tyrannical ruler who would ride roughshod over the views of the political nation. Aware of her own limitations, therefore, she listened to counsel, rejected controversial matches and in the event remained single.

NOTES

1 INTRODUCTION

1 Even Wallace MacCaffrey who recognised the significance of Francis of Anjou's courtship of the queen gave relatively little space in his political narratives of Elizabeth's reign to her matrimonial negotiations with the Archduke Charles of Austria and Henry duke of Anjou. On the Archduke marriage, W. MacCaffrey, *The Shaping of the Elizabethan Regime* (1969), pp.62, 139, 154–5; on the Henry of Anjou marriage, pp.258, 262. For the Francis of Anjou courtship, see W. MacCaffrey, *Queen Elizabeth and the Making of Policy 1572–1588* (Princeton, 1981), pp.243–66 and 'The Anjou Match and the Making of Elizabethan Foreign Policy', in *The English Commonwealth 1547–1640: Essays presented to Professor Joel Hurstfield*, Edited by Peter Clark, Alan G. T. Smith and Nicholas Tyacke (Leicester, 1979), pp.59–75.

2 W. Camden, *The History of the most Renowned and Victorious Princess Elizabeth, late Queen of England* (1688), p.27.

3 J. N. King, 'Queen Elizabeth I: Representations of the Virgin Queen', *Renaissance Quarterly* 43 (1990), p.33.

4 For the speech of Elizabeth to the House of Commons see T. E. Hartley (ed.), *Proceedings in the Parliaments of Elizabeth I* (Leicester, 1981), i, pp.44–5. A fuller discussion of the two speeches can be found in F. Teague, 'Queen Elizabeth in her Speeches', in *Gloriana's Face: Women, public and private in the English Renaissance*. Edited by S. P. Cerasano and M. Wynne-Davies (Hemel Hempstead, Herts., 1992), pp.63–78.

5 C. Levin, *The Heart and Stomach of a King: Elizabeth I and the politics of sex and power* (Pennsylvania, 1994), pp.41–2.

6 Hartley, *Proceedings*, p.112.

7 Document quoted in M. Levine, *Tudor Dynastic Problems 1460–1571* (1973), p.177.

8 *Somers Tract*, i, p.175.

9 For the legal claims of the Greys and Mary Stuart see Levine, *Dynastic Problems*, pp.99–101.

10 Petition of the Privy Council drafted by Cecil, 28 December 1559, PRO SP 12/ 7 fol. 186. To be accurate, the concern here was as much Mary's present claim to the throne as the succession.

11 J. Bruce (ed.), *Correspondence of Matthew Parker, Archbishop of Canterbury*. Parker Society (Cambridge, 1853), pp.129–32.

12 J. B. Gabe and C. A. Schlam (eds), *Thomas Chaloner's 'In Laudem Henrici Octavi'* (Lawrence Kansas, 1979). I would like to thank Dr Jonathan Woolfson for this reference.

13 'Notes taken out of a letter from the earl of Sussex, 28 August 1578', J. Payne Collier, 'The Egerton Papers', *Camden Society*, 12 (1840), pp.74–5.

14 Christopher Haigh has dealt with the inconsistency by arguing that the traditional image of Elizabeth is a myth. See C. Haigh (ed.), *The Reign of Elizabeth I* (1984) and *Elizabeth I* (1988).

15 P. Johnson, *Elizabeth I: A study in power and intellect* (1974), pp.109–11, effectively dismisses this argument.

16 For hostility to change, see Johnson, *Elizabeth I*, p.112 and for her irresolution J. Ridley, *Elizabeth I* (1987), p.214.

17 A. Plowden, *Marriage with my Kingdom: The courtships of Elizabeth I* (1977), p.160.

18 S. Haynes, *Collection of State Papers . . . Left by William Cecil* (1740), p.99.

19 L. J. Taylor-Smither, 'Elizabeth I: A psychological profile', *The Sixteenth-Century Journal* 15 (1984), pp.47–70.

20 P. Wright, 'A change in direction: the ramifications of a female household, 1558–1603', in *The English Court from the Wars of the Roses to the Civil War*. Edited by David Starkey *et al.* (Harlow, 1987), pp.159, 168.

21 J. Hurstfield, *Elizabeth I and the Unity of England* (1960), p.40.

22 P. L. Scalingi, 'The Scepter or the Distaff: The question of female sovereignty, 1515–1607', *The Historian* (USA) 42 (1978), pp.59–75; M. Levine, 'The Place of Women in Tudor Government' in *Tudor Rule and Revolution: Essays for G. R. Elton from his American Friends*. Edited by D. J. Guth and J. W. McKenna (Cambridge, 1982), pp.109–23; C. Jordan, 'Women's Rule in Sixteenth-Century British Political Thought', *Renaissance Quarterly* 40 (1987), pp.421–51; P. A. Lee, 'A Bodye Politique to Governe: Aylmer, Knox and the debate on queenship', *The Historian* (USA) 52 (1990), pp.242–61.

23 Jordan, 'Women's Rule', p.429.

24 S. Bassnett, *Elizabeth I: A feminist perspective* (Oxford, 1988), pp.124–5, 128.

25 A. Heisch, 'Queen Elizabeth I and the Persistence of Patrimony', *Feminist Review* 4 (1980), pp.45–56.

26 Quoted in Levin, *Heart and Stomach*, p.43.

27 'A discourse of the queen's marriage with the duke of Anjou, drawn out by the Lord Keeper', 1570, 'Egerton Papers', *Camden Soc.*, 12 (1840), p.57.

28 D. M. Loades, 'Philip II and the government of England', in *Law and Government under the Tudors*. Edited by C. Cross, D. M. Loades and J. J. Scarisbrick (Cambridge, 1988), pp.177–94.

29 Sarah Duncon of Yale University, who is working on Philip II as king of England, shared some of her ideas with me, in particular how courtly ritual inversed the traditional gender roles of king and consort during the reign of Mary I. The example of the silver and gold plate comes from D. M. Loades, *The Reign of Mary Tudor: Politics, government and religion in England 1553–58*, 2nd edn (Harlow, 1991) p.170.

30 Interest in the portrayal of Elizabeth as the Virgin Queen has grown in recent years, largely thanks to the work of scholars of literature during the 1980s and 1990s. See for example: S. Greenblatt, *Renaissance Self-Fashioning: From More to Shakespeare* (Chicago, 1980), pp.166–8; D. Norbrook, *Poetry and Politics in the English Renaissance* (1984); L. A. Montrose, ' "Shaping Fantasies": Figurations of gender and power in Elizabethan culture' in *Representing the Renaissance*. Edited by Stephen Greenblatt (California, 1988), pp.31–64; P. Berry, *Of Chastity and Power: Elizabethan literature and*

the unmarried queen (1989); S. Frye, *Elizabeth I: The competition for representation* (Oxford, 1993); H. Hackett, *Virgin Mother, Maiden Queen: Elizabeth I and the cult of the Virgin Queen* (1995).

31 Haigh, *Elizabeth I*, p.16.

32 According to Levine, 'The Place of Women', pp.112–13, despite Aylmer's acceptance of the legitimacy of gynaecocracy, modern feminists would find his views insulting as he shared his contemporaries' misogynist prejudices.

33 H. Robinson (ed.), *The Zurich Letters*, 2nd series, Parker Society (Cambridge, 1845), ii, p.35.

34 J. N. King, *Spenser's Poetry and the Reformation Tradition* (Princeton, 1990), p.135.

35 E. C. Wilson, *England's Eliza* (Cambridge, Mass., 1939), p.8.

36 A. Heisch, 'Queen Elizabeth I: Parliamentary rhetoric and the exercise of power', *Signs* I (1975), pp.31–55.

37 D. Cressy, *Bonfires and Bells: National memory and the Protestant calendar in Elizabethan and Stuart England* (1989), pp.50–7.

38 J. N. King, 'The Godly Woman in Elizabethan Iconography', *Renaissance Quarterly* 38 (1985), pp.41–84.

39 'The Passage of Our Most Dread Sovereign Lady, Queen Elizabeth, through the City of London to Westminster, the Day before her Coronation' in *An English Garner: Tudor Tracts 1532–1588*. Edited by A. F. Pollard (New York, 1964), pp.365–92.

2 EARLY SUITORS

1 *Letters and Papers, Foreign and Domestic Henry VIII*, viii, pp.58, 135–9, 151, 211, 253, 297–8, 323, 353, 358. Henry VIII did not demand that Francis I should break with Rome as is suggested in C. Erickson, *The First Elizabeth* (1983), p.26 and elsewhere. On the contrary, he specifically said that he would not ask Francis 'to execute such laws in his realm as we have done in ours, unless the bishop of Rome gave him occasion'. *L. & P. Henry VIII*, viii, p.136.

2 Statute of the realm printed in Levine, *Dynastic Problems*, pp.155–6.

3 *L. & P. Henry VIII*, xii, pt. i, p.361.

4 12 August 1541, *L. & P. Henry VIII*, xvi, p.519; 3 March 1542, xvii, pp.65–6.

5 4 April 1543, *L. & P. Henry VIII*, xviii, pt. 1, p.214.

6 *L. & P. Henry VIII*, xviii, pt. 1, pp. 229, 231–2, 291; pt. 2, p.62.

7 23 October 1545, *L. & P. Henry VIII*, xx, pt. 2, p.294.

8 W. K. Jordan (ed.), *The Chronicle and Political Papers of King Edward VI* (Ithaca, NY, 1966), p.50; 'Instructions given to Sir John Borthwick sent to the King of Denmark', BL Sloane MS 2442 fol. 27.

9 30 August 1551, Sir Anthony Guidotti to the earl of Warwick and 15 February 1553, Sir Richard Morysine to Sir William Cecil, *Calendar of State Papers Foreign 1547–53*, pp.164, 245.

10 The d'Aumâle marriage is mentioned in Jehan Scheyfve's dispatches, June and 6 July 1551, *Calendar of State Papers Spanish 1550–52*, pp.299, 325; see also F. A. Mumby, *The Girlhood of Queen Elizabeth* (1909), p.77.

11 *Cal. S. P. Span. 1553*, pp.38, 46, 55. There were also rumours that Northumberland might put aside his own wife and marry Elizabeth himself for the same purpose.

12 Mary's attitude to her sister is discussed fully in D. M. Loades, *Mary Tudor: A life* (Oxford, 1989), pp.274–314.

13 We do not know the grounds on which Henry's marriage to Anne Boleyn was declared void but it was obviously not because of the legality of his pre-existent marriage to Catherine.

14 28 November, *Cal. S. P. Span. 1553*, pp.393–6.

15 4 November, *Cal. S. P. Span. 1553*, pp.334–5.

16 17 December, *Cal. S. P. Span. 1553*, p.441.

17 28 November, *Cal. S. P. Span. 1553*, pp.393–5.

18 24 December, Charles V to Renard, *Cal. S. P. Span. 1553*, p.454.

19 29 December, *Cal. S. P. Span. 1553*, p.472.

20 For Wyatt's rebellion see D. M. Loades, *Two Tudor Conspiracies* (Bangor, Gwynedd, 2nd edn 1992); and for Gardiner's attitude to Courtenay and Elizabeth see G. Redworth, *In Defence of the Church Catholic: The life of Stephen Gardiner* (Oxford, 1990), p.314.

21 *Cal. S. P. Span. 1554*, pp.197, 231, 233, 276, 308; *1554–8*, pp.4, 23. Rumours of a Savoy match had reached France as early as December 1553, R. A. Vertot and C. Villaret, *Ambassades de Messieurs de Noailles en Angleterre* (Leyden, 1763), iii, pp.1–2.

22 *Cal. S. P. Span. 1554*, p.233.

23 'An account of the negotiations at Brussels of Lord Paget', 14 November 1554, *Cal. S. P. Span. 1554–8*, pp.90, 92; *Calendar of State Papers Venetian 1555–6*, pp.97, 214, 532, 558.

24 With his abdication in December 1555, Charles V divided his empire and left to his son, Philip, his rights in the Netherlands, Spain, Franche-Comté, Italy and the Indies, while his brother Ferdinand inherited the Habsburg lands in Germany. Ferdinand, however, believed that he should also have received the Netherlands which were within the Holy Roman Empire. *Cal. S. P. Ven. 1556–7*, p.1079.

25 *Cal. S. P. Ven. 1556–7*, p.1080; Renard also recommended Savoy in February 1555, C. Weiss, *Papiers d'Etat du Cardinal Granvelle* (Paris, 1841–52), iv, p.398.

26 It has been suggested that negotiations for the match began when the duke came over to England in late 1554, but there is no evidence that marriage with Elizabeth was raised with Savoy at that time and the purpose of his mission lay elsewhere. See G. Claretta, *Il Duca di Savoia e la Corte di Londra negli Anni 1554 e 1555* (Pinerolo, 1892).

27 *Cal. S. P. Ven. 1556–7*, pp.1015, 1023, 1105; *1557*, p.1538.

28 BL Cotton MS Titus B ii fol. 109.

29 *Cal. S. P. Ven. 1557*, p.1538; M. J. Rodriguez-Salgado and S. Adams (eds), 'The Count of Feria's dispatch to Philip II of 14 November 1558', *Camden Miscellany* 28, *Camden Society 4th Series* 29 (1984), p.334.

30 'The Lady Elizabeth's answer made at Hatfield to Sir Thomas Pope', 26 April 1558, BL Harleian MS 444 fols 20–9.

31 Mumby, *Elizabeth I*, pp.236–7; J. M. B. C. Kervyn de Lettenhove (ed.), *Relations Politiques des Pays Bas et de l'Angleterre sous le règne de Philippe II* (Brussels, 1882–1900), i, pp.27, 180–1, 198, 229.

32 'Advertisement for the king touching the state, power and military forces of the kingdom of Sweden and other points on which the king desires to be informed', 16 September 1558, AGS E 8340/ 232 fol. 367.

33 'Feria's dispatch', *Camden Misc.* 28, p.335.

34 The words of Sir Francis Walsingham in 1571.

35 C. Hibbert, *The Virgin Queen: The personal history of Elizabeth I* (1990), p.80; Haigh, *Elizabeth I*, p.12.

36 For Elizabeth I's parliamentary title and its significance, see G. R. Elton, *The Parliament of England 1559–1581* (Cambridge, 1989), pp.175–6.

37 Lettenhove, *Relations Politiques*, i, pp.273, 279, 566; 7 January 1559, Feria to Philip II, AGS E 8340/ 233 fol 20v.

38 5 August 1559, J. G. Nichols (ed.), 'The diary of Henry Machyn, citizen and merchant taylor of London 1550–63', *Camden Society* 42 (1848), p. 206; 'An anonymous mid-Tudor chronicle', BL Additional MS 48023 fol. 357.

39 6 August 1559, Breuner to Ferdinand I, V. Von Klarwill, *Queen Elizabeth and Some Foreigners* (1928), p.113.

40 21 November 1558, Lettenhove, *Relations Politiques*, i, p.295, translated in *Cal. S. P. Span. 1558–67*, pp.1–4.

41 25 November 1558, Philip II to Feria, AGS E 8340/390 fol. 390.

42 21 November 1558 and 14 December 1558, Lettenhove, *Relations Politiques*, i, pp.295, 339, translated in *Cal. S. P. Span. 1558–67*, pp.2, 9.

43 M. J. Rodriguez-Salgado, *The Changing Face of Empire: Charles V, Philip II and Habsburg authority, 1551– 1559* (Cambridge, 1989), p.315. The duke of Savoy married Marguerite, the only sister of Henry II, in 1559.

44 9 December 1558, Lettenhove, *Relations Politiques*, i, pp.327–9.

45 10 January 1559, Lettenhove, *Relations Politiques*, i, pp.398–401, translated in *Cal. S. P. Span. 1558–67*, pp.22–3.

46 Lettenhove, *Relations Politiques*, i, pp.398–401; M. F. Alvarez, *Tres Embajadores de Felipe II en Inglaterra* (Madrid, 1951), p.38.

47 Quoted in C. Martin and G. Parker, *The Spanish Armada* (1988), p.281.

48 28 January 1559, Lettenhove, *Relations Politiques*, i, p.412.

49 2 January 1559, Richard Clough to Sir Thomas Gresham, Lettenhove, *Relations Politiques*, i, p.385.

50 For Elizabeth's policy and the passage of the Bills of Supremacy and Uniformity through parliament see N. L. Jones, *Faith by Statute: Parliament and the settlement of religion* (1982).

51 31 January and 20 February 1559, Feria to Philip II, AGS E 812 fols 20, 28, translated in *Cal. S. P. Span. 1558–67*, pp.25, 28.

52 20 February 1559, *Codoin*, lxxxvii, p.129 translated in *Cal. S. P. Span. 1558–67*, p.31.

53 12 February 1559, *Cal. S. P. Span. 1558–67*, p.27; Rodriguez-Salgado, *Changing Face of Empire*, p.322.

54 G. Ribier, *Lettres et Mémoires d'Estat des Roys, Princes, Ambassadeurs et autres Ministres . . .'* (Paris, 1666), ii, p.777. Many historians have mistakenly assumed that Elizabeth kept alive the marriage hopes of the king for as long as she could. See Erickson, *Elizabeth*, p.185.

55 *Cal. S. P. Span. 1558–67*, pp.25, 28, 31–2, 35.

56 20 February 1559, *Codoin*, lxxxvii, p.134 with a translation in *Cal. S. P. Span. 1558–67*, pp.28, 35.

57 C. G. Bayne, *Anglo-Roman Relations 1558–1565*, Oxford Historical and Literary Studies 2 (Oxford, 1913), pp.235–6.

58 19 March 1559, *Codoin*, lxxxvii, p.137. According to Feria, she said 'ella no podia casarse con V. M. porque era hereje . . . me replicó tantas veces que ella era herética y que no se podia casar con V. M', with a translation in *Cal. S. P. Span. 1558–67*, p.37.

59 *Journal of the House of Lords* (1846), i, pp.563, 565.

60 For example J. E. Neale, *Queen Elizabeth* (1934), p.77.

61 Elizabeth had opened separate negotiations with Henry II on Calais in February. Weiss, *Papiers d'Etat*, v, pp.469, 472–8.

62 11 April 1559, *Codoin*, lxxxvii, pp.156–7, translated in *Cal. S. P. Span. 1558–67*, pp.48–9.

63 Rodriguez-Salgado, *Changing Face of Empire*, p.324.

64 Martin and Parker, *Spanish Armada*, p.84; Bayne, *Anglo-Roman Relations*, pp.33, 239.

65 27 January 1559, Von Klarwill, *Queen Elizabeth*, pp.28–31.

66 Von Klarwill, *Queen Elizabeth*, pp.38, 41, 42, 47.

67 28 April 1559, Ferdinand I to Elizabeth, *Cal. S. P. For. 1558–9*, p.227; 12 April 1559, Philip II to the count of Luna, *Codoin*, xcviii, pp.59–60; 12 and 14 April 1559, Philip II to Feria, AGS E 812 fols 42, 43; 12 and 24 April 1559 Philip II to Feria, *Cal. S. P. Span. 1558–67*, pp.53–5, 60.

68 18 April 1559, *Codoin*, lxxxvii, p.180 with a translation in *Cal. S. P. Span. 1558–67*, pp.57–9.

69 Letter to the count of Luna [May] 1559, *Codoin*, xcviii, pp.78–9; 28 and 29 May 1559, *Cal, S. P. Span. 1558–67*, pp.70–1.

70 de Quadra had been based at the Imperial court before coming to England. Alvarez, *Tres Embajadores*, p.48.

71 7 June 1559, Von Klarwill, *Queen Elizabeth*, pp.78–9; 2 and 5 June 1559, *Cal. S. P. For. 1558–9*, pp.298, 299–300.

72 5 June 1559, AGS E. 650 fol. 6; 'Inquiries to be made by Mundt', 2 June 1559, *Cal. S. P. For. 1558–9*, pp.299–300.

73 23 June 1559, Ferdinand I to Philip II, 'no me pareceria darle mi hijo, caso que ella lo demandase', *Codoin*, xcviii, p.89.

74 22 and 23 June 1559, *Codoin*, xcviii, pp.87–8, 90. Ferdinand's letter to Elizabeth of 22 June 1559 which responds to her wish to remain single is in AGS E. 650 fol. 7.

75 9 July 1559, *Cal. S. P. Span. 1558–67*, p.83; 17 August 1559, Philip II to the bishop of Arras, Weiss, *Papiers d'Etat*, v, pp.637–8.

76 2 and 18 September 1559, Lettenhove, *Relations Politiques*, ii, pp.9–10, 13, 19–22, 28–9; 8 September 1559, AGS E 812 fol. 105; 7 and 9 September 1559, *Cal. S. P. Span. 1558–67*, pp.95–6; 8 September 1559, Von Klarwill, *Queen Elizabeth*, pp.123–6.

77 2 October 1559, de Quadra to Ferdinand I, AGS E 812 fol. 121; summary of letter 5 October 1559, AGS E 812 fol. 141; 15 October 1559, de Quadra to the duchess of Parma, AGS E 812 fol. 149; AGS E 8340/ 233 fol. 186; 29 October 1559, Lettenhove, *Relations Politiques*, ii, pp.69–71; the letters of 2 and 29 October are translated in *Cal. S. P. Span. 1558–67*, pp.98–104, 107.

78 References to the illness of Amy Dudley can be found in *Cal. S. P. Ven. 1558–80*, pp.81, 85.

79 2 October 1559, *Codoin*, lxxxvii, p.245; 2 October and 18 November 1559, *Cal. S. P. Span. 1558–67*, pp.104, 115; 14 November 1559, P. Forbes, *A Full View of the Public Transactions in the Reign of Queen Elizabeth* (1740), i, p.261.

80 4 November 1559, Ferdinand I to Breuner, Von Klarwill, *Queen Elizabeth*, p.151.

81 Letters from Ferdinand I, 24 October 1559, AGS E 812 fol. 221; 4 November 1559, AGS E 812 fol. 223; 23 November 1559, *Codoin*, xcviii, pp.103–4; 6 December 1559, AGS E 812 fol. 224.

82 'Report of Viscount Montague', December 1559, Haynes, *Cecil's State Papers*, i, p.233; Lettenhove, *Relations Politiques*, ii, pp.151–3, 163, 182, 252–5, 289–90, 404; *Cal. S. P. Span. 1558–67*, pp.122–4, 128–9.

83 Philip explained that he was worried about 'los inconvenientes que podrian succeder si por mi parescer, fuesse el archiduque y después á essa gente se le antojasse deternerle', 24 December 1559, L. P. Gachard, *Correspondance de Marguerite d'Autriche, Duchesse de Parme, avec Philippe II* (Brussels, 1867), i, p.82.

84 11 April 1559, AGS E 812 fol. 41, translated in *Cal. S. P. Span. 1558–67*, p.51.

85 I. Andersson, *Erik XIV's Engelska Underhandlingar Studier I Svensk Diplomati och Handelspolitik* (Lund, 1935), p.186; 22 July 1559, Von Klarwill, *Queen Elizabeth*, p.104. De Quadra reported that the courtiers 'burlan dellos en masceras en su presencia', 13 August 1559, AGS E 812 fol. 100, translated in *Cal. S. P. Span. 1558–67*, p.91 but dated July. He made similar comments on 18 August 1559, AGS E 812 fol. 101, translated in *Cal. S. P. Span. 1558–67*, p.93.

86 'Machyn's diary', *Camden Soc.*, 42 (1848), pp.213–4; J. Bruce (ed.), 'Annals of the first four years of the reign of Queen Elizabeth by Sir John Hayward', *Camden Soc.*, 7 (1840), p.37; 1 October 1559, *Cal. S. P. For. 1559–60*, p.5.

87 7 June 1559, Von Klarwill, *Queen Elizabeth*, pp.86–7; 1 October, 2 and 25 November 1559, *Cal. S. P. For. 1559–60*, pp.5, 76, 137; 'Hayward's Annals', *Camden Soc.*, 7 (1840) p.37; 'Machyn's diary', *Camden Soc.*, 42 (1848), pp.221, 223; 20 October 1559, A. Clifford (ed.), *State Papers and Letters of Sir Ralph Sadler* (1809), i, p.507; 22 November 1559, *Cal. S. P. Ven. 1558–80*, p.659; BL Addit. MS 48023 fol. 354.

88 18 December 1559, Lettenhove, *Relations Politiques*, ii, pp.137–8; 2 November and 20 December 1559, *Cal. S. P. For. 1559–60*, pp.75, 211; 14 January 1560, *Cal. S. P. Ven. 1558–80*, pp.659–60.

89 J. Nichols, *The Progresses and Public Processions of Queen Elizabeth* (1823), i, p.79; 8 November 1560, Elizabeth to Eric, and 8 November 1559, Elizabeth to the king of Sweden, BL Royal MS 13 B i fol. 20, translated loosely in *Cal. S. P. For. 1559–60*, pp.86–7; 'Proposals of the king of Sweden presented through the duke of Finland', 14 December 1559, *Cal. S. P. For. 1559–60*, p.190.

90 29 October 1559, Gresham to Cecil, *Cal. S. P. For. 1559–60*, pp.68–9. For Swedish trade see H. Zins, *England and the Baltic in the Elizabethan Era* (Manchester, 1972).

91 11 June 1559, Von Klarwill, *Queen Elizabeth*, p.94. According to de Quadra, 9 October 1559, 'este hijo del Rey ... es ridiculo a la Reyna y a todos los de su casa', Lettenhove, *Relations Politiques*, ii, p. 58; 25 August 1560, Thomas Randolph to Cecil, PRO SP 52/ 5 fol. 53.

92 'Speech of the Swedish ambassador before the Council', 3 April 1560, *Cal. S. P. For. 1560–1*, pp.500–1.

93 16 June 1560, Gresham to Parry, and 8 and 25 August 1560, Randolph to Cecil, *Cal. S. P. For. 1560–61*, pp.119–20, 219, 260. Lettenhove, *Relations Politiques*, ii, pp.442, 461, 496; *Cal. S. P. Span. 1558–67*, p.169; 28 August 1560, *Cal. S. P. Ven. 1558–80*, p.249.

94 M. Roberts, *The Early Vasas: A history of Sweden 1523–1611* (Cambridge, 1968), pp.160–6.

95 Andersson, *Erik XIV*, pp.187, 190–1; Roberts, *Early Vasas*, p.213; 8 October 1560, Brigantyne to Cecil, *Cal. S. P. For. 1560–1*, p.340.

96 *Cal. S. P. For. 1560–1*, pp.443, 556–7; *1561–2*, pp.49, 73.

97 See chapter 3 on Dudley's courtship. For Throckmorton's support of the Swedish marriage, see *Cal. S. P. For. 1561–2*, pp.48, 85, 122; for his earlier dislike of it, see 22 October 1560, *Cal. S. P. For. 1560–1*, p.369. Although at times Cecil seemed undecided about a Swedish marriage, the Spanish ambassador believed that he was furthering the Swedish match in 1560 and 1561; see 13 September 1561, *Cal. S. P. Span. 1558–67*, p.213; 14 July 1561, Cecil to Throckmorton, P. Yorke, *Hardwicke State Papers* (1778), i, p.174.

98 21 May and 3 June 1561, *Cal. S. P. For. 1561–2*, pp.122, 129.

99 A book written by Georg Northe was one such piece of propaganda. Andersson, *Erik XIV's Engelska Underhandlingar*, p.188.

100 27 July 1561, *Cal. S. P. For. 1561–2*, p.208.

101 *Cal. S. P. For. 1561–2*, pp.247, 282, 293, 300, 319; *Cal. S. P. Span. 1558–67*, pp.212–13; 'Minute of Cecil to the Lord Mayor of London', 21 July 1561, Haynes, *Cecil's State Papers*, i, p.368; 8 May 1561, Robert Jones to Throckmorton, BL Addit. MS 35830 fol. 107.

102 T. Wright, *Queen Elizabeth and Her Times* (1838), i, p.40 note.

103 3 and 4 October 1561, 'Machyn's Diary', *Camden Soc.*, 42 (1848), p.223; 28 September 1561, Sir Henry Killigrew to Throckmorton, BL Addit. MS 35830 fol. 205; BL Addit. MS 48023 fol. 366; 29 August 1561, Lettenhove, *Relations Politiques*, ii, p.616 translated in *Cal. S. P. Span. 1558–67*, p.211; *Cal. S. P. For. 1560–1*, pp.324–5, *Cal. S. P. For. 1561–2*, pp.331–2, 327.

104 24 September 1561, *Cal. S. P. For. 1561–2*, pp.320–1.

105 BL Addit. MS 48023 fol. 358.

106 BL Addit. MS 48023 fol. 358. De Quadra also reported that the Lord Mayor and aldermen excused themselves from the banquet to show their dislike of the marriage; 17 January 1562, AGS E 815 fol. 199.

107 29 March 1562, A. Teulet, *Relations Politiques de la France et de l'Espagne avec l'Ecosse au XVIième Siècle* (Paris, 1862), ii, pp.175–6; 2 April 1562, de Quadra to the duchess of Parma, AGS 815 fol. 132, partially translated in *Cal. S. P. Span. 1558–67*, p.233.

108 Andersson, *Erik's Engelska Underhandlingar*, p.188; Roberts, *Early Vasas*, p.213; 'Machyn's Diary', *Camden Soc.*, 42 (1848), pp.127, 130; BL Addit. MS 48023 fol. 355; 13 September 1561, *Cal. S. P. Span. 1558–67*, p.213; 25 May 1562, Jones to Throckmorton, BL Addit. MS 35831 fol. 33; 7 September 1562, AGS E 816 fol. 13; 20 February 1561, Dymock to Cecil, *Cal. S. P. For. 1560–1*, pp.556–7.

109 Francis Goldborne to Mr Harvey, 22 July 1562, PRO SP 70/ 39 fol. 118; 22 July 1562, Ashley and Broadbelt to Guildenstern, SP 70/ 39 fol. 119; 27 July 1562, John Keyle to Geoffrey Preston, SP 70/ 39 fols 175–6; interrogations of Goldborne, Dymock and Keyle, 6 August 1562, PRO SP 70/ 40 fols 62–88.

110 4 August 1562, *Acts of the Privy Council*, ns vii, p.123; 5 August 1562, the Privy Council to Guildenstern, Nichols, *Progresses*, i, p.104; 15 August 1562, Lettenhove, *Relations Politiques*, iii, p.108. Dymock and John Keyle had contacts with Cecil. Letters written to him after the affair was over suggest that they were acting as his agents abroad, and it is possible that he was encouraging them to push the marriage in 1562 in order to thwart Dudley.

111 7 August 1562, Lettenhove, *Relations Politiques*, iii, p.97; Dymock to Cecil, 12 August 1562, PRO SP 70/ 40 fol. 124.

112 12 August 1562, Dymock to Cecil, PRO SP 70/ 40 fol. 124.

113 *Cal. S. P. For. 1562*, pp.384, 389.

114 31 October 1562, *Cal. S. P. For. 1562*, p.412; 15 October 1563, A. I. Cameron (ed.), 'The Warrender Papers', i, *The Scottish Historical Society*, 3rd series 18 (1931), p.36, also in *Cal. S. P. For. 1563*, p.559.

115 *Cal. S. P. For. 1562*, p.412; 18 February and 3 March 1564, *Cal. S. P. For. 1564–5*, pp.50, 69.

116 25 August 1560, PRO SP 52/ 5 fol. 53v; 5 November 1559, *Cal. S. P. Span. 1558–67*, p.109.

117 For Holstein's arrival and entertainments, see BL Addit. MS 48023 fols 352v, 354; Nichols, *Progresses*, i, p.83; 1 April 1560, Lettenhove, *Relations Politiques*, ii, p.291; 23 April 1560, Weiss, *Papiers d'Etat*, vi, p.42. For the reply to his proposal, see 23 August 1560, Holstein to Cecil, *Cal. S. P. For. 1560–1*, p.255.

For Holstein's departure in early May; 13 May 1560, Teulet, *Relations Politiques*, ii, pp.129–30.

118 23 August 1560, Holstein to Cecil, *Cal. S. P. For. 1560–1*, p.255; 17 September 1560, Cecil to Holstein, BL Cott. MS Galba B xi fol. 257.

119 22 December 1560, Holstein to Elizabeth and 20 January 1561, Elizabeth to Holstein, *Cal. S. P. For. 1560–1*, pp.450, 509–10.

120 'They are moche troubled here with the rumour of amity and frendship, which (they say) is like to be betwene the Quene's Majestie and Ferdinando Duke of Autriche', wrote Throckmorton on 10 June 1559. Forbes, *Public Transactions*, i, p.122.

121 These were the words of the Scottish estates to the king of France, 31 August 1560, Teulet, *Relations Politiques*, ii, p.150. On 9 October 1559, de Quadra reported that the French wanted the Swedish match but the previous November Christophe d'Assonleville had written that the enemies of the French favoured a Swedish match; Lettenhove, *Relations Politiques*, i, p.277, ii, p.57. For Cecil's view, see 1 October 1559, *Cal. S. P. For. 1559–60*, p.5.

122 For French support for the duke of Saxony, see *Calendar of State Papers Rome 1558–71*, p.6. For the duke of Nemours, see Forbes, *Public Transactions*, i, pp.135–6.

123 *Cal. S. P. Span. 1558–67*, pp.164, 173; J. H. Pollen (ed.), 'Queen Mary's Letter to the Duke of Guise', *Scottish Historical Society*, 43 (1904), pp.55–7; Lettenhove, *Relations Politiques*, ii, p.647; 14 November 1560, Jones to Throckmorton, BL Addit. MS 35830 fol. 66; *Hardwicke State Papers*, i, pp.163–4.

124 31 August 1560, Teulet, *Relations Politiques*, ii, p.151.

125 The third earl took the title in 1553 when his father, the second earl, also James Hamilton, became styled duke of Châtelherault. 31 August 1560, Teulet, *Relations Politiques*, ii, pp.150–1; 23 October 1560, Peronet de Chantonnay to Philip II, AGS E K1493 B11 no.112

126 Quoted in 28 June 1559, Throckmorton to Cecil, Forbes, *Public Transactions*, i, p.147. See also, 14 June 1559, *Cal. S. P. Scot. 1547–63*, p.215; 28 June and 13 August 1559, de Quadra to Philip II, AGS E 812 fols 69, 100, translated in *Cal. S. P. Span 1558–67*, pp.81, 90.

127 [20] March 1560, Cecil to Thomas Randolph, HMC 58 *Bath*, ii, pp.16–17; 'A motion of the Lords of Scotland for a marriage with the earl of Arran', [December] 1560, PRO SP 52/ 5 fols 127–8v; 20 November 1560, de Quadra to Philip II, AGS E 813 fol. 33, translated in *Cal. S. P. Span. 1558–67*, p.178.

128 13 September 1560, Maitland of Lethington to Cecil, PRO SP 52/ 5 fol. 73v.

129 18 August 1560, Maitland of Lethington to Cecil, PRO SP 52/ 5 fols 37–8v. The Scottish view of the match can also be found in the letter of Randolph, 25 August 1560, PRO SP 52/ 5 fol. 53.

130 AGS E K1492 B10 no.32; 29 September 1560, Chantonnay to Philip II, AGS E K1493 B11 no.102.

131 24 October 1560, Sussex to Cecil, PRO SP 63/ 2 fol. 82.

132 *Cal. S. P. For. 1559–60*, pp.68–9, 102; Lettenhove, *Relations Politiques*, ii, pp.90, 429; Haynes, *Cecil's State Papers*, p.212.

133 31 December 1560, Throckmorton to Dudley, Wright, *Queen Elizabeth*, i, p.58.

134 D. Digges (ed.), *The Compleat Ambassador* (1655), p.63.

3 THE DUDLEY COURTSHIP

1 In his history, Camden wrote that Sussex condemned Dudley 'as a new Upstart, who (as he was wont to say in detracting him) could produce no

more but two Ancestors, namely, his Father and his Grandfather, and those both of them Enemies and Traitours to their Countrey.' Camden, *History*, p.79.

2 6 August 1566, PRO SP 31/ 3/ 26 fol. 134.

3 When Eric of Sweden asked John Dymock why Dudley was 'so muche in favour', the merchant replied that he had sold a piece of his land to help Elizabeth in her trouble under Mary 'as I had hard saye'. Unsupported by any other source, this information is obviously unreliable. 'Statement of John Dymock', 6 August 1562, PRO SP 70/ 40 fol. 72.

4 14 November 1558, Feria to Philip II, AGS E 8340/ 232 fol. 382.

5 S. Adams, 'The Dudley Clientele 1553–63', in *The Tudor Nobility*, edited by G. Bernard (Manchester, 1992), pp.241–55; *Calendar of Patent Rolls 1558–60*, p.61; *1560–3*, pp.189–91.

6 R. McCoy, 'From the Tower to the Tiltyard: Robert Dudley's return to glory', *The Historical Journal* 27 (1984), pp.425–31.

7 18 and 29 April 1559, Feria to Philip II, AGS E 812 fols 44, 48, translated in *Cal. S. P. Span. 1558–67*, pp.57–8, 63; 4 and 10 May 1559, *Cal S. P. Ven. 1558–80*, pp.81, 85; 13 November 1559, *Codoin*, lxxxvii, pp.258–60, translated in *Cal. S. P. Span. 1558–67*, p.112.

8 'An anonymous mid-Tudor chronicle', BL Addit. MS. 48023 fol. 352; 6 December 1559, Lettenhove, *Relations Politiques*, ii, pp.123–4.

9 6 August 1559, Breuner to Ferdinand I, Von Klarwill, *Queen Elizabeth*, pp.113–14.

10 'Draft instructions for the cardinal of Ferrara', July 1561, J. H. Pollen, 'Papal Negotiations with Mary Queen of Scots during her reign in Scotland', *Scottish Historical Society* 37 (1901), pp.60–1.

11 8 September 1559, AGS E 812 fol. 105; 7 September and 29 October 1559, *Cal. S. P. Span. 1558–67*, pp.95–6, 107; 13 December 1559, de Quadra to Philip II, AGS E 8340/ 233 fol. 208; BL Addit. MS 48023 fol. 352.

12 13 November 1559, *Codoin*, lxxxvii, pp.260–1; 27 November 1559, Lettenhove, *Relations Politiques*, ii, p.105; both are translated in *Cal. S. P. Span. 1558–67*, pp.113–14, 117.

13 7 September [1560], Dudley to Sussex, BL Cott. MS Titus B xiii fol. 15.

14 PRO SP/ 12/ 13 no.21.

15 C. Read, *Mr Secretary Cecil and Queen Elizabeth* (1955), pp.199–200; MacCaffrey, *Elizabethan Regime*, pp.74–5.

16 For the death of Amy Dudley, see G. Adlard, *Amye Robsart and the Earl of Leycester: A critical inquiry into the authenticity of the various statements in relation to the death of Amye Robsart* (1870); J. E. Jackson, 'Amye Robsart', *The Wiltshire Archaeological and Natural History Magazine* 18 (1878), pp.47–93; I. Aird, 'The Death of Amy Robsart', *The English Historical Review* 71 (1956), pp.69–79.

17 BL Addit. MS 48023 fol. 353.

18 So wrote Thomas Lever from Coventry [17 September 1560], Haynes, *Cecil's State Papers*, p.362. See also *Cal. S. P. For. 1561–2*, p.3.

19 9 September 1560, Dudley to Blount and 13 September 1560, Blount to Dudley, Adlard, *Amye Robsart*, pp.32–3, 40.

20 There is some other evidence to support the chronicler's view of the foreman. First he wrote to Dudley before the investigation was over to give his opinion that Amy Dudley's death appeared to be an accident. Adlard, *Amye Robsart*, p. 41. Second, a man of his name, Mr Smith, which is admittedly very common but who was also described as 'the quene's man', was the recipient of a gift from Dudley in 1566. I would like to thank Dr George Bernard for this point.

21 BL Addit. MS 48023 fol. 353.
22 10 October 1560, Throckmorton to Northampton, PRO SP 70/ 19 fol. 39; 29 October 1560, Throckmorton to Chamberlain, SP 70/ 19 fol. 132.
23 13 September 1561, de Quadra to Philip II, AGS E 815 fol. 227, translated in *Cal. S. P. Span. 1558–67*, p.213.
24 Adlard, *Amye Robsart*, p.41; Blount to Leicester 1567, HMC 70 *Pepys*, pp.111–12; 9 June 1567, Sir Henry Neville to Sir John Thynne, Jackson, *Wilts Arch. Mag.* (1878), p.78.
25 D. C. Peck (ed.), *Leicester's Commonwealth: The copy of a letter written by a Master of Arts of Cambridge (1584) and related documents* (Ohio, 1985), pp.42–3.
26 Adlard, *Amye Robsart*, pp.35–7. The jury's verdict of 'death by mischance' was possibly a discreet way of acknowledging a suicide. It is worth noting, too, that the death occurred the day before Elizabeth's birthday, a natural time perhaps for Amy Dudley to feel depressed.
27 BL Addit. MS 48023 fol. 353v; 'The declaration and confession of Arthur Gunter', Haynes, *Cecil's State Papers*, pp.364, 365.
28 For Paget see BL Addit. MS 48023 fol. 360; for Sussex see 24 October 1560, Sussex to Cecil, PRO SP 63/ 2 fols 82–3.
29 'Confession of Arthur Gunter', Haynes, *Cecil's State Papers*, p.365.
30 15 October 1560, de Quadra to Philip II, AGS E 814 fol. 40, translated in *Cal. S. P. Span. 1558–67*, pp.176–7.
31 'Machyn's Diary', *Camden Soc.*, 42 (1848), p.252.
32 30 November 1560, Jones to Throckmorton, *Hardwicke State Papers*, i, pp.164–7.
33 'Confession and submission of Arthur Gunter', Haynes, *Cecil's State Papers*, pp.364–5; BL Addit. MS 48023 fol. 353; 13 January 1561, Killigrew to Throckmorton, *Cal. S. P. For. 1560–1*, pp.497–8.
34 31 December 1560, Jones to Throckmorton, PRO SP 70/ 21 fol. 146.
35 30 November 1560, Jones to Throckmorton, *Hardwicke State Papers*, i, p.168.
36 McCoy, *The Historical Journal* (1984), pp.425–31; 9 September 1559, de Quadra to Feria, Lettenhove, *Relations Politiques*, ii, p.23.
37 de Quadra described Dudley on 7 March 1560 as 'el peor moco che yo he visto en mi vida y mas atraydorado y tras esto non nada valiente, ni animoso'. Lettenhove, *Relations Politiques*, ii, p.252.
38 '... conociendo yo que estaba la Reina tan inclinada á este casamiento, se meravillaba que yo no hubiese ofrecido á V. M. esta ocasion para ganar á Milord Roberto, poniéndole hoy de su mano, el cual le serviria y obedeceria como uno de los vasallos propios de V. M.' The dispatches which relay this and succeeding interviews on the subject of the Dudley marriage appear in *Cal. S. P. Span. 1558–67*, pp.178–80 and *Codoin*, lxxxvii, pp.312–16.
39 '... que lo deste Reino esta en muy malos terminos, y que es imposible dejar de remediarlo' and 'estaban determinados restituir Religion por vía del Concilio general'.
40 *Codoin*, lxxxvii, pp.317–19, 'tornóme á hacer grandes ofertas y me certificó que todo esto se pondria en manos de V. M., y aún en lo de la Religion me dijo que sino bastaba enviar al Concilio, iria allá él mismo'.
41 M. Axton, 'Robert Dudley and the Inner Temple Revels', *The Historical Journal* 13 (1970), p.367.
42 K. Bartlett, 'Papal Policy and the English Crown 1563–1565: The Bertano correspondence', *The Sixteenth-Century Journal* 23 (1992), p.651.
43 MacCaffrey, *Elizabethan Regime*, p.78 and *Queen Elizabeth I* (1993), pp.73–4.
44 MacCaffrey, *Elizabethan Regime*, p.72.

45 Bayne, *Anglo-Roman Relations*, pp.74–8.

46 'Memorial to Christopher Mundt', 30 December 1560, PRO SP 70/ 21 fols 109–10v.

47 'Instructions for the earl of Bedford', 20 January 1561, PRO SP 70/ 22 fols 88–97v.

48 17 March 1561, Philip II to de Quadra, AGS E 815 fol. 62, translated in *Cal. S. P. Span 1558–67*, pp.184–6; 17 March 1561, Philip II to the bishop of Arras, Weiss, *Papiers d'Etat*, vi, pp.298–301; 14 April 1561, de Quadra to the bishop of Arras, Lettenhove, *Relations Politiques*, ii, p.548; Bayne, *Anglo-Roman Relations*, pp.87–94.

49 27 January 1561, de Quadra to the bishop of Arras, AGS E 815 fol. 59.

50 'sin la voluntad de los de su reyno', AGS E 815 fol. 65.

51 25 March 1561, de Quadra to Philip II, AGS E 815 fol. 64, translated in *Cal. S. P. Span. 1558–67*, pp.186–91.

52 12 and 14 April 1561, Lettenhove, *Relations Politiques*, ii, pp.546, 548.

53 12 April 1561, de Quadra to Philip II, *Cal. S. P. Span. 1558–67*, pp.191–4.

54 'Examinations of Coxe', 17 April 1561, 19 April 1561, the earl of Oxford to the Council, and 'Further examinations and interrogations', April 1561, PRO SP/ 12/ 16 nos 49–50, 59–68; interrogations to be answered by Lady Waldegrave, *Cal. S. P. Domestic Addenda 1547–65*, p.509.

55 8 May 1561, Cecil to Throckmorton, PRO SP 70/ 26 fols 61–3.

56 28 April 1561, de Quadra to the duchess of Parma, Lettenhove, *Relations Politiques*, ii, pp.559–60; 5 May 1561, de Quadra to Philip II, AGS E 815 fol. 75, translated in *Cal. S. P. Span. 1558–67*, pp.199–203.

57 May 1561, Cecil to Throckmorton, *Hardwicke State Papers*, i, p.171. The original in BL Addit. MS 35830 fol. 109 is dated 10 May 1561.

58 'Consultation at Greenwich', 1 May 1561 and 'Reply to de Quadra to be sent to Throckmorton and Mundt', 5 May 1561, *Cal. S. P. For. 1561–2*, pp.93, 99–100.

59 6 May 1561, de Quadra to the duchess of Parma and bishop of Arras, AGS E 815 fol. 78, translated in *Cal. S. P. Span. 1558–67*, pp.203–4.

60 *Hardwicke State Papers*, i, p.170.

61 1 May 1561, AGS E 815 fols 76, 77.

62 30 June 1561, de Quadra to Philip II, AGS E 815 fol. 86, translated in *Cal. S. P. Span. 1558–67*, pp.208–9.

63 28 September 1561, Killigrew to Throckmorton, BL Addit. MS 35830 fol. 205; 24 December 1561 [the earl of Bedford] to Throckmorton, *Cal. S. P. For. 1561–2*, p.455; the original of this latter document, PRO SP 70/ 33 fol. 60, is badly mutilated and words have been inserted in the calendar.

64 23 August 1561, de Quadra to the bishop of Arras, AGS E 815 fol. 105.

65 27 December 1561, de Quadra to the duchess of Parma, AGS 815 fol. 126; 24 December 1561 [Bedford] to Throckmorton, *Cal. S. P. For. 1561–2*, p.455.

66 28 June 1561, Sir Henry Neville to Throckmorton, PRO SP 70/ 27 fol. 66; 5 December 1561, Thomas Fitzwilliams to Throckmorton, *Cal. S. P. For. 1561–2*, p.424; the original of this latter document is also badly mutilated and words have been inserted in the calendar.

67 The *Dialogue* is printed in J. Strype, *The Life of the Learned Sir Thomas Smith*, Appendix (Oxford, 1820), pp.184–259. For one of the manuscript copies, see BL Addit. MS 48047 fols 97–135.

68 Smith mistakenly wrote down Lady Katherine Grey instead of Elizabeth Woodville – an interesting slip of the pen. This mistake appears in the two MSS I have consulted as well as Strype.

69 J. Phillip, *The Play of Patient Grissell*, edited by R. B. McKerrow and W. W. Greg, Malone Society (1909).
70 L. B. Wright, 'A Political Reflection in Phillip's *Patient Grissell*', *Renaissance English Studies* 4 (1928), pp.424–8.
71 E. Rosenberg, *Leicester Patron of Letters* (New York, 1955), p.47; Axton, *Historical Journal* 13, pp.365–78.
72 Thomas Norton and Thomas Sackville, *Gorboduc or Ferrex and Porrex*, edited by I. B. Cauthen Jr (1970). All the following quotations come from this modern edition.
73 BL Addit. MS 48023 fol. 359v.
74 See for example M. Levine, *The Early Elizabethan Succession Question, 1558–1568* (Stanford, 1966) pp.38–44.
75 R. C. McCoy, *The Rites of Knighthood: The literature and politics of Elizabethan chivalry* (California, 1989), pp.37–40.
76 On 9 January 1561 Dudley told de Quadra 'tenia sus negocios en muy buen punto'. AGS E 815 fol. 186.
77 31 January 1562, de Quadra to Philip II, AGS E 815 fol. 204, translated in *Cal. S. P. Span. 1558–67*, pp. 224–6.
78 BL Addit. MS 48023 fol. 363; 1 May 1562, de Quadra to Philip II, AGS E 8340/ 234 fol. 158v; 30 April 1562, de Quadra to the duchess of Parma, Lettenhove, *Relations Politiques*, iii, p.11. The fullest account of this episode is in Simancas which also mentions 'Ludboro' as a supporter of the petition.
79 25 May 1562, Jones to Throckmorton, BL Addit. MS 35831 fol. 32.
80 1 May 1562, de Quadra to Philip II, AGS E 8340/ 234 fol. 158v.
81 *Cal. S. P. Span. 1558–67*, p.225 says 'more fitting' but the Spanish is 'persona de mejores calidades'; 31 January 1562, de Quadra to Philip II, AGS E 815 fol. 204.
82 6 June 1562, de Quadra to Philip II, AGS E 815 fols 160, 222, translated in *Cal. S. P. Span. 1558–67*, pp.241.
83 1 June 1562, *Cal. S. P. For. 1562*, pp.67–8.
84 28 April and 20 June 1562, de Quadra to the bishop of Arras, Lettenhove, *Relations Politiques*, iii, pp.6, 56; 'The queen's charges against de Quadra', 30 April 1562, AGS E 815 fol. 138; 3 April 1562, de Quadra to the bishop of Arras and 20 June 1562, de Quadra to Philip II, AGS E 815 fols 218, 224. Translations appear in *Cal. S. P. Span. 1558–67*, pp.234, 241–2, 244–5, 247–8, 249.
85 27 November 1561 and 31 January 1562, *Cal. S. P. Span. 1558–67*, pp.219, 224–8; N. M. Sutherland, 'The Origins of Queen Elizabeth's Relations with the Huguenots, 1559–62' in *Princes, Politics and Religion 1547–1589* (1984), p.94.
86 27 November 1561, *Cal. S. P. Span. 1558–67*, p.219; 31 January 1562, de Quadra to Philip II, and 30 April 1562, AGS E 815 fols 140, 204.
87 8 May 1560, *Cal. S. P. For. 1562*, pp.21–2.
88 16 October 1562, de Quadra to the duchess of Parma, Lettenhove, *Relations Politiques*, iii, pp.164–5; 25 October 1562, de Quadra to Philip II, AGS E 816 fols 29, 30.
89 BL Addit. MS 48023 fol. 369.
90 27 October 1562, de Quadra to Philip II, AGS E 815 fol. 190; 15 November 1562, AGS E 816 fol. 43; 25 October 1562, *Cal. S. P. Span. 1558–67*, pp.262–4.
91 15 November 1562, de Quadra to Philip II, AGS E 816 fol. 43, translated in *Cal. S. P. Span. 1558–67*, p.269; 29 November 1562, AGS E 816 fol. 51.
92 J. E. Neale, *Elizabeth I and her Parliaments 1559–81* (1953), i, p.106.
93 W. Murdin, *Burghley's State Papers* (1759), p.755.

94 29 November 1562, AGS E 816 fol. 51.

95 Elton, *Parliament of England*, p.358.

96 G. E. Corrie (ed.), *A Catechism by Alexander Nowell*, Parker Society (Cambridge, 1853), pp.223–9.

97 Read, *Mr. Secretary Cecil*, pp.266–7; Elton, *Parliament of England*, p.358.

98 See the Lord Keeper's opening address, Hartley, *Proceedings*, i, pp.80–6.

99 *Cal. S. P. Span. 1558–67*, p.269; BL Lansdowne MS 102 fol. 18.

100 P. W. Hasler, *The Commons 1558–1603* (1981), ii, p.163.

101 *The Journal of the House of Commons*, i, pp.62–5.

102 Hartley, *Proceedings*, i, pp.90–3.

103 Hartley, *Proceedings*, i, pp.109–10.

104 2 February 1563, Lord Rich to Elizabeth, HMC 70 *Pepys*, p.10; letter to Elizabeth from an unknown peer who was unable to attend the debates in parliament, 10 February 1563, 'The Egerton Papers', *Camden Soc.*, 12 (1840), pp.34–40.

105 Hartley, *Proceedings*, i, p.635.

106 Hartley, *Proceedings*, i, pp.94–5; *C. J.*, i, p.65.

107 7 February 1563, *Cal. S. P. Span. 1558–67*, pp.295–8.

108 Hartley, *Proceedings*, i, p.115.

109 'Interrogations for Francis Newdigate and Lord John Grey', 25 April 1564, Haynes, *Cecil's State Papers*, p.412.

110 S. Adams, 'The Dudley Clientele and the House of Commons 1559–1586', *Parliamentary History* 8 (1989), pp.224–5.

111 *Cal. S. P. Span, 1558–67*, p.313.

112 *Somers Tract*, i, p.175. The queen's letter is misdated as 1583.

113 Professor Elton argued that she was punishing Dudley for his role in the 1563 parliament; Elton, *Parliament of England*, p.363.

114 'Examination of Robert Garrerd', 19 January 1563, *Cal. S. P. Dom. Add. 1547–65*, p.534.

115 For Cecil's views on a Dudley marriage, written somewhat later, see Haynes, *Cecil's State Papers*, p.444; for the Archduke Charles marriage, see 27 January 1563, Von Klarwill, *Queen Elizabeth*, pp.172–3.

116 *Somers Tract*, i, p.175.

117 4 September 1564 and 5 May 1565, *Codoin*, lxxxix, pp.35, 116–17. On 5 May Dudley told de Silva 'nunca la Reina se determinará en casarse conmigo, porque tiene determinacion de casarse con algun gran Príncipe, á los ménos no con súbdito suyo mas no hay con quién fuera del Reino, sino fuese con vuestro Príncipe ó con el Archiduque.' According to de Silva, 'él no podria sin disgusto grande tratar de que la Reina se casase con otro'.

118 Somewhat earlier Chantonnay reported that the French thought of Dudley as pro-French; 23 October 1560, AGS E K1493 B.11 fol. 112. For French support of Dudley marriage, 9 June 1565, AGS E 818 fol. 41, translated in *Cal. S. P. Span. 1558–67*, pp.435–6.

119 22 August 1565, de Foix to Catherine de Medici, Teulet, *Relations Politiques*, ii, p.217; 20 August 1565, AGS E 818 fol. 57; Le Laboureur, *Nouvelles Additions aux Mémoires de Michel de Castelnau* (Brussels, 1731).

120 See chapter 4, p. 78.

121 27 March 1565, Bedford to Leicester and 2 June 1566, Lawrence Humphrey to Leicester, HMC 70 *Pepys*, pp.53, 87–8; 7 April 1565, Parker to Cecil, Bruce (ed.), *Parker Correspondence*, p.237; P. Collinson, *The Elizabethan Puritan Movement* (1967), pp.92–3.

122 C. M. Dent, *Protestant Reformers in Elizabethan Oxford* (Oxford, 1983), pp.25, 29, 292; August 1563, Grindal to Dudley, W. Nicholson (ed.), *The Remains of*

Edmund Grindal, Parker Society (Cambridge, 1843), pp.261–4; Bartlett, *Sixteenth-Century Journal* (1992), pp.646, 656–7.

123 27 October 1563, *Cal. S. P. Rome, 1558–70*, p.153.

124 MacCaffrey, *Making of Policy*, pp.440–1; Collinson, *Puritan Movement*, p.92; Dent, *Protestant Reformers*, p.242.

125 2 January 1565 and 23 December 1566, *Codoin*, lxxxix, pp.70, 420, translated in *Cal. S. P. Span. 1558–67*, pp.401–2, 605–6.

126 For more details of Leicester's relationship with Lady Sheffield, see Peck, *Leicester's Commonwealth*, pp.269–71; G. K. Warner, *The Voyage of Robert Dudley to the West Indies*, Hakluyt Society, second series 3 (1899), introduction.

127 For following quotations see Nichols, *Progresses*, i, pp.426–522; J. W. Cunliffe (ed.), *The Complete Works of George Gascoigne* (1919), ii, pp.91–131. Not all literary critics think that Leicester meant seriously a proposal of marriage. Among those who argue that the main purpose was marriage, see M. Axton, *The Queen's Two Bodies* (1977), pp.61–6; and H. Cooper, 'Location and Meaning in Masque', in *The Court Masque*, edited by David Lindley (Manchester, 1984), p.142.

128 An interesting discussion on the tensions between the rival representations of the queen devised by Leicester and Elizabeth can be found in Frye, *Representations*, pp.56–96.

129 A.W. Pollard (ed.), *The Queen's Majesty's Entertainment at Woodstock 1575* (Oxford, 1903 and 1910).

130 Only the cartoons of the paintings have survived. That for Elizabeth's portrait is inscribed with the date May 1575. R. Strong, *Gloriana: The portraits of Queen Elizabeth I* (1987), pp.85–6.

131 McCoy, *Historical Journal* (1984), p.435.

132 Samaha, *J. Soc. Hist.* (1975) p.69; I. Cloulas, *Correspondance du Nonce en France, Anselmo Dandino (1578–1581)*, Acta Nuntiaturae Gallicae 8 (Paris, 1979), p.516.

4 THE ARCHDUKE CHARLES MATRIMONIAL PROJECT 1563–7

1 A shorter version of this chapter which did not draw upon the archives in Simancas appeared in S. Doran, 'Religion and Politics at the Court of Elizabeth I: The Habsburg marriage negotiations of 1559–1567', *The English Historical Review* 104 (1989), pp.908–26.

2 P. S. Fichtner, 'The Disobediente of the Obedient: Ferdinand I and the Papacy 1555–1564', *The Sixteenth-Century Journal* 11 (1980), pp.25–35; copy of Christopher Mundt's undated letter recommending the Archduke Charles, BL Cott. MS Nero B ix fol. 104.

3 31 August 1559, Breuner to Ferdinand I, Von Klarwill, *Queen Elizabeth*, p.119.

4 5 October 1559, de Quadra to the bishop of Arras, Lettenhove, *Relations Politiques*, ii, p.55.

5 21 August 1565, Cecil to Sir Thomas Smith, Wright, *Queen Elizabeth*, i, p.207; 14 September 1566, *Cal. S. P. Span. 1558–67*, p.580, translated in *Codoin*, lxxxix, p.374.

6 *Cal. S. P. For. 1563*, pp.70, 207, 302; 8 May 1563, Lettenhove, *Relations Politiques*, iii, p.399.

7 19 August 1563, Ferdinand to Martin de Guzman, *Codoin*, xcviii, pp.494–5.

8 12 October 1563, Smith to Elizabeth, *Cal. S. P. For. 1563*, p.551; 28 December 1563, Mundt to Cecil, HMC 9 *Salisbury*, i, p.285.

9 'Report of Allinga', 30 January 1564, Von Klarwill, *Queen Elizabeth*, p.186; 28 December 1563, HMC 9 *Salisbury*, i, pp.285–6.

10 14 October 1563, Mundt to the duke of Württemberg, Von Klarwill, *Queen Elizabeth*, pp.174–7.

11 23 March 1564, the duke of Württemberg to Ferdinand I and the 'Report of Allinga', 30 January 1564, Von Klarwill, *Queen Elizabeth*, pp.177–9, 185–6, 189–90.

12 23 March 1564, Von Klarwill, *Queen Elizabeth*, p.178.

13 H. Horie, ' The Lutheran Influence on the Elizabethan Settlement 1558–63', *The Historical Journal* 34 (1991), pp.520–4.

14 30 January 1564, Von Klarwill, *Queen Elizabeth*, p.180; 24 January 1564, Wright, *Queen Elizabeth*, i, p.163.

15 28 January 1566, *Codoin*, lxxxix, p.254, 'acqui no vivian como turcos, que tenián el Santiísimo Sacramento y seguian la confesion de Augusta, como ella habia entendido que el Archiduque lo hacía'. The translation in *Cal. S. P. Span 1558–67*, p.513 is not entirely accurate.

16 26 April 1565, *Codoin*, lxxxix, p.109; a translation is in *Cal. S. P. Span. 1558–67*, p.422.

17 12 March 1565, *Codoin*, lxxxix, pp.78–9 translated in *Cal. S. P. Span. 1558–67*, p.405.

18 21 April 1565, AGS E 818 fol. 26, she performed the ceremony 'con mucha auctoridad y devocion' with a translation in *Cal. S. P. Span. 1558–67*, p.419.

19 21 April 1565, AGS E 818 fol. 26, translated in *Cal. S. P. Span. 1558–67*, p.419.

20 4 June 1565, Zwetkowich to Maximilian I, Von Klarwill, *Queen Elizabeth*, p.234.

21 The copy of the *Advertisements* is dated 1566 and described as the articles of the English Church. AGS E 819 fol. 17.

22 12 September 1564, Cecil to Smith, Wright, *Queen Elizabeth*, i, p.176; 23 September 1564, BL Lansd. MS 102 fol. 100v; 17 September 1564, de Silva to the duchess of Parma, Lettenhove, *Relations Politiques*, iv, p.106; 18 and 23 September 1564, *Cal. S. P. Span. 1558–67*, pp.380, 382.

23 4 November 1564, Mundt to the duke of Württemberg, Von Klarwill, *Queen Elizabeth*, p.201.

24 1 February 1564, Le Strange to Breuner, Haynes, *Cecil's State Papers*, i, p.430; contents of letters from Chantonnay, March and April 1565, AGS E 653 fol. 23; 4 February 1565, Von Klarwill, *Queen Elizabeth*, pp.203–4.

25 De Silva was told by Spinola who 'es gran cosa del Roberto'. 2 July 1564, de Silva to the duchess of Parma, Lettenhove, *Relations Politiques*, iv, p.46.

26 Charles IX was born 17 June 1550 and was, therefore, nearly seventeen years younger than the queen. De Foix told Catherine de Medici that Elizabeth first broached the topic of a marriage, but Elizabeth informed the Spanish ambassador that de Foix had approached her and she had laughed at it because of their respective ages. 'Report of the French envoy in England to Catherine de Medici', December 1564, HMC *Third Report*, pp.262–3; 9 October 1564, de Silva to Philip II, AGS E 817 fol. 109, translated in *Cal. S. P. Span. 1558–67*, pp.384–7. For Dudley's part in the negotiations see 15 March 1565, de Silva to Philip II, *Codoin*, lxxxix, pp.82–3, translated in *Cal. S. P. Span. 1558–67*, p.407.

27 *Lettres de Catherine de Médicis*, ii, p.256.

28 26 March 1565, *Cal. S. P. For. 1564–5*, p.321.

29 4 June 1565, de Foix to Catherine de Medici, PRO 31/ 3/ 26 fols 1–2; 12 June 1565, Cecil to Smith, BL Lansd. MS 102 fol. 112.

30 14 April 1565, de Silva to Philip II, AGS E 818 fol. 22; 26 April 1565, *Codoin*, lxxxix, pp.102–3; translations appear in *Cal. S. P. Span. 1558–67*, pp.415, 420.

31 18 September 1564, *Codoin*, lxxxix, pp.35–6 translated in *Cal. S. P. Span. 1558–67*, p.380.

32 '. . . yo os prometo que si hoy pudiese nombrar sucesor a este Reino tal como yo querria y convendra, que no me casase, porque no es cosa á que jamás he sido aficionada; pero dándome tanta priesa mis súbditos, que no se podrá dejar de hacer, a lo ménos este otro medio, que será bien dificil.' 24 March 1565, *Codoin*, lxxxix, p.86.

33 28 April and 9 July 1565, AGS E 818 fols 24, 52; translations appear in *Cal. S. P. Span 1558–67*, pp.426, 447.

34 6 June 1565, Philip II to de Silva and 13 July 1565, de Silva to Philip II, *Codoin*, lxxxix, pp.123, 142–3, translated in *Cal. S.P. Span. 1558–67*, pp.434, 447–8.

35 'Summary of the advice given by the Privy Council', 4 June 1565, PRO SP 52/ 10 fols 148–51.

36 3 June 1565, Cecil to Smith, BL Lansd. MS 102 fol. 110; June 1565, PRO 31/ 3/ 26 fol. 20.

37 For the origins of the conflict between Sussex and Leicester, see S. Doran 'The Political Career of Thomas Radcliffe, Third Earl of Sussex 1526?–1583', unpublished Ph.D thesis, University of London (1979), pp.152–5; for Norfolk, 31 March 1565, Randolph to Throckmorton, PRO SP 52/ 10 fol. 68.

38 June 1565, PRO 31/ 3/ 26 fol. 16; undated letter Sussex to Philip II, AGS E 819 fol. 22; 4 June 1565, Von Klarwill, *Queen Elizabeth*, pp.223–5.

39 Von Klarwill, *Queen Elizabeth*, p.232; *Cal. S. P. Span. 1558–67*, pp.407, 517; Haynes, *Cecil's State Papers*, pp.409–10. The Imperial ambassador thought that Pembroke and Shrewsbury were amongst the match's supporters but de Foix thought that they, together with Bedford, were not keen on the match. PRO 31/ 3/ 25 fols 1, 20–1. Arundel was playing little part in political life after his resignation from the Lord Stewardship in the early summer of 1564.

40 Von Klarwill, *Queen Elizabeth*, pp.208–9.

41 'Provisions in the marriage pact as they were indicated by Cecil in the name of the queen 30 May 1565', 2 June 1565, Von Klarwill, *Queen Elizabeth*, p.212.

42 9 June 1565, AGS E 818 fol. 41; 2 July 1565, *Cal. S. P. Span. 1558–67*, p.444; 2 July 1565, Von Klarwill, *Queen Elizabeth*, pp.237–8; 4 June 1565, PRO 31/ 3/ 26 fols 1, 14–15, 20; Teulet, *Relations Politiques*, ii, p.217.

43 4 June 1565, Von Klarwill, *Queen Elizabeth*, p.224.

44 4 June 1565, Von Klarwill, *Queen Elizabeth*, pp.216, 224–5; 4 June 1565, de Foix to Catherine de Medici, PRO 31/ 3/ 26 fol. 2.

45 Haynes, *Cecil's State Papers*, p.444; June 1565, PRO 31/ 3/ 26 fols 14–15.

46 4 June 1565, Zwetkowich to Maximilian I, Von Klarwill, *Queen Elizabeth*, p.225; June 1565, PRO 31/ 3/ 26 fols 13–15.

47 17 June 1565, Sussex to Elizabeth, PRO SP 12/ 36 fol. 152.

48 4 July 1565, Von Klarwill, *Queen Elizabeth*, p.240.

49 4 and 16 July 1565, Von Klarwill, *Queen Elizabeth*, pp.241–4.

50 23 July 1565, *Cal. S. P. Span. 1558–67*, pp.452–3.

51 6 August 1565, Zwetkowich to Maximilian I, Von Klarwill, *Queen Elizabeth*, pp.248–51.

52 'Answers to the inquiries of the emperor's orator', 12 August 1565, Von Klarwill, *Queen Elizabeth*, pp.251–2; 12 August 1565, AGS E 818 fol. 53.

53 Dent, *Protestant Reformers*, pp.34–7.

54 21 August 1565, Wright, *Queen Elizabeth*, i, pp.206–9;

55 27 August 1565, *Cal. S. P. Span. 1558–67*, p.470; 3 September 1565, de Silva to Philip II, AGS E 818 fol. 57; contents of de Silva's letters between 24 September and 15 November 1565, AGS E 818 fol. 62; contents of his letters 9, 14 and 22 October 1565, AGS E 818 fol. 72.

56 6 August 1565, *Codoin*, lxxxix, p.163, translated in *Cal. S. P. Span. 1558–67*, p.461.

57 10 November 1565, Chantonnay to Philip II, AGS E 653 fol. 54.

58 19 November 1565, Maximilian I to his ambassador at the Spanish court, Von Klarwill, *Queen Elizabeth*, p.255; 20 October 1565, Philip II to de Silva, AGS E 818 fol. 76; 10 November 1565, de Silva to Philip II, AGS E 818 fol. 89; translations of these latter two appear in *Cal. S. P. Span. 1558–67*, pp.491, 506–7.

59 27 November 1565, Maximilian to Elizabeth, *Cal. S. P. For. 1564–5*, pp.526–7; 19 November 1565, Von Klarwill, *Queen Elizabeth*, pp.255–7. Reference to the letter as conciliatory can be found in Sussex's letter to Philip II dated 1566, AGS E 819 fol. 22.

60 24 December 1565, Philip II to Chantonnay, Pollen (ed.), 'Papal Negotiations with Mary, Queen of Scots' (1901), p.469.

61 4 February 1565, AGS E 819 fol. 66 names Huntingdon clearly unlike the versions in either *Codoin*, lxxxix, p.259 or *Cal. S. P. Span. 1558–67*, pp.518–20.

62 In June 1565, de Spes had seen a link between the commercial disputes in Flanders and progress of the the archduke's suit in England. Elizabeth saw the marriage negotiations, he said, as a way to 'effectuar conforme a sus desseos los negocios de Flandes', AGS E 818 fol. 32. For the Bruges conference see G. D. Ramsey, *The Queen's Merchants and the Revolt of the Netherlands* (Manchester, 1986), pp.17–29.

63 11 February 1566, *Codoin*, lxxxix, p.272, translated in *Cal. S. P. Span. 1558–67*, pp.525–6.

64 19 February 1566, Throckmorton to Leicester, HMC 70 *Pepys*, pp.78–9.

65 Sir Thomas Smith was another Dudley supporter, who had decided in late 1565 that it would be better for Elizabeth to marry a foreigner rather than not marry at all. HMC 70 *Pepys*, p.67.

66 Bayne, *Anglo-Roman Relations*, pp.206–7.

67 'First draft of the instructions for Thomas Sackville', 25 February 1566, BL Cott. MS Vitellius C xi fols 228–32; 30 March 1566, de Silva to Philip II, AGS E 819 fol. 75. Sackville's father died on 21 April 1566.

68 22 April 1566, de Silva to Philip II, AGS E 819 fol. 80, translated in *Cal. S. P. Span. 1558–67*, p.544.

69 Memorandum entitled 'The inconveniences or difficulties mentioned in the emperor's letters with the answers to the same', 30 April 1566, BL Cott. MS Vitellius C xi fols 238–9; 'Instructions given to Dannett', 30 April 1566, BL Cott. MS Vitellius C ix fols 244–6; 2 April 1566, Elizabeth to Maximilian I, AGS E 656 fol. 39; 1565, Elizabeth to Maximilian I, PRO SP 70/ 27 fol. 937.

70 'Reply of the Imperial Chancery to Thomas Dannett', July 1566, Von Klarwill, *Queen Elizabeth*, pp.259–64.

71 4 July 1566, Dannett to Cecil, PRO SP 70/ 85 fol. 8.

72 4 July 1566, Dannett to Elizabeth, PRO SP 70/ 85 fols 6–7.

73 30 August 1566, *Cal. S. P. Span. 1558–67*, p.575.

74 14 September 1566, AGS E 819 fol. 74, translated in *Cal. S. P. Span. 1558–67*, pp.578. For the masque performed at the wedding of Frances Radcliffe see Bodl. Rawlinson MS 108 fols 19v–35. A fuller discussion on the masque is in

S. Doran 'Juno versus Diana: The treatment of Elizabeth I's marriage in plays and entertainments, 1561–81', *The Historical Journal* 38 (1995), pp.264–5.

75 1566, PRO SP 12/ 40 fol. 195.

76 6 September 1566, *Codoin*, lxxxix, p.369 translated in *Cal. S. P. Span. 1558–67*, p.577; 14 September 1566, AGS E 819 fol. 74, translated in *Cal. S. P. Span. 1558–67*, p.578.

77 BL Egerton MS 2836 fols 36–71.

78 Murdin, *Burghley's State Papers*, p.762. The succession was of course a matter for the royal prerogative.

79 MacCaffrey, *Elizabethan Regime*, p.145. This episode is described in La Forêt's dispatch to Charles IX on 21 October 1566 which I have not seen.

80 Elton, *Parliament of England*, p.366; Hasler, *Commons*, iii, pp.60–1; Haynes, *Cecil's State Papers*, p.444.

81 J. D. Alsop, 'Reinterpreting the Elizabethan Commons: The parliamentary session of 1566', *The Journal of British Studies* 29 (1990), pp.216–40.

82 *C. J.*, i, p.75.

83 19 October 1566, de Silva to Philip II, AGS E 819 fol. 7.

84 *L. J.*, i, p.635; 4 November 1566, *Codoin*, lxxxix, p.394, translated in *Cal. S. P. Span. 1558–67*, p.591.

85 27 October 1566, Murdin, *Burghley's State Papers*, p.762.

86 22 September 1566, PRO 31/ 3/ 26 fol. 172.

87 *C. J.*, i, pp.75–6.

88 Hartley, *Proceedings*, p.147.

89 Hartley, *Proceedings*, p.164; 4 November 1566, *Cal. S. P. Span. 1558–67*, p.592; 6 January 1567, de Silva to Philip II, AGS E 819 fol. 16.

90 BL Lansd. MS 1236 fol. 42.

91 30 January 1567, BL Cott. MS Vitellius C xi fols 240–2v.

92 AGS E 819 fols 26, 38, 54, 56, 80. The Imperial delegation arrived in London on 2 June 1567 with no instructions concerning the marriage.

93 26 April 1567, *Codoin*, lxxxix, pp.473–4, translated in *Cal. S. P. Span. 1558–67*, pp.636–7.

94 In the summer of 1567, the Spaniards and Austrians were blaming the Calvinists for the troubles in the Netherlands and France. AGS E 657 fol. 30.

95 30 January 1567, BL Cott. MS Vitellius C xi fols 240–2. A Latin prayerbook was printed in 1560 for use in the universities and schools of Winchester and Eton.

96 'Instructions for Sussex', 20 June 1567, PRO SP 70/ 91 fols 82–8.

97 For the diary of Sussex's journey, Bodl. Tanner MS 50 fols 190–200.

98 22 July 1567, Sussex to Cecil, PRO SP 70/ 92 fol. 78; 22 July 1567, Sussex to Elizabeth, PRO SP 70/ 92 fol. 81; 'schedule enclosed in letter to Cecil', 22 July 1567, PRO SP 70/ 92 fol. 82.

99 9 August 1567, Cobham to Cecil, Haynes, *Cecil's State Papers*, pp.451–2; letters from Sussex, 11 August 1567, PRO SP 70/ 93 fols 41, 43; 18 August 1567 Maximilian I to the archduke, Von Klarwill, *Queen Elizabeth*, pp.264–6; *Cal. S. P. Ven. 1558–80*, p.403.

100 22 August 1567, the archduke to Maximilian I, Von Klarwill, *Queen Elizabeth*, pp.267–8.

101 20 September 1567, Chantonnay to Philip II, AGS E 657 fol. 68; 27 August 1567, Sussex to Elizabeth, BL Cott. MS Galba B xi fols 300–2; 8 September 1567, Maximilian to the archduke, Von Klarwill, *Queen Elizabeth*, pp.268–72.

102 Von Klarwill, *Queen Elizabeth*, p.272; 16 October 1567, *Cal. S. P. Ven. 1558–80*, p.405; 18 October 1567, Sussex to Elizabeth, E. Lodge, *Illustrations of British History, Biography and Manners* (1838), i, p.445.

103 'Reply to Sussex with reference to his last proposal', 23 October 1567, Von Klarwill, *Queen Elizabeth*, pp.279–82; 'The toleration required for the archduke', 24 October 1567, BL Cott. MS Julius F vi fol. 61.

104 24 October 1567, Sussex to Elizabeth, PRO SP 70/ 94 fols 161–2.

105 Von Klarwill, *Queen Elizabeth*, pp.280–1.

106 29 November 1567, Stanley to the earl of Derby, PRO SP 12/ 44 fol. 112. In my article in the *English Historical Review* I referred in error to the Controller as Edward Rogers who had in fact died the previous year.

107 15 November 1567, AGS E 819 fol. 219, translated in *Cal. S. P. Span. 1558–67*, p.684; 22 November 1567, AGS E 819 fol. 51; 18 December 1567, Norfolk to Sussex, BL Cott. MS Titus B ii fol. 308; 15 November 1567, Norfolk to Cecil, PRO SP 12/ 44 fols 90–1; 15 November 1567, Norfolk to Elizabeth, HMC 58 *Bath*, ii, p.17; N. Williams, *Thomas Howard, Fourth Duke of Norfolk* (1964), pp.128–9.

108 BL Addit. MS 4149 fol. 89. See chapter 8 for a fuller discussion.

109 The sermon itself has not survived but reference is made to it in Stanley's letter of 29 November 1567, PRO SP 12/ 44 fol. 112. The biblical text comes from Joshua 6:26.

110 Bishop Grindal had told Bullinger in June 1567 that 'unless Charles chooses to renounce popery, he has nothing to hope for in this quarter', 21 June 1567, *Zurich Letters*, p.192. Archbishop Parker, on the other hand, continued to support the match in November 1567 and was prepared to see the temporary and limited toleration of the Mass. BL Cott. MS Vitellius C xi fol. 282.

111 There is no direct evidence for Leicester's role in encouraging preaching against the marriage but George Stanley made accusations against him on this score. 21 January 1568, Leicester to Sussex, BL Lansd. MS 9 fol. 214.

112 1 December 1567, de Silva to Philip II, AGS E 819 fol. 217 translated in *Cal. S. P. Span. 1558–67*, p.686; 6 December 1567, AGS E 819 fol. 218; 21 December 1567, AGS E 819 fol. 221, translated in *Cal. S. P. Span. 1558–67*, p.689.

113 1 December 1567, AGS E 819 fol. 217.

114 'Copy of the Lord Keeper's speeches in the Star Chamber', 28 November 1568, PRO SP 12/ 44 fols 109–10.

115 Somerset, *Elizabeth I*, p.200, called it a 'nonsense'.

116 10 December 1567, Elizabeth to Sussex, PRO SP 70/ 95 fols 129–31.

117 12 December 1567, Elizabeth to Sussex, PRO SP 70/ 95 fol. 133.

118 3 January 1568, PRO SP 70/ 96 fols 13–14; 27 January 1568, PRO SP 70/ 96 fol. 99; 11 January 1568, Von Klarwill, *Queen Elizabeth*, pp.284–9; 15 and 22 January 1568, *Cal. S. P. Ven. 1558–80*, pp.409, 410.

119 19 December 1567, Sussex to Cecil, PRO SP 70/ 95 fol. 161.

120 Murdin, *Burghley's State Papers*, p.760; 17 June 1565, Sussex to Leicester, PRO SP 12/ 36 fol. 152; Camden, *History*, p.79.

121 28 January *Codoin*, lxxxix, pp.249–50, translated in *Cal. S. P. Span. 1558–67*, p.511.

122 23 June 1566, *Codoin*, lxxxix, pp.336–7, translated in *Cal. S. P. Span. 1558–67*, pp.560–1; 6 July 1566, AGS E 819 fol. 104, translated in *Cal. S. P. Span. 1558–67*, p.565; 23 June 1566, HMC *7th Report*, p.619.

123 10 May 1567, Throckmorton to Leicester and 1567, Blount to Leicester, HMC 70 *Pepys*, pp.103, 111; 31 May 1567, HMC 9 *Salisbury*, i, pp.345, 350.

124 16 June 1566, PRO SP 63/ 18 fol. 44.

125 June 1566, archdeacon of Essex to Leicester referring to his May Day sermon, HMC 70 *Pepys*, p.90.

126 16 December 1566, *Codoin*, lxxxix, p.416, translated in *Cal. S. P. Span 1558–67*, p.604. She may have been referring to two of the six religious bills introduced

in December 1566; the first proposed to give statutory authority to the Thirty-nine articles and the other was 'for the order of ministers' and would control preaching.

127 In the letters of English Protestants to the divines at Zurich and Geneva in the mid-1560s there are many hostile references to Lutherans, which suggest an anxiety about their influence. *Zurich Letters*, ii, pp.125, 139, 143, 157.

128 Bruce (ed.), *Parker Correspondence*, pp.223–7, 262–3; J. H. Primus, *The Vestments Controversy* (Amsterdam, 1960), p.93; P. Collinson (ed.), 'Letters of Thomas Wood, Puritan 1566–77', *Bulletin of the Institute of Historical Research*, Special Supplement no. 5 (1960), pp.xii–xiii.

129 Contents of de Silva's letter 9 October 1565, AGS E 818 fol. 72; copy of Parker's *Advertisements* in the archives at Simancas, AGS E 819 fol. 17.

130 Undated letter of Sussex to Philip II, AGS E 819 fol. 22: 'Ninguna cosa proba piu la utilita di questo con la casa de Austria che questa che li Franzezi nostri inimici lo repugnano.'

131 It is for this reason that I disagree with Malcolm Thorp's argument that already in the early 1560s Spain was perceived as the enemy. M. Thorp, 'Catholic Conspiracy in Early Elizabethan Foreign Policy', *The Sixteenth-Century Journal* 15 (1984), pp.431–49.

132 7 June 1565, AGS 818 fol. 32; 'solo el medio para conservarse en su estado, y donde ella podra tener al Rey Catolico y al Emperador por sus protectores'.

133 Haynes, *Cecil's State Papers*, p.444; 4 February 1566, *Codoin*, lxxxix, p.259, translated in *Cal. S. P. Span. 1558–67*, pp.517–18; 27 October 1567, Sussex to Cecil, PRO SP 70/ 94 fol. 173; Alvarez, *Tres Embajadores*, p.200.

134 Contents of letters from Chantonnay from 31 March until 25 April 1565, AGS E 653 fol. 23; 6 June 1565, *Codoin*, lxxxix, pp.122–3, translated in *Cal. S. P. Span. 1558–67*, p.434; 9 June 1565, Chantonnay to Philip II, AGS E 653 fol. 33; 20 October 1565, Philip II to de Silva, AGS E 818 fol. 76, translated in *Cal. S. P. Span. 1558–67*, p.491; 3 January 1566, Philip II to Chantonnay, AGS E 656 fol. 56.

135 16 August, 20 September and 16 October 1567, Chantonnay to Philip II, AGS E 657 fols 62, 68, 74b.

136 *Cal. S. P. Span. 1568–79*, pp.2–3, 4–5.

137 Haynes, *Cecil's State Papers*, pp.579–88; 25 March 1568, Bruce (ed.), *Parker Correspondence*, pp.317–18; E. I. Kouri, *England and the Attempts to Form a Protestant Alliance in the Late 1560s: A case-study in European diplomacy*, Annales Academiae Scientarum Fennicae 210 (Helsinki, 1981).

138 Grindal's funeral sermon for Emperor Ferdinand, 3 October 1564, J. Strype, *The History of the Life and Acts of the Most Reverend Father in God, Edmund Grindal* (Oxford, 1821), p.148.

5 HENRY DUKE OF ANJOU

1 The eldest born in June 1550 was only eight at the time of the negotiations. Elizabeth was born in September 1533.

2 Lettenhove, *Relations Politiques*, i, p.432; Le Laboureur, *Mémoires*, ii, p.258.

3 23 June 1568, Sir Henry Norris to Cecil, PRO SP/ 70/ 98 fol. 227; 5 July 1568, *Cal. S. P. For. 1566–8*, p.494; Haynes, *Cecil's State Papers*, pp.473–5; N. M. Sutherland, *The Massacre of St Bartholomew and the European Conflict 1559–72* (1973), pp.69–73.

4 28 June 1568, PRO SP 70/ 98 fol. 245.

5 12 May 1568, PRO SP 70/ 98 fol. 36. Henry was born on 20 September 1551.

6 20 October 1570, *Lettres de Catherine de Médicis*, iv, pp.6–10 which includes the letter calendared in *Cal. S. P. For. 1569–71*, pp.372–3; 22 January 1571, *Cal. S .P. Span. 1568–79*, pp.290–1; Teulet, *Relations Politiques*, ii, pp.358, 418.

7 N. M. Sutherland, *The Huguenot Struggle for Recognition* (New Haven, Conn., 1980), pp.83–4. At this time Admiral Coligny preferred an Italian campaign and was opposed to a Huguenot invasion of the Netherlands unless Charles IX first declared war on Spain.

8 In May 1570 she had raised Elizabeth's marriage in general terms with the resident English ambassador who thought she was opening the suit of Anjou. Catherine, however, remonstrated that he was too young and that Leicester was a more suitable choice, 4 May 1570, Catherine to Fénélon, *Fénélon*, vii, pp.110–11.

9 20 October 1570, *Lettres de Catherine de Médicis*, iv, pp.9–10.

10 9 November 1570, *Fénélon*, iii, pp.357–60.

11 2 February 1571, *Lettres de Catherine de Médicis*, iv, pp.26–7; 5 and 9 February 1570, Alva to Philip II, AGS E K1519 B29 nos 11, 13.

12 7 September 1571, *Fénélon*, iv, p.225.

13 These arguments were presented in 'A discourse on the queen's marriage with the duke of Anjou', of which there are several manuscript copies, thought to be written by Lord Keeper Bacon in 1570. A printed version is in 'The Egerton Papers', *Camden Soc.*, 12 (1840), pp.51–9. Similar points were made in 'Rough notes by Cecil of the considerations for and against the queen's marriage', 14 January 1571, PRO SP 70/ 116 fols 19–20.

14 13 September 1570 and 16 January 1571, Lettenhove, *Relations Politiques*, vi, pp.5, 37. In fact Alva opposed Philip II's policy of encouraging Catholic rebellion in England.

15 14 and 17 September and 21 November 1570, *Cal. S. P. For. 1569–71*, pp.335, 339, 371. The desperation of Elizabeth is suggested by the French ambassador's report that she was even prepared to offer him the free exercise of his religion, 5 September 1570, *Fénélon*, iii, p.300. While Elizabeth would not have agreed to the use of a private Mass, it is likely that she was prepared to make some other new concessions. The Venetians also thought that Elizabeth was offering new terms and that her envoy had been given sufficient authority 'to bind her to whatever he may conclude as to the marriage', 27 September 1570, *Cal. S. P. Ven. 1558–80*, p.458.

16 In fact no final decision had been taken about the treasure, which were Genoese loans to the Spanish king. De Spes believed that Elizabeth had decided to appropriate the money and therefore advised Alva to take preventative action. J. Retamal Favereau, 'Anglo-Spanish Relations 1566–72: The mission of Don Guerau de Spes at London', unpublished Oxford University D. Phil. (1972), pp.98–113; G. D. Ramsey, 'The Foreign Policy of Elizabeth I', in *The Reign of Elizabeth I*. Edited by Christopher Haigh (1984), pp.156–7.

17 Retamal Favereau, 'Anglo-Spanish Relations', pp.154–5.

18 Undated paper entitled 'The commodities that may follow upon the marriage with the duke of Anjou', PRO SP 70/ 115 fol. 96; 'Egerton Papers', *Camden Soc.*, 12 (1840), p.58.

19 An assessment of the actual danger posed by Mary's presence in England appears in P. J. Holmes, 'Mary Stewert in England', in *Mary Stewert Queen in Three Kingdoms*. Edited by Michael Lynch (Oxford, 1988), pp.195–215.

20 30 April and 22 May 1570, Elizabeth to Sussex, BL Cott. MS Caligula C ii fols 201–2, 214.

21 29 September 1570 and 7 and 20 October 1570, *Cal. S. P. For. 1569–71*, pp.346, 350, 359.

22 'Egerton Papers', *Camden Soc.*, 12 (1840), pp.53, 58.

23 J. H. M. Salmon, 'Gallicanism and Anglicanism in the Age of the Counter-Reformation', in *Renaissance and Revolt: Essays in the intellectual and social history of early-modern France* (Cambridge, 1987), pp.160–1.

24 Indeed when the pope initially refused to grant a dispensation for Marguerite to marry Henry of Navarre, Catherine went on with planning the marriage anyway.

25 'Egerton Papers', *Camden Soc.*, 12 (1840), pp.57–8.

26 29 December 1570 and 18 January 1571, *Fénélon*, iii, pp.418–20, 438–9.

27 18 January 1571, *Fénélon*, iii, pp.439–40; 22 January 1571, *Cal. S. P. Span. 1568–79*, p.291.

28 2 March 1571, *Lettres de Catherine de Médicis*, iv, p.311.

29 3 April 1571, Catherine to Fénélon, *Fénélon*, vii, p.200.

30 3 February 1571, Walsingham to Leicester, Wright, *Queen Elizabeth*, i, p.385.

31 F. J. Levy, 'A Semi-Professional Diplomat: Guido Cavalcanti and the marriage negotiations of 1571', *Bulletin of the Institute of Historical Research* 35 (1962), pp.211–20; 29 December 1570, *Fénélon*, iii, pp.416–18.

32 16 March 1571, Buckhurst to Elizabeth, PRO SP 70/ 117 fols 33–40; 2 March 1571, *Lettres de Catherine de Médicis*, iv, p.31. They also took with them Elizabeth's portrait to give to Anjou.

33 14 February 1571, Leicester to Walsingham, Digges, *Compleat Ambassador*, p.47; see also 23 March 1571, pp.70–1.

34 24 March 1571, Elizabeth to Walsingham, Digges, *Compleat Ambassador*, pp.62–6.

35 She was not demanding the immediate conversion of Anjou, as had originally been expected of the Archduke Charles, but she was requiring the same restrictions on his exercise of religion as had been demanded as the Habsburg negotiations progressed.

36 Draft by Cecil of a paper entitled 'Reasonable demands to be required from Monsieur for the preservation of the religion of England' dated 1570, PRO SP 70/ 115 fol. 98.

37 24 March 1571, Digges, *Compleat Ambassador*, p.67.

38 2 April 1571, Walsingham to Burghley, Digges, *Compleat Ambassador*, pp.67–70.

39 19 April 1571, *Fénélon*, iv, pp.58–61.

40 Sutherland, *Massacre of St Bartholomew*, p.60.

41 23 April 1571, Alva to Philip II, AGS K1519 B29 no.65.

42 The French terms appear in Digges, *Compleat Ambassador*, pp.85–6; HMC 9 *Salisbury*, ii, pp.542–3; BN Fonds Français 20153 fols 107–9. For Elizabeth's answers to them see 6 April [1571], BN FF 20153 fol. 107; 'The answer to the eight articles proposed by the king of France on behalf of the duke of Anjou', 16 April 1571, HMC 9 *Salisbury*, ii, pp.543–4.

43 As reported by Walsingham, Digges, *Compleat Ambassador*, p.67.

44 BN FF 20153 fol. 107.

45 C. Read, *Mr Secretary Walsingham and the Policy of Queen Elizabeth* (Oxford, 1925), i, p.128: 'she would concede no more than that he should be excused from attending the English service'. In reality this was a great concession and more than Elizabeth was prepared to grant.

46 19 April 1571, Elizabeth to Walsingham, Digges, *Compleat Ambassador*, pp.83–4.

47 12 June 1571, J. Bernard to Catherine de Medici, BN FF 3253 p.323.

48 19 April 1571, *Fénélon*, iv, p.60; 28 April 1571, Walsingham to Burghley, Digges, *Compleat Ambassador*, p.89.
49 'Conference between Walsingham and Paul de Foix', 28 April 1571, Digges, *Compleat Ambassador*, pp.90–2.
50 Digges, *Compleat Ambassador*, pp.91–2.
51 28 April 1571, Digges, *Compleat Ambassador*, p.90; 10 May 1571, *Fénélon*, iv, pp.92–102.
52 11 May 1571, Elizabeth to Walsingham, Digges, *Compleat Ambassador*, pp.97–9.
53 11 May 1571, Burghley to Walsingham, Digges, *Compleat Ambassador*, p.100.
54 William Strickland's words in the 1571 parliament, Hartley, *Proceedings*, i, p.200.
55 Quote appears in Bayne, *Anglo-Roman Relations*, pp.47, 294; 'preces communes, no contiene dottrina falsa ninguna ny cosa impia, porque todo es escrittura o oraciones tomadas de la Iglesia Catolica'.
56 C. Haigh, *English Reformations: Religion, politics and society under the Tudors* (Oxford, 1993), p.259.
57 25 May 1571, Walsingham to Burghley, Digges, *Compleat Ambassador*, pp.101–3.
58 10 May 1571, *Fénélon*, iv, p.102.
59 Catherine was also seeking to marry her youngest son, Alençon, to the daughter of the duke of Saxony, and told Alva that the marriages of both her sons would weaken the enemies of the king who would be deprived of their help. AGS E K1521 B30 no.42.
60 N. L. Roelker, *Queen of Navarre, Jeanne d'Albret 1528–72* (Cambridge, Mass., 1968), p.354.
61 Sutherland, *Huguenot Struggle*, pp.184–5.
62 23 March 1571, Lettenhove, *Relations Politiques*, iv, pp.92–9, 123; 'Copy of the opinion of the duke of Feria and Prior Don Antonio respecting English affairs', *Cal. S. P. Span. 1568–79*, pp.307–8.
63 5 June 1571, Burghley to Walsingham, Digges, *Compleat Ambassador*, p.104; 2 June 1571, *Fénélon*, iv, pp.125–7.
64 4 June 1571, HMC 9 *Salisbury*, ii, pp.288, 545–7.
65 7 July 1571, Digges, *Compleat Ambassador*, p.116.
66 HMC 9 *Salisbury*, ii, p.288.
67 11 July 1571, *Fénélon*, iv, pp.169–70.
68 9 July 1571, Elizabeth to Walsingham, Digges, *Compleat Ambassador*, pp.112–15; 9 and 11 July 1571, *Fénélon*, iv, pp.165, 171–2.
69 9 July 1571, Digges, *Compleat Ambassador*, pp.111–12; N. M. Sutherland was therefore mistaken when she wrote that 'by June the only thing Elizabeth refused was *open* confirmation that, once in England, Anjou would be permitted the private exercise of his religion'. Sutherland, *Massacre of St Bartholomew*, p.170.
70 22 April 1571, Walsingham to Leicester, Digges, *Compleat Ambassador*, p.82; 25 July 1571, *Fénélon*, vii, p.234; iv, p.209.
71 25 July 1571, *Fénélon*, vii, p.234; 27 July 1571, AGS E K1522 B30 no.31.
72 27 July 1571, Walsingham to Burghley, PRO SP 70/ 119 fol. 45.
73 4 August 1571, the bishop of Dax to Anjou, BN Dupuy MS 658 fols 123–7v.
74 Sutherland, *Massacre of St Bartholomew*, pp.168–9.
75 'Instructions for De Foix', 29 July 1571, *Fénélon*, vii, pp.238–41.
76 3 August 1571, Digges, *Compleat Ambassador*, pp.120–2; N. M. Sutherland, 'The Foreign Policy of Queen Elizabeth, the Sea Beggars and the Capture of Brille 1572', in *Princes, Politics and Religion 1547–1589* (1984), p.191.

77 Digges, *Compleat Ambassador*, pp.126–8.
78 21 September 1571, *Fénélon*, iv, pp.238–41.
79 Leicester to Walsingham, Digges, *Compleat Ambassador*, p.129.
80 Digges, *Compleat Ambassador*, p.131.
81 2 September 1571, Elizabeth to Walsingham and Burghley to Walsingham, Digges, *Compleat Ambassador*, pp.129–31, 133. The concessions she offered were so similar to those recommended by Cecil in late 1570 that it is probable that she was acting upon his advice.
82 31 August 1571, Burghley to Elizabeth, PRO SP 70/ 119 fol. 176.
83 'Answers to the demands made by de Foix', 19 August 1571, PRO SP 70/ 119 fols 105–6; 'Latin reply of Elizabeth to articles about marriage', 24 August 1571, BL Cott. MS Julius F vi fol. 174. HMC 9 *Salisbury*, ii, p.550; Digges, *Compleat Ambassador*, pp.129–32.
84 'New articles for the duke of Anjou', 28 August 1571, HMC 9 *Salisbury*, ii, p.550.
85 In the presence of her Council on 5 September 1571 Elizabeth presented to de Foix her demand for a personal interview with Anjou to discuss the detailed points about religion, *Lettres de Catherine de Médicis*, iv, pp.60–2.
86 23 August 1571, *Cal. S. P. Span. 1568–79*, p.331; 7 September 1571, *Fénélon*, iv, p.226.
87 3 and 12 August 1571, Walsingham to Leicester, Digges, *Compleat Ambassador*, pp.120–1, 127–9; 15 September 1571, Walsingham to Leicester, HMC 58 *Bath*, v, p.184.
88 2 September 1571, Elizabeth to Walsingham, Digges, *Compleat Ambassador*, p.131.
89 16 August 1571, Burghley to Walsingham, Digges, *Compleat Ambassador*, p.129.
90 'Memorandum of Burghley', 6 August 1571, PRO SP 12/ 80 fol. 57; 'The commodities that may follow upon the marriage with the duke of Anjou', SP 70/ 115 fols 96, 110; 'Considerations of a league with France', 22 August 1571, SP 70/ 119 fol. 110.
91 2 September 1571, Burghley to Walsingham, Digges, *Compleat Ambassador*, p.134.
92 5 September 1571, PRO SP 12/ 81 fol. 18.
93 8 and 19 October 1571, Walsingham to Burghley, PRO SP 70/ 120 fols 68–9, 85.
94 26 September 1571, Walsingham to Burghley, PRO SP 70/ 120 fol. 54.
95 28 September 1571, *Fénélon*, vii, p.261; 8 October 1571, PRO SP 70/ 120 fol. 68.
96 *Fénélon*, iv, pp.224–8, 239–40; vii, pp.241–3, 29–51; J. A. E. de Ruble (ed.) *Mémoires Inédites de Michel de La Huguerye* (Paris, 1877–80), i, p.40; Sutherland, *Massacre of St Bartholomew*, p.180.
97 Roelker, *Queen of Navarre*, p.351.
98 Lettenhove, *Relations Politiques*, vi, p.225.
99 With hindsight, historians can appreciate that these three events were far less threatening than contemporaries perceived. Furthermore, at Lepanto the majority of ships fighting against the Turks were Venetian rather than Spanish.
100 PRO SP 70/ 120 fols 54–6, 99; Digges, *Compleat Ambassador*, p.152.
101 'Instructions to Killigrew', 8 October 1571, PRO SP 70/ 120 fols 71–2.
102 C. Read, *Lord Burghley and Queen Elizabeth* (1960), p.63.
103 'Extract from the instructions of Sir Thomas Smith concerning marriage between Elizabeth and Anjou', 1572, BL Cott. MS Julius F vi fol. 168; 'Instructions given to Smith', 3 December 1571, BL Harl. MS 252 fol. 147.
104 3 January 1572, Smith to Burghley and 8 January 1572, Smith and Killigrew to Elizabeth, *Cal. S. P. For. 1572–4*, pp.3, 8–9.

105 8 January 1572, PRO SP 70/ 120 fols 28–9.
106 PRO SP 70/ 120 fol. 29.
107 PRO SP 70/ 120 fol. 31.
108 18 January, 6 February and 9 July 1571, *Fénélon*, iii, pp.440–1, 468; iv, p.167. It is not clear who these 'Catholic lords' could be – possibly Arundel and Norfolk, although neither were attending Council meetings.
109 R. B. Wernham, *Before the Armada* (1966), p.312.
110 A. Labanoff, *Lettres, Instructions et Mémoires de Marie Stuart, Reine d'Ecosse*, (1844–54), v, pp.236–42.
111 Murdin, *Burghley's State Papers*, pp.26–151.
112 *Fénélon*, iii, pp.417–18, 438–9; iv, pp.134–5; Digges, *Compleat Ambassador*, pp.47, 105; HMC 58 *Bath*, v, pp.177–8.
113 For this view, MacCaffrey, *Elizabethan Regime*, p.261 and Somerset, *Elizabeth I*, p.254.
114 'Instructions for La Mothe-Fénélon', 18 June 1571, *Fénélon*, vii, p.228; 7 June 1571, iv, p.129.
115 14 May 1571, Digges, *Compleat Ambassador*, p.96.
116 14 August 1571, de Spes to Alva, Lettenhove, *Relations Politiques*, vi, p.161; 2 June 1571, *Fénélon*, iv, p.127; 3 July 1571, Catherine to Fénélon, vii, p.231.
117 Digges, *Compleat Ambassador*, pp.116, 129, 133–4; Lettenhove, *Relations Politiques*, vi, p.167; HMC 58 *Bath*, v, p.184.
118 PRO SP 12/ 80 fol. 57; SP 70/ 119 fol. 110; Digges, *Compleat Ambassador*, pp.129, 136.
119 3 September 1571, Mildmay to Burghley, PRO SP 12/ 81 fol. 6.
120 Elton, *Parliament of England*, p.374: 'all the indications are against the thesis of an independent initiative promoted from within the House of Commons. It was the Privy Council that originally advised the Queen to marry and name a successor; when it got nowhere with her at the Council Board it used the Parliament to augment the pressure on her.'
121 *Zurich Letters*, p.251.
122 MacCaffrey, *Elizabethan Regime*, p.259.
123 *Fénélon*, iii, 468; iv, pp.167–8, 186–7.
124 'Egerton Papers', *Camden Soc.*, 12 (1840), p.55.
125 Summary of letters 25 December 1570 to 3 January 1571, AGS E K1519 B28 no.2.
126 *Cal. S. P. Span. 1568–79*, pp.303, 306; AGS E K1519 B29 nos 65, 66, 70, 75, 76, 78.
127 7 May 1571, Alva to Alava, AGS E K1521 B30 no.55; 20 June 1571, Philip II to de Spes, *Codoin*, xc, pp.472–4, translated in *Cal. S. P. Span. 1568–79*, p.319.
128 13 July 1571, Philip II to de Spes, *Codoin*, xc, p.477, translated in *Cal. S. P. Span. 1568–79*, p.323; L. P. Gachard, *Correspondance de Philippe II sur les Affaires des Pays-Bas* (Brussels, 1848–79), ii, pp.185–8, 195–7; Sutherland, 'Foreign Policy of Queen Elizabeth', p.191.
129 MacCaffrey, *Elizabeth I*, pp.163–5; Neale, *Queen Elizabeth*, p.222.
130 3 August 1571, Walsingham to Leicester, Digges, *Compleat Ambassador*, p.121.
131 12 August 1571, Walsingham to Leicester, Digges, *Compleat Ambassador*, p.128.
132 22 April 1572, Digges, *Compleat Ambassador*, p.180.
133 8 April 1572, *Cal. S. P. Span. 1568–79*, pp.380–2.
134 Sutherland, 'Foreign Policy of Queen Elizabeth', pp.195–202.

6 MATRIMONIAL DIPLOMACY:
THE ALENÇON MATCH 1572–8

1 9 and 18 January and 12 February 1572, Smith to Burghley, PRO SP 70/ 122 fols 37–41, 50, 211.
2 'A summary of the negotiations of Montmorency, de Foix and La Mothe-Fénélon', BN FF 3253 pp.380, 382, 403; PRO SP 70/ 122 fol. 38.
3 Strype, *Smith*, p.111; 10 January 1572, Smith to Burghley, PRO SP 70/ 122 fol. 50.
4 9 January 1572, Smith to Burghley, PRO SP 70/ 122 fol. 37.
5 10 February and 3 August 1572, *Fénélon*, iv, p.370; v, p.77.
6 8 March 1572, *Fénélon*, iv, pp.395–6.
7 26 January 1572, Elizabeth to Smith, PRO SP 70/ 122 fol. 143.
8 2 April 1572, Elizabeth to Walsingham and Smith, BL Cott. Vespasian F vi fols 10–12. These instructions about their negotiations for a treaty make no mention of the matrimonial proposal.
9 30 March 1572, Digges, *Compleat Ambassador*, p.198.
10 For the English reaction to these events see MacCaffrey, *Making of Policy*, pp.166–8.
11 27 April 1572, *Fénélon*, iv, pp.438–9.
12 'Instructions for the earl of Lincoln', 25 May 1572, Digges, *Compleat Ambassador*, pp.209–10.
13 'Power of Charles IX to the duke of Montmorency and other deputies', 25 April 1572, BN FF 3253 pp.368–70.
14 12 May 1572, letter to Sussex, *Lettres de Catherine de Médicis*, iv, p.101; 12 May 1572, Catherine de Medici to Burghley, *Cal. S. P. For. 1572–4*, p.107.
15 14 May 1572, *Fénélon*, iv, p.449.
16 The following account of the negotiations during the visit of Montmorency and de Foix is based on a French summary of their negotiations found in Fonds Français and probably written by de Foix. There are various copies, some in a sixteenth-century and others in a seventeenth-century hand. The easiest to read is FF 3253 pp.371–410 and it appears to be an accurate transcription of earlier copies. La Mothe-Fénélon also reported on the negotiations of which he was a part: *Fénélon*, v, pp.19–26.
17 The three lords were in attendance with the queen during her talks with the ambassadors. Both Sussex and Burghley had been prepared to cede a private Mass to previous suitors and Lord Howard was a conservative in religion.
18 6 June 1572, Leicester to Walsingham, BL Cott. MS Vespasian F vi fol. 88.
19 'Instructions for Walsingham', 20 July 1572, PRO SP 70/ 124 fol. 99.
20 13 July 1572, Walsingham to Burghley, Digges, *Compleat Ambassador*, p.220.
21 13 July 1572, Walsingham to Burghley, Digges, *Compleat Ambassador*, pp.220–1; BN FF 3253 p.380.
22 10 August 1572, Walsingham to Burghley, Digges, *Compleat Ambassador*, p.233.
23 'A memorial for matters of Flanders', 3 June 1572, Lettenhove, *Relations Politiques*, vi, pp.420–1.
24 Digges, *Compleat Ambassador*, pp.226–8.
25 27 July 1572, Elizabeth to Walsingham, Digges, *Compleat Ambassador*, pp.228–30; 27 July 1572, Burghley to Walsingham, BL Harl. MS 260 fols 277–8.
26 'The queen's answer to the French ambassador', 22 August 1572, HMC 9 *Salisbury*, ii, pp.21–2; 22 August 1572, Smith to Walsingham, Digges, *Compleat Ambassador*, pp.235–6; 22 August 1572, Elizabeth to Walsingham, BL Cott. MS Vespasian F vi fol. 144.

27 21 July 1572, letters from Walsingham to Burghley and Leicester, and 22 August 1572, Burghley to Walsingham, Digges, *Compleat Ambassador*, pp.224, 237; 7 August 1572, *Fénélon*, v, pp.79–80; 'Unsigned letter of intelligence to the duke of Alva', 7 August 1572, *Cal. S. P. Span. 1568–79*, p.403; Elizabeth to Walsingham, BL Harl. MS 260 fols 287–9.

28 10 August 1572, letters from Walsingham to Smith and Burghley, Digges, *Compleat Ambassador*, pp.231–4; *Lettres de Catherine de Médicis*, iv, p.111.

29 22 August 1572, Burghley to Walsingham, Digges, *Compleat Ambassador*, p.237; 22 August 1572, Burghley to Admiral Coligny, SP 70/ 124 fol. 164.

30 5 September 1572, the bishop of London to Burghley, Wright, *Queen Elizabeth*, i, p.438. For other examples of reactions in England see: 14 September 1572, *Fénélon*, v, p.121; 16 September 1572, Bruce (ed.), *Parker Correspondence*, p.399; 30 August and 6 and 8 September 1572, *Cal. S. P. Span. 1568–79*, pp.409–11, 413.

31 7 September 1572, Burghley to the earl of Shrewsbury, Lodge, *Illustrations*, i, p.547.

32 17 September 1572, Elizabeth to Walsingham, BL Cott. MS Vespasian F vi fol. 155.

33 K. Duncan-Jones and J. Van Dorsten (eds), *Miscellaneous Prose of Sir Philip Sidney* (Oxford, 1973), p.48.

34 'Speech against the queen's marriage to the duke of Anjou made at Greenwich', 6 October 1579, BL Harl. 6265 fols 107v–8.

35 9 December 1572, Charles IX to Fénélon, Le Laboureur, *Mémoires*, iii, pp.266–9.

36 Wallace MacCaffrey described Elizabeth's policies, the survival of a Protestant interest and the renewal of the 1572 alliance, as 'two contradictory yet complementary goals', and explained that: 'When the Huguenots seemed most in danger, it was the former objective which predominated; when the Queen Mother was able to re-establish some modicum of stability, it was the latter which the English pursued.' MacCaffrey, *Making of Policy*, p.164. Indeed it is questionable as to whether there was any modicum of stability in France between 1572 and 1577.

37 3 November and 28 December 1572, *Cal. S. P. For. 1572–4*, pp.200, 220; 23 September 1572, Alençon to Elizabeth, HMC 9 *Salisbury*, ii, p.23; 20 November 1572, Walsingham to Smith and undated letter from Elizabeth to Walsingham, Digges, *Compleat Ambassador*, pp.287, 297–8.

38 3 December 1572, Maisonfleur to Alençon, HMC 9 *Salisbury*, ii, pp.29–35.

39 29 September 1572, *Fénélon*, v, p.141; 7 and 11 September 1572, Catherine to Fénélon, vii, pp.340, 345.

40 9 December 1572, Charles IX to Fénélon, Le Laboureur, *Mémoires*, p.269.

41 29 September 1572, *Fénélon*, v, p.143.

42 'Instructions to the earl of Worcester', 11 January 1573, BL Cott. MS Vespasian F vi fols 247–8; 'Answers given to Monsieurs La Mothe-Fénélon and De La Mole', 18 March 1573, PRO SP 70/ 126 fol. 143v.

43 12 February 1573, Walsingham to Burghley, PRO SP 70/ 126 fol. 71.

44 1 April 1573, Walsingham to Burghley, PRO SP 70/ 127 fols 3–4v.

45 22 April 1573, Alençon to Elizabeth and 27 April 1573, Valentine Dale to Burghley, PRO SP 70/ 127 fols 44, 56.

46 21 May 1573, letters from Elizabeth to Catherine de Medici and Alençon, PRO SP 70/ 127 fols 106, 107.

47 'Instructions for Edward Horsey', June 1573, PRO SP 70/ 127 fols 228–30, 243–4.

48 20 June 1573, *Fénélon*, v, p.353; 'Speech of the lords of the Council to La Mothe-Fénélon', 2 June 1573, vii, pp.424–7.

49 7 July 1573, Dale to Elizabeth, *Cal. S. P. For. 1572–4*, p.385.
50 R. M. Kingdon, *Myths about the St Bartholomew's Day Massacre 1573–1574* (1988), p.68.
51 During talks with Catherine's special envoy in September 1573, for example, Elizabeth put forward demands for a free hand in dealing with Mary Stuart and for the Huguenots to be granted the freedom of worship promised in the recent peace. BL Cott. MS Caligula E vi fol. 197v.
52 24 August 1573, *Cal. S. P. Ven. 1558–80*, p.491. Alençon had recently been ill with the measles; Camden, *History*, p.195.
53 Kingdon, *Myths about St Bartholomew*, p.128; 20 September 1573, *Fénélon*, v, pp.403–8.
54 Memorandum of Burghley entitled 'Difficulties against the marriage with the duke of Alençon for M. de Retz', 1573, PRO SP 70/ 128 fols 117–20. A French version is in BL Cott. MS Caligula E vi fols 198–9.
55 HMC 9 *Salisbury*, ii, p.290.
56 24 August and 30 December 1573, *Cal. S. P. Ven. 1558–80*, pp.491, 496.
57 For Alençon's intrigues during this period see M. P. Holt, *The Duke of Anjou and the Politique Struggle during the Wars of Religion* (Cambridge, 1986), pp.34–44 and Sutherland, *Huguenot Struggle*, pp.219–22.
58 16 March 1574, HMC 9 *Salisbury*, ii, p.290; 1 April 1574, Dale to Elizabeth and 12 April 1574, Dale to Burghley, PRO SP 70/ 130 fols 157–9, 187; 26 May 1574, *Cal. S. P. For. 1572–4*, pp.506–7; *Fénélon*, vii, p.456.
59 A. Lynn Martin, *Henry III and the Jesuit Politicians* (Geneva, 1973), pp.58–60.
60 For these negotiations, see MacCaffrey, *Making of Policy*, pp.180–5.
61 3 and 5 September 1575, PRO SP 70/ 135 fols 79–81, 89–90.
62 26 September 1575, Villeroy to Mauvissière, Le Laboureur, *Mémoires*, i, p.668.
63 5 September 1575, PRO SP 70/ 135 fols 89–90. In France the English ambassador was suspected of planning his escape; 15 September 1575, *Cal. S. P. Ven. 1558–67*, pp.536–7.
64 28 September 1575, letter from Dale and [29 October 1575] Dale to Elizabeth, PRO SP 70/ 135 fols 188, 284–5. Navarre followed suit on 5 February 1576.
65 'Instructions for M. de la Porte', 27 November 1575, SP 70/ 136 fols 73–4; 1 January 1576, *Codoin*, xci, p.119, translated in *Cal. S. P. Span. 1568–79*, p.516.
66 [March] 1576, Elizabeth to Alençon and 'Instructions for Randolph', 2 April 1576, *Cal. S. P. For. 1575–7*, pp.297, 302–4.
67 1575, Sussex to Burghley, Lodge, *Illustrations*, ii, pp.66–7.
68 Kervyn de Lettenhove, *Les Huguenots et Les Gueux* (Bruges, 1883–5), iv, pp.633, 638.
69 Holt, *Anjou*, pp.70–92.
70 G. Parker, *The Dutch Revolt* (1975).
71 Holt, *Anjou*, pp.93–101.
72 6 August 1578, Sussex to Walsingham, PRO SP 83/ 8 no.13.
73 'Treaty of alliance between Elizabeth and the States-General', 1 January 1578, Lettenhove, *Relations Politiques*, x, pp.219–21.
74 Lettenhove, *Relations Politiques*, x, pp.421–2, 423, 439–42, 448–9, 456–7, 465, 486, 488.
75 22 May 1578, Walsingham to William Davison, and Dr Thomas Wilson to Davison, Lettenhove, *Relations Politiques*, x, pp.488–90. For Bacon's view, HMC 9 *Salisbury*, ii, p.189 and Lettenhove, *Relations Politiques*, x, pp.384–5.
76 26 May 1578, P. L. Muller and A. Diegerick (eds), *Documents concernant les relations entre le Duc d'Anjou et les Pays Bas* (Utrecht, 1889), i, pp.240–1.
77 28 May and 6 June 1578, Henry III to Mauvissière, M. François (ed.), *Lettres de Henri III* (Paris, 1959–84), v, pp.9, 23; 13 July 1578, PRO 31/ 3/ 27 fols

212–3. There is practically nothing about Stafford's mission in the English sources but a letter from Catherine de Medici to Elizabeth makes clear that he carried a message about the marriage, although his main purpose was to investigate Henry III's attitude towards his brother's project in Flanders. [8] June 1578, *Cal. S. P. For. 1578–8*, p.8 printed in full in *Lettres de Catherine de Médicis*, vi, p.35.

78 29 July 1578, Lettenhove, *Relations Politiques*, x, p.660.

79 17 November 1578, PRO 31/ 3/ 27 fol. 246.

80 6 August 1578, Lettenhove, *Relations Politiques*, x, p.697.

81 Sussex's opinion appears in several letters: Lodge, *Illustrations*, ii, p.118; Lettenhove, *Relations Politiques*, x, pp.696–7, 774–5. See also the letter transcribed in W. J. Tighe, 'The Counsel of Thomas Radcliffe, Earl of Sussex, concerning the Revolt of the Netherlands, September 1578', *The Sixteenth-Century Journal* 18 (1987), pp.327–9.

82 28 May 1578, Henry III to Mauvissière, *Lettres de Henri III*, v, p.9; May 1578, *Lettres de Catherine de Médicis*, vi, p.14.

83 6 June 1578, Henry III to Mauvissière, *Lettres de Henri III*, v, p.22.

84 7 June 1578, *Cal. S. P. For. 1578–9*, p.14; 'Instructions to Cobham and Walsingham', Lettenhove, *Relations Politiques*, x, pp.518–22.

85 18 June 1578, Wilson to Walsingham, Lettenhove, *Relations Politiques*, x, pp.525–6.

86 12 July 1578, Wilson to Cobham, Lettenhove, *Relations Politiques*, x, p.581.

87 23 June 1578, Lettenhove, *Relations Politiques*, x, p.535.

88 29 July 1578, Lettenhove, *Relations Politiques*, x, pp.662–3.

89 21, 23 and 24 July 1578, Lettenhove, *Relations Politiques*, x, pp.622, 630, 636.

90 5 July 1578, Anjou to Elizabeth, HMC 9 *Salisbury*, ii, pp.184; 3 August 1578, Wilson to Walsingham, Lettenhove, *Relations Politiques*, x, p.687. They arrived 30 July 1578. For the visit see Lettenhove, *Huguenots*, v, pp.99–101.

91 23 July 1578, Henry III to Elizabeth, *Lettres de Henri III*, v, p.44; 16 and 27 August 1578, PRO 31/ 3/ 27 fols 221–2.

92 9 and 14 August 1578, PRO 31/ 3/ 27 fols 217–19.

93 16 September 1578, PRO 31/ 3/ 27 fol. 226; 6 September 1578, Burghley to Walsingham, Lettenhove, *Relations Politiques*, x, pp.799–801.

94 14 August 1578, PRO 31/ 3/ 27 fol. 219.

95 Sussex mentioned on 28 August 1578 that the queen had told him to write 'upon all occasions' of his opinion on the marriage. Lodge, *Illustrations*, ii, p.108. Leicester's complaint that he rarely spoke with the queen was made on 1 August; Lettenhove, *Relations Politiques*, x, p.680.

96 1 August 1578, Leicester to Walsingham and 8 September 1578, Burghley to Walsingham, Lettenhove, *Relations Politiques*, x, pp.678–80, 800.

97 8 October 1578, Labanoff, *Lettres de Marie Stuart*, v, p.60; 15 October 1578, Philip II to de Mendoza, Lettenhove, *Relations Politiques*, xi, p.37; 15 October 1578, G. Canestrini and A. Desjardins (eds), *Négociations Diplomatiques de la France avec la Toscane* (Paris, 1865–75), iv, p.205.

98 17 October 1578, PRO 31/ 3/ 27 fols 235v–6.

99 The Norwich entertainments are printed in Nichols, *Progresses*, ii, pp.115–210 and all the following quotations come from there. Leicester's role in arranging the 1578 progress is mentioned in D. MacCulloch, *Suffolk under the Tudors* (Oxford, 1986), p.196; for his connections in Norfolk see A. Hassell Smith, *County and Court: Government and court in Norfolk 1558–1603* (Oxford, 1974), pp.39–41, 79.

100 26 October 1578, *Cal. S. P. Ven. 1558–80*, p.586; BN Dupuy MS 537, fols 119–22.

101 Cloulas, *Correspondance*, p.238.
102 12 November 1578, PRO 31/ 3/ 27 fols 241, 249.
103 17 October 1578, HMC 9 *Salisbury*, ii, p.219.

7 THE WOOING OF FRANCIS DUKE OF ANJOU 1579–81

1 Don John had died on 1 October 1578. For Dutch politics see Parker, *Dutch Revolt*.
2 For Anjou's expedition in the Netherlands see Holt, *Anjou*, pp.101–12.
3 10 November 1578, Canestrini and Desjardins, *Négociations*, iv, p.211; Lettenhove, *Les Huguenots*, v, p.373.
4 Camden, *History*, p.227.
5 On 8 February 1579 she referred to him as her 'singe'; HMC 9 *Salisbury*, ii, p.234.
6 28 February 1579, Lettenhove, *Relations Politiques*, xi, pp.304–5.
7 15 and 27 January 1579, *Cal. S. P. Span. 1568–79*, pp.629, 636. These rumours grew as the year progressed.
8 17 January and 8 March 1579, PRO 31/ 3/ 27 fols 259–60, 282; 5 March 1579, *Cal. S. P. Span. 1568–79*, p.655; 13 February 1579, Gilbert Talbot and his wife to the earl and countess of Shrewsbury, Lodge, *Illustrations*, ii, p.141; 16 January 1579, Elizabeth to Anjou, HMC 9 *Salisbury*, ii, p.231.
9 W. T. MacCaffrey, 'The Anjou Match and the Making of Elizabethan Foreign Policy', in *Essays Presented to Professor Joel Hurstfield*. Edited by Peter Clark, Alan G. T. Smith and Nicholas Tyacke (Leicester, 1979), pp.63–4.
10 *Fénélon*, iv, pp.200, 204, 206; N. M. Sutherland described Elizabeth's gestures on these occasions as 'risquée'. Sutherland, *Massacre of St Bartholomew*, p.190. These included offers to send a stag which she had hunted and killed to the duke, and references to the pleasure they could share by hunting together in the country.
11 February 1579, *Lettres de Catherine de Médicis*, vi, pp.275–6.
12 8 March 1579, HMC 58 *Salisbury*, ii, pp. 234–5.
13 17 and 25 January and 22 February 1579, PRO 31/ 3/ 27 fols 259, 262v, 266, 273.
14 25 January and 22 February 1579, PRO 31/ 3/ 27 fols 266, 273–4.
15 The articles taken by Simier to England which appear in BN FF 20153 demanded a pension of £100,000 yet the article put before the Council in May 1579 referred only to £60,000, the sum originally requested by Henry in 1571.
16 21 October 1578, Canestrini and Desjardins, *Négociations*, iv, p.206.
17 16 February 1579, *Lettres de Catherine de Médicis*, vi, pp.272–3. According to the Venetian ambassador, Henry III had urged his brother the previous October not to go England until parliament had agreed to accept him as king. 26 October 1578, *Cal. S. P. Ven. 1558–80*, p.586.
18 26 February 1579, BL Harl. MS 285 fol. 77.
19 4 April 1579, Gilbert Talbot to the earl of Shrewsbury, Lodge, *Illustrations*, ii, pp.149–50.
20 For the papers relating to these discussions, March, 13 April and 4 May 1579, HMC 9 *Salisbury*, ii, pp.238–45, 249–54. Some are transcribed in Murdin, *Burghley's State Papers*, pp.319–22. The fuller unpublished set of Burghley's memoranda is in Hatfield MS 148. For Mildmay's views, see BL Harl. MS fols 104–10.

21 3 May 1579, Murdin, *Burghley's State Papers*, pp.320–1; Elizabeth to Sir Amias Paulet, N. H. Nicolas, *Memoirs of the Life and Times of Sir Christopher Hatton* (1847), pp.107–8.

22 'Objections 3 and 4 made against the queen's marriage with answers of Cecil', March 1579, HMC 9 *Salisbury*, ii, p.240.

23 'Objections 7 and 8', HMC 9 *Salisbury*, ii, p.241.

24 Cecil produced the example of the duchess of Savoy, Lord Henry Howard that of Queen Catherine of Sweden.

25 Conyers Read implied that Burghley was prepared to put his faith in God and the fitness of the queen, *Lord Burghley*, pp.210–11.

26 8 December 1580, Catherine to Mauvissière, *Lettres de Catherine de Médicis*, vii, p.298.

27 Conyers Read argued that in Burghley's memorandum of 27 March 1579 'the only justification for the marriage was the procreation of children', but Burghley was trying to refute arguments raised by the opponents of the marriage.

28 See chapter 6, pp.146–8.

29 Hatfield MS 148 fols 27–38; HMC 9 *Salisbury*, ii, pp.244–5, 250–2.

30 See chapter 6, p.147. The Spanish ambassador commented that Burghley was 'not so opposed as he used to be' to the marriage; 8 April 1579, *Codoin*, xci, p.365 and a translation in *Cal. S. P. Span. 1568–79*, p.662.

31 13 April 1579, HMC 9 *Salisbury*, ii, p.252.

32 The argument that Burghley's advocacy of the marriage owed much to political opportunism and factiousness is put forward in M. Leimon, 'Sir Francis Walsingham and the Anjou Marriage Plan, 1574–81', unpublished Ph.D thesis, University of Cambridge (1989), pp.14, 32, 147.

33 A paper in Walsingham's hand appears in BL Harl. 1582 fols 46–8 and is summarised in C. Read, *Walsingham*, ii, pp.14–18. Written in the spring of 1579 it follows the structure of Burghley's argument and so would appear to be notes for a speech presented to the Council. There is no official record of the debates held in the spring.

34 Bishop Cox's treatise, BL Lansd. MS 28 fol. 71; for the sermons see 31 March 1579, *Codoin*, xci, p.359, translated in *Cal. S. P. Span. 1568–79*, pp.658–9.

35 4 April 1579, Lodge, *Illustrations*, ii, pp.149–50.

36 31 March 1579, *Codoin*, xci, p.359 translated in *Cal. S. P. Span. 1568–79*, p.659.

37 The incident was reported in the Fugger news-letters and was recorded in Stow's Annals. 25 July 1579, V. Von Klarwill (ed.), *The Fugger News-Letters*, second series (1926), p.28; Nichols, *Progresses*, ii, pp.285–6. A ballad was written celebrating both Elizabeth's courage in the face of the danger and her mercy in pardoning the barge-man. T. Park and W. Oldys (eds) *The Harleian Miscellany* (1808–13), x, pp.272–3.

38 Peck, *Leicester's Commonwealth*, p.18.

39 4 and 5 November 1578, Sussex to Burghley, Lodge, *Illustrations*, ii, pp.131–3; 14 August 1578 and 25 August 1579, *Codoin*, xci, pp.270–1, 418, translated in *Cal. S. P. Span. 1568–79*, pp.606–7, 693.

40 For the so-called 'tennis-court' quarrel where Oxford insulted Sidney see B. M. Ward, *The Seventeenth Earl of Oxford 1550–1604 from Contemporary Documents* (1928), p.168. There is also a reference to it in a letter of 28 August 1579 from Sidney to Hatton, Wright, *Queen Elizabeth*, ii, p.101.

41 Camden, *History*, p.95; 6 July 1579, *Codoin*, xci, p.398, translated in *Cal. S. P. Span. 1568–79*, pp.681–2. The Acts of the Privy Council show that Leicester did not attend any meetings between 15 June and 6 July 1579.

42 4 July 1579, Labanoff, *Lettres de Marie Stuart*, v, pp.94–5. Mary was also informed but in this case incorrectly that Hatton had been married in secret.

43 17 June 1579, Wilson to the earl of Rutland, HMC 12 *Rutland*, v, p.117; copy of the safe-conduct 6 July 1579, PRO SP 78/ 3 fols 62–3.

44 25 March 1579, *Lettres de Catherine de Médicis*, vi, p.319; 3 and 15 August 1579, *Cal. S. P. Ven. 1558–80*, pp.605, 608–9.

45 6 and 8 July 1579, *Lettres de Henri III*, iv, pp.237–8, 241; 12 August 1579, Cloulas, *Correspondance*, p.472; Lettenhove, *Huguenots*, v, pp.389–90.

46 Muller and Diegerick, *Documents*, iii, p.117.

47 *Cal. S. P. For. 1579–80*, pp.45, 48; *Cal. S. P. Span. 1568–79*, p.688; Cloulas, *Correspondance*, pp.465, 469, 472; Canestrini and Desjardins, *Négociations*, iv, pp.260, 261, 265; *Cal. S. P. Ven. 1558–80*, pp.667–8.

48 15, 20, 22 and 25 August 1579, *Codoin*, xci, pp.409–10, 415–17, translated in *Cal. S. P. Span. 1568–79*, pp.688–93.

49 Lettenhove, *Les Huguenots*, v, pp.390–1; P. L. Hughes and J. Larkin, *Tudor Royal Proclamations* (Yale, 1969), p.641.

50 31 August 1579, PRO SP 31/ 3/ 27 fol. 366; 31 August 1579, Mauvissière to Pruneaux, Muller and Diegerick, *Documents*, iii, pp.128–30; [1] September 1579, Mauvissière to Henry III, BN FF 15973 fols 173–4; 22 and 25 August 1579, *Codoin*, xci, pp.415–18, translated in *Cal. S. P. Span. 1568–79*, pp.692–3.

51 9 September 1579, Muller and Diegerick, *Documents*, iii, p.188.

52 Anjou referred to these discussions in two later letters: about his religion on 28 January 1580, HMC 9 *Salisbury*, ii, p.307 and about the Netherlands on 3 November 1579, Muller and Diegerick, *Documents*, iii, pp.158–9.

53 7 September 1579, Villeroy to Mauvissière, Le Laboureur, *Mémoires*, i, pp.670–1. For similar comments see 9 September 1579, *Lettres de Henri III*, v, p.265; 9 September 1579, Muller and Diegerick, *Documents*, iii, p.188.

54 Elizabeth's poem to Anjou, Bodl. Ashmolean MS 781 p.142.

55 For Elizabeth's concern about these events see *Cal. Scot. P. 1574–81*, pp.348–50; *Cal. S. P. Span. 1568–79*, pp.686–7; Muller and Diegerick, *Documents*, iii, p.129.

56 For the Latin verses, see BL Cott. MS Caligula E xii fol. 371.

57 29 September 1579, *Codoin*, xci, p.432, translated in *Cal. S. P. Span. 1568–79*, p.701; F. J. Furnivall and W. R. Morfit (eds), *Ballads from Manuscripts*, ii, (1873), p.114.

58 J. Strype, *Life of John Aylmer* (Oxford, 1821), pp.41–2; 28 September 1578, Aylmer to Hatton, Nicolas, *Hatton*, pp.132–3. Mauvissière reported that the English Calvinists 'ne perdans une heure de temps a prescher, escrire et inciter les peuples de ce royaume'; 29 October 1579, PRO 31/ 3/ 37 fol. 407.

59 4 October 1579, PRO 31/ 3/ 27 fol. 397.

60 The pamphlet is printed in L. E. Berry (ed.), *John Stubbs's 'Gaping Gulf' with Letters and other Relevant Documents* (Charlottesville, Virginia, 1968) and all quotations come from there. Stubbs's arguments are summarised in MacCaffrey, *Making of Policy*, pp.257–61.

61 Holt, *Duke of Anjou*, p.121 described the pamphlet as 'unashamedly Puritan', while Leimon, 'Anjou Marriage Plan', p.125 called it 'a factional book'. I use however different points and quotations to support these descriptions.

62 'Proclamation for calling in the book', 27 September 1579, PRO SP 12/ 132 fol. 11; Strype, *Grindal*, ii, pp.360, 584–5; Strype, *Aylmer*, pp.41–2; 28 September 1579, Aylmer to Hatton, Nicolas, *Hatton*, pp.132–4.

63 No pardon appears in the patent rolls of 1579 or 1580 but Mauvissière reported that he 'a esté pardonné sur les chaffaulx'. K. Barnes, 'John Stubbe, 1579: The French ambassador's account', *Historical Research* 64 (1991), pp.421–6.

64 4 and 29 October 1579, PRO 31/ 3/ 27 fols 397–9, 408v.

65 *Cal. S. P. For. 1579–80*, pp.73, 84, 99. In the spring of 1579, Davison had written a letter to Walsingham, attacking the marriage, BL Harl. MS 288 fols 148–52.

66 27 October 1579, *Cal. S. P. Ven. 1558–80*, p.621.

67 Barnes, *Hist. Research* (1991), pp.422–3.

68 8 January 1580, *A. P. C. 1578–80*, p.357.

69 28 September 1578, Aylmer to Hatton, Nicolas, *Hatton*, pp.132–4.

70 F. A. Youngs, *The Proclamations of the Tudor Queens* (Cambridge, 1976), p.208.

71 Camden, *History*, p.270.

72 14 December 1579, Anjou to Elizabeth, HMC 9 *Salisbury*, ii, p.354. The editor has wrongly catalogued this document as belonging to 1580 rather than 1579.

73 Berry, *Stubbs's 'Gaping Gulf'*, pp.155–94; a small anonymous book written in support of the Anjou marriage, PRO SP 15/ 26 fols 111–63.

74 Youngs, *Proclamations*, p.208.

75 *Codoin*, xci, p.435.

76 4 December 1579, *Cal. S. P. Ven. 1558–80*, p.623.

77 The letter must also have circulated the court, as there are over thirty extant copies of his manuscript including one in the Bibliothèque Nationale Cinq Cent Colbert 465 fols 89–95. The letter is printed in Duncan–Jones and Van Dorsten (eds), *Miscellaneous Prose of Sidney*, pp.33–57. In a letter to Hubert Languet on 22 October 1580, Sidney explained that he had been carrying out the intentions of others in writing the piece. S. A. Pears (ed.), *The Correspondence of Sir Philip Sidney and Hubert Languet* (1845), p.187.

78 The view that Sidney was banished from court in early 1580 because of the queen's anger at his letter has been demolished in *Miscellaneous Prose of Sidney*, pp.34–5. On the other hand Sidney appears to have departed in 1580 of his own accord because of his perceived failure in influencing the queen on the marriage.

79 For frog jewellery see J. Arnold, *Queen Elizabeth's Wardrobe Unlock'd* (Leeds, 1988), pp.75–6. For the unusual cluster of pejorative references to frogs or toads, see D. Adler, 'Imaginary Toads in Real Gardens', *English Literary Renaissance* 11 (1981), pp.235–60.

80 Several manuscript copies are extant. When first published in 1591 it was judged to be politically sensitive because of its portrayal of Burghley and consequently was called in and not printed again until after the death of Robert Cecil. The following quotations come from E. Greenlaw *et al.* (eds), *The Works of Edmund Spenser: A variorum edition. The Minor Poems* (Baltimore, 1947), ii, pp.107–40.

81 The song deliberately uses archaisms which appear in the *Shepheardes Calendar*, thereby drawing attention to its debt to the work of Spenser. The following quotations come from the version of *The Countess of Pembroke's Arcadia* in the Penguin Classics series edited by M. Evans (1977), pp.704–9.

82 P. E. McLane, *Spenser's 'Shepheardes Calendar': A study in Elizabethan allegory* (Notre Dame, Indiana, 1961) contains the fullest interpretation of the work as part of a political campaign against the marriage. His approach and conclusions have been challenged by H. R. Woudhuysen, 'Leicester's Literary Patronage: A study of the English court 1578–92', unpublished D.Phil. thesis, University of Oxford (1980), pp.191–7. King, *Spenser's Poetry*, p.152, takes a sensible middle view in arguing that the *Shepheardes Calendar* 'evokes the political milieu of the Anjou courtship'.

83 The above quotations come from *Works of Edmund Spenser: The Minor Poems* (Baltimore, 1943) i, pp.19–26. This interpretation is discussed more fully in McLane, pp.61–76.

84 The following quotations come from *Works of Edmund Spenser*, i, pp.36–41. King, *Ren. Q.* (1980), p.51 argues that the imagery in the Eclogue is very complex and contains the ambiguity of enhancing Elizabeth's status as an eligible woman together with an appeal for her to retain her unwedded state. To an ordinary reader of the poem, however, it is the imagery of godly virginity which is most striking.

85 A. and C. Belsey, 'Icons of Divinity: Portraits of Elizabeth I' in *Renaissance Bodies: The human figure in English culture c.1540–1660*. Edited by Lucy Gent and Nigel Llewellyn (1990), pp.15–16; Strong, *Gloriana*, pp.101–2.

86 Wallace MacCaffrey suggests that neither Walsingham nor Leicester were present at the meetings to discuss the marriage. MacCaffrey, *Elizabeth I*, p.205. Walsingham, however, is recorded as a commissioner at the Westminster meeting on 4 October 1579 in BL Addit. MS 4149 fol. 104, although it is certainly possible that he did not actually attend. He definitely was absent from the Greenwich meeting on 6 October 1579. On the other hand, the manuscripts mark Leicester as attending both these meetings. For commissioners appointed to and in attendance at the 6 October meeting see BL Addit. MS 4149 fol. 105v and Harleian MS 6265 fol. 104. The Acts of the Privy Council record Leicester as present to attend to routine business on 6 October but not on 4 October. *A.P.C. 1578–80*, pp.273, 276.

87 For the various papers concerning the Council meetings, see BL Harl. MS 6265 fols 104–10; Addit. MS 4149 fols 104–8; Murdin, *Burghley's State Papers*, pp.322–42; HMC 9 *Salisbury*, ii, pp.67–72.

88 Murdin, *Burghley's State Papers*, p.331.

89 A note of Sadler's speech appears in Burghley's papers; for a copy of it see BL Addit. MS 33594 fols 1–3.

90 The Spanish ambassador mistakenly thought that Burghley and Sussex alone of the Council were in favour of the marriage, 16 October 1579, *Codoin*, xci, p.434, translated in *Cal. S. P. Span 1567–79*, p.702. Wallace MacCaffrey mistakenly wrote that Lord Admiral Lincoln supported it, *Elizabeth I*, p.205.

91 Murdin, *Burghley's State Papers*, p.336.

92 Historians have usually put the summer of 1579 as the time when Elizabeth had the idea of changing the composition of the Council, yet reports of the change did not appear until the autumn and winter. It is also more likely that she considered it after her Council would not back the marriage. 29 October 1579, PRO 31/ 3/ 27 fol. 407. Mauvissière wrote that the queen had been thinking of this change 'at one time'. The papal nuncio in Paris reported, 8 December 1579, that Elizabeth was considering this policy; Cloulas, *Correspondance*, p.558.

93 16 October 1579, *Codoin*, xci, p.437.

94 For Walsingham and Hatton, 16 October 1579, *Codoin*, xci, p.437. For Leicester, 12 November 1579, Leicester to Burghley, BL Harl. MS 6992 fols 114–15; 6 and 8 December 1579, Cloulas, *Correspondance*, pp.554, 558. Leicester's confinement took place more than three months after Elizabeth had discovered his secret marriage. It is therefore most improbable that his disgrace took place because of his relationship with the countess of Essex as William Camden implied.

95 PRO SP 78/ 3 fols 133–6.

96 These terms can be found in the various copies of the contract dated 11 June 1581, including BN FF 3253 pp.453–68.

97 HMC 9 *Salisbury*, ii, pp.275–6, 293, 539; PRO SP 78/ 3 fol. 145. The political terms can be seen in the final draft of the treaty BN FF 3952 fols 26–8.

98 HMC 9 *Salisbury*, ii, pp.281–2, 305–7, 308. Parliament was in fact prorogued five times between 20 October 1579 and 29 February 1580 as a result of the uncertainties about the marriage.
99 29 October 1579, PRO SP 31/ 3/ 27 fol. 406v; 8 February 1580, Henry III to Mauvissière, BN FF 3307 fol. 5; 26 October 1579, Paulet to [Walsingham], PRO SP 78/ 3 fol. 115.
100 8 February 1580, BN FF 3307 fol. 5.
101 15 April 1580, Cobham to [Walsingham], *Cal. S. P. For. 1579–81*, p.238; 15 April 1580, Catherine to Henry III, *Lettres de Catherine de Médicis*, vii, p.241; Cloulas, *Correspondance*, pp.52, 708–9.
102 30 January 1580, Anjou to Elizabeth and 26 April 1580, Cobham to Sussex, HMC 9 *Salisbury*, ii, pp.311, 322; 16–18 April 1580, *Lettres de Catherine de Médicis*, vii, pp.243–7.
103 21 May 1580, *Lettres de Catherine de Médicis*, vii, p.261.
104 26 April 1580, Hatton to Walsingham, Wright, *Queen Elizabeth*, ii, pp.107–9.
105 15 July 1580, Walsingham to Leicester, BL Cott. MS Caligula E vii fol. 140; 1 July 1580, Sussex to Burghley, HMC 9 *Salisbury*, ii, p.329; BL Cott. MS Titus B ii fol. 438.
106 I have found no copy of Stafford's instructions. His talks with Anjou are described in a letter from Henry III to Mauvissière dated the penultimate day of July 1580, BN FF 3307 fol. 16 with a copy in CC Colbert 473 fols 70–6.
107 2 July 1580, Stafford to Leicester, HMC 58 *Bath*, v, p.202; 19 July 1580, Anjou to Elizabeth, HMC 9 *Salisbury*, ii, pp.331–2; 24 and 30 July 1580, BN FF 3307 fols 14v, 16 with copies in BN CC Colbert 473 fols 60, 70v–77; 24 July 1580, *Lettres de Catherine de Médicis*, vii, p.273; letters of Cobham, 1 August 1580, *Cal. S. P. For. 1579–80*, pp.371–6.
108 For the negotiations for a Spanish marriage, see Cloulas, *Correspondance*, pp.52–3, 708–9, 733–5. For Henry III's and Catherine's attitude to the dispatch of the French commissioners, see 24 July 1580, BN FF 3307 fol. 14v with a copy in BN CC Colbert 473 fol. 60; 24 July 1580, *Lettres de Catherine de Médicis*, vii, p.273.
109 2 and 3 August 1580, *Cal. S. P. For. 1579–80*, pp.375, 377; 2 and 15 August 1580, *Lettres de Catherine de Médicis*, vii, pp.275, 277; 2 August 1580, Cloulas, *Correspondance*, p.718; BN FF 3307 fol. 18 with copy in BN CC Colbert 473 fols 83–6v.
110 10 August 1580, Burghley to Shrewsbury, HMC 58 *Bath*, v, p.28; 9 September 1580, *Cal. S. P. For. 1579–80*, p.411.
111 30 August 1580, Walsingham to Burghley, PRO SP 78/ 4 no.40.
112 1 October 1580, Henry III to Mauvissière, BN CC Colbert 473 fols 92v–4v; 'A memorandum to Cobham', 18 September 1580, HMC 9 *Salisbury*, ii, p.344. The Peace of Fleix ending this civil war was signed in November 1580.
113 25 October 1580, Henry III to Mauvissière, BN FF 3307 fols 19v–20, 21 with copy in BN CC Colbert 473, fols 99–102.
114 19 November 1580, *Cal. S. P. For. 1579–80*, p.485; 'A memorandum on negotiations with France', 9 November 1580, *Cal. S. P. For. 1581–2*, p.131.
115 10 December 1580, *Cal. S. P. For. 1579–80*, p.503.
116 The commission to draw up a league was left undated except for the year 1580. BN CC Colbert 473, fols 126–31.
117 12 December 1580, Henry III to Mauvissière, BN CC Colbert 473 pp.131–6; 12 December 1580, *Cal. S. P. For. 1580–1*, pp.510–15.
118 BN CC Colbert 473 pp.131–6; *Cal. S.P. For. 1579–80*, pp.510–15.
119 12 and 20 November, 17 December 1580, 6 January 1581, PRO 31/ 3/ 228 fols 190, 200v–2, 206, 213; 21 February 1581, *Cal. S. P. For. 1581–2*, p.69.

120 8 December 1580, Catherine to Mauvissière, *Lettres de Catherine de Médicis*, vii, p.298.
121 BN FF 3308 fol. 1 with a copy in BN CC Colbert 473, p.138. The commission was dated 28 February 1581.
122 *Cal. S. P. For. 1581–2*, pp.5, 47, 53–4, 65; *Lettres de Catherine de Médicis*, vii, p.486; 20 January 1581, BN CC Colbert 473, p.138; Cloulas, *Correspondance*, p.57, Canestrini and Desjardins, *Négociations*, iv, p.348.
123 *Lettres de Catherine de Médicis*, vii, p.367; 28 February 1581, BN FF 3308 fols 1, 48; 3253 fols 441–4.
124 'Commission of the French king', 5 March 1581, *Cal. S. P. For. 1581–2*, p.82.
125 9 April 1581, Mauvissière to Henry III, Teulet, *Relations Politiques*, iii, p.103.
126 Youngs, *Proclamations*, p.208.
127 Neale, *Parliaments*, i, pp.386–92.
128 A draft of a speech in Walsingham's hand, 30 April 1581, PRO SP 78/ 5 no.62.
129 'Deposition of Charles Arundell', HMC 58 *Bath*, v, p.202 and PRO SP 12/ 151 no.51; 9 January 1581, *Cal. S. P. Span. 1580–6*, p.78; 11 January 1581, PRO 31/ 3/ 28 fols 217v–18 printed in J. H. Pollen and W McMahon (eds), 'The Venerable Philip Howard, Earl of Arundel 1557–1595', *Catholic Record Society* (1919), pp.29–30; J. Bossy, 'English Catholics and the French Marriage 1577–81', *Recusant History* 5 (1959), p.8; Peck, *Leicester's Commonwealth*, pp.19–20; J. Waters Bennett, 'Oxford and Endimion', *PMLA* 57 (1942), pp.354–7.
130 22 March 1581, BN Italien 1732 fols 10–11.
131 For the entertainments of the French commissioners see 'The journal of the commissioners 24 April to 1 May 1581', PRO 31/ 3/ 28 fols 272–307; 'Journal of Sir Francis Walsingham', *Camden Miscellany*, vi, *Camden Soc.*, 104 (1871), pp.41–2.
132 An English account of the Triumph appears in Nichols, *Progresses*, ii, pp.312–29 and one in French in a letter in BN Dupuy 33 fols 77–81.
133 'Speech uttered by Lord Burghley jointly with the commissioners of Her Majesty to treat with the French', 24 April 1581, *Cal. S. P. For. 1581–2*, pp.130–1; the French original is in PRO SP 78/ 5 no.59.
134 'Harangue prononcée' delivered in London by Monsieur Barnabé Brisson, 19 April 1581, BN FF 3952 fols 20–5. The date should be 29 April.
135 'Journal of the negotiations', 28 April 1581, PRO 31/ 3/ 28 fols 292–6; 2 May 1581, the commissioners to Henry III, PRO 31/ 3/ 28 fols 314–18.
136 'A draft of the speech delivered to the commissioners in Walsingham's hand', 30 April 1581, PRO SP 78/ 5 no.62.
137 'Preliminaries to the Anjou match', BL Harl. MS 6265 fol. 285; 'Commission given to deal with the marriage', 11 May 1581, BN FF 3253 fols 470–4.
138 BL Harl. MS 6265 fol. 285r; 14 May 1581, Walsingham to Cobham, 'A memorandum in Burghley's hand', 16 May 1581, and 'Substance at what passed at the conference', 17 May 1581, *Cal. S. P. For. 1581–2*, pp.172–4, 175–6.
139 For the debates on the terms of the treaty, see *Cal. S. P. For. 1581–2*, pp.175–6. Strangely, Holt, *Anjou*, p.150, described the treaty as 'general and vague'. Amongst the various French copies of it are: BN FF 3253 fols 435–68; 3952 fols 26–8.
140 19 March 1581, Anjou to Mauvissière, Le Laboureur, *Mémoires*, i, p.672; 30 May 1581, Anjou to Elizabeth, HMC 9 *Salisbury*, ii, p.325. The editor wrongly places this letter in the year 1580. The matrimonial contract was signed on 11 June 1581 and the French commissioners wrote to Henry III that Anjou had had to return to Dieppe on 7 June. PRO 31/ 3/ 28 fol. 366.

141 'Form of the celebration of marriage', BN FF 3253 fols 474–7; 3952 fol. 26. Similar descriptions are in BL Cott. MS Vitellius C xvi, fol. 367 and *Cal. S. P. For. 1581–2*, pp.190–1.

142 'Signed statement of French commissioners', 11 June 1581, BN FF 3253 fols 477–8; July 1581, Elizabeth to Henry III, NLW Porkington MS fol. 1v.

143 This was what de Vray told John Somers a month later, 13 July 1581, Somers to Burghley, BL Cott. MS Galba E vi fol. 59v.

144 'Instructions for Cobham and Somers', 20 June 1581, *Cal. S. P. For. 1581–2*, pp.209–13.

145 BL Cott. MS Galba E vi fol. 47.

146 12 July 1581, Cobham to Walsingham, BL Cott. Galba E vi fols 51–4.

147 12 July 1581, Henry III to Mauvissière, BN FF 3367 fols 32–3 with copy in BN CC Colbert 473 pp.149–59, 163.

148 12 July 1581, BN FF 3367 fols 32–3; BL Cott. Galba E vi fols 52v–3v.

149 24 July 1581, Mauvissière to Catherine de Medici, BN FF 3253, pp.492–4.

150 Read, *Walsingham*, ii, p.57 explains that there are seven different drafts of instructions for Walsingham, some of which are inconsistent in particulars. For the final instructions of 22 July 1581 see Digges, *Compleat Ambassador*, pp.352–6 and NLW Porkington MS fols 2–3. For the drafts of 21 and 22 July see *Cal. S. P. For. 1581–2*, pp.271–82.

151 11 August 1581, Burghley to Walsingham, Digges, *Compleat Ambassador*, p.374.

152 6 and 10 August 1581, Digges, *Compleat Ambassador*, pp.360–70, 395.

153 13 August 1581, Digges, *Compleat Ambassador*, pp.380, 386.

154 23 August 1581, NLW Porkington MS fol. 16.

155 24 August 1581, Digges, *Compleat Ambassador*, pp.397–9; NLW Porkington MS fol. 16v.

156 'Memoir of Walsingham of conversation with the queen-mother', 30 August 1581, *Lettres de Catherine de Médicis*, vii, pp.492–7; 31 August 1581, Cobham to Burghley, Murdin, *Burghley's State Papers*, p.360.

157 'Power given by the French king to his commissioners', 23 August 1581, BN FF 3307 fols 39–40 with copy in CC Colbert 473 p.190; 30 August 1581, Pinart to Mauvissière, FF 3307 fols 40–1 with copy in CC Colbert 473 pp.194–206.

158 11 September 1581, Henry III to Mauvissière, BN FF 3307 fol. 41 with copy in CC Colbert 473 pp.200–3.

159 13 September 1581, Henry III to Elizabeth, BN FF 3307 fols 42–3 with copy in CC Colbert 373 fol. 210–12; *Lettres de Catherine de Médicis*, vii, pp.396–7.

160 17 August 1581, Burghley to Walsingham, Digges, *Compleat Ambassador*, pp.389–90.

161 24 August 1581, Digges, *Compleat Ambassador*, p.397.

162 Holt, *Anjou*, pp.157–9.

163 *Ibid.*, p.163.

164 *Lettres de Catherine de Médicis*, vii, p.416; 16 November 1581, BN Italien 1732 fol. 216; 14 November 1581, Henry III to Mauvissière, BN FF 3307 fol. 47 with a copy in CC Colbert 473 fols 222–3.

165 31 October 1581, Henry III to Mauvissière, BN FF 3307 fol. 45 with copy in CC Colbert 473 fols 216–20.

166 'Instructions to Pinart', 14 November 1581, BN FF 473 fols 47v–8 with copy in CC Colbert 473 fols 226–31; 'letter patent of the king', 14 November 1581, BN FF 3307 fols 48–9 with copy in CC Colbert 473 fols 231–3.

167 Holt, *Anjou*, p.160; 14 November 1581, *Cal. S. P. For. 1581–2*, pp.368–9.

168 Camden, *Annals*, iii, p.12. Other accounts include that of the Spanish ambassador, 24 November 1581, *Codoin*, xcii, pp.193–4, translated in *Cal. S. P. Span.*

1568–79, p.227 and of Marnix printed in Muller and Diegerick, *Documents*, iv, pp.258–60. The Venetian ambassador in France repeated information provided by a servant of Anjou, 14 December 1581, BN Italien 1732 fol. 230.

169 26 November 1581, Canestrini and Desjardins, *Négociations*, iv, p.412.

170 Camden, *History*, p.268. It has been mistakenly assumed that Norton was sent to the Tower for words he spoke in the 1581 parliament some eight months previously, but the Spanish ambassador seems to link his imprisonment with opposition expressed at the time of the public kiss. 11 December 1581, *Codoin*, xcii, p.210; 5 December 1581, HMC 12 *Rutland*, iv, p.130.

171 14 December 1581, BN Italien 1732 fols 231–2, the Venetian ambassador is again repeating what he had heard from Anjou's servant. De Mendoza gives a somewhat different account of Elizabeth's attempts to extricate herself.

172 Camden, *History*, p.268; 4 December 1581, *Codoin*, xcii, p.198 with a translation in *Cal. S. P. Span. 1580–6*, p.229.

173 24 November 1581, *Codoin*, xcii, pp.193–4, translated in *Cal. S. P. Span. 1580–86*, pp.227.

174 Holt, *Anjou*, p.162.

175 12 November 1581, Cobham to Walsingham, *Cal. S. P. For. 1581–82*, p.365.

176 My italics. For Henry III's promise, 12 July 1581, Cobham to Walsingham, BL Cott. Galba E vi fol. 52. It is possible that Henry would have been satisfied; the Tuscan ambassador at the French court reported that those Frenchmen who were the most knowledgeable about England were saying that the giving of a ring had been the most solemn pledge of marriage before the Reformation, and that because of the different religions of the contracting parties, it was in this case the most appropriate form of marriage: 'quanto manco di ceremonia tanto manco di difficolta di accordarne', 4 December 1581, Canestrini and Desjardins, *Négociations*, iv, p.413.

177 For a more positive view of Anjou in 1581 see Walsingham's memorandum 'Whether it be good for her Majesty to assist the Duke of Anjou in the Low Countries', November 1581; BL Harl. MS 1582 fols 38–41.

178 November 1581, [the queen] to Cobham and 18 December 1581, Cobham to Elizabeth, *Cal. S. P. For. 1581–2*, p.388.

179 17 December 1581, BL Cott. MS Cleopatra F vi fol. 201; 19 December 1581, *Cal. S. P. For. 1581–2*, p.409.

180 17 and 21 January 1582, *Cal. S. P. Span. 1580–6*, pp.261, 267–8.

181 Nichols, *Progresses*, ii, pp.344–5. A list of the English delegation appears in *Holinshed's Chronicles* (1807–8), iv, pp.460–1.

182 Especially C. Wilson, *Queen Elizabeth and the Revolt of the Netherlands* (1970).

183 Read, *Burghley*, p.265.

184 6 August 1578, Sussex to Walsingham, PRO SP 83/ 8 no.59.

185 At the peace talks at Cologne from May to November 1579, Philip II's delegates took an intransigent position on these points. Parker, *Dutch Revolt*, pp.195, 197.

186 Burghley made these points in 'Memoryall for the Queen's Majestie tochyng the matters of her marryage', March 1579, HMC 9 *Salisbury*, ii, p.244 following closely the argument of Sussex in his letter to Elizabeth, 28 August 1578, Lodge, *Illustrations*, ii, pp.107–18.

187 MacCaffrey, *Elizabeth I*, pp.212–13.

188 J. Lèfevre (ed.) *Correspondance de Philippe II sur les Affaires des Pays Bas* (Brussels, 1940), i, pp.650, 733.

189 *Codoin*, xci, pp.486, 555.

190 C. Piot, *Correspondance de Granvelle*, p.631.

8 THE UNDERLYING DEBATE

1 'A Discourse that it was not convenient for the Queen to marry with the answer', *Somers Tract*, p.171.

2 Phillip, *Patient Grissell*, lines 171–5.

3 Quoted in P. Crawford, *Women and Religion in England 1500–1720* (1993), pp.38–45. See also K. Davies, 'Continuity and change in literary advice on marriage', in *Marriage and Society: Studies in the social history of marriage*. Edited by R. B. Outhwaite (1981), pp.58–80 and P. Collinson, *The Birthpangs of Protestant England* (1988), pp.65–8.

4 Quoted in H. Hackett, *Virgin, Mother, Maiden Queen: Elizabeth I and the cult of the Virgin Mary* (1995), p.54.

5 *Somers Tract*, i, p.171.

6 *Ibid.*

7 My italics. I Corinthians 7, *The Geneva Bible* (1560), facsimile edn (Madison, Wisconsin, 1969). The following Biblical quotations come from this Bible which was the most common edition used in Elizabeth's reign.

8 'The Common Cry of Englishmen', BL Egerton MS 2836 fol. 39.

9 'The Common Cry of Englishmen' refers to this text. BL Egerton MS 2836 fol. 39v.

10 *Somers Tract*, i, p.171.

11 Strype, *Smith*, p.206.

12 Hatfield MS 148 fol. 25 quoted in Read, *Burghley*, p.211.

13 'Earl of Northampton's Answer to Stubbs's Book against Queen Elizabeth's Marriage with Francis Duke of Alençon', printed in Berry, *Stubbs's 'Gaping Gulf'*, pp.158–64.

14 BL Egerton MS 2836 fols 38–9.

15 'Earl of Northampton's Answer', pp.157–64.

16 PRO SP 15/ 26 fol. 117; SP 78/ 3 no.3; Hatfield MS 148 fol. 54.

17 PRO SP 63/ 2 fol. 82.

18 Strype, *Smith*, p.234.

19 Berry, *Stubbs's 'Gaping Gulf'*, p.174.

20 'Extract from the instructions of Sir Thomas Smith concerning the marriage between Elizabeth I and the duke of Anjou', 1572, BL Cott. MS Julius F vi fol. 168. Elizabeth made the same point in her letter to Walsingham on 11 May 1571; Digges, *Compleat Ambassador*, p.99.

21 BL Lansd. MS 94 fol. 71. This document was a draft letter to the queen.

22 'A tract on the lawfulness of marrying with a papist', Strype, *Grindal*, 'An Appendix of Original Papers', p.472. Strype suggested that Thomas Cartwright might be the author.

23 These particular examples were actually provided by Lord Henry Howard in 1580 and Paul de Foix in April 1571, Digges, *Compleat Ambassador*, p.91.

24 'An inquisition to gather what is meetest to be done in the marriage between Queen Elizabeth and Archduke Charles', 1567, BL Addit. MS 4149 fol. 94. Another copy of this document (which is damaged by fire) has it written by the archbishop of Canterbury in November 1567; BL Cott. MS Vitellius C xi fols 282–94.

25 BL Addit. MS 4149 fol. 93.

26 PRO SP 15/ 26 fol. 143; BL Addit MS 4149 fol. 90.

27 BL Harl. MS 6265 fols 107v–108.

28 BL Lansd. MS 94 fol. 95.

29 Von Klarwill, *Queen Elizabeth*, pp.258–9.

30 'The commodities and discommodities of the marriage to be had between A[njou] and E[lizabeth]', 1579, BL Harl. 1582 fol. 36v. Walsingham had made the same point in April 1575; PRO SP 70/ 117 fols 154–5.

31 Berry, *Stubbs's 'Gaping Gulf'*, p.6.

32 These and the following Biblical references appear in BL Lansd. MS 94 fol. 62 as well as in Stubbs.

33 Genesis 12 and 28. Berry, *Stubbs's 'Gaping Gulf'*, pp.7–12.

34 Genesis 34.

35 Ezra 9–10.

36 Berry, *Stubbs's 'Gaping Gulf'*, pp.12–13.

37 Nehemiah 13.

38 For Mildmay see BL. Harl. MS 6265 fol. 108.

39 Berry, *Stubbs's 'Gaping Gulf'*, p.14.

40 BL Lansd. MS 94 fols 64v–65.

41 'Whether a Protestant may marry with a Papist', BL Lansd. MS 94 fol. 68v.

42 BL Lansd. MS 94 fols 65.

43 *Ibid.*, fols 64, 68

44 *Ibid.*, fol. 64.

45 *Ibid.*, fols 63–4.

46 Protestant attitudes to the Mosaic Law are discussed in J. S. Coolidge, *The Pauline Renaissance in English Puritanism and the Bible* (Oxford, 1970), pp.15–24. The quotation comes from Thomas Cartwright and is printed in Coolidge.

47 Strype, *Grindal*, p.472.

48 BN Dupuy MS 658 fol. 125.

49 *Cal. S. P. Ven. 1558–80*, pp.601–3.

50 BL Addit. MS 4149 fols 89–90.

51 Extracts from the treatise concerning the arguments from scripture were found by John Strype in the manuscript collections of Grindal and Burghley and have been printed in Strype, *Grindal*, pp.472–5. Quotations here come from Strype.

52 Strype, *Grindal*, p.475.

53 See chapter 4, pp.91–2.

54 Berry, *Stubbs's 'Gaping Gulf'*, p.20.

55 P. Lake, 'The Significance of the Elizabethan Identification of the Pope as Antichrist', *Journal of Ecclesiastical History* 31 (1980), pp.161–78; Coolidge, *Pauline Renaissance*.

9 CONCLUSIONS

1 'De matrimonia Reginae Angliae cum extero Principe', April 1566, Haynes, *Cecil's State Papers*, p.444.

2 Haynes, *Cecil's State Papers*, p.444.

3 According to Chantonnay, Sussex said that 'seria gran arrimo para el contra sus contrarios, y si no, podria ser que la Reyna pusiese los ojos en persono de quien no viendra bien al dicho conde'. 16 October 1567, AGS E 657 fol. 74b.

4 For Wilson see 'A treatise of England's perils, 1578', *Archiv für Reformations Geschichte* 46 (1955), pp.243–9; for Hatton see E. St John Brooks, *Sir Christopher Hatton: Queen Elizabeth's favourite* (1946).

5 For Cecil's apocalyptic imagery and anti-Catholicism see M. Thorp, 'William Cecil and the Antichrist: A study of anti-Catholic ideology' in *Politics, Religion*

and Diplomacy in Early Modern Europe: Essays in honor of De Lamar Jensen. Edited by Malcolm Thorp and Arthur J. Slavin (Kirksville, Missouri, 1994), pp.289–304.

6 Quotations from D. Starkey, *The Reign of Henry VIII: Personalities and politics* (1985), pp.29, 128.

7 T. Cogswell, 'England and the Spanish Match' in *Conflicts in Early Stuart England: Studies in religion and politics 1603–1642.* Edited by Richard Cust and Ann Hughes (Harlow, Essex, 1989), pp.110, 112.

8 Simon Adams's views can be found in a number of articles: 'Faction, Clientage and Party: English politics 1550–1603, *History Today* (1982), pp.33–9; 'Eliza enthroned? The court and its politics' in *The Reign of Elizabeth I.* Edited by C. Haigh (London, 1985), pp.55–77; 'Favourites and Factions at the Elizabethan Court' in *Princes, Patronage and the Nobility: The court at the beginning of the Modern Age.* Edited by R. G. Asch and A. M. Burke (Oxford, 1991), pp.265–87.

9 E. W. Ives, *Faction in Tudor England*, Historical Association, Appreciations in History, 6 (1979), p.22.

10 MacCaffrey, *Elizabeth I*, p.360.

11 Quoted in P. Collinson, 'The Monarchical Republic of Queen Elizabeth I' in *Elizabethan Essays* (1994), p.41.

BIBLIOGRAPHY

MANUSCRIPT SOURCES

England

British Library: London

Additional MSS 4149, 20850, 25382, 33594, 35830, 35831, 39866, 48023, 48047
Cotton MSS Caligula C ii, C iii, E v, E vi, E vii, E xii
                      Cleopatra F vi
                      Galba B xi, E vi
                      Julius F vi
                      Nero B ix
                      Titus B ii, B vii, C vii
                      Vespasian F vi
                      Vitellius C xi, C xvi
Egerton MSS 2836
Harleian MSS 36, 252, 253, 260, 285, 288, 353, 444, 787, 1582, 6265, 6992
Lansdowne MSS 27, 28, 94, 102, 128, 1236
Royal MSS 13Bi
Sloane MSS 814, 2442
Stow MSS 143, 145, 147

Microfilm of the Salisbury MSS deposited at Hatfield House

Public Record Office: London

31/3 Baschet's transcripts of the French ambassadors' dispatches in the
     Bibliothèque Nationale
SP 12 Domestic Elizabeth
SP 15 Domestic Addenda
SP 52 Scottish Papers
SP 63 Irish Papers
SP 70 Foreign Papers Elizabeth
SP 78 Foreign Papers France
SP 83 Foreign Papers Flanders and Holland

261

BIBLIOGRAPHY

Bodleian Library: Oxford

Ashmolean MSS
Rawlinson MSS
Tanner MSS

France

Bibliothèque Nationale: Paris

Fonds Français MSS 3253, 3307–8, 3189, 3881, 3952, 4505, 5067, 5140, 15973, 17973,
   20153
Collection Cinq Cents de Colbert 82, 337, 465, 473
Fonds Dupuy MSS 33, 658, 771
Fonds Italien MSS 1732

Spain

Archivo General de Simancas

Estado   650–657 Austria covering the years 1558–68
           812–819 Inglaterra covering the years 1558–67
           K 1491–93, K 1519–22 Francia
           8340 varios docomentos de Paris

Wales

National Library of Wales

MSS of J. R. Ormsby Gore at Parkington

PRINTED SOURCES

All works are printed in London unless otherwise stated.

Acts of the Privy Council. Edited by John Roche Dasent (1890–1907)
Adlard, George. *Amye Robsart and the Earl of Leycester: A critical inquiry into
   the authenticity of the various statements in relation to the death of Amye Robsart*
   (1870)
Arber, Edward. *A Transcript of the Registers of the Company of Stationers of
   London between 1554 and 1640,* vols 1–2 (London and Birmingham, 1875)
Ayre, John. *The Works of John Jewel.* 4 vols, Parker Society (Cambridge, 1845–50)
Berry, Lloyd E. *John Stubbs's 'Gaping Gulf' with Letters and other Relevant
   Documents* (Charlottesville, Virginia, 1968)
Bruce, John, 'Annals of the first four years of the reign of Queen Elizabeth by
   Sir John Hayward'. *Camden Society,* vol. 7, (1840)
—— *Correspondence of Matthew Parker, Archbishop of Canterbury 1535–1575.*
   Parker Society (Cambridge, 1853)
Calendar of Patent Rolls, Elizabeth I

Calendar of State Papers, Domestic Series, of the reigns of Edward VI, Mary and Elizabeth. Edited by R. Lemon and Mary-Anne Everett Green

Calendar of State Papers Domestic Addenda. Edited by M. A. E. Green

Calendar of State Papers, Foreign Series, of the reigns of Edward VI, Mary and Elizabeth. Edited by W. B. Turnbull, Joseph Stevenson A. J. Crosby, A. J. Butler

Calendar of State Papers Rome. Edited by J. M. Rigg

Calendar of State Papers Relating to Scotland. Edited by Joseph Bain

Calendar of State Papers Relating to Scotland and Mary Queen of Scots 1547–1603. Edited by Joseph Bain, William K. Boyd and J. D. Mackie

Calendar of State Papers Spanish. Edited by Royall Tyler and M. A. S. Hume

Calendar of State Papers Venetian. Edited by Rawdon Brown

Camden, William. *Annales: The True and Royall History of the famous Empresse Elizabeth* . . . (1625)

—— *The History of the most Renowned and Victorious Princess Elizabeth, late Queen of England* . . . .(4th edn, 1688)

Cameron, A. I. 'The Warrender Papers' vol. 1. *Scottish Historical Society*, 3rd series 18 (1931)

Canestrini, G. and A. Desjardins, *Négociations Diplomatiques de la France avec la Toscane.* 5 vols (Paris, 1865–75)

Challoner, Thomas. *In Laudem Henrici Octavi.* Edited by J. B. Gabe and C. A. Schlam (Lawrence, Kansas, 1979)

Clifford, Arthur. *The State Papers and Letters of Sir Ralph Sadler.* 2 vols (Edinburgh, 1809)

Cloulas, I. *Correspondance du Nonce en France, Anselmo Dandino (1578–1581),* Acta Nuntiaturae Gallicae vol. 8 (Paris, 1970)

Colección de Documentos Inéditos para la Historia de España. Edited by M. F. Navarete *et al.* vols 2–4, 87–90, 98, 101–3 (Madrid, 1842–95)

Collinson, Patrick. 'Letters of Thomas Wood, Puritan 1566–1577'. *Bulletin of the Institute of Historical Research*, Special Supplement no.5 (1960)

Corrie, G. E. *A Catechism by Alexander Nowell.* Parker Society (Cambridge, 1853)

Cunliffe, John W. *The Complete Works of George Gascoigne* vol.2 (1919)

Digges, Sir Dudley. *The Compleat Ambassador* . . . (1655)

Duncan-Jones, K and J. Van Dorsten, *Miscellaneous Prose of Sir Philip Sidney* (Oxford, 1973)

Fénélon, Bertrand de Salignac, Seigneur de La Mothe, *Correspondance Diplomatique.* 7 vols (Paris, 1838–40). Edited by A. Teulet

Ferrière-Percy Hector de la and Comte Baguenault de Puchesse, *Lettres de Catherine de Médicis.* 10 vols (Paris, 1880–1909)

Forbes, Patrick. *A Full View of the Public Transactions in the Reign of Queen Elizabeth* vol. 1 (1740)

François, Michel. *Lettres de Henri III.* 5 vols (Paris, 1959–84)

Furnival, F. J. and W. R. Morfit, *Ballads from Manuscripts.* 2 vols (1868–73)

Gachard, L. P. *Correspondance de Marguerite d'Autriche, Duchesse de Parme avec Philippe II.* 3 vols (Brussels, 1867–81)

—— *Correspondance de Philippe II sur les Affaires des Pays-Bas.* 5 vols (Brussels, 1848–79)

The Geneva Bible (1560) facsimile edition with introduction by Lloyd E. Berry (Madison, Wisconsin, 1969)

Harrison, G. B. *The Letters of Queen Elizabeth* (1935)

Hartley, T. E. *Proceedings in the Parliaments of Elizabeth I* vol. 1 1558–1581 (Leicester, 1981)

Haynes, Samuel. *Collection of State Papers ... Left by William Cecil* (1740)
Historical Manuscripts Commission *Second Report*
Historical Manuscripts Commission *Third Report*
Historical Manuscripts Commission 9 *Salisbury MSS at Hatfield House* vols 1–2
Historical Manuscripts Commission *Eleventh Report*
Historical Manuscripts Commission 12 *Rutland* vol. 5
Historical Manuscripts Commission 58 *Bath MSS at Longleat House* vols 1–5
Historical Manuscripts Commission 70 *Pepys*
Holinshed's Chronicle. Edited by Henry Ellis. 6 vols (1807–8)
Hughes, P. L. and J. F. Larkin, *Tudor Royal Proclamations*. 3 vols (New Haven, Conn., 1964–9)
Jackson, J. E. 'Amye Robsart'. *The Wiltshire Archaeological and Natural History Magazine* 18 (1978), pp.47–93
Jordan, W. K. *The Chronicle and Political Papers of King Edward VI* (Ithaca, NY, 1966).
Journal of the House of Commons vol. 1 (1803)
Journal of the House of Lords vol. 1 (1846)
Kervyn de Lettenhove, J. M. B. C. *Relations Politiques des Pays Bas et de l'Angleterre, sous le règne de Philippe II.* 11 vols (Brussels, 1888–1900)
Labanoff, A. *Lettres, Instructions et Mémoires de Marie Stuart, Reine d'Ecosse* vols 1–5 (Paris, 1844–54)
Lefèvre, Joseph. *Correspondance de Philippe II sur les Affaires des Pays-Bas.* 2 vols (Brussels, 1940–56)
Le Laboureur, J. *Nouvelles Additions aux Mémoires de Michel de Castelnau, Seigneur de la Mauvissière.* 3 vols (Brussels, 1731)
Letters and Papers, Foreign and Domestic of the reign of Henry VIII 1509–47. Edited by James Gairdner with R. H. Brodie.
Lodge, Edmund. *Illustrations of British History, Biography and Manners ...* 2nd edn vols 1–2 (1938)
Martin, C. T. 'Journal of Sir Francis Walsingham from December 1570 to April 1583'. *Camden Society Miscellany*, vol.6 (1871)
Muller, P. L. and A. Diegerick, *Documents concernant les relations entre le Duc D'Anjou et les Pays Bas*, vols 1–4 (Utrecht, 1889)
Mumby, Frank A. *The Girlhood of Queen Elizabeth ...* (1909)
Murdin, William. *Burghley's State Papers* (1759)
Nicolas, Sir [Nicolas] Harris. *Memoirs of the Life and Times of Sir Christopher Hatton, etc* (1847)
Nichols, J. Gough. 'The diary of Henry Machyn, citizen and merchant taylor of London 1550–1563'. *Camden Society*, 43 (1848)
—— *The Literary Remains of Edward VI.* 2 vols, (1857)
Nichols, John. *The Progresses and Public Processions of Queen Elizabeth.* 3 vols (1823)
Nicholson, William. *The Remains of Edmund Grindal.* Parker Society (Cambridge, 1843)
Norton Thomas, and Thomas Sackville. *Gorboduc or Ferrex and Porrex.* Edited by I. B. Cauthen Jr (1970)
Paris, Louis. *Négociations, Lettres et Pièces Diverses relatives au règne de François II* (Paris, 1841)
Park, T. and W. Oldys. *The Harleian Miscellany.* 10 vols (1808–13)
Payne Collier, J. 'The Egerton Papers'. *Camden Society*, vol.12 (1840)
Pears, Steuart A. *The Correspondence of Sir Philip Sidney and Hubert Languet* (1845)
Peck, D. C. *Leicester's Commonwealth: The copy of a letter written by a Master of Arts of Cambridge (1584) and related documents* (Ohio, 1985)

264

Perry, L. E. *John Stubbs's Gaping Gulf with Letters and other relevant Documents* (Charlottesville, Va, 1968)

Phillip, John. *The Play of Patient Grissell*. Edited by R. B. McKerrow and W. W. Greg. Malone Society (1909)

Pollard, A. F. *An English Garner: Tudor Tracts 1532–1588* (New York, 1964)

Pollard, A. W. *The Queen's Majesty's Entertainment at Woodstock 1575* (Oxford, 1903 and 1910)

Pollard, A. W. and G. R. Redgrave *et al. A Short-Title Catalogue of Books printed in England, Scotland and Ireland and of English books printed abroad (1475–1640)* (1946)

Pollen, J. H. 'Papal Negotiations with Mary, Queen of Scots during her reign in Scotland 1561–1567'. *Scottish Historical Society* 37 (1901)

—— 'Queen Mary's Letter to the Duke of Guise January 1562'. *Scottish Historical Society* 43 (1904)

Pollen, J. H. and W. MacMahon, 'The Venerable Philip Howard, Earl of Arundel 1557–1595'. *Catholic Record Society* 21 (1919).

Poullet, E. and Charles Piot, *Correspondance du Cardinal Granvelle* vols 1–9 (Brussels, 1878–96)

Ribier, G. *Lettres et Mémoires d'Estat des Roys, Princes, Ambassadeurs et autres Ministres sous les règnes de François I et Henri II et François II 1537–1559.* 2 vols (Paris, 1666),

Ringler, W.A. *The Poems of Sir Philip Sidney* (Oxford, 1962)

Robinson, Hastings. *The Zurich Letters.* 2 vols Parker Society (Cambridge, 1842–5)

Rodriguez-Salgado, M. J. and S. Adams,. 'The Count of Feria's dispatch to Philip II of 14 November 1558'. *Camden Miscellany, 28 Camden Society* 4th Series vol.29 (1984)

Ruble, A. de. *Mémoires Inédites de Michel de La Huguerye.* 3 vols (Paris, 1877–80)

Scott, Walter. *Somers Tracts* vols 1–2 (1809)

Sidney, Philip. *The Countess of Pembroke's Arcadia.* Edited by Maurice Evans (Harmondsworth, 1977)

Spencer, Edmund. *A Variorum Edition.* Edited by E. Greenlaw, C. G. Osgood and P. M. Padelford (Baltimore 1932–57)

Strype, John. *Annals of the Reformation . . .* 4 vols (Oxford, 1820–40)

—— *Ecclesiastical Memorials . . .* (Oxford, 1820–40)

—— *The Life of the Learned Sir Thomas Smith* (Oxford, 1820)

—— *The History of the Life and Acts of the most Reverend Father in God, Edmund Grindal.* 3 vols (Oxford, 1821)

—— *Historical Collections of the Life and Acts of the right Reverend Father in God, John Aylmer, Lord Bishop of London* (Oxford, 1821)

Teulet, Alexandre. *Relations Politiques de la France et de l'Espagne avec l'Ecosse au XVIe siècle* vols 1–3 (Paris, 1862)

Tighe, W. J. 'The Counsel of Thomas Radcliffe, Earl of Sussex, concerning the Revolt of the Netherlands, September 1578'. *The Sixteenth-Century Journal* 18 (1987), pp.327–9

Tytler, P. F. *England in the reigns of Edward and Mary.* 2 vols (1839)

Vertot, René A. and C. Villaret, *Ambassades de Messieurs de Noailles en Angleterre.* 5 vols (Leyden, 1763)

Von Klarwill, Victor. *The Fugger News-Letter,* 2nd series (1926)

—— *Queen Elizabeth and Some Foreigners* (1928)

Ward, B. M. *The Seventeenth Earl of Oxford 1550–1604 from Contemporary Documents* (1928)

Weiss, Charles. *Papiers d'Etat du Cardinal Granvelle.* 9 vols (Paris, 1841–52)

Wilson, Elkin Calhoun. *England's Eliza* (Cambridge, Mass., 1939)
Wilson, Thomas. 'A treatise of England's perils, 1578'. Edited by A. J. Schmidt. *Archiv für Reformations Geschichte* 46 (1955), pp.243–9
Wright, Thomas. *Queen Elizabeth and her Times* vols 1–2 (1838)
Yorke, Philip. *Hardwicke State Papers.* 2 vols (1778)

SECONDARY WORKS

Adams, Simon. 'Faction, Clientage and Party, 1550–1603'. *History Today* 32 (1982), pp.33–9
—— 'The Dudley Clientele and the House of Commons 1559–1586'. *Parliamentary History* 8 (1989), pp.216–39
—— 'A Godly Peer? Leicester and the Puritans'. *History Today* 40 (1990), pp.14–19
—— 'Favourites and Factions at the Elizabethan Court'. *Princes, Patronage and the Nobility: The court at the beginning of the modern age.* Edited by Ronald G. Asch and Adolf M. Birke (Oxford, 1991), pp.265–87
—— 'The Dudley Clientele 1553–63'. *The Tudor Nobility.* Edited by George Bernard (Manchester, 1992), pp.241–55.
Adler, Doris. 'Imaginary Toads in Real Gardens'. *English Literary Renaissance* 11 (1981), pp.235–60
Aird, Ian. 'The Death of Amy Robsart'. *The English Historical Review* 71 (1956), pp.69–79
Alsop, J. D. 'Reinterpreting the Elizabethan Commons: The parliamentary session of 1566'. *The Journal of British Studies* 29 (1990), pp.216–40
Alvarez, M. F. *Tres Embajadores de Felipe II en Inglaterra* (Madrid, 1951)
Andersson, Ingvar. *Erik XIV's Engelska Underhandlingar Studier I Svensk Diplomati och Handelspolitik* (Lund, 1935)
Anglo, Sydney. *Images of Tudor Kingship* (1992)
Arnold, Janet. *Queen Elizabeth's Wardrobe Unlock'd* (Leeds, 1988)
Axton, Marie. 'Robert Dudley and the Inner Temple Revels'. *The Historical Journal* 13 (1970), pp.365–78
—— *The Queen's Two Bodies.* Royal Historical Society (1977)
Barnes, K. 'John Stubbe, 1579: The French ambassador's account'. *Historical Research* 64 (1991), pp.421–6
Bartlett, Kenneth. 'Papal Policy and the English Crown 1563–1565: The Bertano correspondence'. *The Sixteenth-Century Journal* 23 (1992), pp.643–59
Bassnett, Susan. *Elizabeth I: A feminist perspective* (Oxford, 1988)
Bayne, C. G. *Anglo-Roman Relations 1558–1565.* Oxford Historical and Literary Studies 2 (Oxford, 1913)
Belsey, A. and C. 'Icons of Divinity: Portraits of Elizabeth I' in *Renaissance Bodies: The human figure in English culture c.1540–1660.* Edited by Lucy Gent and Nigel Llewellyn (1990), pp.11–35
Bergeron, David M. *English Civic Pageantry 1558–1642* (1971)
Berry, Philippa. *Of Chastity and Power: Elizabethan literature and the unmarried queen* (1989)
Bossy, J. A. 'English Catholics and the French Marriage, 1577–81'. *Recusant History* 5 (1959), pp.2–16
Claretta, G. *Il Duca di Savoia e la Corte di Londra negli Anni 1554 e 1555* (Pinerola, 1892)
Clifford, E. 'Marriage of True Minds'. *The Sixteenth-Century Journal* 15 (1984) pp.29–46

Cogswell, Thomas. 'England and the Spanish Match' in *Conflict in Early Stuart England*. Edited by Richard Cust and Ann Hughes (Harlow, Essex, 1989), pp.107–33

Collinson, Patrick. *The Elizabethan Puritan Movement* (1967)

—— *The Birthpangs of Protestant England* (1988)

—— *Elizabethan Essays* (1994)

—— 'The Elizabethan Exclusion Crisis and the Elizabethan Polity'. *Proceedings of the British Academy* 84 (1994), pp.51–92

Coolidge, John S. *The Pauline Renaissance in English Puritanism and the Bible* (Oxford, 1970)

Crawford, Patricia. *Women and Religion in England 1500–1720* (1993)

Cressy, David. *Bonfires and Bells: National memory and the Protestant calendar in Elizabethan and Stuart England* (1989)

Davies, Katherine. 'Continuity and change in literary advice on marriage' in *Marriage and Society: Studies in the social history of marriage*. Edited by R. B. Outhwaite (1981) pp.58–80

Dawson, Jane E. 'Sir William Cecil and the British Dimension of Early Elizabethan Foreign Policy'. *History* 74 (1989), pp.908–26

Dent, C. M. *Protestant Reformers in Elizabethan Oxford* (Oxford, 1983)

Dewar, Mary. *Sir Thomas Smith: A Tudor intellectual in office* (1964)

Dop, J. A. *Elizabeth's Knights: Soldiers, poets and Puritans in the Netherlands* (Alblasserdam, Netherlands, 1981)

Doran, Susan. 'The Political Career of Thomas Radcliffe, Third Earl of Sussex 1526?–1583'. Unpublished Ph.D thesis, London University (1979)

—— 'Religion and Politics at the Court of Elizabeth I: The Habsburg marriage negotiations of 1559–1567'. *The English Historical Review* 104 (1989) pp.908–26

—— 'Juno versus Diana: The treatment of Elizabeth I's marriage in plays and entertainments 1561–81'. *The Historical Journal* 38 (1995), pp.257–74

Elton, G. R. *The Parliament of England 1559–1581* (Cambridge, 1989)

Erickson, Carolly. *The First Elizabeth* (1983)

Fichtner, P. S. 'The Disobediente of the Obedient: Ferdinand I and the Papacy 1555–1564'. *The Sixteenth-Century Journal* 11 (1980), pp.25–35

Froude, James Anthony. *History of England from the Fall of Wolsey to the Defeat of the Spanish Armada* vols 6–11 (1893)

Frye, S. *Elizabeth I: The competition for representation* (Oxford, 1993)

Greenblatt, Stephen. *Renaissance Self-Fashioning: From More to Shakespeare* (Chicago, 1980)

—— (ed.). *Representing the Renaissance* (California, 1988)

Hackett, Helen. *Virgin Mother, Maiden Queen: Elizabeth I and the cult of the Virgin Queen* (1995)

Haigh, Christopher. *The reign of Elizabeth I* (1984)

—— *Elizabeth I: Profile in power* (1988)

—— *English Reformations: Religion, politics and society under the Tudors* (Oxford, 1993)

Hasler, P. W. *The House of Commons 1558–1603 (The History of Parliament)* 3 vols (1981)

Heisch, Allison. 'Queen Elizabeth I: Parliamentary rhetoric and the exercise of power'. *Signs* 1 (1975), pp.31–55

'Elizabeth I and the Persistence of Patriarchy'. *Feminist Review* 4 (1980), pp.45–56

Hibbert, Christopher. *The Virgin Queen: The personal history of Elizabeth I* (1990)

Hill, Christopher. *The English Bible and the Seventeenth-Century Revolution* (1993)

Holmes, P. J. 'Mary Stewert in England' in *Mary Stewert Queen in Three Kingdoms*. Edited by Michael Lynch (Oxford, 1988), pp.195–215

Holt, Mack. P. *The Duke of Anjou and the Politique Struggle during the Wars of Religion* (Cambridge, 1986)

Hubault, Gustave. *Michel de Castelnau, Ambassadeur en Angleterre 1575–1585* (Paris, 1856)

Hume, M. A. S. *The Courtships of Queen Elizabeth* (1904)

Hurstfield, Joel. *Elizabeth I and the Unity of England* (1960)

Ives, Eric. *Faction in Tudor England*. New Appreciations in History Series, Historical Association (1979)

Jenkins, Elizabeth. *Elizabeth the Great* (1958)

Johnson, Paul. *Elizabeth I: A study in power and intellect* (1974)

Jones, N. L. *Faith by Statute: Parliament and the settlement of religion* (Cambridge, 1982)

—— *The Birth of the Elizabethan Age: England in the 1560s* (Oxford, 1993)

Jordan, Constance. 'Women's Rule in Sixteenth-Century British Political Thought'. *Renaissance Quarterly* 40 (1987), pp.421–51

Kervyn de Lettenhove, J. M. B. C. *Les Huguenots et Les Gueux* 6 vols (Bruges, 1883–85)

King, John N. 'The Godly Woman in Elizabethan Iconography'. *Renaissance Quarterly* 38 (1985), pp.41–84.

—— *Tudor Royal Iconography: Literature and art in an age of religious crisis* (Princeton NJ, 1989)

—— 'Queen Elizabeth I: Representations of the Virgin Queen'. *Renaissance Quarterly* 43 (1990), pp.30–74

—— *Spenser's Poetry and the Reformation Tradition* (Princeton, 1990)

Kingdon, R. M. *Myths about the St Bartholomew's Day Massacre 1573–1574* (Cambridge, Mass. and London, 1988)

Koch, E. 'Striving for the Union of Lutheran Churches: The church historical background of the work done on the Formula of Concord at Magdeburg'. *The Sixteenth-Century Journal* 8 (1977), pp.105–21

Kouri, E. I. *England and the Attempts to Form a Protestant Alliance in the Late 1560s: A case-study in European diplomacy*. Annales Academiae Scientiarum Fennicae 210 (Helsinki, 1981)

La Ferrière-Percy, Hector de. *Les Projets de Mariage de la Reine Elizabeth* (Paris, 1882)

Lake, Peter. 'The Significance of the Elizabethan Identification of the Pope as Antichrist'. *The Journal of Ecclesiastical History* 31 (1980), pp.161–78

Lee, Patricia-Ann. 'A Bodye Politique to Governe: Aylmer, Knox and the debate on queenship'. *The Historian* (USA) 52 (1990), pp.242–61

Lehmberg, Stanford E. *Sir Walter Mildmay and Tudor Government* (Austin, Texas, 1964)

Leimon, Mitchel. 'Sir Francis Walsingham and the Anjou Marriage Plan, 1574–81'. Unpublished Ph.D thesis, University of Cambridge (1989)

Levin, Carole. *The Heart and Stomach of a King: Elizabeth I and the politics of sex and power* (Pennsylvania, 1994)

Levine, Mortimer. *The Early Elizabethan Succession Question, 1558–1568* (Stamford, California, 1966)

—— *Tudor Dynastic Problems 1460–1571* (1973)

—— 'The Place of Women in Tudor Government' in *Tudor Rule and Revolution: Essays for G. R. Elton from his American Friends*. Edited by D. J. Guth and J. W. McKenna (Cambridge, 1982), pp.109–23

268

Levy, F. J. 'A Semi-Professional Diplomat, Guido Cavalcanti and the Marriage Negotiations of 1571'. *Bulletin of the Institute of Historical Research* 35 (1962) pp.211–20

Lindley, David (ed.) *The Court Masque* (Manchester, 1984)

Loades, D. M. *Two Tudor Conspiracies*. 2nd edn (Bangor, Gwynedd, 1992)

—— 'Philip II and the government of England' in *Law and Government under the Tudors*. Edited by Claire Cross, D. M. Loades and J. J. Scarisbrick (Cambridge, 1988), pp.177–94

—— *Mary Tudor: A life* (Oxford, 1989)

—— *The Reign of Mary Tudor: Politics, government and religion in England 1553–1558*. 2nd edn (Harlow, 1991)

MacCaffrey, Wallace T. *The Shaping of the Elizabethan Regime* (1969)

—— 'The Anjou Match and the Making of Elizabethan Foreign Policy' in *The English Commonwealth 1547–1640: Essays presented to Professor Joel Hurstfield*. Edited by Peter Clark, Alan G. T. Smith and Nicholas Tyacke (Leicester, 1979), pp.59–75

—— *Queen Elizabeth and the Making of Policy 1572–1588* (Princeton, 1981)

—— *Queen Elizabeth I* (1993)

Martin, A. Lynn. *Henry III and the Jesuit Politicians* (Geneva, 1973)

Martin, Colin and Geoffrey Parker. *The Spanish Armada* (1988)

McCoy, R. C. 'From the Tower to the Tiltyard: Robert Dudley's return to glory'. *The Historical Journal* 27 (1984), pp.425–35

—— *The Rites of Knighthood: The literature and politics of Elizabethan chivalry* (California, 1989)

McLane, Paul E. *Spenser's 'Shepheardes Calendar': A study in Elizabethan allegory* (Notre Dame, Indiana, 1961)

Millward, O. *Religious Controversies of the Elizabethan Age* (Leeds, 1977)

Neale, John E. *Queen Elizabeth* (1934)

—— *Elizabeth I and her Parliaments 1559–1581* vol. 1 (1953)

Norbrook, David. *Poetry and Politics in the English Renaissance* (1984)

Palmer, William. *The Problem of Ireland in Tudor Foreign Policy 1485–1603* (Woodbridge, Suffolk, 1994)

Parker, Geoffrey. *The Dutch Revolt* (1975)

Perry, Maria. *The Words of a Prince: A life of Elizabeth I from contemporary documents* (Woodbridge, 1990)

Plowden, Alison. *Marriage with my Kingdom: The courtships of Elizabeth I* (1977)

Pollen, J. H. *The English Catholics during the reign of Queen Elizabeth: A study of their politics, civil life and government 1558–80* (1920)

Primus, J. H. *The Vestments Controversy* (Amsterdam, 1960)

Pulman, Michael Barraclough. *The Elizabethan Privy Council in the 1570s* (Berkeley, 1971)

Ramsey, G. D. *The Queen's Merchants and the Revolt of the Netherlands* (Manchester, 1986)

Read, Conyers. 'Walsingham and Burghley in Queen Elizabeth's Privy Council'. *The English Historical Review* 28 (1913), pp.34–58

—— *Mr Secretary Walsingham and the Policy of Queen Elizabeth* vols 1–2 (Oxford, 1925)

—— *Mr Secretary Cecil and Queen Elizabeth* (1955)

—— *Lord Burghley and Queen Elizabeth* (1960)

Redworth, Glyn. *In Defence of the Catholic Church: The life of Stephen Gardiner* (Oxford, 1990)

Retamal Favereau, Julio. 'Anglo-Spanish Relations 1566–1572: The mission of Don Guerau de Spes at London'. Unpublished D.Phil. thesis (Oxford, 1972)

Ridley, Jaspar. *Elizabeth I* (1987)

Roberts, Michael. *The Early Vasas: A history of Sweden 1523–1611* (Cambridge, 1968)

Robinson, A. M. F. 'Queen Elizabeth and the Valois Princes'. *The English Historical Review* 2 (1887), pp.40–77

Rodriguez-Salgado, M. J. *The Changing Face of Empire: Charles V, Philip II and Habsburg authority, 1551–1559* (Cambridge, 1989)

Roelker, Nancy L. *Queen of Navarre, Jeanne d'Albret 1528–1572* (Cambridge, Mass., 1968)

Rosenberg, Eleanor. *Leicester, Patron of Letters* (New York, 1955)

Ross, Josephine. *Suitors to the Queen* (1975)

St John Brooks, Eric. *Sir Christopher Hatton: Queen Elizabeth's favourite* (1946)

Salmon, J. H. M. *Society in Crisis: France in the Sixteenth Century* (1975)

—— 'Gallicanism and Anglicanism in the Age of the Counter-Reformation' in *Renaissance and Revolt: Essays in the intellectual and social history of early-modern France* (Cambridge, 1987), pp.155–88

Samaha, Joel. 'Gleanings from Local Criminal Court Records: Sedition amongst the "inarticulate" in Elizabethan Essex'. *The Journal of Social History* 8 (1975) pp.61–79

Scalingi, Paula Louise. 'The Scepter or the Distaff: The question of female sovereignty, 1515–1607'. *The Historian* (USA) 42 (1978) pp.59–75

Sil, Narasingha P. *William Herbert of Pembroke (c.1507–1570): Politique and patriot* (Lewiston Queenston, 1988)

Smith, A. Hassell. *County and Court: Government and politics in Norfolk, 1558–1603* (Oxford, 1974)

Somerset, A. *Elizabeth I* (1991)

Starkey, David, Morgan, D. A. L., Murphy, John, Wright, Pam, Cuddy, Neil and Sharpe, Kevin (eds). *The English Court from the Wars of the Roses to the Civil War* (1987)

Strong, Roy. *The English Icon: Elizabeth and Jacobean portraiture* (1969)

—— *Art and Power: Renaissance festival* (Bury St Edmonds, Suffolk, 1984)

—— *Gloriana: The Portraits of Queen Elizabeth I* (1987)

Strong, Roy and J. A. Van Dorsten, *Leicester's Triumph* (Oxford, 1964)

Sutherland, Nicola. M. *The Massacre of St Bartholomew and the European Conflict 1559–1572* (1973)

—— *The Huguenot Struggle for Recognition* (New Haven, Conn., 1980)

—— *Princes, Politics and Religion 1547–1589* (1984)

Taylor-Smither, Larissa J. 'Elizabeth I: A psychological profile'. *The Sixteenth-Century Journal* 15 (1984) pp.47–72

Teague, Frances. 'Queen Elizabeth in her Speeches' in *Gloriana's Face: Women public and private in the English Renaissance*. Edited by S. P. Cerasano and Marion Wynne-Davies (Hemel Hempstead, Herts, 1992), pp.63–78

Thorp, Malcolm. 'Catholic Conspiracy in Early Elizabethan Foreign Policy'. *The Sixteenth-Century Journal* 15 (1984), pp.431–49

—— 'William Cecil and the Antichrist: A study in anti-Catholic ideology' in *Politics, Religion and Diplomacy in Early Modern Europe: Essays in honor of De Lamar Jensen*. Sixteenth-Century Essays and Studies 27. Edited by Malcolm R. Thorp and Arthur J. Slavin (Kirksville, Missouri, 1994), pp.289–304

Waddington, Raymond B. 'Elizabeth I and the Order of the Garter'. *The Sixteenth-Century Journal* 24 (1993), pp.97–113

Waters Bennett, Josephine. 'Oxford and Endimion'. *Publications of the Modern Languages Association of America* 57 (1942), pp.354–69

Wernham, R. B. *Before the Armada: The growth of English foreign policy,
    1485–1588* (1966)
—— *The Making of Elizabethan Foreign Policy 1558–1603* (Berkeley, Cal., 1980)
Williams, Neville. *Thomas Howard, Fourth Duke of Norfolk* (1964)
—— *Elizabeth I: Queen of England* (1967)
Wilson, Charles. *Queen Elizabeth and the Revolt of the Netherlands* (1970)
Wilson, Derek. *Sweet Robin: A biography of Robert Dudley, earl of Leicester
    1533–1588* (1981)
Woodhuysen, H. R. 'Leicester's Literary Patronage: A study of the English court
    1578–92'. Unpublished D.Phil. thesis, University of Oxford (1980)
Wright, Louis B. 'A Political Reflection in Phillip's *Patient Grissell*'. *Renaissance
    English Studies* 4 (1928) pp.424–8
Youngs, Frederick A. *The Proclamations of the Tudor Queens* (Cambridge, 1976)
Zins, H. *England and the Baltic in the Elizabethan Era* (Manchester, 1972)

INDEX